Praise for *From Culture Wars to Common Ground*

"A breakthrough book in contemporary literature on marriage and the family."

—Barbara Dafoe Whitehead,
author of *The Divorce Culture*

"Drawing on ideas from both the left and the right, this book issues a clarion call for churches to come to the aid of the struggling American family. It brings much sanity, as well as religious, historical, and moral insight, to the American family debate and deserves to be read widely."

—David Popenoe,
Professor of Sociology and Associate Dean for the
Social and Behavioral Sciences, Rutgers University;
author of *Life without Father*

"A formidable marshaling of research and theological insight in the service of families that works for the good of us all."

—Nancy T. Ammerman,
Professor of Sociology of Religion, Hartford Seminary;
coeditor of *Work, Family, and Religion in Contemporary Society*

"A brilliant review and critique of the contemporary debate about the condition and future of the American family. . . . Anyone who wishes to engage in the discussion of the contemporary family should read this book from cover to cover, take notes, and become involved in a radical and personal evolutionary process that is essential to the survival of us all."

—Harville Hendrix, Ph.D., author of
Giving the Love You Want: A Guide for Couples
and *Keeping the Love You Find: A Personal Guide;*
coauthor of *Giving the Love They Need: A Guide for Parents*

"This book builds a unique bridge between scholarship about family dynamics and theology, establishing a powerful, crucial, and much-needed link. The book's command of resources and scope of analysis is of the highest order. We are all in the debt of the authors and publisher."

—Amitai Etzioni, author of *The New Golden Rule*

"Fair-minded, meticulously argued, and comprehensive. The authors offer a carefully thought-out constructive agenda for addressing the current 'crisis of the family.' This book exemplifies practical theology at its best and is a volume that ought to be read by anyone seriously concerned with this crucially important topic."

—Stephen Pope,
Associate Professor of Moral Theology, Boston College

"I welcome this book as a collaborative effort among scholars with clear and cogent convictions concerning the plight of modern American families. The discussion is appropriately enriched by the diversity of insights gathered from church leaders, public policy-makers, and representative American families."

—Cheryl J. Sanders,
Professor of Christian Ethics, Howard University

"Builds the provocative case that a new family ethic can restore order and meaning to the frayed family systems of the late twentieth century. The authors have produced a rich and surprising volume that is sure to spark new debates on the meaning and importance of the family."

—Allan Carlson, Ph.D.,
author of *Family Questions:*
Reflections on the American Social Crisis

"An extraordinary, wise, and timely book. This book will change the ways both church and society think about and enact family values."

—John A. Coleman, S.J.,
Charles Cassasa Chair of Social Values,
Loyola Marymount University, Los Angeles

"A major contribution to ongoing, serious public debate and, ultimately, constructive programmatic change in public policy. A must read for clergy, seminarians, religious and secular feminists, secular therapists and social workers, government policy-makers, and everyone else who cares about the quality of family life as integral to both God's reign and to the overall good of the country."

—Paula M. Cooey,
Professor of Religion, Trinity University;
author of *Family, Freedom, and Faith*

"The breadth of this engaging text offers new arguments to even long-time participants in the family debates."

—Christine Gudorf,
Professor of Ethics,
Florida International University

"This book should interest anyone, secular or religious, who is engaged by recent deliberations about families. The writers challenge narrow and intolerant ideas of 'the' patriarchal heterosexual family that are still prominent in some religious discussion. More important, in argument with each other, they begin to forge new theological concepts that contribute to our shared cultural understandings of familial mutuality and respect."

—Sara Ruddick,
Eugene Lang College, The New School for Social Research;
author of *Maternal Thinking: Toward a Politics of Peace*

"A path-breaking study. . . . Eminently sensible and compelling."

—*Theological Studies*

"Deserves extensive discussion in church, classroom, boardroom, and legislature."

—*Journal of the American Academy of Religion*

From Culture Wars
to Common Ground

From Culture Wars to Common Ground

Religion and the American Family Debate

Second Edition

Don S. Browning
Bonnie J. Miller-McLemore
Pamela D. Couture
K. Brynolf Lyon
Robert M. Franklin

Westminster John Knox Press
Louisville, Kentucky

Book design by Jennifer K. Cox
Cover design by Night & Day Design

Second edition

Published by Westminster John Knox Press
Louisville, Kentucky

This book is printed on acid-free paper that meets the American National Standards Institute Z39.48 Standard. ♾

PRINTED IN THE UNITED STATES OF AMERICA

00 01 02 03 04 05 06 07 08 09 — 10 9 8 7 6 5 4 3 2 1

Library of Congress Cataloging-in-Publication Data

A catalog card for this book may be obtained from the Library of Congress.
ISBN 0-664-22352-4

Contents

Tables

Preface to the Second Edition

The first edition of *From Culture Wars to Common Ground* was finished shortly before the 1996 presidential election. President Clinton defeated Robert Dole, partially because he captured the intense debate over the family that had dominated much of American politics during the 1990s. Concern for the American family had become a liberal political issue during the campaign. It had been viewed as a conservative issue for most of the preceding fifteen years, at least since the early 1980s when Ronald Reagan was elected president.

This second edition, with a new appendix on practical theological method, appears at the time of the 2000 presidential election. In the intervening years, the 1996 welfare reforms, which were passed into law in part to help restore marriage and the two-parent family, have been implemented. They seem to have been effective in reducing the number of people on welfare; it is not yet known whether they will actually reduce poverty. Nor is it clear whether they will encourage marriage, fewer nonmarital births, and less divorce.

But several actions that we called for in the first edition have begun to occur. We called for efforts to bring fathers back into families; the government has now stimulated a wide range of programs to do just that. We called for better enforcement of child-care payments by nonresidential parents, generally fathers; the government has continued to work on this very stubborn problem, stubborn partly because so many poor fathers cannot afford payments at all. Most of our team called for a reduction of the marriage tax penalty; there is today a national political debate about how to take this step without being unfair to singles. We called for more state support of marriage education; several states, notably Florida and Arizona, have mandated such programs. Their effectiveness, however, has not been assessed. We called for a $1,000 to $1,500 tax credit for each child; the Congress and president at least went partway; we now have a $500 credit for each child. Many of the practical initiatives that we called for in chapter 11 are beginning to come into reality.

Although some progress in addressing family issues at the level of political culture has occurred, in other ways there has been retreat and regression. Progress in child care, transportation, and medical assistance for poor families and working single parents is still insufficient, although a few states have done relatively well on these issues. Welfare reform hoped to stimulate marriage, but there is little active effort to make marriage a matter of genuine public policy. This is true in spite of the covenant marriage experiments of Louisiana and Arizona, and Oklahoma governor Keating's move to use Temporary Assistance for Needy Families (TANF) funds for joint government and civil society ventures in marriage education. Even though such initiatives are consistent with what we called for in our book, they are still few in number and too recent to have received careful evaluation. Much has happened on family issues in our society, but there is still a need for the deeper analyses and arguments of this book. It is not clear what any of these new efforts will do to strengthen what we call "the equal-regard family." Our society is still short on fundamental thought about families of the kind attempted in *From Culture Wars to Common Ground.*

But we believed when we first wrote the book, and believe now, that the main initiatives on behalf of families must come from the institutions of civil society with churches taking the lead. We have done some analysis of the family programs of the national offices of mainline denominations, but without a more full-scale study, what is happening on behalf of families among the churches is elusive to document. Furthermore, the structure of large Protestant denominations in recent years is in flux; we can no longer assume that "top down" programming is what a denomination is doing. Initiatives are more likely to be located at a variety of levels—local congregations, middle-level governing bodies, and some national boards and agencies. For instance, at the national level the United Methodists are designing significant new programs to meet the needs of poor children. But there are only a few such programs coming from the national agencies; at the lower levels we see many more.

There is, however, little participation by the churches in the wider public debate. There is public attention beginning to center on Michael McManus's Community Marriage Policy, which we described in chapter 11. This is an ecumenical marriage movement that has continued to grow; churches in over 120 towns and cities in the United States have joined to implement common marriage policies at the community level. Liberal analogues to McManus's program are emerging and many churches at the grass roots are responding.

Our effort to find "common ground" in the American debate over the family was not designed to achieve total agreement among either politicians or churches. Instead, we hoped to focus attention on those forgotten issues—fatherlessness, the economic and parenting difficulties of single parents, the declining well-being of children, work and family issues—in order to increase the scope of overlapping and analogous points of view. We wanted to create at best a rough consensus, especially on those issues so noticeably ignored. But more than that, we aspired to illustrate a model and methodology for moral discourse on family issues. For this reason, we hope that the appendix we have now added will throw further light on the procedures and steps needed for both productive dialogue and good practical theology on family issues.

Don Browning
Bonnie Miller-McLemore
Pamela Couture
Bernie Lyon
Robert Franklin

Preface to the First Edition

The authors of this book met nearly a dozen times for several days from 1991 to 1996 to discuss the dilemmas of families, the outline of the book, and critiques of individual chapters. There were numerous small consultations, countless telephone calls and e-mail messages, and more drafts than any of us anticipated.

The ideas and judgments of all five authors pervade this book: Don Browning and Bonnie Miller-McLemore co-edited all chapters; Miller-McLemore drafted chapter 6 on feminism and chapter 7 on the therapeutic, and made substantive contributions to the Introduction and to chapters 1, 2, 4, 5, 10, and 11; Pamela Couture drafted chapter 3 on the family and religion in the nineteenth century. Browning and Robert Franklin drafted chapter 8 on the Christian profamily movements; Browning and Bernie Lyon drafted chapter 9 on the state and market families; after input from the others, Browning and Couture worked on the outline of chapter 2 and Browning drafted it; and Browning also drafted the Introduction and chapters 1, 4, 5, 10, and 11.

We understand this book mainly as a project in practical theology. But from another perspective, it can be understood as an exercise in hermeneutic social science similar in method to the well-known *Habits of the Heart* by Robert Bellah, Richard Madsen, William Sullivan, Ann Swidler, and Steven Tipton. Our book, however advances far more explicit arguments for its normative religious and ethical perspective.

We soon discovered that to write about the family was to confront our diverse family backgrounds. The families of origin for four of us were small-town, Midwest, and liberal Protestant—one Methodist and three Christian Church (Disciples of Christ); even then, however, there were differences in our respective family constellations and traditions. Franklin, on the other hand, comes from the big city of Chicago and the Church of God in Christ. In our immediate families, there are the usual range of family issues—working long hours, scarcity of time, divorce, and gay parenting. All of us either are or have been married. Not only have we written about families, but our experience and struggles in families pervade the book. Furthermore, as we mention again in chapter 1, although this book is primarily about family and marriage in its hetero-sexual expressions, we all agree that the ideas that follow must not be used to promote heterosexist or homophobic policies and attitudes.

Acknowledgments

A project of this kind would have been impossible without the gener-ous support of the Division of Religion of the Lilly Endowment, Inc., and the wise and genial guidance of Vice President Craig Dykstra, Dorothy Bass, who directs the Lilly Endowment–sponsored Valparaiso Project on Education and Formation of People in Faith, and Jim Lewis, who directs the Lilly-sponsored Louisville Institute—all of whom shared supervisory responsibilities for the Religion, Culture, and Family Project.

We want to thank Ian Evison and John Wall, who arranged our meetings; Carol Browning, who functioned as a research associate and vital consultant throughout the project; Christie Green, who helped with research in the final stages; and Dean Clark Gilpin of the Divinity School of the University of Chicago, who generously supported this project. We thank Dean Joseph Hough of Vanderbilt University Divinity School and Dean William Myers of Chicago Theological Seminary for their support of release time for Bonnie Miller-McLemore. We also thank several scholars who are too numerous to list who pro-vided feedback on our work in progress, particularly the authors in the Religion, Culture, and Family Project. We thank our families, who were neglected, often seriously, as we traveled, debated, and wrote about the family. We thank Professor Ben Zablocki of the Rutgers University Social Science Research Center for directing us in our interviews, Professor David Popenoe of Rutgers and the Council on Families in America for being our liaison with Professor Zablocki; Professor Thom Needham of the Fuller Graduate School of Psychology, for administer-ing and collating our survey on the ethical values guiding family ther-apists; and Corine Kyle, of the George H. Gallup International Institute, who administered our love and marriage survey. We thank Barbara Hofmaier for her careful first editing of the manuscript.

There were times during these years when we thought the book might never be completed, that our differences were too large, or that changes in vocations, residence, and available research time would make it logistically impossible. But the book has been completed, and more than that, a richer argument has evolved because it has weathered the storms of our conflicts and the complexities of our family and work lives. Over the course of the project, we have clashed, held our ground, modified our ideas, and changed our views. Ultimately, a shared con-

viction about the importance of a strong theological voice on the family tipped the scale from dissolution to the final completion of this
book.

Don Browning
Bonnie Miller-McLemore
Pamela Couture
K. Brynolf Lyon
Robert M. Franklin

Introduction

This book addresses two questions: What is the situation of families in the United States? And what does Christianity, interpreted in close association with its origins in Judaism, have to say to families today?

A momentous debate about the present situation and future prospects of families in our society has been raging, primarily at the level of political culture. American churches have had an ambiguous relation to this debate. Mainline Protestant churches have been mostly silent in public discussion, and conservative Protestant and Catholic churches have addressed only a narrow range of issues. The churches' involvement, however, is changing as we write. Religious institutions are beginning to realize that their public voice on issues concerning families is important.

Churches have good reasons both for ministering to families and for speaking publicly about families. Judaism and Christianity have been formative influences on families in Western societies. Their influence over the centuries has touched legal, economic, and cultural understandings of families. For the most part, this influence has been both crucial and positive, although Christianity has had its negative impact as well.

But American churches have been particularly slow to help families make the important transition from the period of the Industrial Revolution to a new postindustrial, postmodern society. Although it existed with some variations, the ideal family of the industrial period was thought to consist of a successful breadwinning father and a dedicated domestic mother, with the mother occupying the sphere of the home and the father the sphere of paid work. This family pattern has been changing for more than fifty years. Although we recognize that variations will exist, we argue that the new postindustrial ideal should be the egalitarian family in which husband and wife participate relatively equally in paid work as well as in childcare and other domestic responsibilities. This family will need new preparations, new skills, new religious and communal supports, and a new theory of authority.

This book is about the *theory, practice, and ecology of this new family ideal, what we call "the committed, intact, equal-regard, public-private family."* Although the entire book is about the meaning of the terms "intact," "equal regard," and "public-private," brief definitions are needed from the outset. By "intact" we mean a family in which mother and father are parenting their own children in a lifetime marriage. (This definition includes children who enter the family through adoption or through various methods of assisted reproduction.) We use "equal regard" to describe a relationship between husband and wife characterized by mutual respect, affection, practical assistance, and justice—a relationship that values and aids the self and other with equal seriousness. The ethic of equal regard, as we will see, has implications for children as well. We use "public-private" to characterize families in which husband and wife have privileges and responsibilities in both the public and private spheres of life.

It is theologically, politically, and strategically important for both church and society to make the creation of a new family ethic central to their agendas. Many public leaders are asking churches and synagogues to make the creation and support of this new family central to their tasks. Family issues are not private issues; they have quickly become the great public issues of our time. We believe there is a theological mandate, as well as a great social need, for churches to address family concerns.

Renewing families is one of society's most urgent and crucial tasks. This book, however, does not simply promote "familism" or a "marriage culture" as such. Familism is a profamily cultural attitude that promotes marriage and family stability at any cost to the individuals involved and neglects to investigate alternatives to the breadwinner-homemaker industrial family ideal.

Rather, our book advances a new *critical familism* and a new *critical culture of marriage*. A critical familism and marriage culture entail a full equality between husband and wife and a commitment to the reflection, communication, and openness needed to implement it. This requires an analysis of the *power relations* between husband, wife, children, and surrounding economic and governmental institutions so that hidden blocks and resistances to a realized equal regard can be uncovered and corrected. A critical familism and marriage culture also require an analysis and restructuring of the ecology of supports for families so that extended family, church, civil society, government, and market can be helpful to the conjugal couple and their children; it also requires, in turn, that families themselves contribute to the common good. In addition, a critical familism entails explicit recognition of those situations of violence, abuse, addiction, and exploitation in which intervention and possibly family dissolution may be necessary. Finally, critical familism involves basic social support for and connection with already existing families of single parents, stepparents, adults called to a vocation of singleness, and gays and lesbians raising children.

In a word, this book is not about stable families in the narrow sense of the word; it is about committed equal-regard marriages and families and the religiocultural vision and social supports needed to inspire and maintain them. Only with such a vision in place can we begin to suggest alternatives to the patterns of family disruption, *nonmarriage,* and *serial marriage* typical of our time.

Although Christianity has sometimes supported unjust family practices, its overall direction has been toward a love ethic of equal regard between husband and wife. Christianity has been an unsteady but realistic force coaxing families toward democratization between husband and wife, parents and children. Although it did not work alone to stimulate these trends, Christianity often has inspired powerful economic and legal forces pushing in this direction and often has interacted constructively with these forces once they emerged. Our intent is to further this process.

The classic expressions of Christianity promoted democratization *within* families by urging respect for women and children, the curtailment of a "double standard" in sexual ethics, and the limitation of arbitrary male authority. Christianity also promoted democratization *between* families. This entailed the just distribution of material resources between families. But it meant more. Historian David Herlihy has argued that medieval Christianity's opposition to polygyny was no accident.[1] Polygyny was seen by the church as turning women into slaves and obscuring their status as made in the image of God. Polygyny enabled wealthy men to monopolize women at the expense of poor men. It is not coincidental that when Christianity spread into Germanic, Celtic, or Arabic territories where polygyny was practiced, these unions declined and wealthy families could no longer hoard marriageable women. Poor men had more opportunities to marry, and a new commensurability of family form began to arise between rich and poor.[2]

We are not, however, triumphalist about the virtues of Christianity. At best, the church has been a "treasure in earthen vessels," and its adherents have distorted the Christian message throughout its history. We can talk only of general directions, of seeds that were planted and grew, and of central ideals about just and loving gender relations and parental obligations that became clearer as the centuries passed. Careful interpretive procedures are required to uncover these central liberating and empowering meanings.

A Psychocultural-economic
View of Families

By profession we are theologians who use a variety of disciplines to advance practical theological arguments. Hence, we take a psychocultural-economic view of families. We are aware of the phrase's clumsiness and promise to use it as little as possible. It signals, however, our attempt to avoid the many reductionisms that plague contemporary discussions of the family. And reductionisms are everywhere. Families are economic phenomena, but religious and psychological perspectives often do not see this. Families are cultural and religious institutions, but economic and psychological analyses seldom understand how this is so. Families are psychological (indeed, psychobiological) realities based on deep human needs and tendencies but also requiring communicative skills that must be delicately tuned to unique emotions. Both economic and religious perspectives, however, often disregard the psychological dimensions of families. We try not to get trapped in any of these reductions. Yet we consider our perspective *predominantly* theological.

We searched for a theological view that embraces families as both psychobiological and economic realities. Although we are Protestants, we found that some Catholic models have attended to these multiple realities of families. Hence, we have developed in these pages a Protestant and philosophically pragmatist reappropriation of Catholic approaches to the family. This approach gives us a way to assess psychobiological and economic consequences within the frameworks of more inclusive moral and theological points of view.

The term "psychocultural-economic" is open to misunderstanding. We do not mean to leave out either *theological* or *sociological* perspectives. Just as we mean *psychobiological* when we say *psychological,* we also mean *economic-social* when we say *economic.* Economic and social patterns are not identical, but they often overlap; they provide the settled patterns that routinize much of our action, even within families. For us, the term "cultural" includes the *religious dimension* because for us culture always contains a dimension of ultimate meaning. Because our interests are mainly theological, we constantly bring interpretations of Judaism and Christianity into conversation with various contemporary cultural voices speaking on the family.

We develop the view that humans are first of all reflective, historical, and cultural selves. Humans are biological and economic creatures as well, but they have access to these material realities mainly through the filters of historical, social, and cultural influences that shape their selves. Although the authors of this book believe that humans are cultural and historical beings, we do not believe that they are wholly "constructed" by cultural norms and practices.[3] We hold that the bodily nature of humans influences their interpretation of experience. Humans have needs and tendencies that history and culture shape but do not create. This is why biological and economic forces are so powerful and influence, although never completely determine, the form and dynamics of families.

To show the complexity of this model, we outline the historical influences on modern families. But we use evolutionary psychology and new formulations in psychoanalytic theory to uncover the psychobiological aspects of families. The discipline of economics—even such diverse schools as Marxism and rational-choice theory—will help us understand their material aspects. Biology and economics are used as "diagnostic tools" (to borrow a phrase from the French philosopher Paul Ricoeur) to uncover the depths of our desires, desires expressed by selves that are also shaped by historical experience.[4] As reflective creatures, humans use imagination and practical reason to redirect the biological, historical, and economic forces that play upon them. Nowhere is that more important than in the study of families. Families are not just passive realities; they shape their environments even as they are shaped by them.

Our Team

The major conceptual tension among the five authors centered on the following question: Does Christianity have a stake in the promotion of intact mother-father partnerships, or should it support all families, regardless of form, where genuine need exists? To put it differently, is it the *quality* of family experience, rather than the *form,* that Christianity celebrates? Or is it both quality and form that it values? Is Christianity interested in family form for what it generally contributes to the quality of family experience?

These are not small questions. Political parties divide, denominations split, and divisions arise between friends at dinner parties when such questions come to the fore. The answer is sometimes thought to depend on assessments of current trends. If the intact family is going out of fashion as some think, perhaps churches and secular institutions should support and help make successful the families that are replacing it. Others argue that it is precisely trends toward the demise of two-parent families that should be resisted. Intact families, some hold, are the will of God. Others argue, in more functional or utilitarian terms, that they "do a better job." Some people simultaneously advance both arguments.

Some members of our team feared that promoting intact families would mean neglecting the support of all families. Some feared that if the church and society emphasized support for all families, these institutions would never get around to restoring the vitality of intact two-parent families and the ecology of institutions required to support them. Furthermore, we felt that stability and intactness are not virtues in themselves if they are accompanied by forms of relating that diminish our humanity, such as patriarchy, abuse, inequality, and exploitation. Hence, to argue for the revival of intact families is to argue for their reconstruction; it is to argue for a new family or, at least, the fulfillment of some old democratizing trajectories.

We finally agreed that faith and critical reflection require us to give central support to the mother-father, egalitarian family in which each partner has flexible access to public and private responsibilities. We recognize that this ideal, like all ideals, will have many variations, just as did the ideal of the middle-class family in the industrial era. Like all ideals, it will be susceptible to demonic distortions, but we believe there are resources within Christianity to guard against them.

Although we affirm the prima facie obligation of church and society to promote this ideal, we also believe that both church and society should minister to and support all family constellations, especially all families with children. By prima facie we mean to offer the idea of the intact, egalitarian, mother-father partnership as "true and valid" in the sense of "sufficient at first impression" until, under certain circumstances, exceptions are shown to be warranted.[5] The prima facie presumption toward intactness does not trump all other values under all conditions. The church should take this stand for theological reasons, but there are philosophical reasons that point in the same direction. However, to support all families with children, regardless of form, means to help make them work as well as possible. There are powerful forces in our society producing family dislocation. Divorce, out-of-wedlock births, single mothers, single fathers, stepfamilies, poor families, marginalized families, and other family experiments will not evaporate even if current trends begin to moderate. Both church and society have before them the huge challenge of supporting these families and helping them to flourish—especially in their task of raising children.

In short, we believe that church and society must go in both directions simultaneously. More particularly, churches must develop a theology, a rhetoric, and a pastoral strategy that adequately addresses both the ideal values of the Christian faith and the realities of modern and postmodern life. Our everyday Christian practice should maintain the creative tension between these two directions. The Christian gospel is uniquely designed to hold such tensions together. The capacity to hold ideals and realities together creatively is what we call the *ironic-realist* element within the Christian message. Churches should protect against the moralism that chapter 3 shows existed in Christianity's idealization of the nineteenth–century middle-class family.

It should be stated at the beginning that two significant issues are not directly addressed in this book—abortion and homosexuality. Every book must have its primary foci and limits. These two issues are so complicated that to address either, in addition to the large number of family issues we do address, would make this book unmanageably ambitious. We advise the reader not to jump to conclusions about what this implies for these issues. As a matter of fact, the five authors go in different directions on these important and well-covered topics.

Long-term trends have been recognizing the ideal of the equal-regard, mother-father, public-private partnership. This is why we are not totally pessimistic about the state of the contemporary family. We believe that women are on the threshold of a new status in families and that strands in both Judaism and Christianity have contributed to these transformations. We believe that creative efforts are being made to re-define the role of fathers. These trends too have some foundations in Jewish and Christian thought. Hence, we speak more about the *crisis* of the family than about the *decline* of the family. The present situation of families is simultaneously full of creativity and promise and full of danger and disruption.

Is the egalitarian mother-father partnership the "Christian family"? We cannot assert this without considerable qualification, but we see values and trajectories in Christianity that point in this direction. Family ideals are complex compromises between economic, biological, and religiocultural forces. Families change as economic and historical patterns evolve. But Christianity shaped family patterns in egalitarian directions in the past and will do so again. Just as early Christianity helped change antique patriarchy into a more egalitarian paternalism motivated by love, Christianity today can turn the forces that are reducing women's economic dependence on men into new possibilities for family democracy.

The nineteenth-century industrial family was not *the* Christian family. The new twenty-first–century equal-regard family will not be *the* Christian family either. The intact, equal-regard, public-private family is consistent with Christianity and reflects certain Christian values, but it will *be* fully Christian only if additional themes of Christian love, forgiveness, and grace surround this family and are acted out within it. Furthermore, families are for Christianity highly important relative goods; they are not to be equated with the kingdom of God or the essential meaning of salvation. Christianity, however, enriched the industrial family, and it may do the same for the postindustrial family.

Mutuality, Sacrifice, and Fulfillment:
Three Studies

This book is an exercise in practical theology, a style of doing theology that begins with practical questions, describes the situations from which the questions come, and searches the classic expressions of the Christian faith for guidance. It moves from a description of practice to theory and then back to a renewed and more critical practice. In the end, it is interested in appropriate transformation of our practices to meet changed circumstances.

Practical theology sees the description of problematic practices as a major part of its task. For this reason we spend time in the introduction and first three chapters charting the recent national debate about the past, present, and future of the family in the United States. For this reason also we report on three empirical studies. We want to look at family practices in greater detail than the national debate generally conveys. Specifically, we want to describe the different *models of love that guide family life in the United States.*

In one study we cooperated with the Social Science Research Center and the Council on Families in America in doing ten hours of face-to-face interviews with members of twenty-seven families from six different parts of the country (New York–New Jersey, New England, Chicago-Milwaukee, Atlanta, Indianapolis, and Texas).[6] The second study, done with the Gallup International Institute, was a national survey (the *Love and Marriage Survey*) on the models of love that Americans think correlate with good marriages. In a third study, we worked with Professor Thomas Needham of the Fuller Graduate School of Psychology on a national survey (see chapter 7) of the ethical values guiding the practice of marriage and family counselors.[7]

In our face-to-face interviews we looked at many issues. But mainly we were searching for the moral ecologies—the models of love and obligation—found in various intact American families. We were concerned to learn which of the three models of love—love as self-sacrifice, love as mutuality, and love as individual fulfillment—couples think they predominantly follow in their marriages. Furthermore, we wanted to know how they compared their marriage to their parents' marriage.

We learned that couples today believe that they enjoy more mutuality and are less self-sacrificial than their parents. They see their roles as far more flexible than those of their parents, although wives today are still tied more to domestic responsibilities than are husbands. Couples today think their mothers were much more inclined to see their role as "serving the husband" than wives today. Far more women work outside the home either full- or part-time, and they share access to bank accounts and checkbooks more than their mothers did.

Couples think they share more completely the raising and discipline of children than did their own parents. Fathers today feel they are more expressive and share more feelings with their children than did their own fathers. They get more involved in moral discussions with their children; they see themselves as "explaining moral issues more" than their parents, whom they perceive as being "more cut and dried." They consider their present families to be disciplined, but they are also more willing to "enjoy" life than were their parents.

They think they are more concerned about women's issues than their parents were. They are more concerned about educating their daughters for an unpredictable future. Their own parents often "sacrificed" to educate their daughters but generally for traditional female vocations.

Two issues surprised us. Although parents feel they talk more with their children, reveal feelings more, and struggle with them more about a greater number of issues, they do not feel they get much help from institutions outside the home. Churches, schools, the media, and neighbors do not help as they did a generation ago. In short, *parents today think that the ecology of family supports has deteriorated.* Because they feel they must compensate for the decline of trustworthy institutions, many concerned parents we interviewed felt they have to do more, not less, in shaping their children's lives. As a consequence, adults today think they "felt freer" as kids and had less parental supervision than is the case for their children today.

The Moral Ecology of
Five American Families

Here are the stories of five representative families, their moral ecologies, and their efforts to cope with the interplay of love as mutuality, self-sacrifice, and self-fulfillment. We introduce their stories now and later examine, in more detail, their struggles to reconcile the tensions of love. These stories also help us put flesh on other important issues facing families.

The Turners live in an upper-middle-class northern suburb of Chicago.[8] They are handsome and well-dressed and live in a roomy, impeccably ordered, and tastefully furnished house. They are Evangelical Christians of European descent. Jim, now a conservative Presbyterian, grew up in a conservative Baptist family. He has both a college degree and seminary education. Sophie, his

wife, has a college degree as well. After working in conservative
Christian youth organizations for several years, Jim became a successful freelance writer.

Jim and Sophie, in contrast to some stereotypes of evangelical
families, are not examples of the working father and stay-at-home
mother. At one time, Sophie was the principal breadwinner, followed by a period during which she was not employed outside the
home. Now she has returned to part-time employment as an interior decorator. But with her college education, her teaching experience, and now her part-time career in interior design, she need
not be economically dependent on Jim. Even as it stands, she
makes a significant contribution to the family income. And the
Turners live well.

The religious life of the Turners came largely from Jim's side of
the family. His parents are depicted as loving, generous, and permissive religious conservatives. "They did not have to tell us what
to do. The church did that." Jim raises his two teenage daughters
very much as he was raised—conservatively. But it doesn't work
out the same way. Although the Turners give hours of volunteer
help to both school and church, they feel they get less help from
these institutions in raising their children than his parents got.
They report having to do more "to help our daughters think it
through for themselves."

The Turners are examples of a family that, in spite of the increased secularization of society, think actively and pervasively in
theological categories. They believe that their children are "gifts
from God" and that they are raising their children "for God." God
is the true authority and they simply "try to do God's will." For
many issues, such as those dealing with sexuality, God's will is
clear. Other issues, such as the kind of careers their daughters will
follow, are mainly a matter of individual choice.

The Turners practice a modified form of the "headship" theory
of the role of husbands and fathers in families. Jim Turner is no absent father. In fact, he is very engaged. His rationale for this engagement comes, he believes, from the New Testament.

Jim likes to refer to Ephesians 5:23 ("For the husband is head of
the wife as Christ is the head of the church") and interprets this to
mean that the husband is the chief servant who has the responsibility for taking the lead in creating a Christian household. Both Sophie
and Jim agree that this does not give him the right to be arbitrary,
authoritarian, or insensitive to her wants and opinions. Jim's involvement with the parenting task of his family leads him to join ac-

tively with Sophie in praying, reading scripture, and enacting family rituals with their popular, attractive, and athletic teenage daughters. There is considerable warmth and intimacy in their home, and their daughters seem to be accepting their parents' values.

The Turners handle the growing participation of both husbands and wives in the wage economy through a myriad of small compromises and maneuvers. Their theology of marriage and parenting, their conservative moral stance, and their deep involvement in church and school provides an ideological and institutional buffer against the values of an outside world they perceive as riddled with materialism and greed, especially the entertainment industry. Neither Jim nor Sophie works full-time outside the home. Jim's career as a freelance writer gives him a flexible work schedule. On the days Sophie works, Jim is home before their daughters return from school. He is the coach of his daughter's high school volleyball team, and he attends the PTA meetings and a wide range of school events. Jim also does most of the cooking.

The Turners feel that God has provided an explicit moral pattern for almost every aspect of their family life. On some family issues, however, they feel entitled to exercise practical discernment, imagining as best as possible what Jesus would do, with no fixed pattern in mind. The Turners' moral thinking is informed by a mixture of divine commands, the moral example of Jesus, and practical—even rational cost-benefit—types of calculation. Once they believe they are within the basic framework of God's will, the Turners calculate quite expediently who brings in the income, who does which chores at home, how to save money for college, how to dress well, and how to take nice twice-yearly family vacations.

Jim and Sophie Turner,
Evangelical Christians

———————

Mary Murphy laments that her four children are not growing up to be good Catholics. She worries that she and her conservative Catholic husband were not forceful enough in stressing the truths of the Catholic church. Born and raised in New York City, Mary and her mother lived with various relatives while her father was in the army during World War II and the Korean War. Her mother was institutionalized for alcoholism when Mary was twelve. Although her parents were not strong Catholics, she spent her teenage years largely in residential Catholic schools.

She loved these schools. She cannot remember her father ever telling her what to do. He never advised her or corrected her for anything. She was a good student who behaved well; it was simply assumed by her father that she would always do the right thing. Jim Turner, as the reader will recall, believed that the church, sometimes even more than his parents, guided his life as a child and youth ("the church told us what to do"). In a very similar way, Mary Murphy learned how to behave from the Catholic sisters who were her teachers. She seldom saw her mother throughout her teenage years. Her father was very permissive and nondirective, although she knew he was delighted when she was accepted into Columbia University.

Although she and her husband sent their four sons to Catholic elementary schools, not one is in the church today. Although the sons have done reasonably well in their vocations, their relationships with their girlfriends and wives have included divorces, cohabitation, and abortions. These acts deeply contradict the values of Mary and Patrick Murphy. For the Murphys, in contrast to the Turners, religion was something you did at church, not at home. Prayers, rituals, and religious holidays were not a conspicuous part of the Murphy household, as indeed they had not been a part of Mary's and Patrick's homes of origin.

Yet the Catholic view of marriage was deeply meaningful to Mary and Patrick. To Mary, marriage is an objective sacrament, a transcending reality, that cannot be altered, no matter what economic, health, or personal frustrations beset it. This sacrament formed their marriage. "It is something you grow into; you learn to love your husband according to the objective requirements of the sacrament. I'm sure that we would have left each other many times if it had not been for our belief in the objective reality of the marriage commitment."

Mary, like Sophie, did not work in the early days of her marriage. As time allowed and financial need dictated, she became an editor at a university press. Her job was always secondary to her roles as mother and wife. Patrick helped with the boys at night, but he was a lawyer and never had the flexibility of Jim Turner's schedule. The Murphys were more nearly a traditional family. Both Sophie and Mary wanted their husbands to do as much as possible around the house, but the work was never divided fifty-fifty, and neither Sophie nor Mary seemed to be terribly concerned. With the Turners, the details of gender roles tended to fall outside the clear mandates of their religion and descended to the realm of practicality, personal tastes, custom, and contingency.

The Murphys, like the Turners, made decisions to organize their priorities around home and children. They wanted to live well, but they placed clear limits on both the quest for individual fulfillment and the seductions of the market. They were successful and perhaps lucky enough to have both their home life and a reasonable share of the "good life." But one does not sense that the Murphys do much active practical thinking about their marriage and family. The structures of marriage were "given"—something to be received and internalized. Childrearing was a different matter. The Murphys often puzzled about what they as parents were doing with their sons.

Mary Murphy,
Catholic

———————

To have both the good life and a home life was much more difficult to achieve for Maria Taylor, an African-American mother of three daughters. Maria works and lives near Trenton, New Jersey. While she was in college, she became pregnant and gave birth to a daughter. Because of health problems, she went on welfare. She identified Robert, who was her good friend, as the father, told him that the authorities might force him to make child-support payments, and asked him what he wanted to do. He proposed that they get married. They did.

Today Robert is a coordinator in a center for emotionally disturbed children; Maria is a teacher's aide. They are Pentecostal Christians. The Taylors now have three daughters, one of whom is nearly a teenager. They live on a very basic income, but they make ends meet. They go to church three to four times a week, for young people's fellowship on Tuesday (which the Taylors lead), Bible study on Wednesday, sometimes Youth for Christ meetings on Saturday mornings, and worship service on Sundays. Maria also directs the choir.

Maria's father was the oldest of ten brothers and sisters, whom he raised after their parents' death. Maria's father, even more than her mother, was "always the one that was there." Maria had five siblings. Two are dead (Annette got "caught in the wrong environment"), one had a child out-of-wedlock, and two are married with children. Maria is the only sibling who went to college.

Maria's theology of marriage and family is not as definite as either the Turners' or the Murphys'. Yet her family practices an intense and joyful daily religious life. During nightly prayers, the children are "invited to express themselves." There is a short prayer in the morning, grace and two scripture readings at the evening meal, and singing together as a family. The girls "seem to like all this. They ask for it."

Maria's and Robert's division of household duties is probably the most egalitarian of the three families we have discussed. The person who gets home first at night is the one who makes the evening meal. Maria pays the small bills; Robert pays the rent out of his paycheck. Robert helps put the girls to bed. Even the girls get into the egalitarian spirit. The Taylors have family meetings during which they create the family rules. These rules are posted on the refrigerator. Then Maria and Robert share equally the responsibility of assuring that everyone lives up to the rules. This includes bedtime for the children at 8:30 P.M., schoolwork before bed, and no snacks before dinner. Maria will occasionally spank but generally uses talking. In fact, she raises her children as she was raised, with one exception: like the Turners, she *talks a lot* to her children—she explains things and tells them "how she felt when she was a child."

Maria holds to the Pentecostal line that the man is the head of the house, but she confessed she would "tell Robert that even if she didn't believe it." But, like the Turners, the Taylors take that to mean mainly that the man is to be responsible. Robert *is* responsible, according to Maria. "He is a very good father. We were friends before we fell in love. That's the way it should happen." Maria does not believe that there is anything in her religion that tells how a husband and wife should divide household duties. "It's mainly a matter of common sense." Fathers are important for families. They can do anything a mother can do, "but they are different, and that is important." Boys and girls should be raised in a spirit of equality and basically in the same manner. Education is important for both, according to Maria, and they should both "be raised to work and raised to take care of the children."

Maria's religiomoral thinking about the family is much like the Turners' but is less structured. It provides a loose canopy over all she does. Beneath this broad religious umbrella are a myriad of practical, democratic, and expedient decisions. She is married to a man who seems to understand and like this style. In Maria's family, Christian ideals are used to bolster the responsibility of the father and husband. But the psychological power is with Maria, as is nearly half of the earning power. Within this model, a style of prac-

tical moral thinking reigns that extends duties, rights, and opportunities with considerable equality to parents and children alike.

Mary Tayler,
Pentecostal

————————

Sarah Miles and her husband Frank are well educated and enjoy an
excellent income. But Frank, an Indianapolis oncologist, makes
most of the money for the household. Sarah, a professional concert
pianist, cannot begin to earn this amount unless she greatly increases
her professional involvement, a step she is reluctant to take. Sarah
would like to have earnings so that she could survive independently
from Frank. She also at times finds her marriage highly limiting. In
an effort to remain in the marriage, she struggles to find her individuality and express her unique personal and artistic gifts.

Sarah describes her family of origin as a tense, fatalistic Jewish
family plagued by memories of hard times as immigrants and by a
dark sadness because of relatives who perished in the Holocaust and
other problematic patterns. She remembers three lessons from her
father: "life is hard," "education is extremely important," and "life is
not fair." She laments that "generally my family existed by hating
other people. I just don't want to hate anybody." Her mother was
also an outstanding musician but sacrificed a career for the family—
something she resented.

Sarah continues to pursue music through selective public engage-
ments and instructing others. But her marriage, her role as mother to
two young children, and her musical career have all been colored by
the attitudes of her family of origin. She and Frank were determined
to make their Judaism more meaningful than it had been to either set
of parents. They intentionally aspired to retrieve and reconstruct their
Jewish identity. They have become more involved than their parents
in their local Reform synagogue. Although they continue to be faithful participants, Sarah finds her synagogue out of touch with people's
lives and insufficiently joyful, spontaneous, and warm.

It has been personal therapy that has helped her really find and
experience God, which has given her an entirely new and accepting attitude toward her everyday life. God, her therapist has helped
her see, is "everything," including "something" within her. She
refers to God and her spirituality as "tools." "When you go the
healing route, the tools that you need are connectedness with
God." Therapy and the experience of God gave her a new sense of

self and helped her with the "dark side" of her personality. Nothing else did this, including the synagogue.

Sarah believes that her therapy has made a huge difference for her family life. It is removing the "negativity" from her relations to her husband and children. Nothing that she was taught by her own family does she want to pass on to her children. Rather than the deep feeling that life is unfair, Sarah wants to teach her children that "there is love," that "there is a God," and that life is a matter of "growth."

For the time being, Sarah has given up pursuing a full-time career in music. She works hard to keep her husband and children from turning her into the "sacrificial, all-giving housewife." She enjoys the standard of living that Frank provides. Her spirituality, however, helps her transcend the irritations of living in a modified form of the nineteenth-century "separate spheres" (paid work and domestic life). More than many of the women we interviewed, Sarah was schooled to ride the economic trends of women's move into the wage economy and professional employment outside the home. Sarah and Frank are more influenced by the women's movement than are the Turners, Murphys, or Taylors, although it influences their lives as well.

But the economic good fortune of her husband and her commitment to her children have led her in another direction. Although Sarah is committed to the ideal of a democratized household, she is as practical as are Sophie and Maria in facing the difficulties of realizing that ideal. Her spirituality gives her the strength to live with the ambiguity of not following her love of music yet feeling relieved to avoid the competitive professional life she once wanted.

Fortunately, Frank does his best within the limits of his socialization and high-powered profession. This is probably good, because if he did not work hard to pull his weight as father and domestic hand (even though he struggles and sometimes falls short), Sarah Miles has the talent and drive to leave him. Frank's sincere intentions go a long way.

Sarah Miles,
Reform Jew

———————

Richard and his wife, Phyllis, have three teenage children, a son and two daughters. A leader in his large Presbyterian church in Milwaukee, Richard is the general counsel of a major national corporation. He has been on the board of Planned Parenthood. He was an athlete in high school and considers himself a team player.

Phyllis has a master's degree in special education but has done little teaching. She is now a part-time interior decorator. Phyllis had wanted a career, but the birth of their children and Richard's good salary conspired to push that ambition aside.

Although Richard considers himself a churchman, it is the organizational aspects of churches and their moral values that attract him, not their theology or spirituality. The theological side of his Christianity never developed. His father was like him—an executive, active in the community, a member of the board of trustees of his church, but never deeply religious. His mother taught Sunday school for a couple of years but for the most part was not very active. It is "more the values" of the church rather than its theology or ritual that attracted them. Richard confessed, "I didn't ever see from any of them a spark of religion." They just "followed the Ten Commandments," "dropped the kids off for Sunday school," and "prayed on Christmas and Thanksgiving."

Richard represents himself as being in the same mold. It is the Golden Rule, honesty, hard work, and the Boy Scout motto that have guided his life. This is what he taught his children as well. Richard has no religious understanding of his marriage or his role as a parent. Yet he considers himself a committed husband who puts "the family first." But these commitments pertain to his values, not his theology. He once turned down a prestigious and lucrative job offer in New York City for the "good of the family."

His children, who attend elite private schools, share Richard's lack of enthusiasm for the beliefs and spirituality of the church. In contrast to Richard, however, they have little interest in the institution of the church. They are deeply involved in their social lives; they are, Richard says, "like free floating particles—we see 'em when we see 'em."

Richard and Phyllis divide their family responsibilities on pragmatic grounds. Once again, it is his "philosophy," not religion, he believes, that determines these responsibilities. Richard believes that he is much like his father. But Richard joins Jim and Sophie Turner, Mary Murphy, and Sarah Miles in seeing their fathers, whatever their other virtues, as far less open, affectionate, and communicative than they believe the men of today should be.

Richard is deeply involved in the technical rationality of the modern and postmodern world as it expresses itself in the logic of the market. His emphasis on the Golden Rule might lead one to think of him as a sort of modern-day Kantian. But one detects in Richard's moral thinking little of the rigor associated with the Kantian sense of duty. Richard's ethic is closer to Robert Bellah's concept of "utilitarian individualism," a kind of individualism that calculates individual utility in close relation to the corporate profits.[9] Richard wants to raise the overall good of society but has a strong interest in making him and his family beneficiaries. Richard keeps his values and commitments in a broad and low-key middle range. This makes it possible for him to deal with a wide spectrum of people in his business and community life. As a lawyer, he is trained to see both sides of every issue but then take the side that favors his client. "I get paid for this," he says. He takes this general attitude into his non-professional life as well. Richard has fewer convictions than most people we interviewed. This seems to be true of his children as well. In spite of their excellent educational advantages, consumerism and social life seem to dominate their lives.

Richard Good,
Liberal Protestant

Struggles over how to define and balance sacrifice, mutuality, and individual fulfillment run throughout these cases. These five families find different solutions, implement different strategies. In addition to the different models of love they display, we see in them different ways of relating to market and bureaucratic forces, different ways of relating to patriarchy, and different ways of handling the intricacies of communication. We return to their stories many times in this volume.

The National Survey
on Love and Marriage

Our study with the George H. Gallup International Institute, the *Love and Marriage Survey,* reinforced much of what we learned from our interviews. We continued our study of the three models of love: mutuality, self-sacrifice, and individual fulfillment. Respondents were asked which of these models of love in their opinion best correlates with good marriages and families. The three models parallel three classic models of love found in the Western theological and philosophical tradition. The first defines love as mutuality or equal regard ("giving your spouse and children the same respect, affection, and help as you expect from them"). The second depicts marital love as self-sacrifice ("putting the needs and goals of your spouse and children ahead of your own"). The third model understands love as serving self-fulfillment ("fulfilling your personal needs and life goals"). See table 1.

Table 1. Views of Respondents and Their Parents on
Models of Love Correlating with Good Marriages*

Model of Love	Respondent's Beliefs	Mother's Beliefs	Father's Beliefs
Mutuality	55	29	28
Self-Sacrifice	38	56	40
Self-Fulfillment	5	9	28

*Numbers represent percentages.

Among the 1,019 randomly selected respondents, 55 percent chose mutuality as the model of love best correlating with good marriages; 38 percent chose the self-sacrificial model; and 5 percent chose the self-actualization model. A cultural appreciation for love as mutuality seems to be on the rise. This is even clearer when we compare these scores with how our respondents think their mothers and fathers would have ranked these models. Twenty-nine percent thought their mother would have chosen mutuality, 56 percent thought she would have chosen self-sacrifice, and 9 percent thought she would have chosen self-fulfillment. Couples today believe their mothers valued self-sacrifice in marriage and family life much more than they themselves do. The fathers of our adult interviewees are seen in more complex ways. Our respondents thought that 40 percent of their fathers would have valued self-sacrifice the most, while self-fulfillment and mutuality would have been the equally ranked choice for 28 percent of their fathers. Some fathers of our respondents were perceived as more oriented toward self-fulfillment than respondents' mothers, although, at the same time, many fathers are seen as valuing self-sacrifice more than their sons do as fathers today.

When the same questions were asked regarding behavior in contrast to belief, the scores changed (see table 2). When we asked which model was used to resolve actual conflicts with loved ones, mutuality went down by 10 points to 45 percent, self-sacrifice went down by ten points to 28 percent, and self-fulfillment went up 8 points to 13 percent. It seems that people have higher regard for mutuality and self-sacrifice than they demonstrate in their actual behaviors. Nonetheless, love as mutuality was still the dominant ideal.

All of these scores vary according to age, education, income, marital status, religious experience, political convictions, and race. The majority of our respondents value mutuality more than self-sacrifice, but appreciation for love as self-sacrifice increases for certain types of people. If people have had certain kinds of religious experience, their appreciation for

Table 2. A Comparison of Perceived Behavior and Attitudes
about Models of Love Correlating with Good Marriages*

Model of Love	Belief in Model	Practicing the Model in Behavior
Mutuality	55	45
Self-Sacrifice	38	28
Self-Fulfillment	5	13

Numbers represent percentages.

self-sacrifice is likely to be higher, even though it will still be less than the value they place on mutuality. One's appreciation for self-sacrifice in relation to mutuality is likely to go up if one is male, is politically conservative, has a low income, comes from a farm or small town, is religiously conservative, or is a Lutheran from the upper Midwest. If one is young, female, well educated, politically liberal, a liberal Protestant, and has a high income, one is likely to value mutuality much more than self-sacrifice. People who are satisfied with their loving relationship are also likely to correlate mutuality, rather than self-sacrifice, with good marriages and satisfying family life. People who are cohabiting are likely to value mutuality in solving conflicts (52 percent) but much more likely than the general population to disvalue sacrifice (17 percent) and twice as likely to value self-fulfillment (21 percent).

In short, large portions of our society are seeing mutuality as the preferred model for marital relationships, and people who are younger, wealthier, more educated, and more liberal politically value mutuality more and self-sacrifice less. Self-sacrifice is valued less in all of these groups, whereas love as self-fulfillment seems to be holding steady at around 5 to 7 percent.

Although there is much more to say about all of this, one thing can be said now with considerable certainty: *Our society is undergoing a profound revolution in its image of good marital and family love.* Mutuality is being perceived more positively; self-sacrifice is being perceived more negatively.

Exciting possibilities lie within these shifts, but also great dangers. Mutuality is more easily talked about than enacted. Furthermore, mutuality as a belief or behavior cannot stand alone; it must be related to other beliefs, values, narratives, and hopes. How did our respondent interpret mutuality? Did it mean treating the other as an end as one wishes to be treated? This was our formulation of the option in the survey, but respondents may have interpreted our question differently. Did it mean to them a conditional and reciprocal "give-and-take"? And must not self-sacrifice continue to play a role if mutuality is to endure? Our survey shows that Americans are struggling to find a language of mutuality. It does not demonstrate that they have succeeded.

The Argument

In chapter 1 we investigate how the family became a liberal political issue in the first half of the 1990s. Liberal politics, liberal social science, and liberal religion during the 1960s, 1970s, and 1980s held that family changes—divorce, out-of-wedlock births, stepfamilies, single parenthood—would increase adult freedoms without harming either children or their parents. In the 1990s, the social sciences began showing that these family changes had been, on average, harmful to children and mothers, and liberal political culture began to assume a new realism about family change in its public policy. In the 1980s, the family had been a conservative political issue; by 1996, it was captured by the neoliberals of the Democratic party. It was not clear where liberal religion stood on this shift.

In chapter 2, we review the massive social and cultural trends that are producing such stunning transformations in American families. These trends are fourfold: (1) the drift in Western societies toward heightened forms of individualism; (2) the spread of market economics and government bureaucracy into the intimacies of families and private life; (3) the powerful psychological shifts that these forces have produced; and (4) the influences of a declining, yet still active, patriarchy. We see these trends as interactive, although the cultural trends toward narrow individualism and market materialism are central in driving the others. Voices in the American family debate usually emphasize one or another of these factors at the exclusion of the others. We believe that all four factors are important and that balanced solutions—most current solutions are not balanced—should address all four. *Our solutions try to do this.*

Many social scientists, policymakers, politicians, and church leaders believe that these trends cannot be resisted, that family fragmentation will continue, and that it will spread from Western societies into poorer countries, where it will have especially devastating results. In short, they believe that *nothing can be done about these forces but to try to mitigate their consequences.*[10]

What we call our ironic-realist perspective on the Christian faith leads us to value the realism of this stance yet seek to transcend it with hope. We believe in the possibility of religiocultural change, the power of cultural movements, and the efficacy of debate and rational persuasion both to alter human behavior and to enable people to devise wise programs of intervention. Our hope is born from our religious convictions and a sense of history.

Chapter 3 presents a picture of how the four trends listed above interacted to produce in the nineteenth century an image of the ideal middle-class American family. This ideal was often thought to be the Christian family, although that conclusion was an oversimplification: many variations on this image of the family existed. Our conflicts over the family today are partially due to the fact that family life in the American Northeast, Southeast, Midwest, upper Midwest, Southwest, and West were shaped by different religiocultural and economic forces. These forces and trends are alive even today.

Chapters 4 and 5 present a first statement of the contributions of Christianity to Western family theory. Throughout the book, we use the ideas of a number of Protestant thinkers—Martin Luther, Emil Brunner, Reinhold Niebuhr, Gene Outka—as well as Catholic feminist theologians—Elisabeth Schüssler Fiorenza, Rosemary Ruether, Christine Gudorf, Lisa Cahill, and Barbara Andolsen. These feminists have one thing in common—they take both nature and experience quite seriously. In this point, they have affinities with Thomas Aquinas, a theologian we use for an important but restricted reason: he illustrates what we have in mind by a psychocultural economic or ecological view of the family. He had an understanding of the natural elements that go into family formation that is amazingly similar to the views of contemporary evolutionary ecology. He had a striking theory of what led human males, in contrast to other mammalian males, to become attached—somewhat against their natural inclinations—to the primordial mother-infant family.

We agree with Aquinas that the naturalistic level of analysis is indispensable but insufficient to understand families. Aquinas subordinated, without suppressing, a psychobiology of families to the values of equality and friendship between husband and wife. But Aquinas went further. He developed a high doctrine of sacrificial love that worked to counterbalance what we call the "male problematic"—the primordial male tendency to procreate but not to care for offspring or mate. Our analysis of contemporary family trends reveals this male problematic to be one of the most pressing national and international family trends of our time. Aquinas understood the foundations of this problematic and addressed it in his theology of the family.

Here we make a sharp distinction between his theology of intactness and his patriarchy. Furthermore, we extend his view of Christ as model for the husband and include wives as well. This helps us construct a theory of family love that makes equal regard or mutuality central and then makes *self-sacrificial love an essential but subordinate moment of love that is mainly in the service of equal regard.* In this model of family love, sacrificial love is not an end in itself. Our view of Christian love when applied to families is in sympathy with the cultural trend toward valuing love as mutuality that we discovered in our interviews and survey. But within a fully Christian perspective on love, self-sacrifice or self-giving plays an indispensable role in renewing love as mutuality. The contemporary move toward mutuality does not necessarily indicate that the relationship of commitment and self-sacrifice in family love has been understood.

Love as equal regard or mutuality is central to the New Testament message. We do not interpret the discussion of the Christian household given in Ephesians 5:21–33 as a Christian justification of "male headship" modeled after the authority of Christ, even though the passage has been misused to say this throughout Christian history. When placed in its proper historical context, this passage should be understood as celebrating a servant model of the husband and father that constituted an assault on the male honor codes of the Greco-Roman world—codes that made males "constitutional" monarchs over their wives and "royal" monarchs over their children.

Love as equal regard is complex: It entails respect for the other but is more than that. It also *wills the good* for the other. Because our model of equal regard encompasses both willing the good and giving respect, we must delve into the issue of the "premoral goods" that many "liberal" models of love as mutuality overlook. Furthermore, love as equal regard is reversible; it accords to the self the same regard it accords to the other. That is the meaning of Christian neighbor love, and it applies to members of the family just as it does to the neighbor, the stranger, and the enemy. In fact, we argue that love for the neighbor, stranger, and enemy is an analogical extension of natural family love.

In chapters 6 to 9 we engage in a critical dialogue with four important voices in the American family debate. Our goal is to illustrate the way a cultural conversation can proceed. This rehearsal of the dialogue is not the dialogue itself; it is designed to show the possibility of a critical conversation between conflicting voices. There is much to learn from all of these positions. Yet we have measured criticisms of each of the four voices we engage—feminists, family therapists, Christian pro-family advocates, and economists. Feminists (chapter 6) have been the strongest advocates for a model of love built on mutuality. Furthermore, religious feminists have advanced important formulations of the relation of mutuality and sacrifice.

Because the external pressures for long-term family cohesion are declining, family stability will increasingly be a result of "communicative competence," and family therapists (chapter 7) can help us to understand and implement mutuality with this competence. Such competence, however, is grounded in a commitment that requires a religious vision. The profamily voices—especially the Catholic church and the black churches—hold insights on how to balance family ethics with social policy. In chapter 8 we bring together the Catholic notion of *subsidiarity* and the Reformed theory of the "orders of creation"—two very central ideas for our social philosophy. Finally, economists (chapter 9) remind us of important economic values that families must respect even if most economists fail to have an adequate ethic to guide their economic insights.

In chapters 10 and 11, we set forth a "practical theology of families" that builds on our descriptive and historical investigation. It is guided by a love ethic of equal regard in which self-giving is in the service of mutuality and not an end in itself. Both husband and wife should equally play the sacrificial role, equally enact the role of Christ to the family, and equally do this on behalf of friendship, *philia* (love), and mutuality. The interplay between self-giving and equal regard is best conceived as a life-cycle ethic—something achieved between husband and wife, parents and children, families and other families amidst the changing rhythms of maturing, having children, and growing old. Families guided by this ethic become communities of dialogue and interpretation. This dialogue occurs within and between families and with the family traditions of their heritages. In doing this, they establish their authoritative values in four areas of family life that are becoming increasingly democratized: shared housework, shared earnings, shared care of children, and shared formation of values guiding the family. The family's beliefs and values should evolve from an inquiry into the classic sources of wisdom about families in our religious and nonreligious traditions. This inquiry should involve both husband and wife, their families of origin, and eventually the children. In contrast to the popular saying, father does *not* always know best and needs all the help he can get.

With regard to the relation of families to church, market, and government, our message is first that these institutions should discover each other and see each other as potential friends and cooperative partners. If they are to be friends, appropriate limits must be placed on each of their roles. Religious organizations need to help construct the values for the egalitarian mother-father partnership of the postindustrial family. Government must confess its negative contribution to family disruption through programs that often contributed to dependency and took over family functions. Rather than making a wholesale retreat, however, government must find innovative ways to support families, especially poor families. Government must make new initiatives in concert with the culture-making institutions of civil society, and churches and synagogues belong in these new partnerships.

Finally, the market must help support committed, intact, equal-regard, public-private families. We have many ideas about how the market can help, not the least of which is the proposal for a new sixty-hour family work week: sixty hours that can be divided in a variety of ways to enable both husbands and wives to be as equally "domestic" and as "public" as they desire.

As early Christianity, the Protestant Reformation, and revivalism in the nineteenth century helped construct new understandings of families—ones that simultaneously elevated the responsibilities of fathers, increased the dignity of women and motherhood, enhanced married life as a vocation, emphasized the importance of marital permanence, and proclaimed that families and marriage were subordinate to the kingdom or realm of God—we must pray for a similar religiocultural *revolution* in our time. We also should hope that a new critical familism will have relevance beyond the United States, especially in poor countries where the developing disruption of families may have even worse consequences than in Western, industrial countries.

This new family revolution will be less pious in tone, less under the auspices of confessing churches, more interdisciplinary and interprofessional, more at the grassroots level, and more dialogical than these earlier revolutions. But if such a revolution is to occur at all, religious institutions, as they did so often in the past, must play a major role.

PART 1

The Issues

1

The Family (1990–1996)

From a Conservative to a Liberal Issue

In the early 1990s, the phrase "family values" was most often associated with a concern to defend traditional families and promoted by religious and political conservatives. By 1996 the phrase had become part of a wider and more complex moral debate addressed by a range of liberals as well. This shift in ownership of the family issue was most apparent at the level of political culture.

In 1992, *Families First* was the title of a report from a Bush-appointed commission for studying America's urban families.[1] But by 1996, "Families First" was the official theme of the Democratic presidential and congressional campaign. Bill Clinton's lead and eventual victory can be partly explained by his artful capture of the family issue from the control of political and religious conservatives. This capture was accomplished by synthesizing religious, cultural, economic, and ecological perspectives on the family. Appeals to the themes of environmental ecology that helped Clinton gain the White House in 1992 were extended in 1996 to ecological relations among family, government, market, and church, all of which he tilted toward the central importance of families, especially the committed, intact family.

The Republicans lost the 1996 presidential election in part because their emphasis on restoring family stability was perceived as too individualistic, too nostalgic for earlier family patterns, and too deeply entwined with a hoped-for revival of the economy. Suddenly the Republicans who formerly had championed "family values" saw everything—restoring marital commitment, reducing the divorce rate, lowering the out-of-wedlock birthrate, advancing the well-being of children, reviving civil society—as following from a tax break and a better family income. The Republican perspective seemed devoid of sensitivity to pressing personal struggles and attention to the ecology of supports that families need in order to survive in a postmodern world. In spite of early efforts by Republicans to free the party from preoccupation with the abortion issue, the Republican message on the family still seemed dominated by that topic. Both parties moved toward the middle on family issues, fought over the middle, and tried to take credit for the realities and symbolism of welfare reform. Whether they deserved it or not, the Democrats won the public relations battle and received most of the credit for their perspective on the American family debate.

Whether ownership of the family issue has similarly shifted from conservative to mainline religious groups is a central question of this book. In the 1996 election, such conservative groups as the Christian Coalition and Focus on the Family suffered a setback; they were ignored by Republican candidate Robert Dole and therefore became unenthusiastic about delivering the vote. At the same time, mainline churches were largely invisible in the public discussion about the family. Although the mainline Protestant denominations have both conservative and liberal members, for the most part the public statements of these churches in the 1990s reflected an older political liberalism dating from the 1960s and 1970s that was concerned more with poverty and economic justice than with the construction of a new egalitarian family ethic. The Catholic church and African-American churches offered the most balanced religious voices in the American family debate, addressing both family ethics *and* public policy.

This chapter describes these recent shifts, leaving to later chapters the task of providing some historical background to the current conversation. We hope in these next pages to plant the seeds of an idea: that just as liberal political groups in the mid-1990s recaptured the family issue as an important one to address, mainline and liberal religious groups might also learn to make family concerns central. We hope, however, that our vision of a critical familism and a critical culture of marriage would guide them in their efforts.

Changing Perceptions
of the Issues

Is the family declining or merely changing? This was a question asked repeatedly as the 1990s began. Before that, many social scientists and cultural liberals had believed that families were simply changing and that the new forms were just as good, and maybe better, than older ones. Religious, cultural, and political conservatives, however, believed that most family changes were harmful. But within a very few years liberal political and cultural opinion makers had moved away from the idea that family changes were benign to a new concern over family disruption. What was behind this swing in national opinion?

Part of the reason for the swing is that a new group of social scientists began to diverge from the dominant social science thinking that had existed for two decades. By the mid-1980s, new research documented the growing poverty and declining well-being of the children and mothers of single-parent households and the children of stepfamilies. A convergence of this research and the diagnosis of conservatives and neoconservatives occurred, even though the social scientists promoting this new perspective were liberal in political orientation.

These social scientists *changed the subject* of the national family debate. They shifted the subject from moral values, homosexuality, and abortion to the declining well-being of children, the impoverishment of women, and the rise of male detachment from families. The New Democrats of the Democratic Party understood these shifts and seized them for their own political advantage. Liberal religious groups were slower in comprehending the significance of this shift of interpretation in the social sciences and the national debate.[2]

Although churches and synagogues on both the right and the left were not visible in stimulating this change of subject, nonetheless both social scientists and politicians began to perceive churches as indispensable to the solution of family problems. More and more, social scientists and politicians were asking the church "to be the church" and to retrieve and reconstruct its classic heritage of thinking on marriage and the family. They especially became interested in the resources that the black churches of the United States brought to family issues.

The Family Debate
in Political Culture

The family became a leading political and cultural issue in the 1992 presidential race between George Bush and Bill Clinton—sparked by Vice President Dan Quayle's famous speech on "family values." In that speech Quayle cited as an example of the continuing decline in values an episode in the *Murphy Brown* television series featuring the lead character's decision to have a baby out of wedlock. For a short time after Clinton's victory, however, it seemed that the family issue would fall off the screen of public attention. But by the summer of 1994, President Clinton brought it back by confessing that he agreed with Quayle in seeing family disruption as a major social problem.[3] By late summer of 1994, only months before the November congressional elections, both Quayle and Clinton gave important addresses with similar diagnoses of the problem.[4] Both saw teenage pregnancies, out-of-wedlock births, and absent fathers as contributing to the poverty of women and children, the

poor emotional and physical health of the young, growing youth violence, and poorer performance in school. Both agreed that although the
causes were complex, an unfavorable shift in American values was a
principal factor behind these trends. Both said that although government was limited in what it could do, it nonetheless should exercise
moral leadership. Both argued that voluntary institutions—especially
churches and synagogues—are the greatest resources available for redi-
recting the values and commitments of American families.

There was one distinction between them: Clinton advocated a larger
role for government programs than Quayle thought necessary. This difference was evident two years later in Hillary Rodham Clinton's *It Takes
a Village: And Other Lessons Children Teach Us* (1996) and Dan Quayle's
and Diane Medved's *The American Family* (1996).[5]

This exchange between Clinton and Quayle portended the future debate. William Bennett on ABC's *Nightline* argued that it was time for
America to begin a new national debate on the meaning of marriage.
Politicians on all sides were inviting churches and synagogues to play a
renewed role as advocates for marriage and the family. Media figures like
Ted Koppel, Robert McNeil, and Jim Lehrer paid Quayle's message new
respect. The family issue seemed no longer simply a conservative ma-
neuver to avoid responsible welfare programs or attack alternative families. Some family changes were now being viewed as harmful to
children, costly to the nation's economy, and damaging to the well-
being of the entire society.

Barbara Dafoe Whitehead's article "Dan Quayle Was Right," published in a spring 1993 issue of *Atlantic Monthly*, cited overwhelming social science evidence that the decline of two-parent families was hurting
children.[6] Whitehead built her argument on a variety of social science
resources, especially the work of Professor Sara McLanahan of Princeton University.[7] The article garnered a sensational response from American intellectuals, columnists, and political leaders, prompting more
letters to the editor than any previous article in the magazine's history.

Whitehead's message was reinforced by other commentators. During
the autumn of 1993, the controversial neoconservative social scientist
Charles Murray of the American Enterprise Institute published an essay
in the *Wall Street Journal* with the arresting title, "The Coming White
Underclass."[8] Murray argued that the phenomenon of out-of-wedlock
births, hitherto associated with the black community, was now developing with great speed in the white lower and middle classes. Murray
pointed out that the birthrate among never-married white mothers was
then 22 percent, up from 5 percent three decades earlier. Twenty-two
percent had been the out-of-wedlock birthrate in the black community

in the early 1960s. In 1993, that rate in the black community was 68 percent and as high as 80 percent in some inner-city neighborhoods.

Murray argued that this explosion of out-of-wedlock births in the white community was precipitating a plunge into poverty of a massive new group of white mothers and children. It threatened to create a white underclass that would be considerably larger than the existing black underclass and perhaps just as resistant to change. In short, Murray, who has since then, with the publication of *The Bell Curve,* generated controversy and in some circles lost credibility, was heeded when he said that the predictions of Senator Patrick Moynihan's much-debated book *The Negro Family: The Case for National Action* (1965) were correct.[9] When a community, for whatever reasons, undergoes a process of family deinstitutionalization, it will soon be in major trouble in other respects. The reasons for these trends may be different for black and white communities, but the consequences, he argued, will be the same— poverty for both mothers and children compounded by delinquency, poor performance in school, and worsened mental and physical health for children.

Although some commentators thought that Whitehead and Murray had overstated their cases, these articles influenced the thinking of such leading liberal columnists as Joan Beck, William Raspberry, Clarence Page, and David Broder.[10] By February 1993, liberal columnist David Broder announced that the "family values" debate was "largely over," that is, most of the members of the Washington establishment, both conservative and liberal, had accepted the claim that many families were in trouble and that it was time for society to help create strong, intact two-parent families.[11]

Whitehead's analysis, more palatable than Murray's, was seen as perceptive but incomplete. She identified cultural individualism as the cause and a cultural revolution as the cure of family disruption. She advocated a cooling of trends toward individualism and a renewed cultural dedication to the importance of intact two-parent families committed to raising children. Whitehead advocated this family form in contrast to the family pluralism celebrated by 1970s theorists like sociologist Jessie Bernard and participants in President Carter's 1980 White House Conference on Families.[12] Many observers agreed with her prescription, as far as it went. Yet Whitehead was considered short on analysis of economic, gender, and power issues, and policy proposals merited only a sidebar in her famous article. Both conservatives and liberals wanted more.

Murray's solution was more radical, even disturbing. He proposed a new cultural emphasis on the institution of marriage as the only context for exercising the rights of procreation, a return to the stigmatization of unmarried fathers and mothers, a removal of welfare supports such as Aid to Families with Dependent Children (AFDC) and food stamps for mothers of out-of-wedlock children (he would retain medical coverage for children), and a new use of adoption and orphanages for children of never-married mothers. More surprising still was the number of national leaders who took his proposals seriously. Shortly after the midterm elections in November, 1994, it was clear that the new Republican majority was considering many of Murray's proposals. The direction congress went in giving welfare to the states and ending entitlements for poor children was in the end, however, far short of Murray's more radical proposals.[13] Murray introduced his extreme solutions with an equally frightening prognosis. If the "illegitimacy" rate among whites reaches a critical level, he predicted,

> we should expect the deterioration to be as fast among low-income whites in the 1990s as it was among low-income blacks in the l960s. My proposition is that illegitimacy is the single most important social problem of our time—more important than crime, drugs, poverty, illiteracy, welfare or homelessness because it drives everything else. Doing something about it is not just one more item on the American policy agenda, but should be at the top.[14]

His solutions seemed draconian to many, but by early 1994 Murray had gained a hearing not only in the United States but in other capitols in the Western world.[15]

How would these poor mothers and their children survive? Murray proposed a new social attitude that would require mothers who kept their children to turn to extended family, church, and community, rather than government, for their financial and emotional support. If civil society—not the government—were assigned this responsibility, care would improve and old-fashioned discouragements of out-of-wedlock births would return. This idea for a new role for civil society was widely discussed in early 1996, but not in the way that Murray had hoped.

The Shift from Blaming Mothers to Blaming Fathers

We dwell on Murray's and Whitehead's articles not because we champion their positions, but because they were decisive in placing the American family debate firmly on the national agenda and before liberal political and cultural leaders. Although the debate sometimes centered on families on welfare, it brought broader issues to light. In spite of their differences, both Whitehead and Murray were concerned about the problem of fathers who procreate but do not support their offspring, and both helped focus attention on the "absent father" phenomenon.

Murray, in contrast to Whitehead and her associates, blamed misdirected government policies and, to a degree, women themselves. "Men will be men," he believed, unless women say no. Furthermore, according to Murray, until government had entered family life through AFDC and other supports, women generally had said no. They knew that they and their extended families could not afford to do otherwise. The emergence of the welfare state, he argued, changed these commonsense judgments by creating an artificial environment that softened the consequences of male procreative irresponsibility.[16]

In his 1992 *Murphy Brown* address, Dan Quayle blamed Hollywood and the countercultural movements of his own generation for championing unwed motherhood. By 1994, however, he claimed to be criticizing not unwed mothers but rather the fathers who have children but do not support them.[17] Beginning in the summer of 1993, leading magazines started reporting social science data on how poorly fathers support their children after divorce and when cohabitation ends.[18] In early 1995, family advocate David Blankenhorn published a book titled *Fatherless America*.[19] He and others argued that behind the statistics about family pluralism, divorce, and out-of-wedlock births was the growing phenomenon of fathers who were emotionally, morally, and financially absent from the lives of their offspring. He argued that powerful new cultural scripts were justifying, even promoting, what social scientists called the "fading father" phenomenon.

A powerful version of the fatherhood argument was based on the "social capital" theory of sociologist James Coleman.[20] It was used to show how parents mediate social capital—that is, social networks, resources, and norms—to their children. When the social capital that fathers convey is absent, children suffer.[21] At another level, evolutionary psychologists argued that it is not just the social capital that is important but the energy, commitment, and "investment" with which it is communicated.[22] Biological fathers, they observed, are more "invested" in transmitting this capital and cannot be easily replaced. Kin-selection theory—the fact that biological parents share 50 percent of their genes with their children—was used in David Popenoe's sociological study titled *Life without Father* (1996) to explain why natural parents, on average, seem more identified with and invested in their offspring.[23] This new interest in fatherhood gave birth in late 1994 to a bipartisan organization called the National Fatherhood Initiative, founded by former Bush administration officials Don Eberly and Wade Horn.

The Progressive Response
to the New Centrism

Not everyone accepted the neoconservative and neoliberal diagnosis that families were in trouble and that the fatherlessness and poverty of the underclass were spreading into the larger society. Progressive authors such as Stephanie Coontz, Judith Stacey, Iris Young, Arlene Skolnick, and Stacey Rosencrantz did not affirm the proposition that two parents (a mother and a father) were always better for children. Nor did they accept the proposition that the rise of divorce and out-of-wedlock births in themselves were central problems and that marriage was the solution.[24] They sometimes endorsed the idea that two parents were generally better than one or none but minimized the negative consequences of raising children in alternative circumstances if proper supports were available. They were wary of uncritical familism and called attention to the hazard of violent, destructive, or male-dominated families.

They also criticized neoliberal and communitarian scholars such as David Popenoe, Jean Bethke Elshtain, Norval Glenn, Amitai Etzioni, and William Galston, who were arguing for a renewed appreciation for intact families.[25] This latter group was associated with organizations such as the Council on Families in America, the New Democrat–oriented Progressive Policy Institute, and Etzioni's Communitarian Network. Between 1988 and 1994, such scholars wrote books and articles documenting the declining well-being of children, lamenting the demise of intact families, and building what former White House Domestic Policy Adviser William Galston called "the liberal-Democratic case for the two-parent family," a formulation that influenced Clinton's family policies.[26] In the spring of 1995, many of these scholars signed *Marriage in America: A Report to the Nation,* released by the Council on Families in America. The report discussed the family crisis but also highlighted the decline of marriage as an institution.[27]

Progressives criticized not only the conclusions of these centrists but also the new emphasis on intact families in the reports of national commissions published in the early 1990s. In contrast to the 1977 Carnegie report that celebrated the new freedom of family diversity, the National Commission on Children's *Beyond Rhetoric* (1991) and *Families First: Report of the National Commission on America's Urban Families* (1993) emphasized the importance of intact families for children.[28] *Beyond Rhetoric,* issued by a committee chaired by Senator John D. Rockefeller IV, represented the new emphasis:

> Children do best when they have the personal involvement and material support of a father and a mother and when both parents ful-

fill their responsibility to be loving providers. . . . Rising rates of divorce, out-of-wedlock childbearing and absent parents are not just manifestations of alternative lifestyles, they are patterns of adult behavior that increase children's risk of negative consequences.[29]

Political scientist Iris Young represented the tone of the progressive critique of centrists. In her 1994 article in *Dissent*, "Making Single Motherhood Normal," she argued that single-mother families are not the cause of poverty; poverty is the cause of single motherhood, especially its unhappy consequences for children.[30] Rather than oppose early single parenthood, society should guarantee that it does not end in poverty. Furthermore, society should lift all stigmatization of single mothers that "makes them scapegoats for social ills of which they are often the most serious victims."[31] Unwed fathers who can afford to should make childcare payments for their children, but marriage is not necessary for procreation and raising children nor "the answer to childhood disadvantage."[32] Institutions—schools, welfare organizations, medical facilities—should accommodate to a new "plurality of women's life plans," some of which entail having children young and outside of marriage and delaying education until some later time. Women, including teenage girls, have a right to bear children outside of marriage if they desire. She writes, "I submit that we should affirm an unmarried young woman's right to bear a child as much as any other person's right."[33]

Progressives such as Judith Stacey in her article "The New Family Values Crusaders" (1994) admitted that the new neoliberals and communitarians had to be distinguished from the likes of Dan Quayle and leaders on the religious right—Pat Buchanan, Pat Robertson, and Jerry Falwell. They did not advocate, for instance, saving the family by confining women to the home.[34] Nonetheless, she was disturbed by the readiness of neoliberals and communitarians to sound an alarm over the "decline" of the two-parent family. She claimed their emphasis on the benefits of a "mother and a father in fostering the emotional well-being of children" was "undocumented."[35] Furthermore, she believed that they unwittingly reinforce the "Christian right" and a "conservative cultural consensus."[36] Toward the end of her essay, however, she moves toward a more centrist position herself by encouraging progressives to understand that advances cannot be made by denying that "many women . . . want committed, intimate relationships with men" and that "teenage motherhood (married or not) often does not augur well for the offspring."[37]

We see several reasons for the impasse between progressives and neoliberal centrists. Neoliberals themselves had not fully developed what we call a *critical* culture of marriage or a *critical* familism. They advocate an egalitarian relationship between husband and wife but do not give a detailed account of the moral logic of equality and how it is connected to their language of commitment and self-sacrifice. As a result, their language of self-sacrifice and fidelity sometimes overwhelms their language of equality. Although they reject a return to the family patterns of the 1950s, they neglect analysis of social and personal power relations of the kind required for a critical familism. Although they pay some attention to the economic, psychological, and patriarchal causes of the family crisis, these factors are often swamped by their strong emphasis on the cultural and individualistic forces driving family disruption. Finally, they do not benefit from the generosity of a distinctively religious language that recognizes, in addition to commitment and endurance, the realities of human frailty, forgiveness, and an empowering grace needed to humanize their call for a firmer family ethic.[38]

Although progressives should be applauded for their attention to economic and class factors in the family crisis, they have been slow to give the restoration of intact families and marriage a high place in their social agenda. The ideas of a critical familism and a critical culture of marriage are suggested by their writings but not fully developed. And last, they too do not benefit from the way religious language balances ideals and frailties with forgiveness and grace in family life.

Political Culture: The Dialogue between Neoconservatives and Neoliberals

In 1991, sociologist James Davison Hunter argued in his book *Culture Wars* that Americans were divided on a host of moral issues between "orthodox" and "progressives."[39] The family was one of the primary issues. In 1994, he published a second book, alarmingly titled *Before the Shooting Begins: Searching for Democracy in America's Culture War*. It proclaimed, in effect, a plague on the houses of both the orthodox and progressives.[40] Showing the moral language of both extremes to be inadequate, Hunter argued that each side misrepresented the other, failed to listen to opposing voices, and fought the cultural war to achieve absolute victory over the opponent. Because Hunter concentrated on the abortion controversy, he was unable to detect the emerging dialogue and alliance, centered primarily in the U.S. Congress, between neoliberals and neoconservatives on other family issues. It was difficult to find, however, an analogous neoliberal-neoconservative dialogue in the official deliberations of American religious denominations.

Hunter overlooked the fact that by 1994, the central topic of the national cultural debate was changing from abortion and homosexuality to a wider range of family issues: divorce, the time pressures on two-income families, the absence of fathers, the growing poverty of women, and the effects of these factors on children. Although abortion and homosexuality resurfaced in the summer of 1996 as the possibility of gay marriage was considered and the Republicans debated softening their stance on abortion, these two issues were moving to the sidelines. Leaders of the conservative profamily Washington think tanks Eagle Forum, Family Research Council, and Concerned Women of America revealed in interviews with us in 1993 that they were intentionally putting these issues on the back burner as they concentrated on other family concerns.[41]

Political conservatives in the 1980s offered a cultural analysis of family problems. They blamed declining cultural values, feminism, secularism, and the welfare state's subversion of marriage. During the same period liberals and progressives, both political and religious, played down the importance of cultural values and focused on economic causes.[42] They blamed deteriorating economic conditions and inadequate welfare supports for the problems of families.

The neoconservatives and neoliberals of the 1990s were different. Neoliberals such as Senator Moynihan, William Galston, President Clinton, and the New Democrats of the Democratic Leadership Conference began to admit that in addition to economic factors there were cultural and moral causes behind the problems families were facing. Even traditional liberals such as Secretary of Health and Human Services Donna Shalala and undersecretaries Mary Jo Bane and David Ellwood began talking like neoliberals and communitarians. Neoliberals remained liberal in their continued belief in a positive role for government in helping families but searched for new ways to express state involvement. At the same time, neoconservatives such as William Bennett, Henry Hyde, and the Family Research Council were much less antigovernment than older conservatives. But they were much more likely to use government-designed tax cuts and special tax incentives, in contrast to welfare, to help and influence families.[43]

After the Republican congressional victory in November of 1994, it was not clear whether this convergence and alliance between neoliberals and neoconservatives would hold. It has so far, but in a strange way. New Democrats and Republicans joined in a massive reform of welfare that could not have been accomplished without the compromises that this alliance was prepared to make. Both Democrats and Republicans competed to take credit for the reforms in the 1996 elections. The spirit of dialogue and compromise was commendable, but the eventual consequences, as we argue in the last chapter, were problematic.

Trying to Change the Subject

During this period, the Christian Coalition, initially perceived by the public as a poorly educated fringe group, became a broad-based, middle-class movement potentially appealing to a third of the population.[44] Although hard-line fundamentalists held fast in America and around the world to the ideal of the hierarchical, patriarchal family,[45] many conservatives, and even the Christian Coalition, were becoming more moderate on a variety of family issues, including gender issues.[46] At one point the Coalition was criticized within its own leadership for its fixation on homosexuality and abortion. None other than Ralph Reed, its executive director at that time, called for the Coalition to set aside these preoccupations temporarily and concern itself with concrete policy issues that might actually benefit families.[47] This was a step he finally took when in May, 1995, he released the Coalition's "Contract with the American Family."[48] The contract was noteworthy for its avoidance of the issues of abortion and homosexuality and its explicit attempts to shore up the declining fortunes of the middle classes by proposing a $500 tax credit per child and a repeal of the so-called marriage tax penalty.

Christian conservatives were trying to broaden their family agenda. Former *Time* magazine correspondent Michael McManus began writing books and articles castigating both liberal *and* conservative churches for being silent on divorce and its consequences for children and women.[49] Congressman Henry Hyde counseled conservative Christians to put anti-abortion initiatives on hold until the coming of a brighter day.[50] Dan Quayle and William Bennett instructed the Christian Coalition at its 1994 annual meeting to focus on the more important issues of divorce and out-of-wedlock birth in contrast to abortion and homosexuality. Bennett summed up:

> I understand the aversion to homosexuality. But if you look in terms of damage to the children of America, you cannot compare the homosexual movement, the gay rights movement, what that has done in damage to what divorce has done in this society.[51]

Some conservatives reacted to these moderating trends. Pat Buchanan, in direct rebuttal of Ralph Reed, called for the Coalition to hold true to its course and continue to make traditional family values (and the evil of homosexuality and abortion) central to its message.[52] In the spring of 1994, Richard Neuhaus, head of the Institute on Religion and Public Life, and Charles Colson joined to form a new Catholic-Evangelical coalition. In their joint statement they promised "to cooperate on questions of common concern like abortion, parental choice in schools, and strengthening the traditional family."[53] Pat Robertson, the president of the Christian Coalition, supported the initiative—raising the possibility of a rift between him and his executive director, Ralph Reed. Reed was severely crit-icized by both Pat Buchanan and Gary Bauer of the Family Research Council for not addressing the issues of homosexuality and abortion in the "Contract with the American Family." In the months after the No-vember 1994 elections, it was not clear who would gain the upper hand in conservative religious circles. At the conclusion of the Republican con-vention in August, 1996, it appeared that the leadership of the Christian Coalition had moderated sufficiently to accept the fact that abortion and homosexuality received hardly a word on the convention floor, signaling that these topics were not central to the Dole campaign.[54]

The 1996 Campaign

As a result of their move toward the middle on family-related issues, Democrats actually helped implement part of Newt Gingrich's Contract with America. The final welfare reform package approved in late July, 1996, promoted government reinforcement of family formation, trans-ferred welfare programs to the states, and eliminated the care of poor children as an entitlement. All of this was done principally to enhance family stability, a work ethic, and marriage. Democrats retained more medical care, childcare, and food stamps for poor mothers and their children than many Republicans wanted. But in the end, saving money was not the point of this legislation. Ostensibly, the point was to move America's moral and cultural horizon to a new culture of responsibility. The strong objections of Senator Moynihan were not to the need for re-form but to the idea of devolution and the failure by congress to develop a coherent national policy that would support poor children no matter what.[55]

Bill Clinton and Al Gore touched almost all the family bases before and during their 1996 campaign. They called for a closer relation between government and religion. They helped pass the 1993 Religious Freedom Restoration Act, designed to give religious organizations more public space to participate in welfare, family assistance, and various forms of fam-ily advocacy.[56] They called for religious organizations to help stop teenage pregnancy and promote family solidarity, hence catching the wave of the new emphasis on civil society. Hillary Clinton in It Takes a Village said that her personal wish was "that every child have an intact, dependable fam-ily."[57] Clearly, the "village" for the Clintons was not solely the federal gov-ernment: churches and other voluntary organizations were also important to their vision. Having herself a husband and mother from disrupted fam-ilies, Hillary Clinton believed that such families could be helped to work if the right supports—including government supports—were in place. This struck a note of hope for divided families.

Moving outward from a visible church-family link, President Clinton argued for a host of other family supports. Although he emphasized commitment and marital permanence, he did not promote these values without the help of social supports. In his Families First campaign, he came out against teenage sex, smoking, and violence on television. He proposed college tuition tax credits, school uniforms (more value-explicit public schools), curfews, better programs to combat truancy, better-implemented programs for obtaining child support from absent fathers, tax breaks for adoptive parents, cheaper insurance coverage for children, portable health insurance for families, and more flexible and creative work-family relations.[58] In June, 1996, Vice President Gore held a major conference in Nashville on the obligations of the marketplace to be more friendly and supportive to families; he announced an extension of the Family and Medical Leave Act to allow time off, rather than wages, to be given for overtime at work. He also advocated a 24-hour-a-year mandatory release from work for parents to take children to medical appointments and to attend parent-teacher conferences. Furthermore, both Vice President Gore and Hillary Clinton introduced the vision of an "ecology" of institutions supporting the nexus of intact families and other families as well,[59] linking the natural ecology theme of the 1992 campaign and the family ecology theme of 1996.

Whether the Democrats meant what they said and could keep their promises was a major issue of the campaign, especially in the final days. The concurrent issue of "character" led in part to the question, Do Bill and Hillary Clinton really mean what they say about families? While we cannot answer that question, we can conclude that their rhetoric and promises were perceived by the public to be more balanced and sensitive to immediate family dilemmas. Robert Dole and Jack Kemp emphasized strong families, a cleansing of seditious Hollywood values, and their own system of tax breaks for families, which would, they thought, also renew civil society. On the whole, however, their message used more economic language than the Democratic message—even more than that of conservative groups like the Christian Coalition—and was perceived as removed from daily family struggles.

Clinton's more multidimensional vision, striking for its vague and symbolic *ecological structure,* seemed more convincing to voters. His speeches ranged from emphasizing the priority of the public marital contract and the importance of biological parents to accentuating the web of institutions that families need to survive and flourish. However general and ungrounded these political speeches are, their arguments and metaphors give us an object to address as we engage this debate in later chapters.

Three Styles of Religious Response:
A Preliminary Review

Religious voices other than that of the Christian Coalition were part of the national debate but not very visible. Three types of Christian theological thinking on family issues can be identified: a liberal Protestant, a Catholic, and a conservative Protestant response. In this chapter we primarily discuss the liberal mainline stance, waiting until chapter 8 to discuss in more detail Catholic and conservative Protestant responses.

We need, however, to say this much now about Catholics and conservative Protestants. First, on Roman Catholicism: in spite of the emergence of what is known as personalism in Catholic moral thinking, Catholic views on the family still reflect most aspects of the church's earlier natural law thinking. This heritage makes Catholicism's role in the American family debate complex. On the one hand, it affirms a conservative sexual ethics and an emphasis on the intact family. It also, however, supports a liberal social philosophy on welfare and the importance of labor unions in fighting for a family wage. We argue that the Catholic church, although exemplary in many ways, never fully came to terms with its inadequate views on gender. In other words, its familism never became a critical familism.

Second, on conservative Protestantism: the conservative Protestant voice in the debate has several strands. It includes fundamentalists, evangelicals, and the so-called Religious Right, mainly represented by the Christian Coalition and Focus on the Family. We also include black Protestant denominations among the conservative voices because they are theologically orthodox although generally liberal in their social philosophy for families. But the conservative Protestant voice also includes a powerful brand of Reformed theologians who think about families and their relation to state and market through appeals to "orders" or "spheres" of creation. Although important insights can be gained from all of these groups, their general failure to argue for gender justice in families and lack of a fully critical familism will lead us in later chapters to register criticism of them all.

Religious Liberalism
and the Family Debate

Being associated in our professional lives with the mainline Protestant tradition, we confess both our appreciation for and dissatisfaction with its recent contributions. We value its trajectory toward justice and universality. We affirm its move toward gender equality in and outside of families. We celebrate its concern for justice for poverty-ridden children and families.[60] We affirm its emphasis on "relationality"—a shared intimacy between husband and wife, parents and children. But we feel these same values, when stated without careful qualification, lead to an inability to delineate the specific goods that distinguish the family from other social organizations.

We search for a more complex model than the one provided by the religious liberalism of the mainline Protestant church. Sociologist Benton Johnson has pointed out that mainline Protestant churches since the mid-1960s appear to have abandoned concern with family stability and children's well-being, at least at the level of their official pronouncements.[61] Instead, from 1970 into the 1990s these denominations have repeatedly turned their attention to the issues of homosexuality and abortion, just as religious conservatives have, leaving concern with the effects of family disruption mainly to politicians and social scientists.

Although all mainline denominations contain a significant proportion of evangelicals, many of their official deliberations in the 1970s and 1980s reflected the liberal contractualism of secular legal theories of marriage and family. With the advent of no-fault divorce in the 1960s and 1970s, marriage agreements increasingly were seen in general society as analogous to business contracts rather than sacraments or covenants.[62] Unilateral divorce—divorce based on the will of one partner even if the other resisted—made marriage contracts even weaker than other contracts.

The reports of the mainline churches on marriage and family issues never accepted the secular contractual view as exhaustive of the religious significance of marriage and family. Their theology of marriage, however, had analogies to contractualism, and, increasingly, to a private contractualism. Rather than speaking of a legal contract as such, some liberal Protestants talked of "marital-type relationships" or of "committed relationships." Their religious meaning was found in the affective quality, justice, and nonexploitative character of the relationships.

Although seldom called contracts, these ideal relations nonetheless possessed features of contracts because they were thought to be voluntarily established and dissolved. Gradually, the classic religious models of marriage—marriage as both contract *and* covenant (as we heard in the language of Sophie and Jim Turner) or marriage as both contract *and* sacrament (as we heard from Mary Murphy) gave way to the idea of marital-type relationships that were essentially contracted privately even if legally witnessed and religiously sanctioned.

The concept of "justice love" between consenting adults—a concept found in the Presbyterian report *Keeping Body and Soul Together* (1991)—is an example of this style of practical theological thinking.

This kind of relationalism became widespread in liberal theological circles; treating partners as ends and never only as means became the goal of the marital-type relationships. This view, finally rejected by the Presbyterians, blurred distinctions between nonsexual friendships, sexual friendships, cohabiting couples, legally contracted marital couples, and couples both legally contracted and covenantally or sacramentally sanctioned. A new democracy of loving and just intimate relationships replaced older boundary-creating understandings of marriage as publicly witnessed covenant, sacrament, and contract.

Setting aside consideration of the merits of its specific recommendations on homosexuality, the Presbyterian report was noteworthy for its tendency to move marriage and family toward models of deinstitutionalized just and loving relationships.[63] In addition to its neglect of the institutional and social aspects of marriage and the family, there was no mention of children, their growing poverty and poor health, the growing absence of fathers, and the new social science claims about the generally unfavorable consequences for children of divorce and out-of-wedlock births. The report tended to characterize the family as a patriarchal institution—violent, unequal, and rapidly becoming a passing sexual arrangement.[64] It focused more on critiquing patriarchy than on helping to construct a new ethic for committed intact families. The report also ignored the growing tensions between work and family and what legal scholar Lenore Weitzman and others had called "the feminization of poverty."[65]

During the autumn of 1993, the Evangelical Lutheran Church in America reviewed a committee report titled *The Church and Human Sexuality: A Lutheran Perspective.*[66] Although this statement presented a more traditional theology of marriage and family than did the Presbyterian report, it too drifted toward a language of poorly defined "committed" and "loving" relationships.[67] It too ignored information on the situation of children, the burdens of mothers doing it all, the absence of fathers, and the emerging culture of nonmarriage and divorce. The statement was tentative about affirming the church's traditional stance on the confinement of procreation to legal and religiously sanctioned marriage. This report at the time of this writing is still under review by the denomination.

A similar move can be found in the recent history of the Episcopal church. Historian Joanna Bowen Gillespie shows that since its 1978 conference titled "Today's Families and the Challenges for the Year 2000," the move of the denomination has been away from the "trap of nostalgia" about the family. She writes, "Today, the former denominational focus on family delimited by sex and marriage has been subsumed under the broader concept of 'family as social institution.'" This concept does not refer to family as a legal, contractual, and publicly covenanted entity but to a more broadly based constellation of familylike groups. "In public forums as well as seminaries, Episcopal thinking about family now includes a broad range of kin and nonkin relationships in a variety of racial and economic settings (households)."[68] Gillespie continues, "The emerging theology of family sports a new terminology: 'household' replaces an outmoded, stereotyped 'family.'"[69]

The United Church of Canada (UCC) followed a similar path. Canadian religious scholars Daphne and Terence Anderson found a major break around 1978 in the subject and tone of its public reports on sexuality, family, and marriage.[70] Studies and documents before that date emphasized the importance of marriage, the problems of divorce, and the centrality of parenthood to marriage. After 1978, the emphasis was on sexuality rather than marriage, "intimacy" in contrast to parenting, personal fulfillment in contrast to communal obligation, and sex and family as matters of private decision rather than public accountability.[71] In these UCC statements, sexuality in marriage referred "only to its unitive function and says nothing about procreation." In the end, these reports' "basic theology of marriage and sexuality . . . severs procreation, children, and family from the core purpose of marriage and sexuality."[72]

It would be wrong to say that relationality at the cost of other values was the only interest of mainline denominations. For instance, since the 1980s the Women's Division of the Board of Global Ministries of the United Methodist Church has been concerned with "the feminization of poverty" and the declining well-being of children. In addition to addressing issues facing working women,[73] Methodist agencies recently have developed an extensive mentoring program for premarital and young married couples. Methodist bishops have unveiled "The United Methodist Bishops' Initiative on Children and Poverty," a comprehensive approach to increasing children's well-being, helping families, promoting congregational interaction with social service agencies, and stimulating congregational involvement in welfare legislation.[74] Roman Catholic bishops have undertaken similar initiatives, and other Protestant denominations have addressed these issues and matters pertaining to domestic violence, although they often lacked the means to make their efforts known.

Nor is concern with the values of relationality and intimacy as such misguided. In fact, these values are central in the health of families today. We discuss this in chapter 7 by introducing the idea of an "intersubjective" understanding of love. Without skills in *communicating* love, families in postmodern societies will collapse because of the decline in customary outside supports. *Mainline denominations have been leaders in articulating the centrality of love as dialogically or intersubjectively communicated equal regard and mutuality.* In this, they should be affirmed.

According to our love and marriage survey, some mainline churches and their educated, well-salaried members value mutuality considerably more and self-sacrifice less than the national average. Although the number of individuals from any one denomination in our national survey was relatively small, the figures are suggestive. When questioned on which model of love they use to solve conflicts with loved ones, half as many Episcopalians value self-sacrifice as do members of the general population, 12.8 to 28.2 percent. Episcopalians chose mutuality as the model correlating best with good marriages and families more than did the general population: 61.2 to 45 percent. A little over 18 percent of Presbyterians correlate self-sacrifice with good marriages, while 28.2 percent of the general population does. Episcopalians and Presbyterians are in the vanguard of the mainline and scored consistently higher in preferring mutuality than the rest of the population and conservative religious groups.[75]

Important feminist impulses motivated this concern for mutuality in the mainline denominations, and from our perspective this is a positive contribution. But love as mutuality, unless carefully defined, can drift into individualistic forms of reciprocity—"I will do good to you *if* you do good for me"—a kind of thinking that can be found in the liberal Protestant Richard Good when he said, "the relationship goes where I go," meaning the relationship was subordinate to following his career. Furthermore, mainline denominations sometimes went too far in emphasizing the value of relational mutuality at the expense of a careful analysis of other goods important for families.

What sociologist of religion William Garrett writes specifically about Presbyterianism may apply to the articulate liberal wing of all mainline denominations.[76] Mainline groups historically were marked by their leadership in adapting Christianity to the dynamics of modernization. Now modernization, Garrett says, has come back to haunt these denominations. Modernization—the spread of "technical reason" even into intimate spheres of life—has tended to undermine most of the external supports for families. In view of this tendency, there is some wisdom behind the strategy to meet the threats of modernity with intimacy and egalitarian relationality and to reduce covenant or sacrament to these interpersonal values. *But by itself, this tactic of the mainline denominations is sadly one-sided.*

Of course, the more liberal statements of the mainline denominations were aimed at other goals as well. Theological liberals, fresh from battles of the 1960s over civil rights for African Americans and educated by the progressive social sciences of the 1970s, analogized a relation between equality for minorities and equality for a variety of family forms. The new family pluralism, they thought, could work for children and adults if only the onus of prejudice could be removed. Hence, a nonprejudicial atmosphere and new levels of public support for poor single mothers and their children were needed to make the new family pluralism viable. The liberal wing of the mainline churches joined with political and social science liberals in their optimism about family change and in accepting the new private and relational contractualism as the basic ethic for families.

It would be unfair to suggest that political and religious liberals have not valued permanent marriage. It is correct to say, however, that increasingly they have seen legal and religious marriage as one among many options for the organization of human intimacy, sexuality, and reproduction[77] and have tended to agree with liberal social scientists in believing that neither private institutions nor public policy can bring marriage back as the socially sanctioned institution for the organization of sexuality and reproduction.[78]

Family, State, Market, and Religion:
The New Cooperation

By late 1993, political figures began encouraging churches to bring a new moral and programmatic leadership to family matters. In November 1993, President Clinton spoke before a national meeting of the black Pentecostal Church of God in Christ. He asked, amidst the growing chaos affecting the nation's youth, "Who will be there to give structure, discipline and love to these children? You (the clergy) must do that and we (the government) must help."[79] Clinton was admitting that government could not address the family issue alone, and that it needed the help—indeed, it needed to follow the lead—of the churches. A month later, Clinton's domestic advisor William Galston gave a major address calling for a policy of "maximum feasible accommodation" between government and religious institutions.

There was little evidence that the broad spectrum of American churches was alert to the calls for a new alliance between civil society, churches, families, and government that emerged in late 1995. Individual churches, especially some megachurches, had strong programs for families, but mainline denominational leaders seemed reluctant, or to be lacking the resources, to make family ministries and public policy a major priority. On the whole, neither conservatives nor liberals, religious or political, were doing the sociological analysis, theological reconstruction, or practical programming required to address the complexity of the issues facing American families, and when they were, they lacked a public voice to make these efforts known. Neither group had a grasp of the history of the family or of how religion, culture, and economics had interacted to create modern and postindustrial family strains. Until deeper historical, cultural, ethical, and theological understanding of the forces pushing toward the democratization of families is attained, confusion will continue to plague the American family debate. It is this deeper analysis that we now attempt.

2

The Family Crisis

Who Understands It?

Diagnosing a problem is as important as prescribing a remedy. The debate over the crisis of the American family is divided as much by different understandings of the issue as by alternative visions of solutions. Four competing social science explanations of the family crisis are being advanced in today's debate: (1) our changing cultural values, especially the increase of individualism; (2) changing economic patterns (Marxists, rational-choice economists, liberal social scientists, and liberal politicians have leaned in this direction); (3) psychological causes such as poor socialization for family life, inadequate communication skills, or a modern aggravation of ancient asymmetrical reproductive patterns of males and females; and (4) patriarchy—declining yet still visible.

Many voices in the American family debate overemphasize one or another of these four factors. Conservatives generally overstate the role of culture (although Bob Dole nearly dropped the cultural analysis from his message). Liberals tend to overemphasize economic causes (although Bill Clinton developed a cultural analysis of his own). Therapists and many average people may overstate the role of psychological factors in causing family disruption. That is understandable: their own feelings, communication skills, and perceptions are factors they can do something about. Patriarchy is often emphasized by feminists, who sometimes do not relate it to the other factors.

We believe that all of these factors are important, along with the pervasiveness of human sin, which underlies all social reality.

Furthermore, these four factors interact, a point often overlooked. *How* they interact is the key issue addressed in this chapter. Their interaction has produced the postmodern context for family formation and maintenance—*a context involving a new fourfold democratization of marriage and families, what we call the democratization of intimacy, work, value formation, and parenting.*

Moreover, solutions should parallel explanations. Solutions should address the cultural (the religiocultural), economic, psychological, and patriarchal aspects of the family crisis, and we try to do this in our concluding chapters. We believe that a Christian perspective not only addresses the four factors producing the family crisis but contributes to the democratization of families needed to resolve the crisis. This is true even though the Christian faith and the democratization process are not the same.

All of these explanations for family crisis have some validity, but the cultural factor of inordinate individualism—the desire to attain more expressive and utilitarian satisfactions for oneself—is critical. This does not mean that individualism in itself is evil or rampant in American society. Our survey on love and marriage suggests that people are struggling to locate their self-regard and individual needs within an ethic of mutuality. But the sociological data in this chapter suggest that they are having trouble accomplishing this. If people are to balance individualism and mutuality more satisfactorily, they must have a clearer and more powerful ethic. This is what the love ethic of equal regard, surrounded by the Christian story, tries to accomplish.

Our five representative families supply evidence for the validity of the four explanations for the family crisis given above. First, more individualism than in their families of origin is seen in these families, but a particular kind of relationality as well. Husbands and wives thought that they were both more demanding and more emotionally expressive with one another than were their own mothers and fathers. They also believed that they were more emotionally expressive with their children than their fathers and mothers had been with them. Second, most of these women earned money outside the home, thereby participating in some of the economic shifts that have put pressure on families. Most of the wives make a significant contribution to the family's wages. All of these wives could support themselves if necessary. Only Maria and Robert (the most economically pressed of the five families) have gone well beyond the two-spheres ideology of the nineteenth-century family. But most of these families—and this is very important—had *more flexibility with their time* than many families in which each parent had a full-time job. In four of the five families the husband and wife had a job and a half between them. And third, they are all aware of the psychological strains of the postmodern family, and the Turners, Miles, and Taylors work hard on communication. Fourth, although the husbands are not heavy-handed patriarchs, all of them, with perhaps the exception of Robert Taylor, have the economic edge and, perhaps, a psychological edge as well. They are excellent examples of the declining, yet still present, reality of patriarchy. Certainly Richard Good—the most socially and culturally liberal of all the husbands—has the economic power in his family.

Yet these families are intact. They have thus far avoided becoming part of the growing negative statistics about families. But positive trends are also visible; our national love and marriage survey, for example, uncovered evidence that a new value is being attached to mutuality in family life. The following trends should be kept in mind as we amplify our explanation of the family crisis.

Trends Affecting Families

Divorce

The divorce statistics are well known but so fundamental that they must be reviewed. The rate of divorce has steadily increased for more than one hundred years. It has risen from 7 percent in the 1860s to more than 50 percent today. In fact, demographers Martin Castro and Larry Bumpass predicted in 1989 that if the rate continued to rise at the level of that decade, 60 percent of new marriages would end in divorce.[1] The rate has, in fact, moderated somewhat.

Out-of-Wedlock Births

When the phenomenon of divorce is placed beside the rising rate of out-of-wedlock births, which has increased from 5 percent of all births in the early 1960s to more than 30 percent today, marital and family stability looks precarious indeed.[2] It is true that the rates for divorce and out-of-wedlock births are higher in lower socioeconomic groups. High rates of divorce, however, occur in all classes. The rate of out-of-wedlock births, although still low among the educated, has actually *doubled* among this group over the last decade. Births to "never-married mothers" ages eighteen to forty-four jumped from 17.2 percent in 1982 to 32.5 percent in 1992. Births to never-married mothers with one or more years of college rose even faster, from 5.5 percent in 1982 to 11.3 percent in 1992. For never-married mothers with graduate or professional degrees, it doubled, moving from 2.2 to 4.1 percent.[3]

Such trends demonstrate that out-of-wedlock births are no longer a phenomenon confined to inner-city black populations. Although the rate of such births in the black community rose from 22 percent in the 1960s to 68 percent in 1994, the rate of increase in the white community during the past decade was greater. The birthrate for unmarried white women was 23 percent by late 1994, 1 percent higher than it had been for blacks three decades earlier.[4] The rate of spread throughout the population plus the increase in cohabitation has led to new talk about an emerging culture of "nonmarriage."[5] These statistics led Charles Murray to write his essay predicting the creation of a "new white underclass."

Poverty, Families, and Single Parenthood

It seems extreme to correlate single parenthood and the creation of an underclass. Unemployment, racial discrimination, and the flight of industry from the inner city certainly contribute to the phenomenon of an underclass. Single parenthood, however, is a significant independent factor that should be added to the causes. For instance, the income of divorced mothers and their children drops precipitously. Single-parent families have less than half the average income of two-parent families.[6] Some studies in the late 1980s found that the incomes of mothers dropped by as much as 47 percent after a divorce; other reports put the figure closer to 30 percent.[7] A U.S. Census Bureau report said that in 1992, 47 percent of families headed by a single mother lived in poverty in contrast to 8.3 percent of two-parent families.[8]

But the consequences of this poverty for mothers and children are another story. Do children and mothers in single-parent homes really suffer? If they do, is it because of the lower income alone, or does single parenthood, independent of income, make a difference?

By the late 1980s, social scientists were reporting that 27 percent of all children at any given time were living in a single-parent home, generally with their mother.[9] For children born between 1970 and 1984, it was estimated that 44 percent would live with a single parent before reaching age sixteen.[10] As we will see more fully later, on average the children of single parents do not do as well on almost all indices of child well-being: physical and psychological health, performance in school, entry into the job market, family formation, and marital stability. The 1993 *Kids Count Data Book,* published by the Annie E. Casey Foundation, points out that only 31 percent of mother-headed households receive any child support or alimony.[11] Forty percent of children who are technically eligible for child support do not gain a legal award, and a quarter of those who receive an award from the courts never actually collect it. Less than a third of the children of a single parent receive the full amount to which they are entitled.[12]

Poverty is a major problem for these mothers and their children. But it is not the only problem. The authors of the Casey Foundation report say it succinctly: "Many single-parent families succeed. But finding the time to parent, run a household, and work is difficult."[13] To emphasize that we are not mounting an attack on single parents in citing these facts,

we assert again that it is a goal of this book to take both parts of this quotation seriously—to help single mothers succeed while enhancing the
conditions that create and preserve intact families.

The Absent Father

The challenge of single parenthood also raises the issue of absent fathers. Since 86 percent of single-parent families are headed by mothers,
what, on the whole, do fathers contribute to the children they bring into
the world but do not live with? Is their contribution important, or can
it be easily replaced?

In addition to the economic loss suffered by mother-headed households, fathers in general do not spend much time with their children after a divorce or separation. A study of divorces in central Pennsylvania
reported that only a third of the fathers saw their children at least once
a week within two years after the divorce. A 1981 national survey found
that the overall situation was worse and that only one child in six saw
his or her father as often as once a week. Furthermore, in the national
survey, close to one-half of the children had not had a visit with their
father in the twelve months preceding the survey.[14]

But the pattern of visitation as such does not tell the story of nonresidential fathers. Sociologists Frank Furstenberg and Andrew Cherlin say
it well: "Even in the small number of families where children are seeing
their fathers regularly, the dads assume a minimal role in the day-to-day
care and supervision of their children."[15] Many fathers who do not live
with their children become marginalized in their children's lives.
McLanahan and Sandefur show that when this happens, a whole range
of social contacts and resources is removed from the lives of children.[16]

Work, Time, and Families

Many social scientists have argued that the most important social
trend of the twentieth century is the move of women into the wage market. This shift from work centered in the home to work for wages outside the home has resulted in greater freedom for women and a greater
sense of participation in the public world—genuine benefits for women.
Associated with this trend are momentous new pressures and temptations resulting from the growing economic independence of husband
and wife from each other, the injection of cost-benefit logic into family
life, time shortages due to increased work outside the home, and the increasing need of couples to be employed not just for fulfillment but for
financial survival. According to the Bureau of Labor Statistics, 75 percent of all mothers whose youngest child was under age eighteen were

employed outside the home in 1992. Fifty-five percent of those with children under three years worked for wages.[17] The percent of women of all ages working in the labor market rose from slightly under 40 percent in 1960 to nearly 60 percent in 1990. In 1980 women made only 69 percent of wages paid to men; by 1990 they received 80 percent. Women during the 1980s had a 10 percent increase in the inflation-adjusted value of their salaries; men had an 8 percent decline. In the academic professions, women earned in 1992 between 95 and 99 percent as much as their male peers.[18] Women's wages, of course, should have parity with men's wages, but as they do, the economic dependency of women on men which once stabilized even unhappy marriages will further decline.

In addition to the fact that both mothers and fathers are now in the labor market, the work week has been extended, and take-home pay has decreased. More people are working longer hours with less time for leisure and childcare. Judith Schor has noted that American companies have been increasing workloads of employees, extending hours, and reducing staff in an effort to remain competitive in the world market.[19] Reinvigorated global competition and inflation have caused most American workers to fall behind. They need to work more to keep up, and industry has readily exploited their vulnerability. For instance, Americans in 1992 worked 320 more hours a year than their French and German counterparts.

This helps explain why parents today spend less time with their children than pre-1960 parents spent. Overwork has created what social scientists call the "parenting deficit"—a lowered capacity of parents to spend sufficient amounts of time with their children. According to a study done at the University of Maryland in 1985, parents spent an average of seventeen hours each week with their children as compared to a total of thirty hours in 1965.[20] This situation has given rise to the controversy over day care: if parents are not with their children, who is with them, and how competent are they to take the place of parents?

The Consequences for Children

By 1987, research began to mount pointing to the declining well-being of children. David Popenoe's comparative study of Western societies (1988) offered one of the first major reviews of the literature.[21] Psychologist Judith Wallerstein's research showed the unfavorable impact of divorce on children, a conclusion that was supported yet qualified by sociologist Mavis Hetherington.[22] Additional sobering research on the effects on children of single parenthood began to accumulate.[23]

Facing the facts about declining child well-being need not mean that women must return to the role of primary caregiver. We propose instead that the work and care patterns of society be reconstructed. Nonetheless, we must ask, is this research true? Do divorce and out-of-wedlock births have bad consequences for children? Is the divorce or the non-marital birth the crucial factor? Does family structure, as such, make so much difference? Do a husband and a wife raising their own biological children do better on average than a single mother, a single father, a stepfamily, or a grandmother? Or are other factors such as income, race, education, and parenting patterns what is really important?

Clearly, parenting patterns are more important than the simple fact of biological relatedness. A warm and wise single mother or stepparent is better than a rejecting, violent, and careless biological father or mother. But that observation is too crude. The question is, does biological relatedness on average contribute to the relational qualities that go into good parenting? Until recently, much of the research into the effects on children of family disruption was not sufficiently sophisticated to answer this question. Child well-being was declining in American society—that was clear. But the reasons were difficult to ascertain.

Social science research is now growing more sophisticated. An excellent example of this can be found in Sara McLanahan and Gary Sandefur's *Growing Up with a Single Parent* (1994), a state-of-the-art statistical analysis of four major national studies of families, three of which are longitudinal (following their subjects over time).[24] McLanahan and Sandefur state their conclusions early in the book—in italics.

> Children who grow up in a household with only one biological parent are worse off, on average, than children who grow up in a household with both of their biological parents, regardless of the parents' race or educational background, regardless of whether the parents are married when the child is born, and regardless of whether the resident parent remarries.[25]

Is single parenthood the only reason some children do poorly? McLanahan and Sandefur say no. It is one very important factor that interacts with a variety of other factors. Income, parenting patterns, neighborhood resources, educational level, race—all count, but they all get a particular boost from the factor of one absent biological parent. For instance, in the 1980s the national high school dropout rate was about 19 percent. For children living with both parents the rate was still a robust 13 percent. Obviously for this 13 percent, factors other than single parenthood are operating to lead youth to leave school. But children of single parents (included in this formulation were children not living with both biological parents, that is, children of divorced or never-married mothers and children living in stepfamilies) are approximately 30 percent more likely to drop out of school, a sizable increase. When examining more recent data from one of their longitudinal studies, McLanahan and Sandefur found that 87 percent of children from two-parent families receive a high school degree by age twenty, compared to 68 percent of children living with one biological parent, a difference of 19 percent. When adjustments for race, education, and place of residence are made, the number of school dropouts that is associated with the absence of one biological parent is 15 percent, still a sizable figure.[26]

McLanahan's and Sandefur's data here are controlled for race, education of parents, number of siblings, and place of residence. Income is controlled separately, but is still accounted for. We discuss the relevance of income separately, as do McLanahan and Sandefur. Many single parents were poor before their divorces or before giving birth to an out-of-wedlock child. But many became poor after these events.

When all the controls (with the exception of income) are put in place, the following comparison between single-parent families and intact two-parent families emerges. The children of single parents do worse on four of five measures of high school performance—test scores, college expectations, grade point average, and school attendance.[27] Furthermore, young people, both males and females, living apart from their biological parents are one and a half times more likely to be idle and to have difficulty entering and succeeding in the job market.[28]

Race and income clearly contribute to explanations of why children of single parents seem to do worse than children of two-parent families. But they do not explain everything. For instance, the school dropout rate for the average white child from a disrupted family is higher than that of the average black or Hispanic child from a two-parent family. The authors of *Growing Up with a Single Parent* emphasize the conclusion: "For the average white child, family disruption eliminates the advantage of being white with respect to high school graduation."[29] Family disruption lowers success in college even more and seems to do so independent of race. For example, the sons and daughters of single-parent affluent blacks do more poorly in college than the children of intact black families with lower incomes. And the daughters of advantaged white single-parent families are five times more likely to have children out-of-wedlock.[30]

Finally, income—especially loss of income—makes a definite difference in outcomes for the children of single parents. It may account for as much as 50 percent of the remaining difference after education, residence, race, and number of siblings are taken into account.[31] But income does not account for the entire difference between intact and disrupted families. If this were so, the children of stepfamilies and intact biological families would do about the same; their incomes are almost identical. McLanahan and Sandefur find that children in stepfamilies do about the same as children of single parents on almost all indices of well-being. And they do significantly less well on average than children living with both biological parents.[32]

Cultural Factors: The Rise of Individualism

These trends did not develop out of thin air but are the results of deep movements in modern history. There is little doubt that Western societies since the Enlightenment have been in the grips of a cultural vision that emphasizes individual rights and fulfillment. Individualism can be traced back to the Protestant Reformation, the Renaissance, the emphasis on consent in Catholic canon law, the Hebrew and early Christian belief that humans reflect the image of God, and aspects of Greek humanism. Since the Enlightenment, community bonds—whether within village, state, church, extended family, or between spouses—have increasingly made fewer claims on our efforts toward self-fulfillment and our control of the material and political means to achieve it.

The so-called nuclear family (wife, husband, and children residentially and economically differentiated from the extended family) is itself an accommodation to this individualistic trajectory. The couple—the conjugal core—in the nuclear family is thought to have obligations primarily to each other and to their children, in contrast to obligations focused on the patriarchal head of the extended family or the extended family itself. Even obligations of the conjugal couple to each other, trends show, have seriously declined.

In *Habits of the Heart* (1985), Robert Bellah and his colleagues explored the depths of American individualism. They argued that Americans have lived out of and often distorted traditions that have led them to pursue an ethic of "expressive individualism" in their intimate relations and "utilitarian individualism" in their jobs.[33] Bellah and his colleagues believe that American individualism is excessive and is destructive of family life. They call for a conversion of values, a retreat from individualism, a rebirth of commitment, and a new appreciation for the importance of institutions—including the legally defined and culturally sanctioned institutions of marriage and the family. Social scientists Jan Dizard and Howard Gadlin in *The Minimal Family* (1990) agree with the authors of *Habits of the Heart* that expressive individualism is the central value that Americans today bring to their marriage and family relations.[34] They see no way to halt this cultural trend.

Historians Edward Shorter and Lawrence Stone organized their seminal interpretations of family history in Europe and England around the move from embeddedness in community and extended family to an increasing quest for individual emotional and sexual satisfaction.[35] Although they, along with social historian Philippe Ariès, overstate the degree to which affection and emotional involvement were absent from families prior to the eighteenth century, they are correct in believing that expectations for individual emotional and sexual fulfillment have increased.[36] The French social philosopher Alexis de Tocqueville in the eighteenth century detected the emerging individualism in American life, felt it was clearly more pronounced in America than in Europe, and described it with a mixture of admiration and anxiety.[37] Even more empirically oriented social scientists such as David Popenoe, Norval Glenn, Sara McLanahan, and demographer Larry Bumpass believe that the cultural trajectory toward individualism has been a powerful engine behind family transformation and disruption.

We see reasons to value but also to criticize this individualistic trend. The cultural trend toward individualism should not be equated with "fault" or "sin," although individualism and sinfulness can interact, with negative effect. Just as there can be ordinate self-concern, there can also be a legitimate and ordinate concern with individuality, autonomy, and freedom. But there can also be an individualism of inordinate self-concern, and many commentators feel this is what Western societies have displayed over the past century and a half. Many analyses, however, fail to distinguish between ordinate and inordinate self-concern.

Ordinate forms of individualism must be affirmed as a fundamental aspect of life. Ordinate individualism—or individuality—has special meaning in our time for women, people of color, and other marginalized groups. But we locate individual fulfillment within an expanded definition of love—what we call a love ethic of equal regard. This model of love rigorously balances the obligations of regard for others with a legitimate and energetic regard for oneself and identifies the social, economic, and cultural elements required to sustain it.

Economic Transformations

Cultural and socioeconomic forces need to be understood in their interactions with each other. Failure to do this has led to errors in standard conservative and even some neoconservative and neoliberal analyses. The long-term Western drive toward individualism feeds many of the economic transformations that have affected families. At the same time, these economic changes have gained a quasi-autonomous life of their own, rebounded on families, and deepened individualistic and materialistic tendencies.

Technical Rationality and the "Colonization of the Life-World"

We cannot understand these social and economic transformations without invoking Max Weber's hypothesis about the "Protestant ethic" and how it shaped the economies of Europe and the United States. Weber believed that the cost-benefit market logic of Western capitalism was a by-product of Calvinism's celebration of systematic activity done for the glory of God.[38] This emphasis on systematic activity gave birth to a form of capitalism that valued long-term investments, rational book-keeping, and the restrained personal use of profits. According to Weber, as the original religious vision that gave birth to this economic pattern became secularized, a narrow technical rationality took its place.

Technical rationality is the application of scientific controls to the material improvement of human life. The logic of technical rationality holds that efficiency is always the best means to the end of satisfying some human desire. Technical rationality can be used in two contexts. As the German social theorist Jürgen Habermas shows, it can be used in a bureaucratic context to enhance collective satisfactions. It can also be used in a market or capitalistic context to enhance individual satisfactions.[39] In both contexts, the bureaucratic or the market, technical rationality tends to strain if not undermine the deeper, more personal interactions of everyday community life, including the interactions of family life.

Wherever technical reason spreads and life is reduced to the rule of efficiency and productivity, the organic, spontaneous, and dialogical aspects of life are deemphasized and disrupted. Face-to-face encounters are reduced to means-ends interactions. The intimate, I-thou relations of families and small communities are overtaken by the logic of efficiency, a process Habermas calls the "colonization of the life-world."[40]

Sociologist Alan Wolfe has applied Habermas's theory of colonization directly to the sphere of family life. He builds a strong case that the cultural dominance of technical rationality, whether in its bureaucratic or market form, often disrupts families. He points to the indices of family disruption in Sweden (with its reliance on socialist bureaucracies to support families) and their analogy to the patterns of disruption in the United States (with its tendency to subordinate family needs to the demands of market economics).[41] The bureaucratic form of technical rationality encourages family dependency on the state. The market form, if unchecked, casts families into competitive isolation, so that family life is dominated by the pressures of the struggle for economic survival.

We saw market pressures on family time in all the families we studied, although it is possible that the Turners, Miles, Murphys, and Goods are intact families partly because in none of these couples were both parents working full-time. For various reasons, they had not immersed themselves fully into the competitive, time-consuming pressures of the market, although the women more than the men were the ones who checked market forces by working less. We also saw evidence of the pressures of competition and work outside the home in the statistics about the reduced time that today's parents spend with their children.

An equally important aspect of colonization theory deals with the impact of government bureaucracies and welfare programs on family stability. The statistics on out-of-wedlock births, especially among welfare populations, raise the question most pointedly. We do not believe that the explosion of out-of-wedlock births can be totally explained by welfare programs that make child-support payments to unwed mothers. Broader cultural trends explain part of this phenomenon; remember that the largest percentage of increase in out-of-wedlock births is among populations not on welfare—older, college-educated middle-class women.

Yet large sectors of the policymaking community now believe that programs such as Aid to Families with Dependent Children do account, in part, for these trends. Even confirmed liberal policy experts David Ellwood and Mary Jo Bane, in *Welfare Realities: From Rhetoric to Reform* (1994), state that welfare programs from 1960 to 1990 created a "culture of dependency" and that this culture has had some impact, along with other forces, on family structure.[42] Charles Murray is partly correct when he argues that welfare supports for single mothers during the 1960s not only encouraged fathers to abandon their children and mates but also helped create a culture of nonmarriage that perpetuated itself in spite of declines in welfare payments in recent years.[43] As we indicated above, Murray's diagnosis is taken with increasing seriousness even though his radical solutions are accepted by very few. But if his assessment is right, his views illustrate one expression of the "colonization of the life-world" by bureaucracy.

Economic Explanations

Habermas and Wolfe provide useful insights into other economic dimensions of families. Although economic patterns do not swamp cultural factors, they do play an important role. Marxist theorists, under the influence of Frederick Engels's *Origins of the Family, Private Property, and the State* (1884), have argued that families everywhere reflect the patterns of work of a given society.[44] Engels argued that the industrial economic patterns of nineteenth-century capitalism brought men into the wage market, paid them salaries, and thereby gave husbands economic control over their dependent wives who were left at home to tend the children. When we look at concrete historical arrangements of the family in nineteenth-century America in chapter 3, Marxist theories will help explain some, although not all, aspects of the rise of the middle-class family. Clearly industrialization had much to do with creating what is variously called the industrial, Victorian, or bourgeois family. Marxists believed that if capitalism and private property were abolished, men would lose power over women, and a new egalitarian relation—indeed, a new kind of free and romantic "sex love"—would emerge between male and female. Marxists had to face the fact that the abolition of private property in the Soviet Union did not radically alter relations between the sexes and left families susceptible to a new kind of external disruption—the colonizations of the state in the form of increased pressure for women to take low-paying jobs outside the home without encouraging new supportive domestic habits in husbands.

Non-Marxist economic theory in the United States has been dominated by what is commonly referred to as rational-choice theory. This view is consonant with the Marxist view at least on one point: economic patterns powerfully shape family life. But this approach, associated with the figures of the Chicago school of economics (which we critique in detail in chapter 9), holds that these economic patterns function as environments within which to exercise individual rational-choice behavior. People tend, according to this school of thought, to act in ways that maximize individual satisfaction. For instance, people make decisions about their spouses and children in the same way that they make decisions about their education, jobs, cars, and financial investments—that is, according to what brings them individual satisfaction.

The emergence of capitalism, the theory goes, altered the environment in which family members made rational choices in the eighteenth and nineteenth centuries. Economists tell us that industrial capitalism brought three massive shifts in our patterns of economic dependency, which in turn produced radical changes in families. First, it brought men out of economic dependency on farm labor, crafts, and extended family to financial reliance on wages paid by factories and offices, creating a new distinction between public workplace and the private family sphere. Second, women became newly dependent economically on men, as they relied totally on wages earned by their husbands, a circumstance that Marxists criticized in the capitalist family. Women's customary economic activity in sewing, doing farm chores, and preparing meals narrowed during this era to childcare and house cleaning, especially in urban centers. Industrial capitalism also forced women into new patterns of consumerism: a reliance on goods and services from outside the home. Third—the most momentous shift of all—was the move during the last half of the twentieth century of women and wives from the private sphere of home into the public wage market, just as husbands and fathers had done many decades earlier.[45]

These three shifts in patterns of economic dependency explain—according to such rational-choice economic theorists as Gary Becker, Robert Michaels, and Richard Posner—most of the family disruption trends we mentioned earlier. They show how capitalism and rational choice thrust both men and women, fathers and mothers, into deeper involvement with competitive and efficiency-driven markets. This is what Habermas means by the colonization of the domestic life-world by the rhythms, logics, competitions, and time pressures of the market. The market, often aided by advanced technologies and the media, began to engulf and invade all.

Rational-choice theorists believe that their model of economic action can explain a host of family ills. Take divorce. Because women have paid jobs, they are no longer as economically dependent on men, these theorists argue. If marital satisfaction is not present, women can divorce and still survive economically. Indeed, men can divorce women and believe that their former wives can and should survive without their help.

Take out-of-wedlock births. A mother who has her own livelihood may choose to keep an out-of-wedlock child because she can support herself and her child. A mother who has fewer of the skills valued in the marketplace may keep her child because she assumes that the state will support them. This last explanation is highly debated, but some theorists believe it to be true.[46]

It does appear to explain the rise of absent fathers. Fathers can leave their families because mothers and children seem less dependent on them economically. Furthermore, pressures from extended families and the community, which once functioned to keep unhappy couples together, lose their moral influence when no longer reinforced by the sanctions of economic rewards and penalties from families of origin.

Finally, rational-choice theory appears to explain why the birthrate has been declining over the last century. Children cost money, take time, and contribute less to their parent's financial well-being than they once did when they contributed to the family farm or trade. Children are no longer profitable.

The rational-choice economic explanations for these family changes, we must admit, *are powerful.* But, as useful as they are for predicting and explaining broad trends, they are incomplete.

Individualism and
Rational-Choice Theory Combined

Rational-choice theory is not sufficient in itself to account for family disruption. But it is not necessary to choose between rational-choice theory and the cultural interpretation with its emphasis on individualism. The two, surprisingly, converge very nicely. Demographer Ron Lesthaeghe has argued that the march toward individualism and the march toward capitalism with its emphasis on rational choice have gone hand in hand. After amassing data tracing parallel trends in declining fertility and marital stability in most Western countries, he concludes that "the underlying dimension of this shift is the increasing centrality of individual goal attainment, that is, the individual's right and freedom of defining both goals and the means of achieving them."[47] This Enlightenment thrust toward individualism is institutionalized and aggravated, he argues, by market logic in capitalist countries. Rational-choice theory appears to have predictive and explanatory power because historical and cultural forces have in fact molded us to become rational-choice individualists. In contrast to being innately rational-choice creatures, humans may *have become* such creatures because historical, cultural, and economic forces have molded us that way.

If the broader and deeper reality of human anxiety and sin is also acknowledged, it may be that Enlightenment individualism, capitalist economic individualism, and the reality of human anxiety and inordinate self-concern have mixed together to make personal human relations, in or out of marriage and the family, increasingly subordinate to our individual satisfactions, increasingly subject to the cost-benefit mentality of the market, and increasingly prone to being handled as we try to handle the buying of cars, houses, television sets, and the other transient goods of modern life.

Racism, Poverty, and Discrimination

Lesthaeghe makes an interesting observation that should be kept in mind as we assess the role of poverty in producing family disruption. The two great spurts in divorce and out-of-wedlock births in Western societies, he points out, occurred during the last quarter of the nineteenth century and during the 1960s and 1970s, both times of unusual economic growth and affluence.[48] Furthermore, as economists Victor Fuchs and Diane Reklis have demonstrated, the declining well-being of children in the United States dating from the 1970s came at a time of unprecedented per capita increases of income for children from both private and governmental sources.[49]

But the relation of the cycles of wealth and poverty to family disruption must be at least interactional, as McLanahan, Sandefur, and others argue. McLanahan and Sandefur believe that *family disruption leads to poverty but that poverty, whatever its causes, can further exacerbate family disruption. For instance, poor couples get divorced at a higher rate than middle-class couples, and rates of nonmarital births are higher among the poor as well.*[50]

Furthermore, one must remember that much of inner-city poverty has been produced by systemic racism that isolated black males from economic opportunity when industry, banks, and commerce fled the inner city after World War II.[51] Racism is a particularly intractable and lamentable cultural reality that is further aggravated by individualism and rational-choice motivations. It is another way in which cultural values—in this case racist cultural values—get mixed with our increasing drive to maximize individual satisfactions, both economic and expressive. Hence racism itself, as real as it is, interacts with cultural individualism and the colonization of families by market and bureaucratic forces.

The Democratization of Families

As we argue in chapter 9, the love ethic of equal regard does not demand the total rejection of either the cultural trend toward individualism or the move toward economic rationalism. Both trends have their positive and negative aspects. How they manifest themselves depends on the more encompassing ethic within which they are placed. In this book, we critique both individualism and the market yet preserve dimensions of both.

The interaction of cultural and economic explanations of family trends has important implications for the future. Individuals increasingly will marry and form families out of a free decision to do so. Less and less will people marry and stay married because women are economically dependent on men. Less and less will men marry women believing that women have no other economic choices. This shifting cultural and economic situation will lead either to a new *democratization* of families or to further disruption. In fact, we believe this mixture of cultural and economic forces is *pushing families toward a democratization of intimacy, work, value formation, and parenting:*

1. The democratization of *intimacy* has meant a new demand for *mutuality* in intimate exchanges of sexuality and affection.

2. The democratization of *work and domestic chores* has meant a new demand for equality in performing and sharing these tasks.

3. The democratization of *value formation* has meant a new expectation that husband and wife will contribute equally to the values of their new family by preserving and reconstructing their respective traditions of origin.

4. The democratization of *parenting* has meant an increased need for husband and wife to become equally involved and equally authoritative in the tasks of parenting.

Not all couples and families will achieve greater democratization in all of these spheres of life. But, as our love and marriage survey indicates, the value that couples place on mutuality should be understood as an effort to find an appropriate ethic for dealing with the forces pushing toward democratization. As we argue below, democratization as such does not capture the full range of values associated with a Christian perspective on marriage and family. Nor, for that matter, does love as mutuality. But the economic and cultural pressures that once put women in a subordinate position of power in families are, it seems, declining. Relations are held together, if they are at all, more nearly by genuine attraction, free consent, mutuality, uncoerced economic security, and religiocultural commitment and sanction. The unique Christian contribution comes in at precisely this point. It formulates the nature of commitment that guides the flourishing and promotes permanence in the context of increasing democratization.

One question emerges: Do individuals in our society have the interpersonal skills, the moral values, the cultural inheritance, the communal supports, and the religiocultural commitment needed to manage marriage and family life in a cultural-economic environment that stimulates deeper democratization of family life? This question requires that we turn to a more psychological mode of analyzing the current family situation.

Psychological Transformations

A third explanation for the crisis of the family points to psychological causes. If our analysis is correct, increasingly marriages and families will stay together because individuals bring *rich* and *flexible* selves to their relationships. Both qualities are crucial—richness (which includes a consolidated religiocultural identity and interpersonal skills) and flexibility (the capacity to relate to difference, otherness, and change). This does not mean that economic conditions can be ignored. In fact, for strong, flexible, and communicative selves to emerge, economic conditions between the sexes must be just. Psychological development and economic patterns must reinforce each other as, indeed, must culture and economics. But adding the psychological to the cultural and economic causes means that neither of the latter two is sufficient for either diagnosis or solution. The psychological perspective must be added because it is often the most readily undervalued, as it is in liberationist, Marxist, and some heavily cultural interpretations of family disruption.

Psychoanalytic Psychology and the "Parental Problematic"

To introduce the concept of the self is to introduce the discipline of psychology. This is why we have called our point of view a psychocultural-economic perspective on families. Of course, the discipline of psychology is not the only vantage point from which to view the self. Selves are formed not only in relation to intimate others and institutions but by the biological needs people bring to these relations and the cultural responses that further define these needs.

In industrial and post-Victorian society, the separation of paid work and home life instituted patterns of socialization for children that made the ideal of the intact, democratic family described above difficult to achieve. Political scientist Susan Moller Okin has argued that gender justice in the socialization of males and females in families of origin is essential if justice is to prevail in the families they form and, indeed, in the social patterns of the wider society.[52]

This argument builds partly on psychological work done by Nancy Chodorow and Jessica Benjamin, who have provided elaborate psychoanalytic discussions of the difficulty of achieving equality between the sexes in a world where mothers are the primary caregivers for both boys and girls.[53] Chodorow has developed powerful descriptions of how the separate spheres of paid work for fathers and childrearing for mothers led to distortions of the self for both boys and girls. When mothers raise children in isolation from father and wider community, both boys and girls overidentify with the mother. The boy's prolonged attachment to the mother undermines his later identification with adult males and sometimes fuels hostility between mother and son. This same deep attachment to mother makes growth to adult independence difficult to achieve for girls. Both boys and girls miss the emotional contributions of the father and the independence and sense of autonomy of the mother. The selves of both sexes—their capacity for initiative, self-regard, and healthy identifications with others—are impaired when they are socialized in the patterns of the classic modern or industrial family.

The psychological perspectives of Chodorow and Benjamin are just another angle of vision on one of the most central problems in the contemporary crisis of families: *the growing absence of fathers from mothers and children and the increasing necessity for mothers to raise children by themselves.* The psychological perspective uncovers the inner developmental deficits brought about by socioeconomic splits between home life and paid work. This line of thought gives further credit to the explanatory power of the economic point of view, whether rational-choice or Marxist. In its extreme forms, the father is absent altogether, as happens in many families after divorce and for most children born out of wedlock. This unwillingness or inability of fathers to care for their children—with the exception of the limited number of "new fathers"—is an unprecedented, worldwide phenomenon, as new research by the Population Council has shown.[54] The absenteeism of fathers correlates with poverty for both children and mothers. It further disrupts the psychological, biological, and educational development of children.

Evolutionary Psychology and the "Male Problematic"

The social-psychological analysis suggested by Chodorow helps us understand the consequences of this absence of fathers from childrearing. Evolutionary psychology and ecology contribute another level of analysis. Evolutionary psychologists remind us that males give care to their offspring in only 3 percent of the mammalian species: the general mammalian pattern is that the females of a species raise offspring with little or no assistance from male procreators. How did the change come about at the human level? What is at stake in the contemporary drift back to the childrearing patterns of our mammalian cousins where females provide the care and socialization? Is this the reality that Senator Moynihan was speaking about when, predicting a 40 percent nonmarital birth rate by the year 2000, he worried about humans becoming a "new species"?[55] Was he really talking about the possibility of reverting to a very old species—the original mammalian condition that humans thought they had left behind?

The rise of individualistic values, the split between paid work and domestic life, and the impact this split has on the socialization of children are aggravated by deep-seated tendencies in human nature. In later chapters, especially chapter 4, we supplement our psychological explanations with the theory of the asymmetrical reproductive strategies of mammalian males and females. We separate what is important about these psychobiological insights from the disastrous and oppressive use to which they have sometimes been put throughout human history.

The theory of asymmetrical reproductive patterns, increasingly accepted in the social sciences, holds (1) that male mammalians have an almost unlimited capacity for reproduction but have difficulty determining when an infant is theirs, and (2) that female mammalians, especially human females, can give birth to only a limited number of offspring but have definite knowledge that an infant is theirs. This simple anthropological insight, explained below in more detail, says much about why responsible fatherhood is precarious, difficult to achieve, and easy to dislodge and why the tasks of motherhood have sometimes expanded to undesirable limits. It also throws further light on why postmodern societies are failing to produce the conditions for shared parental responsibility between males and females and how classical religio-ethical traditions helped, long ago, to create these necessary conditions.

The Influence of Patriarchy

The fourth factor—declining yet still-present patriarchy—is given special emphasis by feminists in explaining the family crisis. Patriarchal family structures have assumed the subordination of women and have sometimes led to exploitation, injustice, violence, and abuse. The feminist analysis is correct: patriarchy is an important factor in current family problems, even if it is declining. Part of the reason it is important is because *it seems to be declining*. The more moderate exercise of patriarchy by men and the response by women are therefore fraught with ambiguity. This ambiguity, in turn, becomes a powerful factor for family disruption in itself. Women increasingly do not trust men. Men do not trust themselves. Some men, for fear they will appear patriarchal, become weak and ineffectual in an attempt to compensate. Some women in turn are disappointed when men fail to take appropriate initiatives and carry out their responsibilities. Indecision, confusion, ambivalence, and discontent abound. When patriarchy interacts with cultural individualism, market economics, and the problems of socialization, communication, and asymmetrical male-female reproductive patterns, the difficulties are aggravated even further.

But the subtleties of this explanatory factor are best illustrated with the use of examples from history. The influences of a weakening patriarchy and the struggles for equality and justice are a major theme in chapter 3, where we discuss families in American history.

Causal Explanations
and Reality of Sin

The best social-science explanations, as important as they are, do not give us a full account of family disruption. A missing factor is the reality of sin—a harsh and, for some, an incomprehensible concept. However important the four causes we have listed, they have power and the range of their devastation is expanded because they interact with the human proclivity for sin. But sin is a complex and sophisticated concept, not a flat, moralistic idea.

A theological point of view locates the deeper problem of families in the fallibility and fault of the human will: in the susceptibility of the human spirit to distortion and self-preoccupation. By *fault,* we mean the human tendency toward inordinate self-protection in the face of anxiety that manifests itself in both pride and, as feminists have argued, self-effacement or self-loss. The language of fallibility and fault, borrowed here from Paul Ricoeur, is a more abstract way of talking about the Christian concept of sin.

We hold—along with Kierkegaard, Reinhold Niebuhr, and Ricoeur—that humans are sinful because their capacity for freedom and imagination leads them to be creatures of great anxiety.[56] Humans are anxious about their finitude, status, self-cohesion, relationships, wealth—about anything that they believe important for their existence. Humans invariably try to protect themselves from anxiety (which is not in itself sin) through excessive control, pride, and aggressiveness or, as theologian Valerie Saiving Goldstein once argued, by self-renunciation and fusion with others—a common response of oppressed women and minorities.[57]

We agree with the Protestant theologian Reinhold Niebuhr that the reality of sin is empirically knowable, in the broadest possible meaning of *empirical.* The Christian tradition tells us that all humans are sinful, but the simple power of human observation tells us much the same thing. Furthermore, sin enters into all aspects of human relations, including—perhaps especially—the intimate aspects of marriage and family life. Anxiety suffuses our relationships, and we then use any number of strategies—pride, protectiveness, manipulation, submissiveness, self-loss, and deception—to alleviate the anxiety.

Although sin independently accounts for many of the difficulties of families, it interacts with cultural values, economic patterns, psychological needs, and patriarchal structures. Theologians use sin to explain human difficulties; social scientists search for a range of other causes. Because sin is simultaneously a theological and a broadly empirical category, it can be related to other causal factors to explain human problems, including family problems.

Unless social-science explanations are informed by the reality of sin, causes are converted into *excuses*. Yet, mean-spirited moralism can be avoided if we place the reality of sin within the context of the multiple pressures that work upon it.

The Importance and Limits of the Intact Family

In the chapters that follow, it is easier to define philosophically and theologically a family ethic of equal regard than to specify the concrete conditions that make this ethic possible to live out. We do not dismiss the power of grace and conversion in changing the lives of couples who work out their marital vocations within a religious context. In fact, we argue that such Christian realities are essential. Nonetheless, these transformative religious powers work in actual cultural, economic, and psychological conditions. The difference between this book and standard philosophical and theological texts is that we work hard not only to state the theological and ethical ideals that should govern families but also to speak of the actual developmental and social conditions that allow them to be made manifest in the lives of persons.

We develop our love ethic of equal regard in close relation to the concept of kin altruism, the preferential treatment people tend to give to their biologically related family members. This helps us show why the family with intact, biologically related parents should be given a prima facie priority in our cultural, ethical, and educational scale of values. *The fundamental family issue of our time may be how to retain and honor the intact family without turning it into an object of idolatry and without retaining the inequalities of power, status, and privilege ensconced in its earlier forms.* The prima facie importance to children of being raised by their biological parents is stated clearly by McLanahan and Sandefur:

> If we were asked to design a system for making sure that children's basic needs were met, we would probably come up with something quite similar to the two-parent family ideal. Such a design, in theory, would not only ensure that children had access to the time and money of two adults, it also would provide a system of checks and balances that promoted quality parenting. The fact that both adults have a biological connection to the child would increase the likelihood that the parent would identify with the child and be willing to sacrifice for the child, and it would reduce the likelihood that either parent would abuse the child. Last but not least, the fact that

two parents had connection to the community would increase the child's access to information about the opportunities outside the household and would, at the same time, strengthen social control. While we recognize that two-parent families frequently do not live up to this ideal in all respects, nevertheless we would expect children who grow up in two-parent families to be doing better, on average, than children who grow up with only one parent.[58]

This statement points to core realities of healthy families. But many qualifications must be added before it can become an adequate working model. There is no mention of the need for equality between father and mother, no mention of how it is achieved or its impact on children, no mention of the role of culture and religion in creating such a family, no mention of the moral resources needed to make this family work, and no mention of what to do when this ideal is not realized. There is, furthermore, no mention of a larger vision of life which makes singleness an honorable vocation and supports all kinds of families in need. A narrative framework must be added to this statement so that we can value it as an important relative truth but not elevate it to an idolatrous absolute, as some conservatives are inclined to do. This book is about both affirming this statement and setting it in a better context of meaning.

To introduce the essential qualifications, we must set this statement within the history of family thinking in the Western world—first within American history. Then we will work backward in quest of the origins of Western family thinking—to Reformation and medieval Christianity, and finally to the Bible, Greece, and Rome. The chapters that follow amplify this statement by McLanahan and Sandefur, place it within a theological context, and show its meaning and limitations within a variety of historical situations.

3

Religion and the Ideal Family

Nineteenth-Century Variations in North America

In this chapter, we turn to the concrete events in American history that have shaped our contemporary view of families. We do this for two reasons: to give examples of the ambiguity of the notion of an ideal family and to illustrate how individualism, economic changes, psychological strains, and patriarchy—the four factors discussed in chapter 2—played out in American history.

What is meant by "the ambiguity of the notion of an ideal family"? The purpose of an ideal is to point us beyond the immediacy of our concrete existence toward a vision for which we can hope. A family in which equal regard prevails between the members is such an ideal. Few people, however, have attained their ideals, either in previous centuries or in this one. The way we live out ideals depends on the actual circumstances of our lives. The powerful ideal of the nineteenth-century middle-class family contrasts with the actual circumstances in which people lived and reminds us of the possible ambiguities of the equal regard, intact, public-private family for today.

The present culture wars over the family are no surprise when we consider the different notions of family that have been held throughout American religious history. The traditions of the northeastern, southeastern, middle, and western states shaped family ideals in different ways. Puritan family traditions of the Northeast varied from Anglican and Calvinist patterns of the Southeast, and revivalism and Wesleyanism later wrought separate transformations in both areas. When adopted by African-American slave families, Protestantism and Roman Catholicism also underwent adaptation. Roman Catholicism brought its beliefs and practices to Native Americans of the Southwest and later to a New England that was once solidly Puritan. Europeans shaped these various North American subcultures but were reshaped by them in turn.

As our psychocultural-economic model implies, families are shaped by religiocultural traditions but also by events like wars, depressions, and famines. As a result, a notion of the ideal family of one region is not equally powerful in other parts of the country. For instance, New England Puritanism influenced significantly the family patterns of the United States, but some areas were fed by other traditions and only lightly touched by this one.

We need to distinguish between cultural ideals and their concrete variants. In the following sample of American family images and practices, we discover that ideals can be dangerous when invested with ultimacy. Ideals of the family thought to be Christian were imposed on unique situations as absolute demands even when the implementation of that ideal actually violated Christian love and justice.

When ideals are flexibly held and graciously presented, they can provide a vision of the future out of which new patterns of family life can emerge that bring cohesion and hope. Social ideals can, however, become oppressive when powerful people use them to judge those who cannot possibly attain them; this misuse of ideals has occurred across race and class lines. Ideals can also be used subversively by less powerful groups to claim the symbols of upward mobility or challenge old stereotypes.

In groups with European backgrounds, the nuclear unit of mother and father raising children was assumed. Generally, this nuclear unit lived separately from the extended family, as demographer Peter Laslett has shown was the case for centuries in Western countries.[1] In contrast to the belief that the family before the Industrial Revolution was essentially extended and living under one roof, historian John Demos, echoing Laslett, has observed that "small and essentially nuclear families were standard from the very beginning of American history, and probably from a still earlier time in the history of Western Europe."[2] Nonetheless, the patterns of permeability between nuclear family, extended family, and wider community varied substantially.

Colonial Puritan Families
of the Northeast

The Puritan family is important because its heritage figured significantly in the founding religious, political, and legal systems of the United States. New England Puritanism, and European Calvinism before it, influenced American Presbyterians, Congregationalists, Baptists, and Methodists—in short, major portions of American Protestantism. The Puritan theology of the family reveals some of the deeply rooted ideals of American family life, even though it is not the source of all our thinking about families.

The Puritan family had a patriarchal structure and value system,[3] yet it exhibited degrees of egalitarianism and a permeability to surrounding institutions. The Puritan marriage ideal upheld a norm of "subordination and equivalence," words used by historian Kari Børresen to characterize the positions of Augustine and Thomas Aquinas.[4] This norm justified the social hierarchy of men over women even though each sex was assumed to have equal spiritual worth before God. Puritans took at face value Ephesians 5:21–33, which appears to make males the heads of families. They added the caveat that patriarchy should be benevolent, "as Christ loved the church." The community expected spouses to live together permanently, to live peacefully and harmoniously, and to engage in normal and exclusive sexual relations. When this ideal was translated into everyday practice, even grievous oppression did not necessarily free a woman to disobey her husband. When spouses did not live up to Puritan ideals, the husbands and wives were disciplined differently. Mild physical chastisement of wives by husbands was frequently accepted, but not the reverse. Married women and men who committed adultery were severely punished, but court records provide no evidence of a married man being punished for committing adultery with a single woman.[5]

John Demos claims that within this patriarchy there existed certain egalitarian ironies. Even though husbands were the family's legal agents and most laws assumed that wives did not have separate legal identities, wives could under some circumstances enter into legal contracts. That wives could make independent contracts was unprecedented in British law. "But in the New World," as Demos writes, "this situation was perceptibly altered."[6] Especially when women were married a second time, they might retain control of inheritances and gain custody of children.

If patriarchal marriage embraced some incongruities, so did fathering. Historian Philip Greven gives an example of what we have called the declining yet still-present significance of patriarchy. He demonstrates the extent to which patriarchal control over sons and daughters yielded, in the course of four generations, to a new individualism, in this case defined as the desire for personal autonomy from parental control.[7] In Andover, Massachusetts, the first generation of fathers kept tight control over their property, giving their sons the inheritance rights to the land and property they needed only in order to marry. The second generation of fathers was more likely to give their sons deeds of sale that relinquished the father's property rights in return for an agreement that sons would care for them in their old age. Sons of the third generation did not wait for their fathers to deed property to them but bought it, insuring their parent's security in old age while gaining control over the property during their adult lives. This further freed them from the exacting expectations of aging parents. These sons also began moving away from Andover when portions of the family property became too small to be divided or sold to several sons. In the fourth generation the population in Andover declined as sons sought livelihoods in neighboring towns. Downward mobility, one might say, brought the decline of strict patriarchal control.

These practices concerning property generally created nuclear families, although not always. When fathers gave sons a portion of their property in order to marry, the sons built additional homes and established a differentiated nuclear family, whereas when sons inherited the family homestead, three generations often lived under the same roof and ploughed the same fields. Sons and daughters in their own homes, though they still lived within close range of kin and close friends, were more independent of their fathers. Growing individualism, changing economics, and variations in patriarchal control interacted.

Other parenting practices moved Puritan children in and out of the households of their parents. Although parents were ultimately responsible for their children's needs, meeting those needs required help from other families in the community. In the Plymouth Colony children were frequently "put out": families sent a child to live with another family to be a servant or to learn a trade.[8] The new family cared for all of the child's needs as if he or she were a family member. This entailed providing shelter, food, clothes, education, and religious instruction. This practice created permeability in the structure and relations of the various households organized around the nuclear family core.

Other forms of interdependence between family and community existed. Family members could appeal to the courts to bring violent spouses into conformity with community standards and to discipline unruly children.[9] In contrast to most present-day nuclear families, these Puritan families had to provide not only for themselves but for the needs of the community. In the absence of the monasteries of the Middle Ages or the social service institutions of the modern state, courts sought families who would house orphan children, provide homes for single women and men, care for the sick or disabled, provide correction for the criminal, and oversee the affairs of the financially destitute.[10] In the Massachusetts Bay Colony, young single men were required to live with families. Although this was generally the rule in Plymouth, young males occasionally were permitted to form temporary living arrangements together as long as they lived "civily" and under court supervision.[11]

Central to this interaction between family, society, and environment was the idea of the family as a "little church" and "little commonwealth"—a teacher to children of the meaning of their covenant responsibility to observe God's rule in church, state, and home. The father was the instructor. In this, he represented church and state. But more than these, he represented a direct relation to God, mediated by scripture. The family was a divinely instituted order of creation, just as were state and church. Although each order had its own line of authority directly from God, the divine will was believed to demand a unified ethic bringing these diverse spheres of life into coherence. We heard in the thinking of Jim and Sophie Turner echoes of this view of families: the modified authority of fathers, the divine institution of the family, and the necessity of moral congruence between state, church, and family. The Turners were once Baptists and are now conservative Presbyterians, both successors to the Puritans.

Southern Slave and Slaveholding Families

The slave and slaveholding families of the Southeast offer an alternative example of how patriarchy organized nuclear families into a larger household controlled by the *paterfamilias* (the male head). This kind of patriarchy controlled families through benevolence and brutality. Despite the power of this patriarchy, slave families maintained distinct cultures and practices within the larger patriarchal system. The slaveholding family presents yet another perspective on how patriarchy changed over the generations.

Slaveholders considered their households to be "my family, white and black." Several nuclear families, free and slave, were incorporated within the concept of the family under the patriarchal head of the household. The master controlled a household, and the household consisted of the senior patriarch and his spouse (the conjugal couple), their children, their grandparents, their slaves, and sometimes the families of their adult children.[12] The slaveholder's nuclear family was a comparatively closed, endogamous family system in which slaveholders married among a limited number of families of their own class. Although affection between spouses was probably more readily expressed than among the Puritans, the rule of patriarchy in the South was stricter, with fewer of the egalitarian alterations than were found in the Puritan family.[13]

Slave families were generally exogamous, following the practice of not marrying first cousins.[14] Although some slaves chose partners within the plantation, many coupled with slaves from nearby plantations, relying on a father's weekend pass to the neighboring plantation to maintain family togetherness. The larger the plantation, the more distance the slaves had from their owner's cultural system and the more likely they were to maintain their own practices regarding family life.

The closed patriarchal structure of the slaveholder's family was reinforced by a culture of honor and shame. Although we claim no causal relation, the honor-shame culture of the colonial South had analogies to family honor codes of the Greco-Roman world at the time of early Christianity. The honor system of the southeastern colonies, according to historian Bertram Wyatt-Brown, was based on public reputation. One's sense of self was dependent upon the self's presentation in public and how the public in turn confirmed that self.[15] The patriarch was bound to protect from violation the women of his household and be ready to defend in duels, even to death, the integrity of his supervision of resources, household, wife, sister, or mother.

Slaveholding women felt the consequences of this honor code in the isolation, unchallenged assumptions, and rigid structures that framed their world.[16] In marriage, romance was heightened. But only rarely did a woman have the education that would lead her to assume that she had rights apart from her husband, that she could exercise an equally valid and divergent opinion apart from his pleasure, or that she might have appealed to the larger community for intervention on behalf of her discontents. Because her companionship was class-bound, she often had few confidantes other than her husband. She focused on him, although she had significant supervisory responsibilities for the domestic life of the plantation. He focused on his public responsibility, although he might be quite affectionate toward her.

Scholars of southern women's history have debated whether the proximity of slaveholding women to slave families created countercultural sympathies in women. No consensus exists. Furthermore, unlike antebellum New England, in the Southeast religion provided few avenues for change. Northeastern biblical interpretation often undermined a strictly hierarchical society; in the Southeast, biblical interpretation reinforced strict hierarchy.[17] Neither women's religious associations nor educational opportunities provided a vehicle for women to make known their discontents.

Slave families faced severe obstacles in creating an enclave for their own family life and the ideals to govern it. Although some benevolent masters tried to keep slave families together, the social system of slavery did not respect—in fact, did not legally acknowledge—the slave family.[18] Slaves could not take oaths, so they could not formally marry. Whether they were sold, separated, or permitted to live together depended on the master's will and financial need. Black women were subject not to their own husbands but to the white male master. A black woman could be sexually dominated by her master, so that her children were often his children. The black slave husband could not assume his own paternity. A black husband who protected his wife against being beaten, sold, or raped did so at the risk of his life. Such a defense was an act of treason. Slave parents did not always live harmoniously; they too had marital strife and difficulty with children. But in light of their oppression and what we will say later about the natural conditions for family formation, the durability of the slave marriage and family, as documented by historian Herbert Gutman, is particularly notable.[19]

Plantation records reveal strange combinations of economic supports and threats to the stability of slave families. If a slave owner lived a long time or successfully passed his land to his children, slave families might enjoy the stability of this orderly succession. If, however, the slave owner died or became severely indebted, his estate was sold or divided among his sons and heirs. Slave families could then enter a new phase of instability, as creditors and heirs felt few obligations to keep families together.[20]

Slave families, however, created unique family cultural practices. In addition to marrying outside of their own kin, they often delayed permanent commitments until after the birth of a first child. Marriages were recognized through religious ceremonies alone. Slaves practiced various forms of "jumping the broomstick," a public ritual recognition of spousal commitment. In addition, they often declared their marriage before Christian slave ministers and their owners with accompanying marital festivities. When slaves married in young adulthood, and their age was close to that of their master's, the slaves' chance of marital stability was maximized. If their owner lived a long and prosperous life, slave marriages usually endured for a lifetime as well—even without the recognition of the law.[21]

The Native-American Matrilineal Family and Roman Catholicism of the Southwest

At about the same time that the Puritan family was developing its variation on European Calvinist practices and slavery was initiated in the Southeast, the families of southwestern Indians encountered Spanish explorers. These Native-American tribes had descended from a civilization of considerable complexity. Even though the European invasion disrupted family and community for Native Americans across the continent, the encounter between the two cultures in the Southwest was different from that of Native Americans and Europeans elsewhere. The Spanish brought armies in search of gold rather than communities of settlers seeking freedom from established religion. They brought a

Roman Catholic faith whose priests established missions, evangelization efforts, and schools rather than a Protestant faith with parish ministers and congregations with resident families of European origin. The invaders in the Southwest included more men than families, and the natives they encountered had substantially different family structures from those of Europeans.

Among the Pueblos, for example, the Spanish encountered matrilineal families who lived in nuclear arrangements but whose first obligations lay with the wife's family and clan.[22] In the terms of evolutionary ecology, the dynamics of kin altruism and kin investments worked out differently than they do in patrilineal family systems. Although children lived with their fathers, other blood-related males such as maternal uncles or grandfathers were often their first source of help. Women had economic power because property was handed down through a mother's lineage. Political and military power, however, lay with men and they held the positions of community leadership, and men moved to the homes of their wives after marriage.[23]

Christian theology and ritual figured significantly in the realignment of Native-American and Spanish family systems. Native Americans were often baptized because they were captured during war as infants or children and sometimes made slaves. In times of peace, children were brought by their families for baptism as a final, desperate cure for illness. Once children were baptized, the church did not allow them to return to their tribes during war or peace.[24] Rather, the church took on the responsibilities for physical care and catechism. For religious, military, and political reasons the boundaries between the family practices of southwestern Native Americans and the Europeans were extremely permeable. Captured and baptized Indians often intermarried with the Spanish.

The matrilineal kinship structures of Native Americans interacted with a Roman Catholicism in which Mariology played a significant role.[25] A religion that emphasized the importance of Mary the mother of Christ and a matrilineal family structure may have united to heighten the centrality of women and the permeability of family and community structures. Family styles in New England and the Southeast were quite different.

The Enlightenment Attack on Patriarchy

Some of the differences in the style and decline of patriarchy in families of New England and the Southeast reflect the different literature read by the elites of each area. Southeasterners studied the Greek classics, in which patriarchy was assumed to be normative, but New Englanders of the eighteenth century were reading the avant-garde theories of the Enlightenment in which patriarchy was under attack. Relations in the family served as a metaphor for Enlightenment philosophers' intellectual challenge to political patriarchy.

Enlightenment philosophers of the eighteenth century—Hobbes, Locke, Montesquieu, and Condorcet—might be called the deconstructionists of the monarchy. For them, monarchy was patriarchy, and the philosophers challenged both. They did this by hypothesizing that in the family in the state of nature, both father and mother participated in the governance of children and household.

Historian Linda Kerber has shown that these thinkers drew freely from their perceptions of companionate relations among husbands, wives, and children to argue for shared political power.[26] Political power should be shared with the people, according to Locke, just as parents share power in the family.[27] Locke built his argument on the biblical doctrine of creation. The Ten Commandments tell us to honor both "father and mother," not just the father.[28] The father's rule over wife is a result of the Fall, a prediction about the consequences of sin and not a command from God.[29] Political responsibilities, according to Condorcet, were originally created from mutual attachments within the family which extended outward to the clan. Hobbes taught that mothers were by nature the rulers of the family and that fathers ruled only by social convention.[30] In varying degrees, the philosophers called on reciprocal affections within the family to rationalize shared power among men in politics. This contrasted with political theorist Robert Filmer's tendency to analogize from the patriarchal father alone outward to the political order and not outward from the mutual relation of husband and wife.

Although these philosophers used the family to make analogies about the political order, they rarely envisioned or practiced a genuinely democratic family life. Nevertheless, they laid the philosophical groundwork for changes in the family and helped create democratic images of the family that the philosophers may not have expected or intended.

The ideologies of democracy and individual dignity interacted with socioeconomic trends to influence further the shape of families. Before the Revolutionary War, women were fused into the political and legal identities of their husbands or fathers. Women of the northern and middle colonies, however, began to create political and legal identities for themselves partly as a result of economic shifts that occurred during the Revolutionary War. Before the war women helped wean the colonies from dependence upon British goods by making products in their homes. During the war women ran farms while their husbands were

fighting. When Tories or revolutionaries tried to commandeer their
farms for headquarters or supplies, women had to decide their political
alliances for themselves.[31] These experiences forged a more independent identity for wives and influenced the transformation of the economic and legal systems of the New England and Middle Atlantic states.
The growth of a philosophy of republicanism and the economic contributions of wives and mothers went hand in hand. These trends stimulated a new interest in women's education. If mothers were to be capable
of educating sons for the republic, they would need education themselves, first at home and later at women's academies.[32] Democratic theory and practice were reshaping the gender identities and civic
responsibilities of mothers and giving them a domestically based civic
role, "Republican Motherhood."[33]

Missionaries, Patriarchy, and the Native-American Matrilineal Family System

The movement in families from patriarchy toward democracy was not
uniform. In fact, patriarchy was reinforced in some communities even
as it declined in others. Christian missionaries generally found the matrilineal clan systems of Native-American families strange and unacceptable. According to historian William McLoughlin, missionaries
often were unable to recognize the value systems operating within
Native-American families.[34] Furthermore, even though many tribes had
been hunters, the U.S. government wanted to contain Native Americans
on individual family farms so that their wider territories could be settled
by European migrations. Because missionaries were often also agents of
the federal government, their reconstruction of "Christian" Native-
American families also served the government's purposes.

As in the Southwest, many southeastern Native-American tribes had
exogamous, matrilineal family systems in which the men hunted and
fought. The women farmed, shared domestic power and responsibilities,
and depended on their brothers rather than their husbands for assistance.
Europeans, accustomed to patrilineal, patrilocal, and patriarchal systems
where men farmed or conducted business and women worked in the
home, found all of these features difficult to understand.

In the name of Christianity, missionaries sought to reconstruct this
family system. The Cherokees provide an example of how this reconstruction occurred. The Cherokees had been impoverished and weak-
ened by the Revolutionary War and by guerrilla warfare between natives
and white settlers. Traditionally, they had relied on hunting. As traders

entered the area, Cherokees became dependent on trading skins and furs. Game was dwindling, threatening both forms of livelihood. Single European men who were deserters from the war began moving into the area and intermarrying with Cherokee women. Such men gained full civil rights in the Cherokee nation but raised their children according to white familial practices. Under these pressures, cohesive native rituals and family practices declined.

White settlers, including missionaries, brought access not only to alternative livelihoods such as cotton farming but also to additional religious and supernatural powers. Christianity therefore held interest for many Cherokees. Yet American Christianity brought with it values that challenged the Cherokees' matrilineal clan system. Missionaries did not go into Cherokee towns but established their own settlements with their own behavioral rules. Cherokee converts to Christianity were expected to move to the missionary towns. When Cherokees began farming, often out of economic necessity, the organization of farms challenged traditional gender assumptions. The women could no longer till the fields in communal groups, as they had previously done—an activity that reinforced relationships between women. Men no longer gained male identity and status through skills in hunting. To the missionaries, women tilling the fields represented barbarism, whereas men farming and women spinning and weaving represented civility. To the Cherokees, farming was "women's work," and men who farmed failed to gain the respect of traditional Native-American males.

The intermarriage between Cherokee women and white men posed a severe threat and introduced the formation of patriarchal families. Cherokee women often sought white husbands as a route toward upward economic mobility, but white men who married Cherokee women raised their children according to patrilineal economic practices. Often, the intermarried Cherokee women and their *métis* children became property owners and even slaveholders. Their white husbands and fathers did not want this property to revert to their wives' clans.[35] Husbands wanted to control their economic assets by leaving inheritances to their children. For this system to work, patrimony became important, and white husbands reverted to traditional patriarchal assumptions— that at marriage wives became their property, that the value of a woman depended upon her chastity, and that marriage had to be monogamous, at least for women.

This story is significant for our study. It shows that the decline of patriarchy was not a straight line. It also shows the tenacity with which patriarchy, patrilineality, fixed gender roles, and rigid understandings of the relation of nuclear to extended family were held to be uniquely and unalterably Christian. As we will see in later chapters, Christianity's understanding of the father's responsibility and of his servant role must be distinguished from the patriarchy, patrilineality, and patrilocality with which this message frequently was associated. Christianity has something special to say about the responsibility of fathers, but this message was not carried by the Protestant missionaries to the Cherokees in such a way that it could be adapted to their unique family strengths.

Industrialization and Evangelical Religion on the Bourgeois Northern Frontier

Even as Native-American family structures were being transformed during the transition from hunting to farming, industrialization was contributing to the restructuring of agricultural families of European descent. What historians call the nineteenth-century middle-class, or Victorian, family began to emerge. This family, generally thought to be *the* Christian family, was nuclear and consisted of fewer children, a wage-earning husband, and a housewife who raised the children and supervised the purchase rather than the production of household goods.

This model became the ideal of the middle-class family. Distinct virtues became associated with each gender role. In this family form, industrial and market expressions of technical rationality converged with a new entrepreneurial individualism and a reshaped patriarchy. This ideal arose first in the industrial, Protestant Northeast, but analogous variations developed among both Protestant and Catholic immigrants, free blacks and freed slaves, pioneer settlers, and pioneer entrepreneurs.

In a study of the New York frontier of the early nineteenth century, historian Mary Ryan shows how religion and economics interacted to produce the nineteenth-century middle-class family.[36] The evangelical religion of the Second Great Awakening released an expressive, affective religious style unknown to the more staid Puritans. At the same time, the development of industry created gender relations far different from those of the Puritans. In the Puritan family, production was located in the home; now, fathers became wage earners outside the home. Parenting styles changed. Formerly, the father was considered the primary custodian and disciplinarian who ruled by guilt and the manipulation of consequences; now the mother, the parent at home, ruled by shame and withdrawal of emotional support. Economic relations changed. The husband provided a family income; the wife supervised her family's consumption of goods. Education changed. No longer did boys learn a trade by doing adult tasks at the sides of their fathers; now a concept of "boyhood" developed, in which they were considered boys until they

were educated and learned a trade. The concept of housekeeping developed, now identified as a woman's task.

The revivalism of this era, popular first among lower-class Baptists
and Methodists, was originally perceived by Presbyterian church elders
as a threat to patriarchal order in the family. In the end, as revivalism
became popular among women of the Presbyterian middle classes (who
were direct descendants of the Puritans), it converted women, children,
and some men not only to Christ but to responsible and energetic participation in the roles of the new industrial Victorian family.[37] For some,
revivalism infused these roles with a sense of Christian vocation.

The functions of this new family in relation to the community
changed. With adult males absent from the home, families were no
longer able to take in orphans, prisoners, the sick, and the elderly. As
family privacy increased and gender roles diverged, the first era of
women's associations developed. These associations cared for the needs
of persons outside the immediate nuclear family, and they created and
funded the first institutions for the care of persons who required more
care than it was thought families could deliver.

Women's associations also developed movements for women's rights
and contributed to abolitionism. They created women's first public and
political agendas. Women of the emerging middle class evangelized and
provided charitable services among poorer groups. Middle-class single
women earned their first wages as teachers, although not on the pay
scale of men. The "cult of domesticity," as the ideal of middle-class womanhood, provided a model for married women at home and in associations. It provided a model for single women who began to be paid to
perform family functions that had moved outside the home. It also constituted a guiding image for domestic servants, both immigrants and
freed slaves, who sought economic security and upward mobility.

A parallel associational life for men began to emerge, contributing to
the caring activities of communities and the psychological development
of men. Numerous fraternal associations, generally secret and religious,
were formed that offered men companionship with other men, opportunities to provide caring service in their communities, and support
from other men for their psychological development and entrance into
the stresses of a competitive market economy. As fathers were now more
absent from the home, young men faced new challenges in their development of gender identity. Now predominantly under their mothers'
tutelage, young boys had fewer opportunities to observe the tasks, responsibilities, and identities of adult men. Fraternal associations like the
Masons and the Knights of Columbus provided young men with a peer
group that could help them through the rites of passage from boyhood

to manhood. Men's participation in fraternal associations, however, increasingly substituted for their activity in churches. As a result, by the end of the nineteenth century, Protestant churches were populated predominantly by women.[38]

A particular pattern of the nuclear family became the mark of the middle-class family. The ideal nineteenth-century nuclear family consisted of a wage-earning father, a mother presiding over domestic life, children, and sometimes servants. The family lived in its own home where the mother spent her time caring for children, managing the home, and volunteering in various activities. The father relinquished much of the childcare and guidance to the mother and did his best to earn a good wage. Not all nuclear family constellations followed this form, of course, not even in the nineteenth century, nor are nuclear families today Victorian in form. This pattern is often referred to in the American family debate as the "traditional family," meaning something very old and classic; the nineteenth-century ideal family is mistakenly equated with the family of biblical times. It is important not to equate the terms "nuclear family," "conjugal couple," and "traditional family," with the term "Victorian family," as is often done by all sides of this debate. Each of these terms can have specific meanings somewhat different from the others; they are not simple equivalents to the Victorian family.

The notion of the Victorian ideal family was flexible enough to be adapted to different socioeconomic realities in various regions of the country. Historian Colleen McDannell, in *The Christian Home in Victorian America, 1840–1900* (1986), has compared northeastern Protestants to Irish Catholic immigrants and has demonstrated that these Catholics created an analogous Victorian ideal that responded to their economic and religious differences.[39] McDannell argues that the Victorian ideal provided stability for Catholic families in the midst of the socioeconomic changes created by urbanization and industrialization. Even when families could not live up to the middle-class ideal, they were led by popular literature, much of it religious, to aspire toward a "proper" home. This home declared itself to the community by its outward appearance—its gingerbread architecture, absolute cleanliness, and religious decoration.

In order for poor Catholics to adapt for their purposes the middle-class, evangelical Protestant concept of the ideal family, many issues had to be negotiated. Irish Catholics emigrated from an impoverished Ireland, only to find themselves in similar straits in the United States. They competed with free blacks, sometimes violently, for jobs on the lowest rung of the northeastern labor structure. Class often determined family structure; many single immigrants, men and women, sent money to their families in the Old World. Poverty prevented them from marrying. When they could not depend on marriage in their future, what were young women and men to do, especially in a society that increasingly valued domesticity? Some attached themselves to middle-class families as servants; others married late in life. Many took religious vows, an act that usually raised their social standing, at least within their own communities. Traditionally, Roman Catholic theology taught that celibacy was preferred to marriage, and in the nineteenth century record numbers of young people declared religious vocations. Like volunteer associations among Protestant women, Roman Catholic religious orders provided arenas for public domesticity in teaching or caring for the sick. Roman Catholic young people saw in their religion a life's path that did not depend on marriage.

Roman Catholic religious practice, however, created an ideal of domesticity different from that found in evangelical Protestantism. Northeastern Protestants created religious space by gathering together, reading the Bible, and expounding the scriptures. Because these practices could take place at home as well as in church, the practice of family worship and religious education sacralized domesticity. In contrast, Roman Catholics created religious space less through seeing or hearing the Word and more through attending mass and taking part in sacramental life. Although aristocratic Roman Catholic homes had their own family chapels, poor Irish Catholics worshiped together in the parish church where they could see the sacramental process of the liturgy. Even today we see a similar pattern in the evangelical Turners, who have a rich devotional life at home, in contrast to the Catholic Murphys, whose worship life was centered in the church around the celebration of the Eucharist.

Furthermore, the patterns of religious leadership in Protestant and Catholic homes differed. Both Protestants and Catholics, according to McDannell, offered maternal and paternal models of family leadership.[40] Among New England Protestants, the father of the household served as priest, prophet, and king, one whose responsibility it was to gather the household, including children and servants, for prayer and exhortation. As fathers became more distant from their families under the effects of industrialization, mothers became the religious leaders of the family, not in the role of priests but as religious educators and mediators of God's sustaining love. In the maternal model, mothers instructed children intimately and individually, and remote fathers provided stability for the mother-infant bond. In both cases, Protestant parents more than Catholic parents believed they directly represented

God and scripture in the home without the mediation of priest and church.

Catholic fathers had few religious role models. Priests held the sacramental authority, were celibate, and were outside the family system. Most saints provided the ideals of a celibate religious life. Even so, as lower-class Roman Catholics adopted the middle-class family model, the Holy Family became important. Joseph became more prominent as a patron saint, a positive father figure within Roman Catholic religiosity. The mother and infant relation was given even deeper sacrality through the images of Mary as Queen of Heaven and Mother of God. Worship did increase among Catholics at home, often centered on individual devotions such as praying before a shrine to the Holy Family.[41]

As some Catholics came under the sway of the ideal of the Victorian family, they began to criticize lower-class members of their own ethnic communities for their inability to create "proper" families. Furthermore, Catholics began to publish their own advice literature on true womanhood and true manhood. Pope Leo XIII (1878–1903) published encyclicals that encouraged family devotions, linked the health of the family to the health of society, denounced divorce, attempted to protect the family from incursions of the state, and yet asked the state to help provide a family wage.

Much of twentieth-century culture considers as natural and God-given what the nineteenth century created: homemakers, wage earners, consumerism, gender-role specialization, and smaller family units that needed to fend for themselves.

The Victorian Family of the Middle States

The emerging ideal of the Victorian family in the frontier of the middle states and the Ohio Valley coincides with the emergence of Methodism as a significant religious tradition in America. Some background on American Methodism helps set the stage for understanding the issues that became significant for Methodist families. During the Revolutionary War, Methodism experienced a period of explosive growth, reaching fifteen thousand converts. Methodism, with its roots in Anglicanism and English Puritanism, first assumed a celibate clergy and a hierarchical lay family structure that coexisted with a spiritual egalitarianism before God. John Wesley broke with the Anglican pulpit tradition: he took the gospel into the fields and mines of England in defiance of Anglican church law. Nonetheless, he did not formally break with Anglican polity. When Wesley sanctioned the irregular ordination of Francis Asbury in 1784 in order to provide clergy for the new American nation, the American church hierarchy he created, though independent of the Church of England, was still reminiscent of the monarchy.

As Methodism spread into the Ohio Valley, so did the peculiarities of Methodist family life. Like the Puritan families who immigrated westward into upper New York State, the Methodists were often the poorer brothers, sisters, sons, or daughters of wealthy families of the upper southern or middle states. Like their northeastern counterparts, many of them were swept up in the evangelical fervor of the Second Great Awakening. Economically, they had more in common with Southerners who depended upon agriculture than with Northerners who were beginning to undergo the transformations of industrialization. Like Roman Catholics, Methodist clergy first practiced celibacy. Like their Protestant counterparts, however, they soon married, and married clergy became normative. Like Roman Catholics, Methodists stressed a regular, common ritual life, creating and celebrating "class meetings" and the "love feast." But like their Protestant kin, they stressed the ministry of the laity, and with clergy few and far between, married laity became leaders in religious life.

When the status of their families of origin did not guarantee their place in frontier society, these new immigrants to the Ohio Valley had to establish at least an *internal* sense of honor, self-mastery, and control. Historian Gregory Schneider argues that the theological rhetoric of self-sacrifice and self-abnegation, combined with serious explorations of members' spiritual life in class meetings, moved Methodists from depending upon the community for honor to finding their identity in the internal psychological acknowledgment of one's guilt and one's forgiveness and redemption by God.[42] Sharing and confessing in home-based class meetings produced a family intimacy that was carried back to their everyday home life. As Methodists adopted these ritual practices not only in the class meeting but within the family, they began to think that the ideal class meeting should be found in the family.

We argue in chapter 5 that analogies exist between this process and the way that early Christians modeled home life after the love feast practiced in their house churches. Like early Christians, Methodists also partially undermined the honor-shame codes of their surrounding culture—specifically the remnants of the Old South's patriarchy, control of women, confinement of women to an isolated domesticity, and willingness to duel in defense of public status. The Methodist family increasingly was built on intimacy, moral scrupulousness, mutual affection, and a greater voice for women, all modeled on an appropriation of patterns experienced in the class meetings and love feasts.[43]

Gradually, however, the family itself replaced the class meeting as the center of small-group religious life. Ohio Valley Methodists created their own version of nineteenth-century family piety. As the class meeting and love feast languished, the family gained significance as sacred space apart from the worshiping community. This helped set the stage for what some recent scholars have called the evangelical "idolatry of the family."[44]

The Victorian Family
of the Southern Frontier

Because the Deep South experienced little industrialization until after the Civil War and evangelical religions flourished only among lower classes, little transformation of the middle-class family occurred in these territories. The southern household, with its gendered conventions of plantation aristocrats and its denial of the family rights of slaves, endured even on its frontier.

The South was not all plantations, however; yeoman farmers and small farmers with fewer than three slaves also worked the soil. Evangelical religion, as elsewhere, took hold among these classes but was looked on with suspicion by the aristocracy. Aristocratic women provided food, clothing, and other aid for poor white and black families, but they did so as ladies of the aristocratic household rather than as women grouped into associations as had happened in the industrialized North.

Historian Elizabeth Fox-Genovese has summarized the difference in conditions between the antebellum North and South. While northern society was creating separate gender spheres, southern society was reinforcing the centrality of the plantation and farm households.[45] The northern model of womanhood was based increasingly on the ideal of equality, even though roles were highly differentiated; the southern model was tied closely to social rank. No southern aristocratic women shared education with men as northern bourgeois women did. While northern women's education for "Republican Motherhood" produced not only educated mothers but teachers who were paid for their work, southern aristocratic women were educated privately and never taught for pay. Despite the fact that it was lived out by only a small number of women, the model of the plantation lady loomed large as the southern cultural ideal of womanhood, much as the middle-class homemaker did in the North. The Civil War destroyed the social structure for this ideal, but perhaps not the ideal itself.

Yet the distance between cultural ideals and real life holds the potential for much variation. Is it possible to find in the slaveholding frontier of the Deep South evidence of Methodist evangelical domesticity? Although Presbyterians, Baptists, and Episcopalians made inroads into southern religion, Methodists had the most widespread and fervent evangelical appeal, bringing the Second Great Awakening into the plantations, particularly to the slaves.[46] Southern Methodists emphasized the importance of missionary work, declaring that slaves had human souls before God. They directed their appeals for benevolence and virtue to slave owners and to slaves, careful also to construct their ideal of the family within a vision of benevolent and virtuous relations between master and slave.[47]

Evidence exists that southern Methodists drew upon the ideal of the Victorian family, recasting it for their own economic and cultural situation. The Southern Methodist Publishing House published tracts for the literate classes on the virtues of family life, and preachers and missionaries reiterated the "family values" of these tracts to slaves and the poor. In a Methodist advice manual called *Family Government*, Bishop James Andrew tried to speak to slave owners who were suspicious that the preachers would incite a rebellion, to northern abolitionists who wanted to reject slavery, and to slaves to whom he felt called to bring a gospel of God's love, dignity, and self-respect.[48]

Andrew's popular advice columns appeared in the denominational newspaper the *Southern Christian Advocate* before the Civil War, and they were collected and reprinted in his widely read book. His message resonated with the virtues of Victorian religion. He stressed the importance of family to church and nation, the goal of mutual affection, the proper roles of a gentle husband and a submissive and helpful wife, the necessity of attentive parenting, and responsibilities to aging parents. He argued, in contrast to analogous British manuals of that era, that the moral education of servants and slaves was as important as the care of children and parents.[49] In addition, the marriages and family relations of slaves were to be given the same regard as one's own marriage and family. Just as one must not arrange a marriage for one's daughter to increase one's wealth, so one must not separate a slave family for one's own financial gain. The virtues espoused by Victorian domestic religion, ironically, may have contributed to a particular form of "subordination and equivalence" for slave families—slaves were treated more humanely even as their lot in life was justified by this same ideology.

In our interviews, we found contemporary manifestations of southern black Methodism in Maria and Robert Taylor. Methodist revivalism is part of the background to the modern Pentecostal movements. In Maria, we saw the willingness to use the language of the Victorian ideal suffused with the intimacy and directness of Methodist spirituality, but now in a family structure at odds with this ideal, which always may have been the case in poor, dual wage-earning black families of the post–Civil War era.

Moving West: Three Variations

Settlers sought to realize their hopes and ideals in the West, and they created new family patterns as they responded to the challenges of different environmental and economic conditions. Individualism, freer markets, and declining patriarchal restraints are all themes in these westward moves. Even the psychological stresses of radical change and loneliness are evident.

For our purposes, we compare three patterns of westward family movement. First, middle-class families, largely from the frontiers of the Northeast and Midwest, migrated as nuclear families, anticipating that they could improve their lives on the cheap lands of the Oregon Territory. Second, when gold was discovered in California, single and married men migrated as individuals who did not intend to settle but hoped to return to their eastern homes with new wealth. Third, Scandinavian farmers, escaping poverty and famine in Europe, settled the upper Midwest in the company of their extended families and significant portions of their entire communities. These three movements created a variety of family patterns and interactions.

In 1831 the American Society for Encouraging the Settlement of the Oregon Territory was established with the explicit intent of repeating "with appropriate variations the history of the Puritan Colony of the Massachusetts Bay."[50] The first mass emigrations to the West, however, were actually initiated by the 1837–39 depression. From 1840 to 1866, families gathered at their point of departure, Independence, Missouri, to form groups for the western journey. Until the 1860s, most of these families came from lower-middle-class or middle-class families, those who had enough property to pay for passage. The story of their travel records the transformation of the Victorian family model, gender roles, and family relations under extreme stress.

Husbands and fathers who were struggling to be breadwinners for their families became hopeful that money could be made in the West. Such a trip fulfilled social expectations that men should provide for their families and "make something" of themselves. A man's job was to build and repair the wagon, hunt for food, determine a route, and get his family to the West before the snows came. In the intensity of that responsibility, men left family concerns, including the births and deaths of children, largely to the women.[51]

Wives and mothers usually went west reluctantly and mourned leaving their original families and established networks. Their diaries record what we know about family life and women' efforts to maintain the attributes of the middle-class Victorian woman. Even in rough terrain, women sought to dress properly, in long skirts, and not speak of—much less reveal—their bodies, unless conditions made that impossible. They cooked over campfires, laundered in streams, and treated the sick.[52]

Middle-class gender attributes were often tested and modified, sometimes humiliating mature mothers and wives. Mothers and wives frequently had to learn male tasks, such as driving a mule team, when their husbands became sick or died. Younger women who felt fewer responsibilities for families and children met the westward journey with enthusiasm more like that of the men. They could embrace new friendships and generally were thrilled by the opportunities to learn the tasks of both genders. For them the trail offered a more carefree independence, not just a grim struggle for self-sufficiency.[53]

A second pattern emerged around the gold rush. The social chaos already created by westward expansion was only intensified by the discovery of gold in California. In the words of historian Laurie Maffly-Kipp, "the lure of El Dorado separated families, tore communities apart, caused enormous losses of life owing to diseases and accidents, and witnessed family savings augmented (though more often diminished) in a short period."[54] As individual men left families, communities, and institutions behind, the stabilities and values created by these forms of common living also faded. Because the migration was motivated more by the desire for quick wealth than by the search for land on which to settle, the value of money dominated all other goals. Institutions and communities were difficult to establish.

Maffly-Kipp argues that a sojourn in California often represented a phase of "liminality" in men's lives, a time set apart when they experimented with behavior that would have been unacceptable at home. Men who had left their families behind were drawn into drinking, gambling, and frequenting prostitutes, but they also learned new domestic tasks, such as sewing. Missionaries wrote home that California needed women to civilize it and to bring spirituality to its wildness and chaos. Women rather than male missionaries, they seemed to say, were the ones who could really bring the taming influence of religion to the miners. In so doing, male writers may have romanticized womanhood in its scarcity even more than it was idealized in its abundance. They also perpetuated the notion that men could not take responsibility for their own lives.

The women who did arrive in California were only modestly successful in bringing the ideals of the Victorian family to the miners. Acting as partners in their husbands' ministries, missionary wives, if they had homes, entertained scores of single men. Prostitutes decorated their brothels in Victorian fashion, recalling memories of home.[55] In most ways, however, the Victorian ideal was not realizable; the social and economic conditions did not permit it. Most women, especially missionary wives, had to contribute economically to the household. For some, this situation meant the burden of overwork, ill health, constant concern about hungry children, and bare survival. For others, the dearth of women increased the economic value of their domestic skills, and their sojourn became an economic opportunity. They enjoyed a measure of economic success and freedom unlike that of their eastern counterparts.

Other conditions that women would have taken for granted in the East were nonexistent. Middle-class evangelical women's religious lives in the East depended on their associations with networks of other women; same-sex friendships were highly valued. With women scarce, female companionship, much less a network of associations, was hard to find. While their middle-class counterparts in the East took on the role of supervising the family's purchase of goods and relying on a servant for domestic assistance, mothers and wives in California found themselves responsible for producing the family's goods without a paid servant or other forms of community assistance.[56] This may have been the seed of a kind of western individualism in family affairs that is with us even today.

The third move to the West by families came with Scandinavian immigrants who settled the old Northwest (or upper Midwest). In contrast to the first two migrations, this did not disrupt family and community stability. Emigration from Scandinavia was motivated by poverty and political and religious concerns. As in Puritan New England, family farms in the old country were no longer capable of feeding additional families; the upper Midwest offered cheap land. Religious and political dissent from state churches created discomfort for some; the upper Midwest allowed religious and political freedom. In such a climate, the practices of families, communities, and religion were relatively easy to transplant.

Many early Scandinavian emigrants were single men who then returned for their families. With fairly reliable information about conditions in the upper Midwest, Scandinavians gathered together, usually at the regional churchyard, for the trip over land and sea. Frequently whole families emigrated with other families from their community. Once these communities were settled, they had networks already in place to assist with obtaining food, shelter, and livelihood. Settlers sent requests to their home communities for clergy; clergy therefore entered stable communities that already had been organized into congregations.[57]

The contrasts between these migrations echo contemporary differences. In the recent debates on the family, the West and Northwest have emerged, for good or ill, as places of individualism, experimentation with family structure, and the readjustment of law and economy to account for women's economic independence. Western states along the Oregon trail tend to value local and personal autonomy. The states in which Scandinavians settled around the turn of the twentieth century, Minnesota and Wisconsin, developed ambitious, government-sponsored family support programs, as did Sweden, Norway, and Denmark. Even today, Wisconsin has been proactively developing policies and programs designed to lead the emerging phase of welfare reform in the United States.

Evangelical Religion and the Welfare State

The ideal of the Victorian family, as we have seen, was shaped by and in turn spawned many variations in the lives of North American families. As it reached the height of its power, this ideal provided a vision not only for smaller organizations of families or church groups, but also for the society as a whole. In so doing, the ideal of the Victorian family contributed to the emergence of the social assistance that we now know as "Social Security" or "welfare." At the end of the nineteenth century, the ideal of the Victorian family became the metaphor for society: society, it was thought, should be homelike.[58] At the apex of what some writers called the feminization of American culture, the metaphor of society as a home provided an international cultural ideal for new forms of public and professional domesticity such as education, social work, and public health. In some cases, the evangelical women's groups of the late nineteenth century broadened their vision to include politics. In other cases, secular women promoted the values of the homelike society without using explicitly theological language. Women began to believe that their vision could not be achieved without government involvement.

The Civil War produced new conditions that required creative answers. A quarter of the male population was dead or maimed. Many mothers were widowed and children orphaned. A significant portion of the younger female population could not depend upon marrying. Legislators developed the first federal social security legislation to provide for those persons who had risked their lives or died in the service of their country—soldiers on the battlefield and mothers on the birthing bed. As historian Theda Skocpol has shown, the earliest form of Social Security was born in the United States after the Civil War.[59]

In the United States, single women who had adopted the late–nineteenth-century Victorian ideal became involved in public mothering, particularly in the settlement house movement. In Scandinavia, where emigration had left behind more women than men, single women still sought to become biological mothers; the number of single mothers increased. Scandinavian countries began experimenting with their first family support programs as early as the 1890s. Only active political involvement on the part of women later brought these programs into fully developed family policies.

Family support in the United States had been largely the domain of church and community throughout the nineteenth century. As the settlement house movement developed, women's associations became active in the support of children and needy mothers. As in the case of temperance, women realized that business and government often created social conditions that left children, women, and families destitute. As federal welfare legislation developed, women argued that protections for children and women also should be included. Social conditions had changed so that families, churches, and women's and men's service associations could not provide adequate care for the destitute. On the coattails of legislation to protect working men, the Children's Bureau was formed; it created the first, although minimal, family support programs available to destitute families in the United States. These were the seedbeds of the extensive welfare programs of the twentieth century.

Twentieth-Century Families
and North American Churches

Regional variations of family ideals, carried by evangelical religion, contained some of the seeds of our twentieth-century tensions regarding the family. In spite of progressive impulses held by nineteenth-century evangelicals, patriarchy reasserted itself in some of these churches. During the last decades of that century, some Christians discovered that men were leaving the churches. Conscientious evangelical men sought to bring men back to the churches from the streets and male lodges— in itself, a laudable goal. Women who had been educated, had leadership roles in the church, and had preached in the mission fields gradually were pushed back into traditional roles. This process began at the end of the nineteenth century and continued until well after World War II. In some fundamentalist groups, this trend continues today. Fundamentalists are among the most cohesive religious groups on family issues, but as with the missionaries' treatment of the Cherokees, they generally promote patriarchy's reascendance at the expense of other important elements of the Christian faith.

In the 1890s the evangelical leader of the Women's Christian Temperance Union, Frances Willard, was fundamentalist in her opposition to alcohol, evangelical in her promotion of Christlike sanctification, and liberal in her eventual embrace of Christian socialism. Her vision of a Christian marriage, expressed in the evangelical language of her era, comes close to our ideal of marital equal regard:

> (They say) "Husband and wife are one, and that one is the husband."
> . . . (I say) Husband and wife are one, that one is—husband and wife.
> . . . One-half the world for (each). . . . co-education to mate them
> (in) mind, equal property rights to make her God's own free woman,
> not coerced into marriage for the sake of a support, not a bondslave
> after she is married . . . ; free to go her honored and self-respecting
> way as a maiden in perpetuo rather than marry a man whose deterioration . . . is a menace to herself and the descendant . . .
>
> Man in the home will have a larger place in the proportion that
> women, in the constant homelike world, gains larger standing room.
> Motherhood will not be less, but fatherhood a hundred-fold more
> magnified. . . . For when to the splendor of their intellectual power
> and the magnificence of their courage shall be added the unselfish devotion that comes of "child-ward care," we shall see characters more
> Christ-like than the world has known save in its calendar of saints.[60]

Willard's image of a Christ-centered family in which each partner showed equal regard to the other was simple: the joining of two partners who partake equally of culture and education, who have equal legal and economic rights, who honor mothering and fathering and share in the nurture of children. Furthermore, Willard suggests, society must change so that men and women would not be forced into marriage under less than ideal conditions; indeed, a genuinely homelike society would encourage such marriages and families to flourish. This is part of the nineteenth-century evangelical vision that patriarchal fundamentalism forgets. Indeed, Willard's evangelical energy and high regard for marriage are elements that today's Christian liberals sometimes forget.

Today's parachurch evangelicals like the Promise Keepers, Focus on the Family, and the Christian Coalition, in spite of their more benevolent patriarchy, have continuity with the late–nineteenth-century male fundamentalist reaction. Such groups tell men to be kind, gentle, and fair, but they fail to understand, as we will show, the necessarily dialogical character of these concepts. Such groups "allow" women to work outside the home. Yet they propose little to bring about the kind of social change needed to make paid employment for both sexes compatible with family obligations.

This century's religious liberals emerged from another side of late–nineteenth-century evangelicalism—the Social Gospel movement.

Associated with the theologian Walter Rauschenbusch, this movement emphasized making changes in society to bring in God's reign and deemphasized individual conversion. The heirs to the Social Gospel movement are most often associated with the mainline denominations in the American family debate. They often join with Roman Catholics, at least in resolutions and pastoral epistles, to hold government responsible for its share of care for families in need.

Mainline Protestants have wrestled publicly with the reality of families at the outer boundaries of family change. In so doing, liberal Protestant denominations carried on the evangelical tradition of providing public forums for passionate debates. As they once fought over the issues of abolition, temperance, and the shape of the family in an industrial society, they have continued to host debates over abortion, homosexuality, family structure, divorce, remarriage, single parenting, and recognizing "families of choice" and "domestic partners." As we have observed, however, the first two issues, abortion and homosexuality, have received the most attention in recent years. In the midst of these discussions, the ideal of the patriarchal father gave way to a relational justice that was sometimes indistinguishable from the secular contractualism of the wider society.

In retrospect, American Christianity prior to the nineteenth century aided in creating an ideal of marriage and family life that provided cultural cohesiveness despite differences that become apparent when we look at particular regions, social classes, and ethnic groups. Some people, but not all, were well served by this ideal. Respecting our cautions regarding the misuse of ideals, we propose that a new flexible ideal may be found in what we have called critical familism—the equal regard, intact, public-private family.

PART 2

Traditions

4

Love, Christian Family Theory, and Evolutionary Psychology

The competing images of love found throughout the history of Christianity have implications for a Christian view of families and for current family dilemmas. We saw the outlines of these different models of love in the tensions of the nineteenth century, especially in the subtle ways in which patriarchy exploited appeals to sacrificial love.

At one extreme, some Christians have identified love with self-sacrifice on behalf of the "other," be that other husband, wife, child, neighbor, stranger, or enemy. This meaning of Christian love has been associated with the Greek word *agape*. In its most radical form, summarized by Anders Nygren in his *Agape and Eros* (1953), this view disconnects self-sacrificial love from enjoyment, delight, pleasure, or self-fulfillment.[1] Love becomes, in this view, largely duty, commitment, and fidelity without thought of return from the other.

At the other extreme, love is identified with the fulfillment of the individual who loves. To love another is to feel elation, enrichment, passion, even pleasure. This form of love is associated with the Greek word *eros*—a word prominent in Greek philosophy and Catholic theology but absent in the New Testament.[2] Erotic love, as philospher Alan Soble calls it, is "reason based"; it is grounded in an assessment of the admirable qualities of the object of love.[3]

Another "middle" view defines love as mutuality—what this book often calls love as "equal regard." Some scholars believe this is the meaning that medieval Catholic theology gave *agape* when they translated it into the Latin word *caritas* (charity).[4] Love as equal regard, as we use it, includes elements of *eros* and sacrificial self-giving, although it subordinates both to equal concern for other *and* self. We believe that love as equal regard also was central to the meaning of *agape* as this word was used in the New Testament, although some Protestant theologians such as Nygren have overlooked this meaning and associated Christian love too strongly with self-sacrifice. Most important for this book, we believe that love as equal regard is the most adequate view of love for families.

Other forms of love are recognized, even in the Christian tradition. There is love as *philia* (friendship), *libido* (lust), *cupiditas* (love for the temporal), *storge* (parental love), and *amor sui* (self-love or self-regard). But what model of love is genuinely Christian? What model of love provides the most adequate understanding of love for families? Which models of love do we detect in the moral ecology of our five families?

Love in the
Moral Ecology of Families

At first glance, both the Turners and Mary Murphy appear to build their family life around agapic or self-sacrificial love. In neither family, however, is *agape* totally severed from affect, delight, and pleasure as it is in more extreme statements of agapic love. Sarah Miles and Richard Good seem on the boundary between love as self-fulfillment and love as some form of mutuality. Maria Taylor regards love primarily as mutuality but retains a lesser emphasis on sacrifice and fulfillment as well. Is there a way of holding these three emphases together in one coherent view?

When Jim and Sophie Turner talk about love, they are typically Protestant in their thinking. Secularization has not made deep inroads with them. (Nor has it eroded the faith of Mary Murphy who is as classically Catholic as the Turners are Protestant.) The Turners talk about marital love as a "covenant" or "commitment" of a man and woman "before God." "The glue is really the commitment," Jim says. In the same vein, Sophie says marriage is a "pledge before God." For both Jim and Sophie, the family is grounded on a covenantal commitment that is called forth and witnessed by God. Once the commitment is made, the couple "grows into the commitment." "The truth is," Jim says, "you should always marry the one you love, but you always have to love the one you marry." Affection first, yes: but then commitment, which leads and educates affection. Jim believes love is a "deed, not an emotion or word. Really love is a reaction, a kind of selflessness."

Is there a place for sacrifice? Jim answers, "I'd say yes, yes, and yes." Is there a place for self-fulfillment and mutuality? Jim believes that self-fulfillment has a place, but "it's more of a by-product." So is mutuality. Both mutuality and self-fulfillment occur if both husband and wife are "really working at giving themselves to the other person."

Commitment, pledge, a covenant that includes God, "learning how" to love, not just "being in" love—these features mark the way that love functions in the Turner family. It is, as we have learned, *very Protestant, very agapic.* From another perspective, the strong emphasis on duty makes it close to the thought of the Enlightenment philosopher Immanuel Kant, who historians say was quite Protestant in tone as well.[5] But in contrast to Kant, the juicier goods of love—sexuality, delight in children, fun, vacations—are also important in the Turners' view. They are secondary, however, to the central features of pledge and commitment, which must stay in place even if these other goods and satisfactions deteriorate or vanish.

The Turners

Sarah Miles and Richard Good give us a very different picture of marital and family love. For Sarah, the word *sacrifice* holds dark and unhappy meanings. It reminds her of the unhappy experiences of her childhood. Life is "not a bowl of cherries," her parents told her as they constantly spoke about how immigration, hard times, and the Holocaust had affected their relatives and friends. Is there a place for self-fulfillment in family life? She answers, "Yes. . . . There's not only a place, that's what it's all about." And mutuality? "There's totally a place for it." Then she adds, mutuality comes about by her "complaining that things are not mutual."

Sarah admits there is a role for love as self-sacrifice, but at most it's a "necessary evil." On the whole, "self-sacrifice is the pits." Although she has sacrificed much for her marriage—especially her career as a musician—she admits that she has gained as well. Even though Sarah and her family attend synagogue, her Judaism is "meaning less and less to her marriage, and her therapy is meaning more." "Fidelity is the main thing I get from my Judaism," she explains. The issue of fidelity, however, is not at the center of family issues she worries about.

Richard Good goes a bit further. What is love in families for Richard? It is a "mutual sense of giving each other freedom to be what you want to be." This is Richard Good's understanding of the Golden Rule—a kind of reciprocal freedom or reciprocal psychological space. Richard doesn't believe that anybody "really sacrifices themselves." Sacrifice "is too strong a word. Compromise is a better word." To change oneself for a relationship "means that the relationship isn't it. . . . The relationship goes where I go. Otherwise there would be some sort of indication that there was something significantly wrong with me."

Richard holds positions of responsibility in his church, but he confesses that religion informs his understanding of love only "modestly—not much." What is important is "not trying to control one another." At that moment, Richard Good's wife happened to come in and volunteered, "He's right. Richard has never tried to change me."

For Sarah Miles and Richard Good, marital love seems to be primarily a tool of self-expression and self-fulfillment. Mutuality is important but is defined mainly as a contract designed to enhance the fulfillment of the partners. The language of self-sacrifice is totally absent for Richard and only hesitantly used by Sarah. For Sarah, self-sacrifice is a tool that supports the process of "negotiation." When she feels she is giving up too much, "she stops to talk and negotiate." She likes her therapist's observation that "everything is negotiation."

Sarah Miles and Richard Good

The polarities of self-sacrifice and self-fulfillment are not authentic options for Mary Murphy. Nor are they strongly contrasted by Maria Taylor. When Maria was asked what she gave up for marriage, she replied, "Marriage is the better thing I ever had. I love my husband to death." Mary Murphy's formulation is even more arresting. In fact, she had difficulty separating self-fulfillment and self-sacrifice conceptually; she wasn't able to choose between them. The whole idea of marriage as a sacrament means for her "that you are not going to be able to tell the difference between where one ends and the other starts." The sacramental view means that you are not able to talk about the alternatives "in the ordinary way. There is not that much difference between giving and getting. Some things that look like sacrifice are really fulfilling."

Although Mary is older than many of our interviewees, she has worked outside the home since her sons entered high school. Yet marriage, children, a husband—these were the things she has always wanted. She does not see her marriage as entailing much sacrifice. Throughout the interview, however, Mary seemed to place all of these finite fulfillments in the context of some higher fulfillment centering on her vision and relation to God and the virtues that help her pursue that vision.

Marriage entails a third party for Mary, as it does for the Turners. This third party is God. "The relationship to God is more important than the relation to each other," she explained. This is the meaning of the Catholic understanding of marriage as a sacrament: "It means that the tangible, everyday contact between the two of us can be a real vehicle of divine love." The love between Mary and her husband Patrick is anchored in a divine love that "is bigger than both of us." This divine love has objectivity and boundaries: "it cannot be broken."

Mary believes that one can fall out of love but that subjectively falling out of love does not mean you should get a divorce. You can get a civil divorce, but "you are still married in the eyes of God." When the Murphy's daughter-in-law told them that she had fallen out of love with their son, they responded, "that will probably happen . . . and it does not necessarily mean that it has to be the end of this marriage." Mary and Patrick were once falling out of love, but this did not mean the end of their marriage. In fact, Mary confessed once falling in love with another man. The belief that her marriage was an objective reality that could not be broken led her to pull back from leaving Patrick. In spite of her view of marriage as an objecive and divinely empowered reality, Mary sees her marriage as full of specific goods: "romance and sexual attraction," "doing things together," "enjoying her sons," and "being pleasant" to one another.

Mary, like Jim Turner, feels that her marriage and family have been a matter of growing into the reality of the marital sacrament. Her feelings have gradually taken the shape of this sacramental reality, a reality that comes from God, locks into our natural affections, and then shapes them to conform to this supernatural gift. But Mary does not use the words "pledge," "commitment," "covenant," and "fidelity" in the way the Turners do. These words would have a far too decisional, voluntaristic, perhaps even narrowly ethical tone for Mary. She uses the words "love," "grace," "sacrament," and "objectivity."

Maria Taylor's understanding of love in marriage and family, we think, closely approaches what Christian love in families is all about. She sees marital love as a matter of mutuality and equal regard with sacrifice serving the end of mutuality. But we should say more about Christian love historically and theologically before returning to Maria.

Mary Murphy and Maria Taylor

Evolutionary Psychology
and Paternal Investment

Regardless of the differences between these families, each is holding together, at least for now. Large numbers of contemporary families are not so fortunate, including some that we interviewed. A complex set of interlocking causes have led to what we call the "democratization of marriage and family." This new situation puts a high premium on the commitments and communicative skills needed to make families cohere. Especially important are the commitment and skills of males. If our analysis is correct, much of the needed cultural and educational reconstruction must begin with them. This means acknowledging how Christian love functioned throughout its history to counter what we call the *male problematic,* the tendency of men to drift away from families. But we speak as well of a *female problematic,* the tendency of females under some conditions to suppress their own needs and raise children without paternal participation, sometimes under great stress and at great cost. Neither male nor female problematics are sinful as such, but they become involved in sin when measured by historically emergent ideals of committed husband-wife relations, ideals that Judaism and Christianity have associated with the unfolding will of God. Understanding these problematics and the desires that motivate them shows why *eros* should be a fundamental part of an adequate definition of Christian love.

Because old social supports are not present for many families, and new communicative skills have not been learned, an explosive situation is developing worldwide in which husbands and fathers are becoming increasingly absent from their mates and offspring.[6] In spite of the many fathers who are very involved in parenting, the trends toward father absence are disturbing. For nearly two decades, leaders who celebrated the new family pluralism overlooked the fact that in most of the new family forms, original fathers were absent.

According to McLanahan and Sandefur, fathers' residential absence does harm to their children for two reasons. The first has to do with with what sociologists call *social capital*: the likelihood that the father has resources in social networks, friends, contacts, family, education, and skills that won't be adequately conveyed to children if he is not present. Of course, other people who might take the father's place—friends, neighbors, aunts, uncles, mothers' boyfriends, stepfathers—have social capital as well, but the evidence indicates that on average none of these does the job as well as the natural father.

McLanahan and Sandefur then gave a second explanation—a biological one—that does not replace but supplements the first. They wrote, "The fact that both adults have a biological connection to the child would increase the likelihood that the parent would identify with the child and be willing to sacrifice for the child, and it would reduce the likelihood that either parent would abuse the child."[7] In short, *biological connectedness, they are suggesting, adds intensity of affection, identification, and investment, and, when it is missing, something important is lost.*

If this is true, what is the theory behind it? Why does biological relatedness make a difference even though, as we argue, its contribution must not be overstated? And what does this difference show about the importance of *eros* to Christian love? Our theses in what follows are twofold: *first, eros must play a part in Christian love, and, second, our modern theories of desire have been too thin, built too much around pleasure and intimacy and not enough around fuller ranges of human motivations, such as parental affections.*

Evolutionary psychology helps McLanahan and Sandefur amplify what their data implies about the importance of fathers, throws light on a forgotten aspect of *eros*—parental investment—that is an essential part of *caritas,* and helps us understand the natural conditions of family formation, conditions that theology should not ignore. Catholic natural law arguments and the Reformed idea of the orders of creation had insights into these natural conditions, but their insights need revision.

Evolutionary psychology goes back to the work of Charles Darwin on sexual selection and the emotions.[8] Darwin was certain that the factors shaping evolution—free variation and natural selection—also influence our mental and emotional life. Most evolutionary psychologists today reject the idea that humans are moved only by genes and environment.[9] The term "sociobiology," because of its association with reductionism, has fallen out of favor and been replaced by evolutionary ecology, behavioral biology, behavioral ecology, or evolutionary psychology. In this book we frequently use the term "evolutionary ecology" to remind the reader that this discipline holds a view of families that sees them as a part of an interlocking environment. Evolutionary theory influenced the psychology and ethics of American pragmatism—Peirce, James, and Dewey—who in turn inform the philosophical stance of this book.[10]

Evolutionary psychology is influencing the field of academic ethics, as can be seen in the work of Mary Midgley, Peter Singer, Richard Alexander, and Robert Wright.[11] Evolutionary ecology can contribute to all ethical issues, including family ethics, for one simple reason: every ethical system must make judgments about how existing central tendencies of humans should be organized for the well-being of individuals and the just harmony of the community. Rough biological judgments—some powerful, some mistaken—were in the background of Aristotle's thinking on the family.[12] Aristotle, in turn, influenced early Christianity and both Thomas Aquinas's and Luther's theology of the family. In short, implicit biological assumptions, both mistaken and accurate, are part of the theological tradition—part of its view of human *eros,* desire, and striving.

Evolutionary psychology's central contribution to family theory is its theory of the asymmetrical reproductive patterns of male and female mammals. This theory accounts for the strikingly different ways males and females go about reproducing themselves. Three concepts explain how these asymmetrical patterns work and especially how human males came to care for their children in the course of evolution: the theories of *inclusive fitness, kin altruism,* and *parental investment.* Inclusive fitness is the key concept. It has replaced an older idea in evolutionary theory which held that natural selection works only on the individual. Early evolutionary theory taught that it was individuals—or more properly their genes—that successfully reproduced themselves (were naturally selected) when they stood up to the pressures of the environment. The theory of inclusive fitness alters this formulation.

Since the monumental work of W. D. Hamilton in 1964, the individual—this basic unit of evolutionary change—is seen to be more complicated than was earlier thought. According to the theory of inclusive fitness, the individual includes the genes that he or she shares with close kin (50 percent with one's siblings, parents, and children; 25 percent with nephews, nieces, and grandchildren; 12.5 percent with first cousins, and so on).[13] Individuals, according to this perspective, do not fight just for their own survival; they also work for the survival and flourishing of the biological relatives who carry their genes. They do this because these genetically related individuals are literally extensions of themselves. Inclusive fitness is not just the fitness of the individual, it is the fitness of the *extended family.*

This leads to the second basic concept—the theory of kin altruism or kin selection. Under some circumstances, individuals are willing to sacrifice their own inclusive fitness on behalf of a relative, and they tend to do this in proportion to the degree of relatedness of the relative. Since parents and their biological children share 50 percent of the same genes, people are more likely to sacrifice for a son or daughter than for a nephew or niece, although they will often do that as well. Biologically related siblings are more likely to sacrifice for one another than for a cousin, although that too can happen. Age has something to do with these calculations of sacrifice. Children, for instance, are less likely to sacrifice for their parents because their parents have little reproductive life before them.[14]

Evolutionary psychology tells us why both biological parents and members of the extended family are so important to a child's well-being. It is kin who are most likely to contribute to the flourishing and defense of children. It is not just mother and father who are important to children but the whole crowd: grandparents, siblings, aunts and uncles, and so on. They all tend to be concerned, at least more than other people, about the children to whom they are related. This explains, even today, why the great bulk of childcare not done by parents is done by members of the extended family.[15]

It is important to assert that *kin altruism, as important as it is, does not explain all human love and self-sacrifice.* Cultural symbols and meanings, most generally religiocultural ones, extend and reshape these inclinations. Although humans are embodied creatures, they are also selves. Insofar as they are embodied, some of the tendencies humans share with other creatures are evident in the desires, inclinations, and behavior— the *eros*—of humans, even if their reflexive selves do not consciously know this is so. The theory of inclusive fitness doesn't explain everything about human sacrificial love, *but it may throw light on what it is designed to explain—the higher natural willingness of parents and blood relatives to sacrifice for related offspring than for nonkin.* As we show in chapter 5 kin altruism is both a great human strength and a monumental source of evil, depending on the wider moral context in which it is set.

The theories of inclusive fitness and kin altruism have relevance for understanding the grounds of parental investment, or, if you prefer, parental commitment. *Investment* is the word used by evolutionary psychologists and has the advantage of fitting a wide range of species for which the term commitment seems too anthropocentric.

Parental investment is a concept developed by biologists Ronald Fisher and Robert Trivers (1972). Trivers defines it as "any investment by the parent in an individual offspring that increases the offspring's chance of surviving . . . at the cost of the parent's ability to invest in other offspring."[16] To say it simply, energy put into one child not only takes that energy away from a parent but limits that parent's ability to nurture another possible child. In short, keeping offspring alive and thriving is a tremendous endeavor but at the same time one of the many expressions of *eros* or desire. Why do parents do it? They do it partly for themselves. This may seem inconsistent with Christian parental love. Indeed, in contrast to what evolutionary psychology imagines, Christians and Jews *also* care for their children because these children reflect the image of God.

The ecological description of the love of parents and extended family for children captures the meaning of the Greek concept of love as *storge*. If evolutionary ecology is correct, *storge*, or kin altruism, is a foundational element in all love.[17] If the primary parental investment is not made in a person, that person does not develop the other forms of love.

Now comes an important twist that throws light on the evolutionary origins of what we call the male and female problematics. The strategies of inclusive fitness and parental investment are quite different for males than for females of mammalian species. Females, because of their limited periods of childbearing capacity and the energy required to carry infants to birth, put their investment in relatively few offspring. The males of most mammalian species, however, follow a different strategy. They are inclined to mate with several females and to produce as many offspring as their life span permits, a potentially limitless number.[18] Males of almost all mammalian species make little or no parental investment in their offspring. For the males of most species, inclusive fitness is enhanced by inseminating as many females as possible and letting the females raise the offspring.

It is tempting to believe that none of these behavioral tendencies applies to humans. But the evidence is against such self-congratulation. These asymmetrical patterns appear to explain some of the sexual behavior of contemporary men and women. This is true in spite of inherited patterns of socialization, be they traditional, egalitarian, or feminist. David Buss's *The Evolution of Desire* (1994) summarizes a vast new scientific literature documenting behavioral differences between males and females in sexual and reproductive matters.[19] Buss's work uncovers patterns based on the study of more than ten thousand people of all ages from thirty-seven cultures. These patterns parallel the "antagonistic" reproductive strategies between males and females outlined above. Males seek more sexual variety; females are comparatively more cautious in their sexual selections, although under certain circumstances they too can be interested in variety.[20] Males are aroused more easily, especially by visual stimuli; females require more intimacy and touching for arousal. Males are sexually attracted to females that are young and appear fertile; females tend to be more attracted to males who have qualities relevant to fatherhood—men who command resources, are intelligent, and are stable.[21]

These theories, easily used for ideological purposes on the right and left of the family debate, must be carefully interpreted and qualified. Furthermore, they say nothing about the comparative intelligence, talent, or moral rationality of men and women. These concepts refer only to reproductive and sexual strategies. Their empirical status, however, is growing in credibility, and, *if equality between the sexes is a worthy moral goal, it can be accomplished better by facing these behavioral tendencies than by acting as though they do not exist.* As distinguished evolutionary psychologist Bobbi Low said in an interview, "I'm not quite sure what these insights mean for ethics, but I'm certain that we cannot achieve equality between the sexes without acknowledging that these differences exist."

We must face these tendencies, not to conform to them but to appropriately build on and modify them. Through a variety of biocultural steps, this has happened to some extent in the course of human evolution. According to evolutionist Donald Symons, by the time hominids had left the forests and become hunter-gatherers in the open grasslands, males had for the most part put behind them the promiscuous pattern of inclusive fitness typical of their chimpanzee ancestors; they had become attached to a single female, formed a relatively egalitarian conjugal couple, and were helping to care for their children.[22] Their primary contributions to their children and mate were protein and protection. However, studies of contemporary hunter-gatherers such as the !Kung San of Northwestern Botswana in Africa suggest that these earliest fathers also cuddled, fed, played with, and taught skills to their children.[23]

Since the time of these earliest hunter-gatherers, human males have generally joined females and followed what evolutionary theorists call the K-strategy of inclusive fitness. The K-strategy invests a large set of resources into raising only a few children to adulthood. This contrasts with the R-strategy, which procreates a large number of offspring (as is the case with fish and tadpoles) and leaves it to luck as to how many will survive.[24] The question is, how did this transition from what evolutionists call the "cad" strategy to the "dad" strategy occur for the human male? How deeply grounded in male human nature is the "dad" strategy? Is the "cad" strategy lying just below the surface of the male ego, ready to manifest itself in contemporary social behavior?

Evolutionary psychology argues that four factors worked together to bring the "dad" strategy into existence and lead human males to join the primordial mammalian mother-infant family. Today we may be undergoing a reversal or an undoing of some of these conditions.

The Four Conditions for Fatherhood

The first condition was the extreme vulnerability of human infants due to their long period of dependency in comparison with other mammalian newborns.[25] Human infants, because of their enormous heads, must be born before they become too large to slide down the birth canal. They are born, therefore, virtually helpless. This put enormous pressure on the hominid mother to feed and care for dependent children, often at the expense of her own needs. Yet for aeons that is exactly what mammalian mothers did. Infant dependency, however, stimulated females to turn to their male consorts for assistance, protection, and food. At the same time they turned to males for assistance, females also developed strategies to *actively* resist manipulation by the male.[26] Families were formed, first of all, to help the infant and mother, even though this arrangement often functioned to oppress them as well.

Second, according to Robert Trivers, conditions supporting "paternal certainty" began to emerge.[27] Paternal certainty refers to the recognition by a male that an infant is his and not the offspring of another male. Mammalian females knew with certainty that the infants moving in their wombs were theirs; this was true until the advent of surrogate motherhood. But males could never be completely certain that they were indeed the father.

Trivers and others have argued that human males became parentally invested when they acquired the capacity to infer that a child was biologically theirs. They developed a dim sense that their parental investment in a child who was partially themselves contributed to their inclusive fitness.[28] In those societies where paternal certainty was difficult to achieve because of female sexual freedom or male absence during war, the mother's brother, who was genetically related to both child and mother, often became the surrogate father.[29]

Third, paternal investment, the theory continues, was part of a wider pattern of male helpfulness calculated to win one of the most sought after goods of life: the pleasures of sexual exchange. Males found sex an integrating experience, esteemed the person that gave them such delights, and were inclined to give up their promiscuous ways and R-strategy and develop regular relations with a single consort.

Finally, evolutionary ecologists believe that males helped females for reasons beyond the desire for sexual pleasure. They also helped with infants in return for help from females in tasks primarily assigned to males. Paternal investment was part of a wider reciprocal helpfulness between males and females. Trivers's early theory about the importance of paternal certainty for male investment in their children is now seen as only part of the story. It was a necessary, but not sufficient, condition for the emergence of paternal care. Sexual exchange and reciprocal helpfulness were also necessary.

An example of the interrelation of these conditions can be seen in the Aka pygmies of central Africa, who show the highest level of male care for infants in the world. Aka husbands and wives earn their livelihood by fishing together. According to anthropologist Barry Hewlett, an Aka male takes care of children as a trade for both his wife's sexual favors and her help with the tasks of fishing.[30]

These natural conditions do not exhaust the qualities that go into parental commitment at the human level. Nor do they constitute a full account of what makes up love between a husband and wife or parent and child. In addition to these factors, marital love entails complex combinations of attraction, equal regard for the person of the other, and capacities for commitment and self-sacrifice. To identify these pervasive natural factors, however, is to inject an element of realism that many discussions of marital and family love omit. For this reason we turn to Thomas Aquinas. In spite of our disagreements with aspects of his theory of the family, he teaches us much about how to keep these diverse elements together.

The evolution of high levels of paternal investment in children among *Homo sapiens* is important for the flourishing of children, notwithstanding the contemporary voices arguing the contrary.[31] In addition to McLanahan and Sandefur's extensive statistical correlations supporting this claim, psychologist John Snarey's four-generation study in *How Fathers Care for the Next Generation* (1993) shows how engaged fathers contribute to the cognitive, emotional, and physical maturation of their children.[32] Snarey follows the psychoanalyst Erik Erikson in using the term "generativity" to refer to the commitment to children that evolutionary psychology calls "parental investment."[33] Snarey's research showed that a father's reading and playing with his children benefits daughters as much as sons, a point that McLanahan and Sandefur confirm.[34] David Popenoe and David Bakan go even further in their claims: they believe that the addition of fathers to the primordial mother-infant family was a key to the rise of civilization among *Homo sapiens*. They also believe that the decline of this male generativity and paternal investment is one of the greatest threats to civilization.[35]

Thomas Aquinas and the Male Problematic: A Psychotheological-Economic Approach

Aquinas's family theory depends, in part, on several observations he made on the basis of the comparative psychobiology of his day, primarily the work of Aristotle and his teacher Albertus Magnus.[36] Furthermore, he was keenly aware of the economic aspects of marriage and families. Finally, he understood the role of religious symbols in transforming human energies. These insights make Aquinas's thought an early example of our psychocultural-economic model of families. In his case, however, it should be called a psychotheological-economic view.

The mediating term between psychobiology and economics was not just culture, as it is for modern social scientists; the middle term was God: all elevating symbolism and meaning ultimately pointed to the divine reality.

Aquinas's psychobiology contains many errors when measured against modern standards, but it also contains important insights when measured by these same sources. Aquinas stood in the Stoic-Augustinian tradition that saw sexual pleasure as clouding human reason; hence, his distrust of it.[37] Aquinas also shared Aristotle's patriarchal view that women are weaker than men physically and mentally and therefore need the guidance of males.[38] Finally, he held that the primary role of women was procreative, thereby overlooking their other potentials.[39] To his credit, his misogyny was softened by the theological idea that women were made in the image of God, an idea that Aristotle would have found puzzling. But even so, Aquinas thought women were less completely made in this divine image than men.[40]

We reject both Aquinas's and Aristotle's subordinationism.[41] Yet there is value in Aquinas's synthesis of Greek and Christian ideas on marriage and family and in his subtle combination of naturalistic, ethical, and theological lines of argument. This model of moral thinking about the family has much to offer contemporary interdisciplinary discussions. As much as possible, we hope to isolate and separate Aquinas's patriarchy and subordinationism from his more lasting insights into why families form. In his naturalistic arguments, Aquinas is surprisingly close to the evolutionary perspective described above. Furthermore, his larger philosophical vision can balance some of the philosophical narrowness of evolutionary psychology.

The Dialectics of Desire
and the Symbol of Christ

Aquinas had his own understanding of the male problematic. He also had a vision of how the symbols of the Christian faith work to overcome these male tendencies. This vision has relevance for women as well, but only when carefully interpreted and amended. Philosopher Paul Ricoeur developed a theory of symbolism that helps us understand Aquinas's use of Christian symbols to address the male condition. In his magisterial *Freud and Philosophy* (1971), Ricoeur argues that, in order to interpret a symbol, one must understand the unconscious archaeology (the unconscious motivation) that is brought to the symbol and, to a degree, transformed by the symbol. A religious symbol, he argues, contains a "mixed language" with two levels: (1) a primitive archaeology (based on an analysis of deep natural inclinations) and (2) a teleology or direction in which these inclinations are being transformed.[42] In the symbolic reading of Aquinas that follows, we do not use Freud to interpret the archaeology of the symbols we find. We use, instead, evolutionary psychology's theory of our unconscious desires.

Symbols have to do with the transformation of instinctuality. This statement in itself assumes a nondeterministic view of human action. We are not determined by our desires. We are instead profoundly shaped by the symbolic universes that attract, help define, and then restructure our desires. Nonetheless, our desires do exist; however much they are shaped by the symbols through which we view them, the symbols themselves do not create our desires.

It needs to be said from the beginning that Aquinas's naturalism does not determine his theory of the family. Rather, it sets forth certain naturalistic conditions—what moral philosophers call premoral values—that are refined and restructured by his ethical and theological argument.[43]

Aquinas's Naturalistic Argument: The Psychoeconomic Level

Aquinas's argument about the family had three levels: naturalistic or psychoeconomic, ethical, and narrative-theological. Aquinas saw the family as a natural institution grounded in deep human inclinations. In order for these inclinations to become fully human, he thought, they had to be refined by will, culture, and divine revelation.

At the naturalistic level, Aquinas discussed four conditions for family formation analogous to the ones found in evolutionary psychology, namely, infant dependency, paternal certainty, mutual assistance, and sexual exchange. In emphasizing these conditions, Aquinas made assumptions about humans' natural preference for blood-related family, ideas similar to the modern-day theory of kin altruism.

First, infant dependency: in the Supplement to the *Summa Theologica,* he writes that humans share with all animals an inclination to have offspring. Having asserted this, Aquinas introduces a very modern-sounding distinction:

> Yet nature does not incline thereto in the same way in all animals; since there are animals whose offspring are able to seek food immediately after birth, or are sufficiently fed by their mother; and in these there is no tie between male and female; whereas in those whose offspring needs the support of both parents, although for a short time, there is a certain tie, as may be seen in certain birds. In

man, however, since the child needs the parents' care for a long time, there is a very great tie between male and female, to which tie even the generic nature inclines.[44]

Aquinas believed (as evolutionary ecologists do today) that humans form families in part because of the months and years needed for vulnerable human infants to grow to independence. In the *Summa contra Gentiles* he writes, "in those animals in which the female alone suffices for the rearing of the offspring, . . . the male and female do not remain together after coition."[45] The human female, he insists, is "far from sufficing alone for the rearing of children, since the needs of human life require many things that one person alone cannot provide."[46] For this reason, it is "in keeping with human nature that the man remain with the woman after coition, and not leave her at once, indulging in promiscuous intercourse."[47] It never dawned on Aquinas that in human prehistory, females did raise the children.

This last quotation suggests, as William James and Mary Midgley have argued so cogently in the twentieth century, that human beings are creatures of multiple impulses that sometimes conflict.[48] Aquinas recognized that under certain conditions, males have inclinations to form families and assist females in raising highly dependent infants. But they also have other inclinations toward promiscuity or something akin to what evolutionary ecologists call the R-strategy (procreation of a large number of offspring). In the *Summa contra Gentiles,* he writes that male animals desire "to indulge at will in the pleasure of copulation, even as in the pleasure of eating." For this reason, they fight with one another for access to females and they "resist another's intercourse with their consort."[49]

This leads to the second set of conditions. Aquinas recognized the role that paternal certainty and recognition play in forming a lasting bond between a male, his consort, and their offspring: "Man naturally desires to be assured of his offspring: and this assurance would be altogether nullified in the case of promiscuous copulation. Therefore the union of one man with one woman comes from a natural instinct."[50] This is Aquinas's rather wooden way of saying that males prefer not to unknowingly take responsibility for another male's children. A system of monogamous bonding heightens a male's certainty that a particular child is his and makes it more likely that he will care for his offspring and remain with the mother.

Aquinas taught that fathers care for their children as a way of enhancing their own immortality, a concept similar to the theories of inclusive fitness and kin altruism. With a distinctively masculine bias typical of his day, he wrote, "Since the natural life which cannot be preserved in the person of an undying father is preserved, by a kind of suc-

cession, in the person of the son, it is naturally befitting that the son succeed in things belonging to the father."[51] Aquinas's main source for this
insight was Aristotle's *Politics*.[52] In one place Aristotle wrote, "In common with other animals and with plants, mankind have a natural desire
to leave behind them an image of themselves."[53]

These protoevolutionary theories of reproductive fitness and kin altruism led Aristotle to oppose Plato's proposal in *The Republic* that civil harmony and true equality would be enhanced if a child were taken from its
parents after birth and raised by the state. Parents, according to the proposal, were to be kept ignorant about which child was actually theirs.
Plato argued that such an arrangement would lessen competition between
families and clans, lead adults to treat all children as their own, and encourage children to relate to all grown-ups as to their own parents.[54]

Aristotle believed that Plato's proposal would lead to the general neglect of all children. He wrote, "That which is common to the greatest
number has the least care bestowed upon it."[55] For Aristotle, parental
investment comes with parental recognition that a particular child is his
or hers. He thought that in Plato's state, "love will be watery. . . . Of the
two qualities which chiefly inspire regard and affection—that a thing is
your own and that it is your only one—neither can exist in such a state
as this."[56]

Aquinas sided with Aristotle in his argument with Plato, thereby tilt-
ing Christian thinking on family issues in the Aristotelian direction. Although he agreed with Aristotle that parental certainty and recognition
contribute to parental investment, he would concur with today's evolutionists that this recognition is more easily achieved by females than
males. Monogamy, he thought, contributes to paternal certainty and is
associated with paternal care for offspring.

> In every animal species where the father has a certain care for his
> offspring, the one male has but one female, as may be seen in birds,
> where both unite in feeding their young. On the other hand where
> the male animal has not the care of the offspring, we find indiffer-
> ently union of one male with several females, or of one female with
> several males: such is the case with dogs, hens, and so forth.[57]

There can, of course, be too much emphasis on the role of parental
certainty for producing long-term commitment to children. Qualifications of this rule apply to most couples who adopt. Such couples are
highly motivated to become parents—more so than most people.
Hence, they often make excellent, highly invested parents. Furthermore,
evolutionary theorists tell us that we become attracted to nonkin infants
partly because they activate parental potentials which have been se-

lected and retained over the course of evolution for their relevance to children. Insights into the evolutionary conditions for male involvement in families should not be used to undercut an understanding of why adoption and even the formation of stepfamilies can often work.[58]

Did Aquinas recognize the roles of *mutual helpfulness* and *sexual exchange,* the third and fourth factors identified by evolutionary psychology as important for family formation? He did, but in a distinctively medieval way. Procreation was for him the primary end of matrimony, but he recognized nonprocreative purposes as well. One of the purposes "is the mutual services which married persons render one another in household matters."[59] Here Aquinas reminds us of contemporary anthropologists who teach that husbands and wives, like the Aka pygmies referred to above, stay together partly because they help each other. This is what moral philosophers call the teleological dimension of marital love; love between a husband and wife increases the *goods* experienced by each member of the couple. We hold that this element of "doing good things" for the other is an important subordinate dimension of the ethics of equal regard and mutuality. This is one of the reasons that males got involved in families aeons ago; they got help from their mates just as their mates got help from them.

But did Aquinas see a place for sexual exchange? He did, but not in a very positive way. Aquinas, as did Paul and Augustine before him, spoke of the need to pay the "marital debt."[60] Not all sexual exchange, for Aquinas, was for procreation. Some was done to avoid the lustful pursuits of nonmarital sex. To avoid this catastrophe, a spouse was to render sex to a partner who desired it.[61] If pleasure was experienced in doing this, it was excused by the force of the marital blessing.[62] But mutual helpfulness and sexual exchange, however negatively the latter was viewed, were both essential parts of the family theory of Aquinas. In short, Aquinas had his own way of stating the naturalistic conditions for family formation. His ethical and theological views assumed and surrounded these conditions.

Aquinas's Ethical Argument

Aquinas's theory of marriage and family rapidly moves from this naturalistic level to the next two levels.[63] The psychobiological discussion helps identify a variety of premoral and natural goods that contribute to human flourishing. A more properly moral argument based on appeals to freedom, dignity, and the status of persons is also a part of his family theory. At this moral level, Aquinas is still developing arguments that are not fully theological. They have to do more with his view of creation than redemption.

Aquinas's moral arguments emerge when he argues for the superiority of monogamy over polyandry and polygyny. He immediately rejects polyandry because it does not provide for paternal certainty: "man naturally desires to know his offspring, and this knowledge would be completely destroyed if there were several males for one female."[64] This is the major reason, according to evolutionary psychologists, that polyandry has not been widely used as a family form in the history of the human race. If a father's emotional and financial investment in the lives of his own children is experienced as a good, then polyandry, according to Aquinas and contemporary evolutionists, is not likely to bring it about.

Polygyny itself, according to Aquinas, *does* provide a degree of paternal certainty and some degree of paternal investment in children. Aquinas's major criticism of polygyny is advanced, then, as a moral rather than a strictly biological argument. He rejects polygyny because it is *simply an unjust institution for women.* He writes:

> Besides. Equality is a condition of friendship. Hence a woman may not have several husbands, because this removes the certainty of offspring; were it lawful for a man to have several wives, the friendship of a wife for her husband would not be freely bestowed, but servile as it were. And this argument is confirmed by experience; since where men have several wives, the wives are treated as servants.[65]

For Aquinas, because women are made in the image of God—although a little less perfectly—they enjoy a kind of equality with men. They are fit candidates for friendship with their husbands. Elsewhere he writes, "If the wife has but one husband, while the husband has several wives, the friendship will not be equal on either side; and consequently it will be not a freely bestowed but a servile friendship as it were."[66] Here we see the rudimentary beginnings of Aquinas's view of marital love as mutuality and equal regard.

Aquinas reinforces this moral argument with a second based on scripture. He quotes Genesis 2:24 and develops an argument that Protestants would say is based on the "orders of creation": "*They shall be two in one flesh.*" He writes that with this verse, the ancient Hebrew custom of "having several wives is set aside, and also the opinion of Plato who maintained that wives should be common."[67] The "one flesh" verse, of course, is repeated many times in the New Testament.[68] Aquinas interprets it to mean that husband and wife are to have a friendship of equality that binds them together in their task of raising and educating their children.

We believe that Aquinas is right here. (In addition, however, as we discuss in chapter 10, part of the meaning of the "one flesh" covenant is that husband and wife treat each other "as if" they were blood relations, even though they are not. Kin altruism thus becomes a fictive model for the equal investment of husband and wife in the well-being of the other.)

Aquinas's emphasis on friendship is part of what he called mutual assistance—his third purpose of marriage.[69] Mutual assistance for Aquinas cut across two levels of human reality. It included the mundane exchange of favors that evolutionists call reciprocal altruism (I'll help you *if* you help me), observed in beasts and humans alike. It also included for Aquinas a moral level where friendship is based on a love for the virtuous self of the other—a selfhood that demands to be treated as an end and never as a means only. For him, marriage is primarily a friendship of mutuality and only secondarily one of utility.[70] Genuine mutuality for Aquinas contained, yet subordinated, utility.

Aquinas's idea of mutuality and equality between husband and wife was proportional, however, to the supposed respective rationality of husband and wife. Since the husband was accorded a higher rationality in the ideologies of the day, the theory of spousal friendship did not provide for the egalitarianism that moderns associate with liberal, contractual models of marriage or the egalitarianism demanded by the Christian faith, properly conceived. The point for now, however, is this: monogamy for Aquinas brought into existence a new level of care and investment by males in their children and created greater equality and friendship between wife and husband.

Aquinas's
Narrative-Theological Argument

The third level of Aquinas's argument for matrimony and family is what we call the narrative-theological level. To be exact, however, the first two levels—the naturalistic and ethical—also have their theological dimensions. They have to do with the doctrine of creation rather than the doctrine of redemption. Aquinas saw God's purposes in nature and in our created ethical constitution as well as in God's desire to redeem us.

Aquinas assumes that nature is the way it is because God *created* it. Even then, he is aware of the conflicting tendencies of nature. The monogamous family is superior, he argues, because it includes a wider range of natural values even though it may deemphasize some of them. His understanding of the multiple tendencies of nature has analogues to modern evolutionary ecology, even though he assumed a final-end tele-ology that evolutionary theory would reject.

At both the naturalistic and ethical levels, Aquinas's argument assumes that the image of God in males and females is a part of creation. We love our children, according to Aquinas, for *two reasons, not just one*. We love them first because, as Aristotle also taught, we love the image of ourselves that we find in our children.[71] God, he believed, implants this impulse within us. But we also love our children because they, like all other humans, contain the good of God (the image of God) within them.[72] This is the second, even more profound reason we love our children. The second, more explicitly theological reason, however, does not eliminate the first, the naturalistic reason. Both reasons have to do with God's work in creation, and God's intentions are behind them both.

The third level of Aquinas's argument concerning the order of redemption was the realm of supernatural grace and sacrament. Here the narrative of Christ's sacrificial death on the cross was used as an analogy to the role of Christian fathers in their families. The following reading of Aquinas does not disparage the Catholic doctrine of marriage as sacrament but shows its profound insights by bringing another angle of vision. Chapter 123 of the *Summa contra Gentiles*, the key text, dramatically weaves together an analysis of natural human inclinations, a theory of sexual justice, and a rendering of the Christian narrative that reinforces marital permanence.[73] The argument is stated from the male point of view, but rather than dismissing it for this fault, we should see it as an effort to overcome the male problematic (the tendency of males to mate without parental investment). Aquinas's arguments can be restated from the perspective of both parents—with both the male and female problematics in mind.

Marital Permanence and the Analogy of Christ

Aquinas makes seven points about the permanence of matrimony, some of which we have encountered. The first three are premoral and deal with the value of paternal investment. First, because fathers care for their children as a way of extending their own lives, they should give this care indefinitely—as long as it is needed. And marriage should be indissoluble because it provides the context for this lifelong investment.[74] Second, because of the long years of human childhood dependency, children need parental, including paternal, help indefinitely. Third, if couples exchange partners, paternal certainty will become obscured, and fathers will care less for their progeny.[75]

The next arguments are distinctively moral. In the fourth Aquinas asserts that to dissolve a marriage is an affront to equity and fairness toward the wife. Aquinas assumes that men tend to dispose of older women and take as mates younger, more fertile females. He writes, "If a man after taking a wife in her youth, while she is yet fair and fruitful, can put her away when she has aged, he does her an injury, contrary to natural equity."[76] Aquinas repudiated patriarchal divorce, a widespread ancient practice that Jesus had rejected as well.

Fifth, in addition to procreation, marriage is for friendship, and this friendship will be all the more stable if it is thought to be indissoluble.[77] Sixth (and most out of tune with the modern mind), Aquinas thought women were necessarily financially dependent on men and "naturally subject" to the man's superior wisdom. Therefore neither women nor men should be allowed to initiate divorce since this would deprive women of the resources and guidance they need.[78] The contemporary slide of single mothers into poverty, in spite of their increased economic independence, suggests that his economic analysis had more merit than his assessment of women's need for male wisdom.[79]

Aquinas's seventh argument for the indissolubility of marriage makes a direct appeal to revelation and is the cornerstone of his understanding of marriage as a sacrament. It points to a paradigmatic narrative action that Christian husbands and fathers are charged to imitate in relating to wives and children. Furthermore, it shows that Aquinas saw narratives about divine action as supplementing both natural human inclination and the positive law in regulating marriage. Both human law and divine revelation should be based on, yet remedy the defects of, natural inclination. Not only do divine laws "express the instinct of nature, but they also supply the defect of natural instinct."[80] Divine law adds to human law "a kind of supernatural reason taken from the representation of the indissoluble union of Christ and the Church, which is union of one with one."[81]

This indissoluble union refers to Christ's sacrificial love for the church described in Ephesians 5:21–33, a sacrifice that Christian men are to model in their relations to wife and children. Aquinas calls this a "sacrament (Eph. 5:32),"[82] which meant to him both indissolubility *and* supernatural grace. We focus, however, on another dimension of Aquinas's understanding of *sacramentum*. This dimension is more dramatic than the somewhat mechanical infusion of grace to overcome concupiscence and immoral behavior; it invites imitation or participation in the archetypal pattern of divine action. Aquinas is addressing this dimension when he writes, "Although Matrimony is not conformed to Christ's Passion as regards pain, it is as regards charity, whereby He suffered for the church who was to be united to Him as His spouse."[83]

This means that the husband is to imitate Christ both in the husband's unbreakable commitment to the family but also in his capacity for sacrificial love or charity (*caritas* in the Latin and *agape* in the Greek). The purpose of this sacrificial love is to endure in the relationship and restore it to the equity of friendship. Friendship with one's spouse, friendship with the neighbor, and finally friendship with God—these are the purposes of Christ's passion, according to Aquinas. The sacrifice is not an end in itself; it is a means for restoring friendship with spouse and parental commitment to children. When Aquinas invokes the narrative analogy between Christ's redemptive passion for the church and the love of fathers for family, he has verses from Ephesians in mind:

> Husbands, love your wives, just as Christ loved the church and gave himself up for her. . . . In the same way, husbands should love their wives as they do their own bodies. He who loves his wife loves himself. For no one ever hates his own body, but he nourishes and tenderly cares for it, even as Christ does for the church, because we are members of his body. (Eph. 5:25–30)

Aquinas's use of Ephesians to elaborate on male sacrificial commitment was the theological counterpart to his theory of male sexual ambivalence (his prescientific view of the male R-strategy). It assumed his naturalistic views on the needs of dependent children and his economic views on the vulnerability of wives. That males should serve the family as Christ did the church was the last of seven otherwise prudential and moral reasons for male commitment. Aquinas in effect tells his reader that this commitment should rest on a grand analogy between the love of husbands, the servant love of Christ, and indeed the very nature of God.

Both the letter to the Ephesians and Aquinas's ideas are carriers, to some extent, of an ethic of love paternalism (which we later critique). Aquinas's was a chastened patriarchy that emphasized responsibility, commitment, and care, but the power was nonetheless in the hands of the husband. Aquinas mitigated the oppressiveness of ancient patriarchies, but he did not reject them altogether. Admitting this, however, should not blind us to the way he developed the analogy between Christ and husband against the background of the ambivalence of male desire and the male problematic. Margaret Mead once observed that without powerful cultural reasons for men to invest in their children and remain with the women who give them birth, human males have deep desires to follow another sexual strategy.[84] Aquinas formulated a powerful religiocultural symbol that reinforced unsteady male inclinations toward paternal investment and monogamy.

Aquinas's symbolic reinforcement of marriage was classically religious: It illustrates Mircea Eliade's respected phenomenology of the sacred. It made matrimony a recapitulation of the action of a divine being in its creation of sacred space and time.[85] The meaning of the husband's identification with Christ's sacrificial union with the church is striking when understood, using Ricoeur's dialectic between archaeology and teleology, as the reinforcement of some and the transformation of other basic male inclinations. The symbol of Christ's steadfast and sacrificial love for the church becomes, as Ricoeur calls it, a "figure of the spirit" attracting inchoate male inclinations and shaping them into a new organization.[86]

The idea of marital commitment as the recapitulation of a divine drama is visible in papal encyclicals and communications beginning with Pope Leo XIII's *Arcanum* (1880) and continuing to John Paul II's *Familiaris Consortio* (1981). Pius XI's *Casti Connubii* (1930) exemplifies this regularly repeated theme: "For matrimonial faith demands that husband and wife be joined in an especially holy and pure love, not as adulterers love each other, but as Christ loved the Church."[87] In most of these documents, however, the drama of male servanthood also was used to bolster male authority. But even in these Catholic documents, which mostly forgot the logic of Aquinas's original use of this narrative, mutuality and equal regard have increasingly been used to characterize the relation of husbands and wives.[88]

Luther, Love, and the
Male Problematic

Luther and Aquinas had similar ways of relating the symbol of the cross to the male's self-sacrificial attachment to families. But Luther differed with his Catholic predecessor on many other matters. Luther taught that marriage was a worthier Christian vocation than celibacy; he emptied German monasteries and nunneries and encouraged marriage between Catholic priests and religious. He also rejected the Catholic sacramental view of marriage. Even though he never transcended patriarchy, he saw both motherhood and fatherhood (even male care for infants) as divine vocations. He repudiated the medieval practice of secret marriage, seeing marriage instead as a public affair under the control of the state, although given meaning and blessed by the church.[89]

Yet Luther's theology of the family was closer to Aquinas's than is commonly thought. Luther referred, however, not to biology but to the Genesis creation stories and their restatement in the Gospels. "So God created man . . . male and female he created them" (Gen. 1:27). Males and females were not made to "be alone" (2:18) but to become "one flesh" (2:24) and "be fruitful" (1:28). Furthermore, these divine intentions were not "commands" of the kind God addresses directly to the individual conscience; they were "ordinances" stamped into the very fabric of creation. Luther wrote,

> It is a nature and disposition just as innate as the organs involved in it. Therefore just as God does not command anyone to be a man or a woman but creates them the way they have to be, so he does not command them to multiply but creates them so that they have to multiply. And wherever men try to resist this, it remains irresistible nonetheless and goes its way through fornication, adultery, and secret sins, for his is a matter of nature and not of choice.[90]

Both Aquinas and Luther made use of arguments based on the structure of nature. Luther did it from the perspective of God's ordinances revealed in Genesis; Aquinas did it on the basis of prescientific naturalistic observations. Both, however, saw God's hand in creation. Both believed that God's will for marriage and family gives additional order to certain regularities of nature.[91] Both theologians helped identify the features of nature that the institutions of marriage and family build on and complete. Luther's view of nature was built on faith and needs to be supplemented by more careful naturalistic description; Aquinas makes careful descriptions but contaminates them with subordinationism and patriarchy. *Both views need reconstruction.*

Modern Christian thinkers should consider the following strategy. They should use the disciplines of biology last, not first. They should begin with the scriptures of the communities of faith that form them, with the Genesis ordinances about male and female leaving their families of origin and becoming one flesh. These scriptures contained intuitive wisdom. Aquinas's naturalistic explanations should then be used to show that what scriptures assert by faith can be given a reasoned account. Although Aquinas's specifications of the natural conditions of matrimony are rough, contemporary evolutionary ecology helps show their plausibility. The eyes of faith should then follow Aquinas in placing these explanations within a theology and ethic that find a place for the hand of God.

Luther, like Aquinas, had his variation of the male problematic. Like Aquinas, he aims his theology of parental responsibility toward fathers more than mothers, partly to counter the male disdain for married life among the celibate Catholic clergy of his day. Luther believed that the mundane and distasteful things that mothers and fathers do for their children are "adorned with divine approval." In "The Estate of Marriage" (1522), he offers a prayer of thanks for his paternal vocation:

> O God, because I am certain that thou hast created me as a man and hast from my body begotten his child, I also know for a certainty that it meets with thy perfect pleasure. I confess to thee that I am not worthy to rock the little babe or wash its diapers, or to be entrusted with the care of the child and its mother. How is it that I, without any merit, have come to this distinction of being certain that I am serving thy creature and thy most precious will? O how gladly will I do so, though the duties should be even more significant and despised. Neither frost nor heat, neither drudgery nor labor, will distress or dissuade me, for I am certain that it is thus pleasing in thy sight.[92]

Luther, as did Aquinas, invoked the Ephesians drama but applied it mainly to men. In his "Order of Marriage for Common Pastors" (1529), he gives prominence to the analogy between Christ and the church and the servant relation of husband to the family (Eph. 5:25–29). He then concludes with a prayer that thanks God for creating man and woman, ordaining them for marriage, and typifying "therein the sacramental union of the dear Son, the Lord Jesus Christ, and the church, his bride."[93]

A final difference between Luther and Aquinas cannot be ignored. Aquinas saw a strong place for the cross and sacrificial love in marriage. But the task of sacrificial love was to restore relations to friendship. Luther, on the other hand, held a strong agapic understanding of love. Luther explicitly rejected the equal-regard interpretation of "Love your neighbor as yourself" (Matt. 19:19) that we promote in this book. Luther writes that "one can take it to mean that both are commanded: we shall love our neighbor and ourselves as well."[94] Luther goes on, "But another way to understand it is that it commands us to love only our neighbor and this according to the sample of our love for ourselves. This is the better interpretation."[95] We concede that neighbor love, as a paradigm for family love, must contain sacrificial love. But the ethic of equal regard gives equal weight to regard for self and regard for the other and provides a more solid ground for love in families than does Luther's view.

The question remains: *Is it possible to remove the patriarchy in Aquinas and Luther and the strong agapism in Luther without losing the paternal and maternal commitment that their understanding of Christian symbols and narratives invite?*

Christian Love and the Female Problematic

Ephesians, Aquinas, and even Luther should be criticized for primarily identifying the marital love of husbands with the drama of Christ's love for the church. Wives and mothers too should be permitted to play the role of Christ, not as subservient martyrs as in the past but as authoritative participants in a redemptive action that only men have hitherto been privileged fully to represent.

In saying this, we quickly invoke a theory of love that makes it possible for us to identify women with the cross of Christ in spite of the way this idea has been abused in the history of the church. It is a view of Christian love that makes sacrifice transitional to the restoration of equal regard, that makes sacrifice primarily a matter of self-giving, sometimes even self-assertion, in the name of restoring mutuality. When this view of love is in the forefront, Christ's relation to the church can function as a counter to the primal female problematic just as it did to the primal male problematic.

For good reasons, most of contemporary theological feminism has resisted models of Christian love that prominently feature self-sacrifice. Theological feminists have been reluctant to identify Christian love too completely with the symbolism of sacrifice or the cross.[96] They have critiqued extreme agapic models of love, fearing that women would once again be asked to play the role of sacrificial worker, denying their own selfhood, needs, and potentials.

It is true that an ideal of sacrifical and self-giving love can be abused. But sacrificial love—by either husbands or wives, fathers or mothers—cannot be eliminated from Christian understandings of love. The cross has an unavoidable role in the Christian life and in Christian families. Our strategy, and that of most of the New Testament, is to locate self-sacrifice *as a moment within a love ethic of mutuality*. When this is done, the sacrificial or Christic moment can be understood as equally appropriate for both husbands and wives, males and females.

Even then, sacrificial or self-giving love in the service of mutuality has its limits, especially for vulnerable women, children, and minorities. When a partner no longer has the capacity or freedom to respond to enduring love or when evil is so deep that finite human love connot hope to transform it, then the vulnerable and defenseless need to acknowledge the limits of their love. When this happens, the Christian story tells us that such persons should ground their worth not in winning the love of another human but in the inexhaustible and unchanging love of God.

Mutuality, Sacrifice, and Families

Is this protracted discussion of love in the family relevant to the concrete lives of the persons we studied? We think that it is. Jim Turner said "yes, yes" when we asked whether there is a place for self-sacrifice. Aquinas, however, holds self-fulfillment and self-giving love together more tightly than does Jim Turner. Mary Murphy is closer to Aquinas in believing that when self-sacrifice is properly conceived it is an ordering of priorities in one's assent to the final good, the love of God.

Richard Good, on the other hand, would not agree with Aquinas about love as either mutuality or self-sacrifice. Nor would he agree with Jim Turner. Recall that he earlier said: people "don't really sacrifice themselves." Although his marriage was stable, Richard held that if you had to sacrifice, the relationship wasn't very good. By contrast, Jim Turner holds to an older Protestant world of meaning that existed before individualism, technical rationality, and market logic swept into our lives. He represents the strengths and weaknesses of Christian paternalism; he is a dedicated father who comes home early to be with his daughters, coach their soccer teams, and sponsor their youth groups. He is evidence of how the Christian faith has helped many men modify, if not completely overcome, the male problematic. But his self-understanding is still marred by traces of male headship.

The gradual disappearance of religious reinforcements for the servant role of husbands and fathers raises an important question: Will our modern, liberal, and contractual models of male-female relations address the male problematic with the same power as this older paradigm? Will the contractualism and individualism of a Richard Good be as durable as it needs to be? As reinforcements for families disappear, will the archaic male and female problematics emerge once again?

5

Honor, Shame, and Equality in Early Christian Families

We found in chapter 4 that within Aquinas's patriarchal view of male "headship" lay a grave concern for the problem of male tentativeness about family formation. In this chapter we ask more directly, how should Christians and others read the scriptures that pronounce men to be the heads of their families? This is one of the most perplexing issues facing a family theory informed by a Christian perspective.

When these passages are read against the background of the honor-shame culture in which they took place, they become far more complex, and early Christianity is seen as one of the least patriarchal movements of its day. In fact, early Christianity emerges as encouraging movements toward what we call the intact, equal-regard, public-private family—movements that are still unfolding today.

We had this issue in mind when in an interview we asked one man, Phil Green, whether his religion influenced the way responsibilities were divided in his family. He answered: "It [the Bible] outlines things that the husband is supposed to do, it outlines things that the wife is supposed to do, it outlines things that the children are supposed to do." The Bible, he believed, offers a divinely authorized plan. To illustrate this, he recounted a skit that was enacted at his Jehovah's Witness church.

> Well, the skit that we are having this week deals with the role that each person plays scripturally. . . . it says . . . that the wife is supposed to be in subjection to the husband and the husband is in subjection to Christ, but not in a chauvinistic way, because it also says the husband is supposed to love his wife as he loves his own self. So if he treats her as he would like to be treated, then there should not be any problems in her being subjected to him.

The wife's role, he continued, is also outlined,

> covering the "things that she's supposed to do." She's supposed to
> teach her children, since she will have more time to be with the
> children . . . that will be a big role for her with regards to the chil-
> dren's raising.

The Jehovah's Witness tradition is a brand of fundamentalism that
sanctions a hierarchical pattern of the family. Its views on the family,
however, are complex.

> Phil Green's wife works outside the home. His household, in its
> economic pattern, is not traditional in the nineteenth-century
> sense. In addition, Phil thinks he is raising his son and daughter
> by his present marriage (he was married before, to another Jeho-
> vah's Witness) "in the same way, i.e., equally." Women in the Je-
> hovah's Witnesses can preach, pray, lead worship, and develop
> considerable skills at these tasks. But they are not permitted to do
> these things when a male leader is present. When they are allowed
> to preside, they must wear a veil on their heads.
>
> Phil even perceives himself as exercising what we call a love
> ethic of equal regard—one that functions, however, within the
> prerogatives and responsibilities of male headship. Phil and his
> wife read biblical passages such as Ephesians 5:21–33 at face
> value—much as Christians have throughout history. He reads
> such passages in much the same way as did New England Puritans,
> southern colonial plantation owners, and late–nineteenth-century
> evangelical males who paved the way toward contemporary Amer-
> ican fundamentalism. Even Aquinas and Luther, who at least un-
> derstood how these passages countered what we have called the
> male problematic, still did not get them quite right.

Phil Green and Thomas Aquinas have something in common. Both
use the language of equality to describe relations between husband and
wife. On this score, however, Phil appreciates equality more than
Aquinas. Aquinas took only a few steps beyond Aristotle's theory of proportional friendship between husband and wife. Aquinas could use the
language of equal friendship, but he limited what was meant by it. There

is, however, no evidence of equality as proportionality in Phil's language. Phil at least *says* that a husband should treat his wife in a thoroughly egalitarian way—as he would want to be treated himself.

Phil and Aquinas have other things in common. Both see the husband as a servant modeled on the sacrifice of Christ. Both repudiate masculinity modeled on the heroic and highly agentive patterns that were so dominant in the Greco-Roman world.

At first glance, then, Phil and Aquinas look pretty good. Where's the catch? The catch is this: *both believe that judgments about equality and friendship should be, finally, in the hands of the husband.* The husband makes the determination about what is equal. Phil does this because he thinks the Bible tells him to do so. Aquinas stacks the deck in favor of the husband for two reasons: because he thinks that the Bible tells him this and because he thinks that women are naturally deficient in deliberative powers. Neither understands equality and justice as being a matter of what Jürgen Habermas calls "intersubjective judgment"—a judgment requiring the dialogue and mutual criticism of both husband and wife.[1]

When the so-called headship passages of the New Testament (Eph. 5:23; Col. 3:18; 1 Peter 3:1) are read flatly, literally, and noncontextually, interpreters have only two choices. Either they accept these passages as a "divine plan" to be obediently followed (as do religious conservatives) or they reject them (as do religious liberals). *But there is a third alternative.* This requires a more nuanced and historically contextual reading of such passages. Advances in the study of the family in the Mediterranean areas make such a reading possible. When placed within its full historical context, early Christianity appears as a progressive influence on the family: in contrast to the surrounding Greco-Roman world, it inspired heightened degrees of female equality, a chastened patriarchy, higher levels of male responsibility and servanthood, less of a double standard in sexual ethics, and deeper respect for children. *But all of this progress was accomplished with ambivalence, hesitation, compromise, and some defensiveness.*

An unresolved tension exists in early Christianity between an ethic of gender equality and a softened patriarchal ethic of male responsibility and servanthood. However, both of these competing ethics challenged the male honor code that dominated family life in the surrounding Greco-Roman world. The more patriarchal pole (sometimes called "love paternalism" or "love patriarchy") looks less oppressive if we compare it to Greco-Roman views of the family—views that were themselves quite complicated and at the time of Paul were giving birth to new degrees of gender equality.[2]

Both the love ethic of equal regard between husband and wife *and* the ethic of male "headship" are visible in Ephesians 5:21–33. The tension between them can be lessened only if one remembers: (1) that the husband as head was humbled and modeled after the sacrifice of Christ, and (2) that the initial egalitarian directions of the Jesus movement were gradually compromised. Both points should be understood in relation to Aristotle's description of the family and his pervasive influence.

Aristotle's theory of the relation of family to *polis* was felt throughout the Mediterranean world, especially in the urban centers of Israel and Asia Minor. This Aristotelian ethos, even among followers of Jesus, helped shape how the Christian self-sacrificing husband could view his wife as equal before God yet needing, as Aristotle would have said, male guidance because of her supposedly inferior deliberative capacities. In comparison to the surrounding culture, early Christianity could exhibit higher servant responsibility on the part of males and enhanced equality for women but seem deficient on gender equality, at least from the perspective of modern liberal views.

It would be an error to reject early Christianity because of its ambivalence on gender issues. Early Christianity displayed an important new understanding in the area of gender relations that needs to be reappropriated, and some of the tensions therein may be lessened when submitted to careful reflection. Achieving this coherence is the task of theology, both systematic and practical. In this chapter we present the biblical background for such reconciliation and in chapter 10 take up the more properly theological task.

Families and the Kingdom of God

In its earliest stages, Christianity was a reform movement within Judaism that consisted of men and women who followed Jesus in his itinerant ministry of preaching and healing. Jesus' preaching announced that the kingdom of God, long awaited in Judaism, was beginning to unfold in the midst of his ministry. He claimed that his ministry and person were an early sign of the coming of this kingdom.

This movement had a complicated relation to families. On the one hand, Jesus was depicted as an enthusiastic wedding guest who blessed the wine at the marriage in Cana. He also was pictured as an opponent of divorce and thereby a proponent of family stability. On the other hand, the Jesus movement is portrayed as conflicting with the *patriarchal family clan* of the Hebraic and Greco-Roman worlds. Both the words *patriarchal* and *clan* are important in this sentence. The word *family* comes from the Latin *familia* and signifies "all persons subject to the control of one man, whether relations, freedmen, or slaves."[3] The Greek word used to describe family, *oikos*, or household, has a very similar meaning. In Hebrew, the word most frequently used for family is *mispaha*—the intermediate clan standing between tribe (*sebet, matteh*) and household (*bayit bet ab*).[4] The family that Jesus sometimes criticized was not the modern, nuclear, companionate family, differentiated in varying degrees from the extended family. The family in Jesus' time was a patriarchal clan and kinship structure that functioned as a religiopolitical unit, valued the blood relatedness of both nuclear and extended family, and was generally in tension with other clans, the state, and the national cult. This kind of family structure could readily resist other superordinate wholes such as the kingdom of God.[5] It was sometimes polygynous.

The modern nuclear family looks weak, puny, and extremely fragile in comparison to the clan structures and households of the ancient world, although it can sometimes have ideological control over people similar to that which Jesus criticized. To be liberated from the ancient *mispaha* or *familia* was to be freed from a cohesive, powerful structure of lifelong nurture, guidance, and economic control. To be liberated from the modern nuclear family is to be freed from a social entity that is much more isolated, diffuse, and ambiguous in its authority.

More specifically, the family pattern assumed by early Christianity was patrilineal (the bride lived with or near the groom's family) and endogamous (marriages were arranged between closely related families of the same blood-related *mispaha*). A typical Hebrew household would consist of conjugal couple (the mother and father and their young children), the family of the firstborn son, other unmarried sons and daughters, servants, and sometimes other relatives. Frequently the married sons and daughters shared the same courtyard with the senior conjugal couple.[6]

Since the days of the postexilic period when Israel tried to reestablish its national, religious, and ethnic identity, there had existed among Jews what Bruce Malina calls a "defensive" family strategy, one emphasizing both monogamy and the restriction of marriage to other Jews faithful to Israel's ancient covenant with the Lord. In the Old Testament, Malachi 2:10–17 expresses this strategy with its new emphasis on the honor and purity of Israelite families, a strategy that still held among Jews into the time of Jesus and Paul.[7] Such families were political-religious entities, centers of cultic worship, deeply concerned with their own honor; they felt that they lived in a world of limited goods for which they needed to compete and were generally distrustful of other clans, tribes, and nations. Furthermore, these Hebrew patterns shared the general contours of an honor-shame ethic similar to one found throughout neighboring Greek and Roman societies. This made it possible for Hebrew family patterns to fit with some ease into the Aristotelian theory of the relation of the family to the *polis*—with its emphasis on the superiority of master, husband, and father over slave, wife, and children—that ruled the urban centers of the Mediterranean world during the Hellenistic and Roman Hellenistic periods.

It is in the context of these meanings of family that we should understand Jesus' words when he said, "For I have come to set a man against his father, and a daughter against her mother" (Matt. 10:34–35; see also Matt. 10:21–23; Mark 13:12–13; Luke 21:12–17). These passages are not attacks on families in any simple sense, and certainly not attacks on the conjugal couple or the nuclear family in our modern sense of these terms. They were, first of all, criticisms of ancient family clans that functioned as patriarchal, religiopolitical units that inhibited their members from becoming a part of the kingdom that Jesus was proclaiming. Early Christianity relativized this patriarchal clan as a family form. The records of the early church represent Jesus as wanting families, and individuals within them, to submit their lives to the rule of the kingdom of God rather than to the codes and cults that were the center of family clans. Some of the criticisms of families attributed to Jesus reflect divisions created in Christian families when they were arrested and jailed by civil authorities.[8] Under such conditions, family members often would disown each other. In such times, the early Jesus movement demanded faithfulness to the kingdom over loyalty to household and clan.

This tension between loyalty to households or clans and loyalty to the kingdom of God has been pervasive throughout Christian history. It was generally resolved by converting entire families and then refashioning the purpose and inner relations of these families to conform to the mission and relational patterns of the house church or *ecclesia*. This often meant a wider scope for the leadership of women, a pattern that may have flowed from house church back to the gender roles of home life.

The tension between patriarchal cult families and the kingdom of God often had a liberating effect for women. Some women left oppressive families for a higher life dedicated to God. When the tension between fidelity to kin and fidelity to the kingdom mixed with the ascetic neo-Platonism of the second to fifth centuries, it functioned to elevate monastic life over marital life. As historian Peter Brown has shown, celibate orders provided women with an alternative to the reasserted patriarchy of both church and state.[9]

The Kingdom and the Discipleship of Equals

The earliest days of the Jesus movement, however, contained an ethos of genuine egalitarianism between men and women. Jesus is portrayed as objecting to the patriarchal patterns of unilateral divorce of Jewish wives by their husbands, a practice that filled the ranks of the poor primarily with rejected women. Jesus is reported as saying that Moses allowed husbands to divorce wives because of "your hardness of heart." From the beginning, he continues, "'God made them male and female.' 'For this reason a man shall leave his father and mother and be joined to his wife, and the two shall become one flesh.' So they are no longer two but one flesh. Therefore what God has joined together, let no one separate" (Mark 10:5–9). Although Jesus is pictured as standing against divorce, his stand is consistent with the "defensive" family strategy of the postexilic period. It was a strategy designed to keep Hebrew men from divorcing their Hebrew wives in order to marry local, wealthier, non-Jewish women of families who had occupied Israel during the exile.[10]

Elisabeth Schüssler Fiorenza's *In Memory of Her* (1983) offers a pivotal egalitarian reading of Jesus' stand against divorce.[11] Fiorenza claims that the pre-Markan and pre-Q sources of the Gospels depict the early Jesus movement as "a discipleship of equals" between men and women. She argues that Jesus was claiming that in the beginning God did not create patriarchy and did not intend that women be given into the power of men to continue their family line. Instead, God intended "that it is the man who shall sever connections with his own patriarchal family and 'the two shall become one *sarx* (flesh).'"[12]

Support for the existence of a discipleship of equals in the early Jesus movement has been advanced by biblical scholar Warren Carter in his *Households and Discipleship: A Study of Matthew 19–20* (1994).[13] These two chapters in Matthew tell of Jesus' repudiation of divorce (19:3–9), his use of children to symbolize discipleship (19:13–15), his teachings about wealth as incompatible with the kingdom of God (19:23–29), his parable about the generous landlord (20:1–16), and finally his instruction that discipleship is like being a slave—"the last will be first" (20:20–28).

Carter advances a novel interpretation of these four groups of scriptures. To him, they assume an audience that has been shaped by the hierarchical Aristotelian family codes so pervasive in the ancient world. Jesus' listeners would have known customs sanctioning the male householder's aristocratic rule of wife, royal rule of children, and tyrannical rule of slaves—ideals outlined in Aristotle's *Nicomachean Ethics*.[14] Carter believes that the teaching and parables in these chapters of Matthew undermine this ancient pattern and promote a radical equality of discipleship in both household and economic life. He sees this in Jesus' strictures against patriarchal divorce, his proclamation in this context of the principle of neighbor love (19:19), his use of the innocence of children as a symbol of life in the kingdom, his disassociation of discipleship from the customary honor accorded wealth, and his use of slavery as a symbol of discipleship ("whoever would be first among you must be your slave").

Following the anthropological studies of Victor Turner, Carter depicts discipleship in Matthew as a permanent or idealized "liminality." Hierarchy and status are replaced by a new community of equality between husband and wife, rich and poor, and a new respect for childhood.[15] The introduction of the rule of neighbor love—"You shall love your neighbor as yourself" (19:19)—immediately after Jesus' prohibition of unilateral divorce by husbands is suggestive. It implies that the principle of neighbor love has special significance for relations between husband and wife—the conjugal core of families.

Much of the life of the pre-Pauline Jesus movement took place in house churches. These important rites enacted dramas of radical equality—at least radical for that day. Galatians 3:28 is thought to refer to a widely practiced baptismal formula that announced the new status of those who "have clothed yourselves with Christ": "There is no longer Jew or Greek, there is no longer slave or free, there is no longer male and female; for all of you are one in Christ Jesus." This formula reveals how relations between husband and wife, master and slave, Greek and Jew were restructured in these early Christian house churches. These redefined relationships may have radiated outward from the gathered *ecclesia* and into both the broader public life and private homes of Christians. All of these pairs enjoyed a heightened equality in the house church because they were thought to be equal in Christ, thereby having equal status before God.

New Testament scholar Stephen Barton states well how these little Christian clubs enacted rituals that had egalitarian consequences for gender relations in the actual families of early Christians:

> It is most likely that the potential created by church-in-house for the extension of the social range of female activity, represented at the same time a potential for redefining the women's social world generally (which, *ipso facto,* included that of their men as well). I mean by this that the ways in which women perceived themselves and expressed themselves within the sacred time and sacred space of the gathering-for-church-in-the-house will have *carried over* into secular time and space, especially because sacred time and space were linked so closely with secular time and space by virtue of the fact that church time constituted a segment of household time and church space was identical with household space.[16]

The way nineteenth-century Methodist class meetings and love feasts restructured family relations—making husband-wife relations more equal, allowing women to be more articulate, and overcoming inherited honor codes of the plantation South—may have had some precedence in the scriptural record of these pre-Pauline house churches or clubs. Both these Methodists and the first-century Christians met in private homes in intense small groups. In both cases, women were functioning in their own space and took far more initiative and authority than they were allowed in other contexts. Both functioned to undermine honor-shame codes in the surrounding society.

As we have pointed out, entire families often joined these early Christian clubs. Although the house churches themselves functioned as a "new family of God" into which all members were "adopted," these associations were not ascetic. Natural family relations were rarely renounced. Paul, in fact, specifically discouraged Christians from seeking divorce, even from their non-Christian partners (1 Cor. 7:10–16). Barton argues that although Mark and Matthew show Jesus as wanting to subordinate the family to the kingdom of God, they did not depict him as antifamily in ways found, for instance, among the Cynics, Essenes, and certain Greek philosophers. He writes, "On the contrary (to take but one example), Jesus' prohibition of divorce presupposes the continuing validity, indeed, the radical renewal—of household relations, at least in the present age."[17]

Family relations among early Christians may have received a new meaning and become more egalitarian when families began to imitate at home the gender relations implicit in the Galatians 3:28 baptismal formula enacted in house churches. New Testament scholar David Balch points out that although Paul's interest in equality between the sexes was less than that shown by the pre-Pauline church, he still made remarks on this topic that were rare in antiquity. Although he could write in one place that "the husband is the head of his wife" (1 Cor. 11:3), he also could write, "For the wife does not have authority over her own body, but the husband does; *likewise the husband does not have authority over his own body, but the wife does*" (1 Cor. 7:4, italics added). Balch calls the last half of this statement giving the wife authority over the husband's body "astounding in Greco-Roman culture," visible, perhaps, only in some similar passages in the moralist Musonius Rufus's *On Marriage*. The early Christian community thus limited the Greco-Roman emphasis on male agency, ownership, and dominance.[18]

As the Jesus movement became a missionary movement to the Greco-Roman world, evidence of this new equality could be found in the prominence of women as leaders in the early Christian house churches. Some of these women were wealthy and hosted meetings of the church in their homes. Some, like Priscilla, were married but achieved distinction independently of their husbands as founders of important churches throughout Asia Minor—a leadership role rare for women in the Greco-Roman world (Acts 18:1–4, 18–21; Rom. 16:3).

Biblical scholar Turid Seim warns us, however, in *The Double Message: Patterns of Gender in Luke and Acts* (1994), not to overstate the equality achieved by women in the early church.[19] Luke-Acts presents women more favorably than do the other Gospels, but it still depicts their servant leadership as centering in the home rather than in the temple or on the street. Priscilla's role in instructing the male Apollos (Acts 18:24–28) and Anna's witness to Jesus in the public space of the temple (Luke 2:36–38) were notable exceptions.[20] It required a special argument, she points out, for Luke-Acts to establish that male leadership in the church should be conceived as servanthood.[21] The servant character of women's contributions, although granted some christological significance, was simply assumed and confined to the inner life of home and house church. Women simultaneously were respected as having a special openness to the faith and ironically held at a distance from the more robust public witness of men.

Seim concludes her assessment by noting that the author of Luke-Acts "transmits a double message. In his narrative he manages the extraordinary feat of preserving strong traditions about women and attributing a positive function to them, while at the same time harbouring an ironic dimension that reveals the reasons for masculine preferences in Acts' presentation of the organization of the Christian group."[22] In the last words of her book she conveys a lasting point: "The double message nurtures a dangerous remembrance."[23] It is a dangerous remembrance of an emerging but ambiguously realized equality for women—in marriage and out of it, in the private domestic sphere and in a wider public sphere. It is a memory that was and is unsettling to old hierarchies and customary segregations.

The Galatians 3:28 pre-Pauline baptismal formula unleashed different consequences depending on the location of the Christian community. For instance, in the Corinthian church, the new equalities of the baptismal formula inspired some women to experiment with wearing their hair loose, keeping their heads bare, and participating in provocative forms of ecstatic behavior. Such behavior was troubling to the outside pagan world. Christians were seen as undermining normative Aristotelian and Neopythagorean models of the Greco-Roman family that gave authority to the father over slaves, wives, and children. This pagan criticism of Christians, and sometimes other "new religions," rose to become an overt physical threat to the Christian community, one of the deepest challenges that this young and fragile movement faced. The movement met this challenge with an apologetic strategy: they denied or minimized the gender and family changes that were occurring in the early Christian movement. The use of the household codes in 1 Peter, as we note below, is an example of this strategy. In the process of making these denials, however, Christians tacitly acknowledged that something new was happening in their ranks.

Paul, in an effort to minimize this criticism, made a distinction between inner and outer freedom. He advised Christians to remain the same in their public roles: slaves should remain slaves, Jews should remain circumcised, and wives should remain obedient to their husbands in spite of their new equality in Christ. In fact, it is precisely in this context that Paul compromised the gender egalitarianism of Galatians and asserted that the divine image in the wife was mediated through the husband. The man, he insisted, "is the image and reflection of God; but woman is the reflection of man" (1 Cor. 11:7). External conformity was of little importance, Paul counseled, in comparison to the deeper freedom and equality that all Christians enjoyed through their identification with Christ (1 Cor. 7:17–24). Paul hoped to earn Christians protection from outside hostility by advising them to conform to the public honor codes of the Greco-Roman world. At the same time, he subverted this very world by developing ideas that led Christians to contradict this code in their private lives.[24]

This advice and Paul's attempt to deflect the criticism of the Greco-Roman world suggest that *Christians in the privacy of their house churches and homes were experimenting with new freedoms and equalities that were affronts to the stability of the official order.* Early Christianity was full of a complex compromise language, sometimes contradictory, that both asserted and restrained a more egalitarian family model in relation to its surrounding culture.

A similarly complex language can be found in Pauline views about the goodness of sexuality and marriage. Paul agreed with most of antiquity that sexuality was somewhat dangerous and that to achieve spiritual purity in the eschatological end time, it was better to be abstinent (1 Cor. 7:1–7). Nonetheless, he never made this preference into a general rule; he believed that marriage was natural and need not be sinful.[25] In fact, Paul spent much time, as Balch points out, explaining the mutual obligations of Christian spouses (1 Cor. 7:1–16).[26] He saw marriage as an individual decision. It was not a necessity for everyone, as was thought in ancient Judaism. There were Christian vocations besides the vocation of marriage.[27]

The impulse toward gender equality in the early Christian communities had social consequences, though these should not be understood in modern, liberal terms. In addition to the distinction between inner-ecclesial roles and outer-public roles, there was also the tendency of that day to interpret the language of equality in terms of the Aristotelian concept of proportional justice. In *Nicomachean Ethics* Aristotle writes, "In all friendships between unequals, the love also should be proportional, i.e., the better should be more loved than he loves."[28] This for Aristotle was the form that equality should take between people who were in his view not of the same status, such as parents and children, husbands and wives. Even though early Christianity reacted against this model, it was also influenced by it.

Husbands and wives throughout the Hellenistic world were believed to have different degrees of deliberative excellence. We saw the remnants of this belief in Thomas Aquinas, who used it to protect women from divorce, arguing that they needed the continuing guidance of men. Carolyn Osiek and David Balch show that the divided spheres and unequal privilege of husband and wife were stamped into the very architecture of the Greco-Roman home. It sharply separated male and female household quarters, divided functions along gender lines, and separated public and private space, with men functioning in the former and women confined to the latter.[29]

Both cultural ideals and architectural space everywhere witnessed to these alleged differences between men and women. After the early days of Christianity, a gradual return was made to the language of male headship and the associated idea that wives required the guidance of husbands. The author of Ephesians, along with Paul, said outright that the "husband is the head of the wife" (1 Cor. 11:4; Eph. 5:23). This means, however, something quite different from the Aristotelian theory of male rational superiority.

This much can be said: early Christianity constituted a two-edged challenge to the patriarchies of the ancient world. It was a challenge that moved from the semiprivate space of the house church to the public space of the *polis*. Christianity was not the only challenge to the ancient world. For instance, certain Stoic authors (Seneca, Plutarch, Musonius Rufus) accepted women more nearly as equals and emphasized friendship (*philia, amiticia*) between husband and wife. But they seldom excited the ire of political authorities as did the early Christians, nor did they enact their views around powerful religious rituals like baptism. The early church's actions and beliefs seemed to constitute a particularly irritating affront to the settled ways of the Greco-Roman *polis*.[30] Theologian John Milbank says it well:

> Where neither women, slaves, nor children were citizens, then the relationship of *oikos* to *polis* was *external,* and mediated by the father.

> But where, on the other hand, women, slaves and children . . . are equally members of an *ecclesia,* then the relationship of every part of the *oikos* to the public realm is a much more direct one. . . Inversely the domestic . . . becomes 'political,' a matter of real significance for law, education, religion, and government (although this has only been spasmodically realized in Christian history).[31]

Even though these transformative impulses were only "spasmodically realized," there may be much to learn from the way domestically based Christian associations indirectly influenced the wider public realm.

The Honor-Shame Codes and the Early Christian House Church

A vexing issue remains. What was the meaning in the early church of the call to husbands to "love your wives, just as Christ loved the church and gave himself up for her" (Eph. 5:25)? And how did this idea modify the headship passages of this same section of Ephesians (5:21–33)? Was this cosmic analogy found in Ephesians and elsewhere intended only to bolster male authority, or was it a genuine reversal of ancient heroic models of male authority in families?

There is evidence that the second reading is the more accurate, even though in Christian history the first interpretation has often been more influential. To understand how this might be true, we must examine more closely the logic of male authority that functioned in official circles throughout the Mediterranean world during the period of Roman Hellenism. Many scholars believe that this was an honor-shame code based on the heroic military virtues of dominance and submission—virtues rooted in the culture that was reflected in the poetry of Homer and reinforced in modified ways by Aristotle.

In such a culture, individuals were defined in relation to their families and the reputation and honor that they had earned. Honor was maintained through the praise of respected equals. This honor was established in political life and in war through achieving dominance in situations of challenge and riposte. Such interaction was a distinctively male activity. If the person who was challenged failed to respond, he was dishonored. If he responded to the challenge but lost in either conflict or public debate, he was still dishonored. Honor was gained through winning, dishonor or shame through losing.

Anthropologists call societies dominated by honor-shame ethics "*agonistic* cultures."[32] Public life was conflictual to its core; private life was under constant threat of being dishonored by intrusive agents outside the family. A male's private sphere—his wife, children, mother, sister, and slaves—were in danger of being insulted, molested, raped, seduced, or stolen. Yet his honor was increased if he could intrude without detection into the private space of another male outside his own extended family.

Men were shamed if their space was challenged and they lost. For women, however, shame was a positive thing; they were to "have shame" and resist losing their shame or being "shameless."[33] For a man to avoid shame and for a woman to keep her shame, men had to protect, control, guide, and circumscribe the lives of their women so that their private space would not be dishonored. Such an ethic celebrated the virtues of active dominance for males and passive conformity for females.

The virtues of male activity, as opposed to passivity, seem also to have been part of the widespread, but controversial, practices of pederasty, whereby young adult males would take boys for their lovers until their own marriages, at which time such relations often subsided.[34] In these relations, the honored position was the dominant position, and the shameful, and hence feminine, position was the subordinate and passive one—the position occupied by the younger partner. The honor-shame code also legitimated a double standard for male sexual activity after marriage. Males could with ease have access to female slaves, possibly young boys, or even their neighbor's wife if they were clever enough to go unchallenged. It was a sign of their agency and dominance to enjoy these relations and intrude on the private areas of others.

Although this characterization of family relations under the honor-shame code is generally accurate, recent research qualifies it in some respects. Although most women in Hellenistic societies led lives confined mainly to the inner spaces of their living compound and to associations with other women, they had surprising freedom and power within these limits.[35] They also made important contributions to household economy through cooking, sewing, household management, and some commercial activities. It is also wrong to think that because free males enjoyed extensive control, no genuine love, affection, and friendship existed between husbands and wives, fathers and children.[36] These relationships, however, were friendships on male terms.

In spite of these qualifications, we should observe that honor-shame patterns generally held true in Roman Hellenism and even in Jewish circles before the victories of Alexander the Great introduced Greek culture to Semitic societies.[37] The honor-shame ethic provided the cultural background against which an alternative family ethic (and an alternative understanding of the relation of *oikos* to the *polis*) began to emerge in early Christianity, albeit in a fragmentary way. It was precisely this new ethic that put early Christianity into a defensive stance with the surrounding culture.

Ephesians, Aristotle,
and the Honor-Shame Code

Early Christianity was exploring an alternative ethic to the honor-shame code. In addition to attempts toward creating an ethic of equal regard between husband and wife, a new model of parenthood was also emerging. Since its earliest days, Christianity has on several occasions been in tension with honor-shame cultural patterns in various parts of the Western world.[38] We use the word "fracture" to convey our judgment that the Christian family revolution was uneven, setting up trends that were both creative and ambiguous and which even today the faithful are trying to harmonize.

The Epistle to the Ephesians—which influenced Thomas Aquinas, Luther, and modern Catholic and evangelical theologies of family—helps us understand how early Christianity engaged the honor-shame culture. Written to a group of second-century urban Christians living in cities in the Lysus valley, the author (probably not Paul but perhaps someone close to Paul) was attempting to save them from sinking back into the pagan existence of the surrounding culture. *The pagan culture that Ephesians was addressing can be best understood as a continuing manifestation of the honor-shame code with its belief in conflict and dominance as a method for achieving dignity and respect.* For rhetorical purposes, the author borrows, even though he transforms, the metaphors of the male culture he opposes. In contrast to the armor and weapons of the heroic culture he criticizes, the author tells his readers to "take up the whole armor of God . . . the belt of truth around your waist . . . the breastplate of righteousness. As shoes for your feet put on whatever will make you ready to proclaim the gospel of peace" (Eph. 6:13–15).

The new male ethic, like the new male armor, is an ethic of peace. More specifically, it is an ethic "with all humility and gentleness, with patience, bearing with one another in love, making every effort to maintain the unity of the Spirit in the bond of peace" (Eph. 4:2–3). The opposing pagan ethic is an ethic of contest or "wrath," which follows the desires of the "flesh and senses" (Eph. 2:2–3). It is not just simple immorality that Ephesians opposes; it is a systematic male ethic that enshrined the virtues of courage, strength, dominance, and conflict as means for achieving domestic order and public honor. Ephesians assumes, is embedded in, yet also critiques the honor-shame code of the Greco-Roman world.

It is within this context that Ephesians addresses the Greco-Roman form of the male problematic. By making Christ's sacrificial relation to the church a model for the husband's relation to his family, it partially reverses the honor-shame ethic guiding male behavior in antiquity. Rather than being the agent who guarantees domestic order through challenge and riposte in the public world, the husband is now admonished to imitate the peace of God and the self-giving love of Christ. It is over against the heroic ethic of the Greco-Roman world that we should understand the words, "Husbands, love your wives, just as Christ loved the church and gave himself up for her" (Eph. 5:25). While the model of male headship is retained in this passage, the ancient heroic code of male dominance is challenged.

It is worthwhile to compare Aristotle's *Politics* and *Nicomachean Ethics* to Ephesians. Both make use of the so-called Aristotelian *Haustafeln,* or household codes. Both follow the pattern of instructions about how masters should relate to slaves, husbands to wives, and fathers to children. Both seem to give a priority to the authority of the male in all of these relations. But much of the logic of the Aristotelian formulation is changed, if not subverted, in the Ephesians pattern. Early Christian family thinking was indebted to, yet partially transformative, of the Aristotelian pattern.

Aristotle called the rule of a master over his slaves "tyrannical" because it was ultimately for the good of the master. Aristotle made the relation between husband and wife parallel to his favorite form of government, the "constitutional" aristocracy. The presupposition behind this arrangement was bluntly stated: "For although there may be exceptions to the order of nature, the male is by nature fitter for command than the female."[39] Aristotle's understanding of family governance was aristocratic because the husband was thought to have more deliberative power—more rationality—and therefore could better guide the wife. His governance of his wife was constitutional because she had her areas of responsibility, and the husband was to rule partly for her benefit. The relation between father and children was "monarchical"; it was "paternal rule," but the father had obligations to govern for the good of "his children."[40]

Ephesians differs from Aristotle on several important counts. First, the pre-Pauline equality between male and female, husband and wife, is present in this passage. In 5:21 we read, "Be subject to one another out of reverence for Christ." Admittedly, grounding equality in being "subject" sounds strange to the modern ear, but it is an equality of *mutual* subjection. Although Aristotle could conceive of a kind of proportional friendship between husband and wife, he could not imagine a fully mutual or equal friendship. It would have been unthinkable for him to have subscribed to any kind of submission on the part of the husband.

Second, the Greek verb for "be subject" is *hypotassomai,* often translated as "be submissive" or "be subordinate." The latter (and stronger)—

be subordinate—is probably closer to the true meaning.[41] *Hypotassomai* is used to describe a soldier's subordination to his military commander or a citizen's subordination to state authorities. The passage in Ephesians is striking and unique; both husband and wife were to honor the other as fit to rule or take turns in leadership in the relation. Husbands were at times to subordinate themselves to wives just as the wives were to the husbands. In contrast, Aristotle's constitutional aristocracy granted such leadership only to the husband.

Third, for Paul husband and wife are to subordinate themselves to one another out of "reverence [sometimes rendered "fear," *phobos*] for Christ." The authority of the husband or wife is not based on either's respective rational capacities, as it was in Aristotle, but on the belief that both are ruled by the spirit and truth of Christ. One can trust the other to take the lead because the other acts in accordance with the Lord—a Lord or Messiah who is the author of one's redemption and therefore deserving of reverence, respect, trust, gratitude, and, when qualified by these words, fear.[42]

Fourth, it is within the revolutionary framework of mutual subordination that we should read admonitions for the wife to be subordinate to the husband. From one perspective, this is merely a continuation of the idea of mutual subordination, where the accent was intended to be more on the husband's responsibilities since they need, in this context, the most drastic redefinition. Because in this culture male honor and agency is the source of family authority, most of Ephesians 5:21–33 concentrates on redefining the husband's role in the family, even though over history it is this accent on male subordination that has been most overlooked.

A stunning idea, in contrast to the Aristotelian assumptions of Roman Hellenism, comes when the author of this passage tells husbands to love their wives "as Christ loved the church and gave himself up for her" (5:25). This introduces the great theme of *agape*—Christ's (hence God's) self-giving love for the church. The love of Christ casts the pattern for the husband's love of his wife and children. Aristotle would have found distasteful the concept of mutual subordination between husband and wife and disliked even more the idea of the male sacrificing himself for the good of his spouse.

Fifth, an element of the second half of the Great Commandment, "You shall love your neighbor as yourself" (Matt. 19:19), enters the text, putting it at odds with the Aristotelian understanding of proportionate friendships between husband and wife. Ephesians asserts, "Husbands should love their wives as they do their own bodies" (5:28). We can hear the principle of neighbor love in the background of this more earthy formulation. This principle, as Warren Carter pointed out, is presented in

Matthew 19–20 in the midst of passages that question the family hierarchies of the ancient world.

Many theologians believe that the principle of neighbor love is the center from which all New Testament ethics should be understood, indeed the key to biblical hermeneutics. It first was thought to apply primarily to the neighbor (even the stranger), but not necessarily to family members themselves. The author continues,

> He who loves his wife loves himself. For no one ever hates his own body, but he nourishes and tenderly cares for it, just as Christ does for the church, because we are members of his body. "For this reason a man will leave his father and mother and be joined to his wife, and the two will become one flesh." This is a great mystery. (Eph. 5:29–32)

In short, the end and goal of the husband's Christlike sacrificial love was not sacrifice as such but the treatment of his wife as equal to his own body.

The words about husbands loving their wives "as their own bodies" contrast strikingly with Aristotle's admonition that "in all friendships implying inequality the love also should be proportional, i.e., the better should be more loved than he loves."[43] Or again, "The friendship of man and wife, again, is the same that is found in an aristocracy; for it is in accordance with virtue—the better gets more of what is good, and each gets what befits him; and so, too, with the justice in these relations."[44] It is clear in these texts who would get the better deal.

But the author of Ephesians never fully escaped the patriarchal language of antiquity. The writer did not return to the central theme of the passage—the mutual subordination of husband and wife—or elaborate the new roles that wives would occupy if this central theme were taken seriously. *This failure to return and tell the second half of the story indicates the extent to which the epistle still reflected the androcentrism of the ancient world.* It said nothing about how the wife might be to her husband as Christ was to the church—a logical implication of the idea of mutual subordination. In addition, it assumed that only the husband would need to treat the wife as he treats himself, as his own body. It says nothing about the need for the wife to treat her husband as she treats her own body. Finally, perhaps most important, it is devoid of the idea of intersubjectivity—the idea that the concrete realization of love and justice between husband and wife requires dialogue and communication.

Ephesians tried to reconcile the idea of male servanthood with the egalitarian accents of the early Christian movement, but it accomplished this synthesis in an unstable way. Ephesians left to posterity a passage difficult to interpret and susceptible to being read in a variety of ways. It has been misused frequently to bolster the crudest forms of Western patriarchal family ethics. It also has been misapplied (by Phil Green and Jim and Sophie Turner, for example) as giving a divine blueprint for the ordering of husband-and-wife relations. This was a turn that fundamentalists, some evangelicals, and much of official Catholicism made historically and make even today.

Placed in its proper context, the letter to the Ephesians provocatively but incompletely challenges unilateral male authority in families. Our complaint should be that it did not complete its trajectory. It did not tell succeeding generations how the wife can be an equal, transformative, Christic figure to husband and children and do so in the *sense of leading as well as following*. Nor did it address the issue of what to do when mutuality seems totally impossible.

The Family and the Retreat of the Post-Pauline Church

One can detect that the pre-Pauline and Pauline church experimented with new models of family relations by noting the apologies of the post-Pauline conservative retreat. This retreat of the *ecclesia* is recorded in what scholars call the pastoral epistles: 1 and 2 Timothy, Titus, and 1 Peter. These letters reveal how the pre-Pauline and Pauline churches deviated from the surrounding Greco-Roman world in family matters just as they also played down and excused this deviation. David Balch's *Let Wives Be Submissive: The Domestic Code in 1 Peter* (1981) tells the story better than any other source.[45] Balch was one of the first scholars to show the extensive influence on New Testament authors of the Aristotelian household codes. He also has documented the criticism that came from Greco-Roman authorities when any religious or philosophical group strayed from the official sanctioning of the male householder's authority over slave, wife, and children.[46]

Christians were one target of this criticism, which took the form of harsh public condemnation and overt persecution. Peter's concern about the opinion of the Greco-Roman world is evident when he told Christians, "Conduct yourselves honorably among the Gentiles, so that, though they malign you as evil-doers, they may see your honorable deeds" (1 Peter 2:12). Furthermore, the letter says, "For the Lord's sake accept the authority of every human institution, whether of the emperor as supreme, or of governors" (1 Peter 2:13). As did Paul, the author of 1 Peter advises overt conformity to the honor codes governing citizenship in public life just as he recommends compromise with the honor codes governing the family.

Immediately after these injunctions, the author sets forth his version of the official household codes. After instructing slaves to be obedient to masters, he says this to wives: "Likewise you wives, be submissive to your husbands" (3:1). Now comes the tip-off to the apologetic strategy of the text: "so that some, though they do not obey the word, may be won without a word by the behavior of their wives" (3:1). Wives should be submissive to impress others, indeed to convert others—either Gentile husbands or Gentiles in general.

Balch's telling argument is this: there would be no need for an apology if the charges were not somewhat true, that both wives and slaves did have different roles in the early Christian church and family when compared to the pagan world.[47] This new behavior in the Christian community, according to 1 Peter, needed to be both disguised and excused so that Christians could fit less defensively into the surrounding hostile community.

A pattern similar to that of 1 Peter is also present in the other pastoral epistles, especially 1 and 2 Timothy and Titus. The apology is there, but so is the return to a more hierarchical model of both church and family. Increasingly, the structure of the early church began to reflect the hierarchical patterns of the middle-class patrons in whose homes the *ecclesia* met.[48] The process began to reverse the pre-Pauline pattern: there *ecclesia* shaped family, but in the later church traditional family patterns began once again to influence *ecclesia*. But it would be a mistake to assume that the second-generation church returned to simple conformity to the honor-shame, agonistic, hierarchical, and tightly gender-separated worlds that it had modified in the early days of the Christian movement. A new twist on family relations had been introduced, a twist that we are struggling with even today.

New Testament scholar Karl Sandnes has stated well the new church-family relation in the era of the pastoral epistles. In his *A New Family: Conversion and Ecclesiology in the Early Church with Cross-Comparisons* (1994), he shows how conversion to the church in the honor-shame culture of the ancient world was risky, fraught with deep fears of abandonment not only by father and mother but by one's entire extended family or clan.[49] The *ecclesia* needed to offer "family-like" supports to converts in order to sustain them. This was true to a degree even when entire households were converted, as was often the case. Even then, these households would be removed from the psychological, social, and economic supports of old friends and the wider family.

Family systems in the ancient world not only provided individual and nuclear family identity but functioned as social security systems providing loans, emergency assistance, and help in old age.[50] The pervasive use of family and household language in the early Christian *ecclesia* to refer to Christian friends is not incidental. Although these were fictive family relations, and not actual family ties, they modeled actual family ties even as they redefined them. The house churches did provide assistance to vulnerable families, widows, mothers, children, orphans, prisoners, and slaves, much as immediate and extended families helped each other.[51]

Even in the house churches of the pastoral epistles, however, there is a difference between natural family and the "household" or *familia* of God. The hierarchical patterns of the Greco-Roman world, if not totally absent, were at least mitigated. Church members were called "brothers" and "sisters" (*adelphoi*) in the Lord and "children" of God. There was a higher degree of mutuality, friendship, brotherly love (*philadelphia*), and concrete assistance in these churches than in the outside world. These churches provided for their needy members a kind of "generalized reciprocity," a mutual giving that did not always expect a return. This kind of reciprocity, in contrast to the kind that does expect immediate return, worked to enrich the pool of shared resources for the entire community. This was the kind of reciprocity practiced in families but now found in the Christian *ecclesia*.[52]

The *ecclesia* was not a literal family, but, as Sandnes points out, it was "family-like."[53] It did not replace natural families, although in extreme instances it provided familylike friendship and social security for converts estranged from their families. In the terms of modern sociological theory, these churches provided converts with friendship and "social capital," a network of people who loved them and offered resources to help them survive. In joining a house church, the new convert was accepting a "new familyhood," and like Jesus, the new convert hoped that his own family would "find [its] place within the new family."[54]

Pagan and Modern Forms of the Honor-Shame Code

The pagan world had a form of the "male problematic" different from that seen in modern societies. The male problematic in modern societies is only partially one of domination and agency in the Greco-Roman sense. If our earlier analysis is correct, it is increasingly a matter of neglect, absence, and failure of responsibility due to a combination of cultural, economic, and social-systemic changes. The ancient honor-shame code may have been a particular cultural elaboration of a deeper male strategy. It was a way of controlling wives, investing in a relatively small number of children, but still having freedom for wider sexual expression. According to anthropologist David Gilmore, honor-shame codes have appeared from time to time all around the world; they are not just confined, as it was once thought, to the Mediterranean area.[55] Historian Lawrence Stone has found honor-shame patterns in pre-Puritan England, patterns against which Puritanism reacted.[56] In chapter 3, we found similar codes in the Old South and saw how Methodism, as in the case of the house churches of early Christianity, exercised a transformative influence on them. Sociologist Elijah Anderson has found a peculiarly anomic honor-shame code in the male street culture of American inner cities.[57]

For all its deficiencies, the honor-shame code in antiquity tended to recognize and cherish paternity. If the modern form of the male problematic is more a matter of neglect and absence than domination, *the fundamental ethical challenge of families in the postmodern era is to renounce all forms of the honor-shame code (antique patriarchal dominance or modern individualistic paternal absence) and promote a new family ethic of equal regard that relates to both domestic and public realms.*

Maria Taylor and
Love as Equal Regard

Maria Taylor's family ethic has similarities to the ethics of Christian scripture and the ethics taught by Aquinas. On the whole, she reads her Bible well. But she, like many Christians, has difficulty putting the headship passages of the New Testament in a proper context. Although she is clear that love as mutuality and equal regard, rather than sacrifice, is central to her marriage, she sometimes uses headship language to refer to the authority of her husband. She does this, we believe, because she has no alternative theological language for talking about male responsibility.

Maria is quite clear about the kind of love that is central to her marriage. Mutuality is the central goal. At the same time, she admits that the language of self-sacrifice has an essential *but limited* role in families. A couple has to "sacrifice in order for your marriage to work." For example, Robert's "mother had to move in with us. Now that is a sacrifice. And his cousin, a young teenager. Whoo, Jesus." And self-fulfillment? Maria feels that she has more of this than her mother did in her day.

Maria stands between Richard Good's and Sarah Miles's emphasis on love as self-fulfillment and Jim Turner's and Mary Murphy's emphasis on commitment and sacrificial love. Maria emphasizes self-fulfillment more than Jim and Mary do but sees more of a role for self-sacrifice than do Richard and Sarah.

Maria believes there is a high degree of mutuality in her relation with Robert. There is also much trust. Maria repeatedly refers to Robert as her "friend." He is someone she can "trust and talk to." Marriage was no sacrifice for her: it was "the best thing I ever had. I love my husband to death. Each year gets better and better." *Eros,* indeed passion, marks their relation. As short as they are on cash, they do something special for their wedding anniversary: "We spend a weekend at the Embassy Suites, or something like that."

Love for Maria means "no one can destroy what you have." Maria is Protestant in ways she does not realize; marriage is a *sacramentum* in the sense of permanence but not as supernatural grace. It is a covenant witnessed by God. She can't imagine ever getting a divorce. Nor does she agree with divorce except for situations of "beating or verbal abuse." Her Pentecostal religion is for both Maria and Robert a source of strength, renewal, and forgiveness. She admits that at times mutuality gets out of balance—"Robert lays down on the bed when I'm coping with the kids." When this happens, Maria turns to the Bible and prayer. So does Robert. When they have their difficulties, "We pray. We never go to bed mad."

Clearly, self-sacrifice is for Maria a part of love in families, but it is not the primary thing. Like many people in our national survey, Maria feels the women of her mother's generation sacrificed more than she does. Yet she feels Robert, like her father, sacrifices even more than Maria. "Robert would do anything for his family— take two or three jobs if necessary." This was the way her father was; he worked all the time. This is one of the reasons that "her parents did not have the mutuality that she and Robert enjoy." Her mother did not work; the entire financial burden fell on her father.

Maria does not find a detailed model for the family in her Christian faith. In this, she is an exception to most conservative Christians we interviewed. They believed that the Bible does give such a plan. Phil Green was an articulate example of a widespread conservative Christian belief. By contrast, Maria observes, "My religion does not tell me anything about male and female roles." "Who does what, is just a matter of common sense." As religious, indeed spiritual, as Maria is, she—surprisingly—sees much of her thinking about families as simply being good judgment and nothing unique to her biblical faith. Yet her faith does make a huge difference. She reads the Bible when she feels her relations with Robert are strained. Does it give her answers to her daily trials, especially answers about who does what around the house? "No, it just keeps me in line so I won't blow my top basically. Common things to understand him [Robert] a little better." Her faith preserves her psychic equilibrium—her faith, hope, and forgiveness. It does not give her a divine prescription for family roles.

Maria's economic situation helps explain how she differs from most of the other people we interviewed. Women today have more economic independence than Aquinas ever imagined possible. This is one reason that love as equal regard is not only an ideal for Maria but more nearly a lived reality than it might have been if she were economically dependent. Maria earns approximately the same salary as Robert. Their economic contributions to the family are roughly equal. They both work full-time, except for summers when Maria is off from her job. Although the Taylors command fewer economic resources than our other four representative families, Maria is less economically dependent on her husband than Sarah, Sophie, Phyllis, or Mary. Maria illustrates how working-class wives throughout the industrial era have often had more power in the home than dependent middle- and upper-class women.

Maria also knows something about the contribution of paternal certainty for creating paternal investment. Maria and Robert were best friends before they got married. They were also lovers. Maria became pregnant with their first child before they were married—in fact, before they even planned to marry. Maria, a skeptic about welfare today, was nonetheless on welfare for a while herself.

When she and Robert finally decided to marry, Robert's family tried to talk him out of it. They raised the question of paternal certainty. "Are you sure that the child belongs to you?" They argued that if it was not his child, he shouldn't take on the responsibility of another's offspring. As Maria says, "They tried to break our trust." This may have been part of what trust was all about for Maria and Robert. It may have meant, at least in part, that Robert thought he knew the child was his and that Maria trusted that he knew.

Maria, as we have noted, retains the language of headship to speak of Robert's role in the family. She does it with irony and calculation. She says that she would tell Robert that he was the family head "even if she didn't believe it." Indeed, by virtue of her actions we have reason to believe that she does not believe it. Yet she finds it useful. Is the rhetoric of headship used by Maria

Taylor designed to overcome the male problematic, replace the role of anomic patriarchy with the language of responsible paternalism—a paternalism that may not actually exist in their family? Would Maria jettison this language if she had a better way to interpret the New Testament material? Would she relinquish her charade if she had deeper insight into an alternative language, one just as realistic and even more adequate to the inner meaning of the New Testament witness?

We believe that the ideal of love as equal regard, as we interpret it, provides such a language. It puts the New Testament language of male headship in perspective and shows its direction toward mutuality. It finds a place for self-sacrifice, a sacrifice that Maria is ready to acknowledge as important for families. But it does not make self-sacrifice central. It makes mutuality—something close to the mutuality that Maria enjoys—a central moral value of families.

A Summary and Look to the Future

What have we learned from these historical chapters? Are there common motifs that can inform a practical theology of family? We mention four themes here that are significantly expanded in the next chapters, especially in chapter 10. These themes also serve as reference points for our dialogue with the four voices in the chapters immediately to follow.

First, Christian love (*agape*), even as applied to families, should point in the direction of love as mutuality or equal regard. Equal regard, as we define it, is a strenuous ethic: one respects the selfhood, the dignity, of the other as seriously as one expects the other to respect or regard one's own selfhood. One also works for the *good*—the welfare—of the other as vigorously as one works for one's own. But one can expect the reverse as well, that the other works for one's own good. Self and other are taken with equal seriousness in a love ethic of equal regard. This is the meaning of the command, "You shall love your neighbor as yourself" (Matt. 19:19).

Furthermore, equal regard must be achieved intersubjectively—a point we argue in the chapter on the therapeutic voice. Not only does it entail a mutual process of empathically sensing the needs of both self and other, but it involves a process of *intersubjective communication and mutual decision* about what equal regard concretely means among the specific people involved. No person alone can determine adequately what equal regard means for another person.

Second, self-sacrifice or self-giving is an important part of love as mutuality or equal regard. But it is subordinate to and supportive of love as equal regard. As neo-Thomist Louis Janssens has said, self-sacrifice is "derived" from love as equal regard. Even in Ephesians, the sacrificial love of Jesus is for the purpose of building up the church. By analogy, the sacrificial love of the husband has the goal of treating the wife with the same love as he does his own body.

Third, the concrete meaning of love as equal regard must be determined in the concreteness of specific contexts within the human life cycle. This point goes beyond what we have derived from historical studies in this chapter and our study of the nineteenth century in chapter 3, even though those chapters hint at it. Love as equal regard enhances and equally distributes a range of premoral values and disvalues that shift in meaning according to contexts and stages in the life of families and individuals. The formal structure of equal regard is invariant, but the concrete goods that it organizes and enhances vary from situation to situation. That is why, when one is discerning the meaning of equal regard in families, a *life-cycle perspective* must be taken. Love as equal regard means different things for different family members at different points in family and individual life cycles.

Fourth, families, as important as they are, are subordinate to the larger common good, whether this is the idea of the kingdom or reign of God or the common good of the civil society. Families are important but relative goods in relation to the righteousness and goodness of the reign of God.

We believe that both human experience and the central direction of the Christian witness confirm these four propositions, which we expand in the remainder of the book. These same sources also give rise to the ideal of the intact, equal-regard, public-private family. Furthermore, this is an ideal for which the trends of culture and history seem to be calling.

PART 3

The Voices

6

Feminism, Religion, and the Family

Characterizing North American feminist voices on the family is complicated by several factors. Feminist positions on the family frequently are stereotyped, cast as monolithic, and misunderstood. Feminism is often wrongly blamed for a host of family problems. It is easy for social critics to brush off feminist perspectives on the family by simply quoting words rejecting reproduction and family life from Shulamith Firestone's dated work *The Dialectic of Sex* (1970).[1] But Firestone's claims were an extreme response to particular problems and certainly not exhaustive of the rich variety of feminist approaches to the family. Feminists, especially feminist theologians, have made important contributions to new views of families that need better understanding.

It may be true that secular feminist theorists have been more successful in undermining patriarchy than in developing alternative family ideals. When we examined secular feminist theories, we discovered a series of impasses on family matters which in the 1970s and 1980s separated humanist from gynocentric feminists and in this decade divided progressive and conservative profamily feminist views. Those interested in feminist contributions to the family debate, we concluded, should attend more seriously to the contributions of religious feminists.

Feminist theory on the family since the 1960s has taken several forms. It can be traced from the early individualism of secular humanist feminism to an emphasis on women's nature in secular gynocentric feminism, to a humanist emphasis in early theological feminism, to a gynocentric religious feminism, and finally to a new ecological religious feminism that celebrates both the personhood *and* embodied love of both women *and* men. The authors of this book have contributed to and identify with these last two moves, which we believe are the direction for the future.

Religious feminists offer viable ways to address the impasses of secular feminism for two principal reasons. First, in contesting the idealization of female self-sacrifice, feminist theologians have focused on an

ethic of radical mutuality, even if only a few have applied it specifically
to family relations. Second, feminist theologians have repudiated the
conventional dualism that places, blame for family disruption on either
culture or the economy, and the dualism that portrays the family as either strictly natural or strictly socially constructed.

Religious convictions stand behind these two premises. Religious
feminists of different theological backgrounds share the conviction that
Christian and Jewish traditions are important sources of empowerment
for families, despite their male-dominated and male-defined narratives
and symbols. As part of this stance, feminist religious thinkers make a
number of theological affirmations that have implications for family
ideals. Feminist theologians emphasize the creation of women in the image of God and hence their inherent worth as partners and cocreators in
life. They write about the imperative of egalitarian relationships of love,
justice, and shared responsibility within family and society. They warn
against the dangers and violence of patriarchy for families but feel that
Christianity when properly understood holds an array of antipatriarchal
values. They speak about the necessity of redefining religious doctrines
of love, sexuality, sin, and redemption. They seek a holistic view of creation and redemption that holds body and mind, material and spiritual
needs in dialectical relation. They are sensitive to individuals and groups
that have been relegated to the margins of social existence. Finally, they
connect the reconstruction of the family with the reformation of society
so that it supports egalitarian husband-wife partnerships in domestic,
economic, and cultural realms. These themes receive different interpretations, but their presence is pervasive among feminist theologians.
They suggest important new norms for families.

Does Sarah Miles
Need Feminist Theology?

Sarah Miles would find some of these feminist theological texts a
source of rich religious and moral ideas relevant to her family
dilemmas. Although Sarah does not refer to herself as a feminist,
she provides an example of how the women's movement has influenced the lives of almost all of our interviewees. She does not
claim feminism in the same way she might claim her motherhood
or her Jewish identity. She does see discrimination against women
as an "extremely serious problem." She likens it to a "toxin" limiting her own personal choices in marriage and work and polluting
the entire "system of healthy beings in the society."

Yet in nearly ten hours of conversation Sarah used the term

"feminist" only twice, and then slightly negatively. Explaining a divorce between her husband's cousin and wife, she calls the former wife "really feminist—it's like 'No! I won't do your socks!' and fighting tooth and nail." She links her own early feminism, prior to marriage, with rebellion; she was "repulsed" by the pomp and ceremony of fawning over the bride, and intentionally planned a wedding that played down the traditional wedding march. In these remarks, she challenges the limited options for women in marriage still represented by the father giving away the bride and by the view of marriage as a woman's sole goal in life.

She readily acknowledges, however, the problems her early feminism created in her own life. As for many women and men today, feminism has left Sarah with "mixed messages" about her place in the world. "The rules sort of changed in the middle of . . . our growing up lives," she observes. At the same time that her aspirations for herself and her work expanded, her domestic horizons narrowed, until "here I am cooking basically all the meals, doing the groceries, doing the laundry, responsible for the kids, doctor appointments, getting them to school, their clothes, their friends, all of our social interactions, anything that happens with the house . . . the household domain is mine."

Like Sarah, none of our other interviewees had much to say, either positive or negative, about feminism per se. Yet, almost without exception, their family lives reflect the impact of feminist assumptions and causes. On the one hand, many people had experienced a discernible shift in roles. Forty-eight percent of our interviewees characterized the division of domestic responsibilities in their family of origin as one in which the mother played a supporting role for husband and children, whereas only 4 percent found this the case in their present families and 52 percent were attempting a more equal distribution of responsibilities. On the other hand, Sarah explicitly raises the question of the actual extent of the changes. Does the routine use of language about egalitarian relationships simply cover a host of subtle inequities between women and men in the particularities of their care for the home and children?

Sarah has difficulty relating her feminism to her religion. We do not believe this is simply because her religion is a form of Judaism. Sarah has difficulties with the doctrines of obedience and self-sacrifice espoused by religion. She is looking for a religious language that balances self-sacrifice with self-affirmation and mutuality. So far Sarah has not found that language. Theological feminism may have something to offer Sarah Miles and many like her.

Feminism and the Survey

The most surprising finding of our national survey on love and marriage may throw light on Sarah's conflicts about the language of sacrifice. The finding was this: men value sacrificial love more than women, or at least they say they do. Although both men and women correlate good marriages more with mutuality than sacrifice, 61 percent of women rank mutuality higher, while only 48 percent of men do (table 3). Of those who rank sacrifice as the highest value, 44 percent are men, and only 33 percent are women. Six percent more women associate mutuality with good marriages and families than does the general population. Five percent fewer women associate self-sacrifice with good marriages and families than does the population at large. Seven percent fewer men value mutuality, and six percent more men value sacrifice than does the general population. Men and women are responding quite differently to the language of self-sacrifice and mutuality in family love.

Table 3. Comparison of Different Models of Love
in Relation to Good Marriages

Beliefs	Respondents* (percent)	Male (percent)	Female (percent)
Mutuality	55	48	61
Self-Sacrifice	38	44	33
Self-Fulfillment	5	5	4

*The total number of respondents surveyed is 1,019.

Several explanations come to mind. Perhaps men say they value sacrifice more because they feel they give up more in marriage. Or perhaps when they associate sacrifice with good marriages they are thinking of women's sacrificial giving. Women, however, may value mutuality more because they are wary of the excessively sacrificial roles they think their mothers played. Maybe they have been influenced by the rhetoric of modern feminism which, as we will see, has written eloquently on love as mutuality. In Ephesians and throughout subsequent Christian thought on marriage and family, husbands and fathers were to recapitulate in their family life the sacrificial love of Christ for the church. Unfortunately this sometimes took the form of autocratic domination. Women were to be self-sacrificial, but unfortunately that sacrifice had more to do with submission and endurance than it did with a sacrificial leadership that was redemptive. We have argued that both mutuality and sacrifice should be symmetrical for both husband and wife and that Christianity, properly understood, points in that direction.

It is clear, however, that women today are retreating from the language of sacrificial love. If our analysis of the male and female problematics is correct, the constructive task is not to repudiate the language of self-sacrifice; it is, instead, to locate it precisely with reference to the central value of mutuality or equal regard. To repudiate it completely will be to lose religiocultural meanings that are essential to the capacity for commitment and the demands of caring for offspring.

Although feminism aims at transforming ideals, most secular feminists categorically reject religious traditions as patriarchal, that is, as calling for unjustified sacrifices by women in deference to men. This may lie at the heart of Sarah Miles's discomfort with her Judaism. The secular feminist dismissal of religion, however, has left it open to criticisms that it promotes egotistic, individualistic, anti-men, anti-children, or antireligious values. Sociologist Judith Stacey raises an important question: Beyond proposals to eliminate the family entirely or simply tolerate instability and diversity, with what do feminists propose to replace the failing nuclear family?[2] Political scientist and psychotherapist Jane Flax agrees that "the absence of a normative theory of the family is a central problem in feminist theory and practice."[3]

Feminism cannot deepen its reflections on the family without coming to terms with religion. This will entail a reconstruction of religious resources. Feminists in religious ethics and theology serve as important allies in this process. Feminist theologians themselves should be forthright in claiming distinctive religious ideals capable of negotiating the complexities of family life—a concrete language by which freedom, care, mutuality, equal regard, and carefully stated and prescribed sacrificial giving between women, men, and children can be envisioned institutionally.

Whereas many secular feminists develop their family theory in a historical vacuum, religious feminists believe that sexuality and family are so entwined with religion that attempts to change either must begin with religious traditions themselves. Furthermore, theological feminists point out to secular skeptics that there are streams of thought in Judaism and Christianity that actually contest norms of male dominance and suggest models of radical equality.

The Family and North American Feminism

From the start, there were feminists who proclaimed the centrality of motherhood and family. There were also those who were impatient with domestic distractions. The tension between women's concerns as mothers in families and their concerns for equality as individuals in the public sphere has been endemic to feminism from the beginning. Although feminists have been preoccupied with patriarchy as the chief problem for family life, some have also had insights into the other three factors we have touched on: individualism, technical rationality, and psychological shifts.

Humanist and Gynocentric
Feminists and the Family

Philosopher Iris Young identifies a movement in late–twentieth-century feminism from what she calls humanist to gynocentric feminism. Despite the blending from time to time of these two forms of feminism in both the nineteenth and twentieth centuries, humanist feminism predominated from the 1960s to the late l970s. Although its dominance was limited, humanist feminism captured the public imagination and is often the position with which feminism is identified. Humanist feminism also has a decidedly white, North American bias, shaped by democratic ideals of equal participation and self-sufficiency. It was responsive to the isolation and disempowerment of middle-class, college-educated housewives in the 1950s and 1960s.

Simone de Beauvoir and her vision of liberation in *The Second Sex* (1974) exemplified humanist feminism at its best and its worst.[4] In response to a patriarchy that ascribed to women an essential and inferior nature that justified male dominance, Young writes, humanist feminism defined "femininity as the primary vehicle of women's oppression, and called upon male dominated institutions to allow women the opportunity to participate fully in the public world-making activities."[5] For the first time, sexual relations were seen as determined by neither nature nor divine decree but as socially constructed political relations. Male-defined family structures where women functioned primarily as sexual objects, childbearers, and decorative charmers benefited men at women's expense. Unequal power based on ideas of women's procreative destiny corrupted human relations. In the 1960s and 1970s, Betty Friedan in *The Feminine Mystique* (1963), Shulamith Firestone in *The Dialectic of Sex* (1970), and Kate Millett in *Sexual Politics* (1970) joined de Beauvoir in portraying female biology, the biological family, childbearing, and child-rearing as problematic obstacles to women's individual achievement and fulfillment.[6] They identified female reproductive organs as problematic, pregnancy as an ordeal, housekeeping as a debilitating imprisonment, and children as a hindrance to the development of a woman's full potential. And for many women, this was and is decidedly the case.

Humanist feminism deemphasized the role of biology in family formation. Although they rightly rejected essentialism or naive realism about female nature, they had difficulty formulating a more balanced critical realist perspective. De Beauvoir argued that woman's proximity to nature should be transcended, and Firestone gave this concrete embodiment by suggesting alternative technologies of reproduction that would relieve women of the burden. Gender differences were seen as socially constructed; they needed to be eliminated because they prevent equal participation in public life. Definitions of the female body as sexual, receptive, and maternal were seen as inhibiting human aspirations for women. Whereas in American history, entrepreneurial individualism was sustained for men but forbidden for women by the Victorian separate-spheres ideology, humanist feminism advocated an individualism for women as well. This sometimes meant placing women's duty to self over duty to husband and children.

One of the most important contributions of humanist feminism was its sensitization of the public to domestic violence. Overt physical and sexual violence against women has several causes, but the remnants of the patriarchal control of women continue to play a major role. Without the protests of the women's movement, the public might still be largely unaware of the statistics on battering and incest.[7] Moreover, there are connections between violence toward women and beliefs, sometimes religiously sanctioned, about male dominance and headship. As religion historian Margaret Bendroth observes, "Modern studies have found the highest incidences of spousal and child abuse in families that are . . . characterized by rigid sex-role stereotypes, poor communication, and extreme inequities in the distribution of power between family members."[8] The discussion of the family in humanist feminism has centered more on uncovering previously hidden abuses—violence, sexual abuse, genital mutilation, marital rape, child and adult prostitution—and less on the reconstruction of a healthy domestic life.

Historian Karen Offen develops a typology somewhat different from Iris Young's. She distinguishes between "individualist" and "relational" feminism. More than Young, Offen is concerned about the negative implications of the Anglo-American individualistic tradition of feminism and its claims for personal autonomy, choice, self-realization, and its relegation of motherhood, relationships with men, and children to the sidelines.[9] She wonders about palpable resistance to feminism, especially among women who have chosen marriage and motherhood. According to Offen, North American feminism is distinct from French feminism in its celebration of individual human rights and its minimization of sex-linked qualities, including childbearing and related familial responsibilities. Celebration of woman's maternal role is not new for European feminists and existed in American nineteenth-century activists such as Elizabeth Cady Stanton. In Europe, as a precondition to seeking admission to male-dominated society, women have focused on sexual difference as compatible with human equality and demanded that the commonwealth change to accommodate women's distinctive contributions as childbearers and nurturers. The individual is not an end in itself; the gender-differentiated but egalitarian couple is the primary building block of society.

Young agrees that a shift in feminism was demanded by women who felt disenfranchised by humanist feminist assumptions and even by the injustice of treating women and men alike. A distinct development in feminist views of the family occurred in the mid- to late 1970s. Women began to recognize the ideals of power, competition, and individual mastery—with the associated repression of body and relationality—as male-defined ideals. Men, not women, had defined pregnancy and female bodies as sources of shame and degradation. Feminists should not join in this denunciation; indeed, they had access through their own biology to alternative values of bodily and ecological preservation. These voices located women's oppression not in femininity per se but in the denial by a masculinist culture of the female body, nature, and maternal thinking.[10] Feminists still wanted equality with men but began to talk about an equality that encompassed sexual differences, including the differences associated with motherhood.

Black feminists like bell hooks and Patricia Hill Collins pointed out that the feminist critique of domestic exploitation and women's struggle to enter the male world makes little sense to women unable to establish safe homes, prepare their children for survival in a discriminatory environment, or marry husbands with viable places in political and economic life.[11] Hooks questions the agenda of bourgeois humanist feminism with its emphasis on individual equality; it ignores, she claims, the systems of domination that involve racism and classism as well as sexism. Biological and social motherhood are viewed as critical sources of strength and survival, not as an obstacle to freedom. Feminist agendas should include securing the right of families to effective child care and the restructuring of society so that women do not exclusively provide that care. Instead of seeing public employment in modern bureaucracies as the key to women's liberation, hooks and others identify the improvement of conditions for all women in the workplace as the more essential aim.[12]

Political scientist Susan Moller Okin's *Justice, Gender, and the Family* (1989) and the more recent writings of Iris Young provide examples of the impasses involved in humanist and gynocentric discourse on the family. Okin modifies the more liberal humanist stance by claiming the centrality of the family in the civil order. Yet she retains its criticism of distorted social constructions of femininity, its rejection of innate sexual differences, and its demand for equal opportunity. A reconstituted family with internal justice is the essential site for rearing citizens capable of creating a just society: "until there is justice within the family, women will not be able to gain equality in politics, at work, or in any other sphere." To achieve such justice, Okin advocates a genderless society and a gender-free family:

> A just future would be one without gender. In its social structures and practices, one's sex would have no more relevance than one's eye color or the length of one's toes. No assumptions would be made about 'male' and 'female' roles; childbearing would be so conceptually separated from child rearing and other family responsibilities that it would be a cause for surprise, and no little concern, if men and women were not equally responsible for domestic life or if children were to spend much more time with one parent than the other. It would be a future in which men and women participated in more or less equal numbers in every sphere of life.[13]

Okin defines gender as "the deeply entrenched institutionalization of sexual difference." She spends more time undoing social institutionalizations of femininity than exploring sexual differences that might influence human interactions in ways that toe length and eye color do not—for instance, the asymmetrical reproductive differences that have much to do with women's vulnerability to pregnancy and abandonment. Although she neglects this level of analysis, Okin is correct when she argues that most family roles have no natural basis but have as their source historical and social mores. As she puts it, "Surely nothing in our natures dictates that men should not be equal participants in the rearing of their children."[14] Her case for equal participation is compelling:

> Unless the first and most formative example of adult interaction usually experienced by children is one of justice and reciprocity, rather than one of domination and manipulation or of unequal altruism and one-sided self-sacrifice, . . . they are likely to be considerably hindered in becoming people who are guided by principles of justice.[15]

Although Okin is mostly right here, she overstates the ease with which the dynamics of biological childbearing and social child rearing can be dismantled and isolated from each other. Splitting body and mind in a way characteristic of much liberal thought, she regards physiological tendencies and the embodied context of human interaction with little seriousness. Furthermore, Okin disregards class and ethnic worldviews that value biological motherhood. And because she views the family as the fundamental basis for all moral education, she mostly overlooks the necessity of correcting injustices in other social contexts.

Iris Young, on the other hand, is an example of a more radical shift away from humanist feminism. In the essay mentioned above, she cautiously mixes what she considers to be the best of both humanist and gynocentric traditions. But when she compiles a book of essays five years later, she climbs "off the fence to the gynocentric side" and claims the importance of gender differences in contrast to the "gender blindness" of both male theory and humanist feminism.[16] From this position, she explores rich experiences of pregnancy, motherhood, and female embodiment essentially discounted by Okin. These furnish wonderful insights into human relationships, bringing "privileged knowledge" that challenges "the way Western philosophy has typically described the relationship of self and other as opposition and confrontation." In pregnancy, the boundary between self and other is fluid. The other is both other and oneself; rather than negation of either self or other, the mother experiences human relationality as "continuity in difference."[17]

Both the power and the problems with Young's new stance become apparent in her essay in *Dissent* sparked by the fury surrounding Dan Quayle's remarks about the *Murphy Brown* episode. She reminds readers that Quayle's original comments were not just a pitch for family values but an attempt to explain the disorder in the black communities of Los Angeles as the consequence of single motherhood. Neoliberals promoting the two-parent family employ similar monocausal arguments naming unmarried and single mothers as principal factors behind poverty, crime, and declining performance in school. Such reductionist explanations of family problems, she contends, restigmatize single mothers. Punitive policies to ensure marriage and prevent divorce are limited at best and destructive at worst, and sometimes operate with implicit racist and classist standards about what constitutes adequate parenting. The United States has "plural childbearing cultures" that lead women with fewer financial and social resources to enter into childbearing at earlier ages.[18] Ultimately, adequate educational and employment opportunities are the solution to teen pregnancy and not marriage per se.

Young makes several points with which both sides might agree: childrearing is hard work. No one should be penalized for performing it. Nonparents bear social responsibility for the welfare of children. Yet neither Young nor some neoliberals she mentions, for that matter, seem able to argue forcefully for a social policy that simultaneously promotes two-parent families yet supports single mothers.

Young's fitting desire to stop discrimination against women who have plenty of other problems leads her to advocate public policy that makes single motherhood normal. She asserts that *in principle* a woman, regardless of her age, has a right to bear a child. Her position exemplifies an odd mixture of both humanist and gynocentric principles. She combines a gynocentric appreciation for female reproductive processes with a humanist advocacy of individual rights and autonomy. Personal liberty should not be restricted; maternal subjectivity must be inherently respected.

The result is an implicit notion of *separative motherhood.* The rich ecology of human commitments and biological inclinations that create a family between mother and child, mother and father, father and child, child and other children, family and relatives, and family with other social institutions is reduced to a stark ideal of motherhood as an inclination and then as an individual and unfettered choice. While embodied motherhood has a powerful place in her thinking, embodied fatherhood has little meaning. Young finds it "plausible" that two parents are more effective than one, but the second adult need not be a "live-in husband." Although "men should be encouraged to involve themselves in close relationships with children," this need not "necessarily" involve "their biological offspring."[19] She assumes that men will generously commit to children not their own, even when many in fact fail to care even for their biological offspring. What will motivate them to do so? She does not tell us. Her gynocentricism, built upon humanist premises, results in the preservation of unaccompanied motherhood and not the ecological nexus of family, parental unit, and community or marriage as a significant social institution. In an understandable desire to protect women's reproductive rights from further encroachment by governmental authorities, she empties marriage of any relational or social value. In place of the republican ideal of a civil society with visions of the common good, she envisions a heterogeneous public in which people are affirmed in their particularity with few guidelines for a common family life.

Okin and Young reflect certain trends in secular feminism and illustrate the contributions and problems of these trends for families. Okin wants to restructure family life in an egalitarian fashion, less for the sake of enhancing family life itself than for the sake of giving women more equal public influence and participation. This remains an important cause. Unfortunately, she presumes that it requires a dismissal of biological differences between women and men, a sharp distinction between women as public figures and women as mothers, and a distinction between childbearing and childrearing. Young argues that reproductive biology is significant, but she largely excludes fathers from her analysis. Her goal is to create a women-centered politics in which the biological family as a formative social institution is valued primarily as it relates to women's freedom.

Ultimately, for all their insights, neither Okin nor Young spend time asking what children need in order to develop and how these needs can best be met. Questions remain unsettled about the relation between (1) the equality of women and men in the family and society and (2) the needs and justifiable claims of offspring.

Progressive and Conservative
Feminists and the Family

In the 1980s, one group of feminists—"conservative profamily feminists"—did begin to give more attention to the needs of children and the tensions between family equality and civil democracy, with decidedly mixed results for feminism. Progressive feminist Judith Stacey coined this descriptive label, which reflects her critique. She is justifiably worried about conflicts within feminism being initiated by a conservative profamily feminism that jettisons the core beliefs and politics of the women's movement. Conservative profamily feminists are characterized by their repudiation of "sexual politics" and affirmation of gender differences and traditional feminine traits. She identifies recent literature by Betty Friedan, Jean Bethke Elshtain, and Germaine Greer as examples, despite their differences.[20]

Of particular interest is Elshtain. As part of the communitarian movement, cochair of the Council on Families in America, and a recognized scholar, she is a prominent voice in current public policy debates. She is also interesting as a transitional figure between secular and religious feminists; she acknowledges that her Christian upbringing and ethic motivate her thinking but seldom presents them directly for analysis and critique.

It is not clear to what extent Elshtain understands her recent family proposals either as religious or as feminist. In her preface to *Public Man, Private Woman* (1981), she says she thinks as "a political theorist . . . influenced, for over fifteen years, by her involvement with the feminist movement."[21] This third-person statement suggests that she is more feminist-influenced than feminist. In her eyes many feminists have lost sight of the crucial issues. She sees feminist protest of the "irredeemable hell" of present familial arrangements as inappropriate and counsels a kind of Freudian distinction between the misery-producing aspects of existence that can be changed and those that cannot. Not surprisingly, her work appeals to nonfeminist intellectuals more than to self-identified feminists. A grave fear that the intimate realm of basic family ties will be politicized separates her from others who share concern for much on the feminist agenda. In particular, she fears the negative dimensions of state intervention in family life and the destruction of "our capacity for sociality," an apprehension she shares with social critic Christopher Lasch, whom she admires. Like the boys in *The Lord of the Flies,* humans will become hopelessly nasty, ugly, and brutish without dedicated mothers and fathers. Preservation of the sanctity of childhood as well as the dignity and purpose of a private-familial sphere should have a central place in the corpus of the "reflective" or "social feminist": "The reflective feminist must be as concerned with the concrete existence and self-understandings of children as she is with female subjects."[22]

In contrast to Young, Elshtain wishes to revitalize motherhood for the sake of familial and societal preservation and only secondarily for the sake of women themselves. Previously, Elshtain used language like the "private-familial sphere" known especially by women; now she talks about the sanctity of stable "two-parent households."[23] The preservation of either entity is more important than the liberation of women. Moreover, it requires recognizing the value of natural female and male traits—and ultimately, of heterosexuality. Part of Elshtain's attraction to selected aspects of psychoanalytic theory (not feminist psychoanalytic theory, however) is its confirmation of the body as a natural bedrock upon which the ego-self builds its being.

With these claims, Elshtain criticizes a major feature of the women's movement, at least humanist feminism. This is the transfer of family and sex roles from the realm of biology to that of society and history. An absolutely critical element in progressive sexual politics is the contention that female gender is socially constructed in ways that jeopardize democracy. Elshtain's argument is that "the family" is a basic, inherent constituent of our "common humanity."[24] Sexual roles are less social, historical creations than largely nonmalleable, biological foundations of human action. The imperatives of gender and family have, in her view, a universal, cross-cultural status. The nuances of a critical realist position of the kind we hold seldom enters into the debate, on either side.

It is important to notice how Elshtain and Okin diverge over the role of the family in democratic polity. While they both believe that the family is important for a democratic society, Elshtain has greater faith that two-parent households, with minimal adjustment in the distribution of domestic labor between mothers and fathers, have inherent abilities to teach the lessons of reciprocity and trust. This may have to do with her interest in protecting the private realm from state and market intrusion. In contrast to Okin, she does not spend much time arguing for a just renegotiation of household labor as essential for the development of justice in children. For Elshtain, the renewal of democracy depends more on the vitality of the two-parent family and parental authority than on equality between husband and wife. Families, because of the immaturity of children, cannot be democratic in the same way that other institutions of civil society can.

However, her argument for parental authority overlooks the ongoing inequities between mother and father in caring for children and in their public and private authority, especially when the mother continues to have primary responsibility for children, thereby remaining more vulnerable socially and economically. The greater status of men, she assumes, need not influence children. Elshtain perceptively takes the viewpoint of the child. Each parent "can be more or less a private or a public person, yet be equal in relation to children."[25] But we wonder if, in saying this, she fully understands the connection between justice in the family and justice in the public sphere. Influenced by Nancy Chodorow and others, Okin argues, by contrast, that an egalitarian family is an essential underpinning for political democracy. Morality does not develop in children in a domestic space that has no continuities with the public sphere. Domestic and political inequities—their lack of equal regard and the greater authority of men—make it difficult for families to produce citizens capable of genuine empathy, reciprocity, trust, and respect.

In chapter 10 we will argue that parental authority must be created through a dialogue between the family traditions of both father and mother, guided by the love ethic of equal regard and mutuality. Although it is wise to refrain from petty bickering over just divisions of domestic responsibilities between husband and wife, isn't this in fact an issue to be addressed if women are to participate freely in the public domain? In short, Elshtain, in her critiques of the excesses of humanist feminism, may sound more traditional than she realizes. From our standpoint, her emphasis on the two-parent family and family stability, although laudable, is somewhat short of a genuinely critical familism that seeks *both* family stability and gender equality.

As we have said in earlier chapters, justice, empathy, and social solidarity flow outward from the energies of kin altruism and related family patterns to the wider society. But for this to happen, mediating institutions must come into the picture. For kin preference and family interaction to become organized around just relations and then generalized outward to others, religious institutions must come into play with visions of the universal family, all members of which are equal before God. This is the way the house churches of early Christianity both created higher gender justice and helped spread family love outward to others—indeed, to the family of the entire *ecclesia*.

Judith Stacey finds troubling such profamily arguments as Elshtain's that retreat from challenging women's systemic subordination. Yet Stacey admits "backlash feminists are responding, however poorly, to genuine social problems as well as problems in feminist theory."[26] The threefold traumas of involuntary singleness, involuntary childlessness, and single parenthood have fueled antifeminist sentiment. This creates a challenging agenda for feminists: feminists must reassess the antifamilism within their own ranks and ask difficult questions about what children need, recognizing that the needs of women and children are not always compatible. Stacey acknowledges that feminists have been better at dismantling family hierarchy than reconstructing egalitarian practices and better at criticizing a distorted heterosexuality than appreciating its complexity and continued validity.[27]

Stacey recognizes that attempts to create a more democratic gender and kinship order have met with more resistance than feminists expected. Why? These attempts create incredible marital and parental instability. Until alternative protections heretofore provided by traditional family arrangements are replaced, they make women more vulnerable. Furthermore, the "inequalities of postindustrial occupational structure [and] the individualist, fast-track culture . . . [make] all too difficult the formation of stable intimate relations on a democratic, or any other basis."[28] Religion, particularly fundamentalist varieties, may serve as a source of support during these turbulent times, as she learned to her surprise in her ethnographic study of two families in her *Brave New Families* (1990).

In this book, Stacey is less disturbed than Elshtain with the direction of everyday families and more prepared to live with the ambiguities of the postmodern family. Although divorce, premarital pregnancies, wandering fathers, disturbed children, and altered living and working conditions plague both of the families she studies, she encounters in her interviews a satisfaction with family life rather than a sense of "decline." In the postmodern interlude, she is willing to tolerate the "multiplicity of family and household arrangements that we inhabit uneasily and reconstitute frequently in response to changing personal and occupational circumstances" as preferable to a return to rigid ideals of family.[29]

Stacey voices a widely shared premise that we found as well in the family theology of the liberal churches: the quality of familial relationships is more important than family structure. But Stacey's optimism in her *Brave*

New Families came before evidence of the declining well-being of some children of single mothers and stepfamilies and the recent insights that, on average, family structure contributes enhanced qualitative investments by parents in their relations with their children.

In the end, the secular conversation between progressive and conservative feminists ends in a seemingly unresolvable impasse. At this point, one must wonder whether Okin, Elshtain, and Stacey have all overestimated the capacity of the family alone to effect either justice (Okin), sociality (Elshtain), or a democratic kinship order (Stacey). All three fail to attend sufficiently to other social institutions that bridge public and private domains, especially worshiping religious congregations. The complex way in which kin altruism was projected into the early Christian Eucharist, the way more egalitarian gender relations at the Communion table were internalized backward into the family thereby equalizing family relations, and then newly defined kin preferences were projected outward into the life of the house church and beyond—these kinds of insights seem absent in both conservative and progressive discourse on the relation of private and public.

Neither Stacey, Okin, nor other secular feminists have the tools needed to initiate this kind of discussion. Okin associates religion with patriarchy and is unable to avail herself of more subtle readings of either Judaism or Christianity. Stacey is deeply suspicious of clerical and religious authority and is genuinely puzzled, even if appreciative, when she learns that evangelical Christianity is a support to her two troubled families. Even though Elshtain sees Christianity as a resource for cogent criticisms of early liberal feminism, she tends to be indirect about her own theological commitments.

This leaves us with an important question. Do feminist theologians have any solutions better than those of progressive and conservative feminists for the problem of the relation of public and private spheres and the relation of mutuality, self-sacrifice, the dependency of children, and the authority and equality of parents— especially as these tensions play out in a democratic capitalist economy?

Christian Feminists and the Family

Although feminists in religion have not completely resolved these questions and few attempt comprehensive reconstructions of family life, they provide cornerstones upon which sound family theory can be built. These cornerstones do not prevent controversy among them, but they do provide grounds upon which conversation and transformations may continue—a definite improvement over the public debate at large. Their voices have been neglected by both secular feminists and those participating in the wider American debate over the family.

Approaches to the family in Christian theology can be placed in three groups, roughly corresponding to developments in secular feminist theory: white liberation feminists, womanists, and conservative or evangelical feminists. Chronologically, white feminist theologians joined the early humanist critique of religiously upheld family dynamics of domination and submission. During the past decade, womanist theologians have changed the conversation about the family. Identifying their threefold experience of sexism, racism, and classism, they called the feminist dismissal of motherhood and family not only problematic but racist. At about the same time, more "conserving" evangelical and Catholic feminists entered the family discussion. They used two strategies. First, they claimed some feminist tenets but shifted the discussion from sexism to gender. Second, they aligned themselves more closely with particular religious traditions.

The differences among these three groups are not as important as the theological convictions they share, noted at the beginning of this chapter. Because theological feminists are in conversation with classic religious traditions, they have a common ground, something to interpret, and something to rework. They may well be able to traverse the impasses between secular feminists.

Liberation Feminists and the Family

Roman Catholic theologian Rosemary Radford Ruether has called consistently for the revitalization of a feminist voice on the family. As early as 1980, she stated the "*imperative need* vigorously to contest the claims of the New Right to represent the interests of the 'family.'" Feminists would do well to keep the issue of the family in their camp, she argued, and not allow the political and religious right to accuse them of being against the values of families and children.[30]

Ruether is aware that many white middle-class feminist theologians have worked harder to discredit patriarchal Christianity than to identify alternative Christian ideals of the family. Yet until the contributions of womanists and conservative feminists, feminist theological discussion of the family tended to stay on the back burner.

But Ruether sparks the discussion. Her classic work challenging patriarchal theological doctrines provides counterproposals to some of the impasses mentioned above. Ruether identifies extremes and argues for a mediating position. *Sexism and God-Talk* (1983), one of the first full-fledged feminist theologies, contests the inevitability of an impasse between humanist and gynocentric feminist family theory. Her Christian sensibilities lead her to reject both the liberal feminist idealization of the male sphere *and* the romantic feminist idealization of the female sphere.

She desires a more comprehensive vision that encompasses "liberal feminist" ideals of civil rights, "socialist feminist" ideals of economic independence, and "radical feminist" ideals of the value of female self, body, and reproduction.[31] The ecological view of the family in this book incorporates most of these emphases and does so in ways that include males as well as females.

Ruether's analysis of the source of problems for families is close, but not identical, to our own. The crisis is caused, she believes, by the combined forces of patriarchy and industrialism. She insists that the "single most important source" of family difficulties is a profit-driven economy characterized by inflation and a sharp separation of home and work.[32] She characterizes the contradictions of contemporary economic life as follows:

> A cultural and economic system that insists that women are equal, while at the same time structuring its economic and social life to make women economically dependent or marginal, as well as the primary parents, results in an increasingly large sector of impoverished women left without male support and without sufficient means to support themselves.[33]

In contrast to Elshtain, Ruether protests the sharp dichotomy of the public and private spheres, which she sees as integrally related to dualisms of male-female and nature-culture. The private realm is far from an inner sanctum. Rather, the nineteenth-century divisions between private and public realms created a privatized domestic culture from which men were alienated and where women bore the chief burdens of domestic responsibility. Most important, she grounds this analysis theologically. The industrial, patriarchal division of labor is not just a problem for families, it is a sin. The division dictates that men and women become overspecialized in their lives, limiting the respective ranges of their human experience (a kind of idolatry) and distorting the human nature of both genders.

Christian feminism means neither a call to androgyny nor the exclusive reclamation of feminine values. It calls for an ideal of "humanity." Authentic human nature created in God's image and the redemptive action of God in Jesus both confirm a fundamental egalitarianism at the heart of reality. These truths ground the dignity and equality of both men and women.[34] We say much the same when we argue that the foundation of love as equal regard is the love that God has for all humans, whether male or female.

What role, then, do biology and physical reproduction have in Ruether's definition of humanity? Ruether maintains a place for the in-

tact, biologically related family and recognizes some biological differences between males and females. But she is rightfully ambivalent about
biological differences because women have been more oppressed by
such claims than have men. Although we wish she had paid more attention to human asymmetrical reproductive patterns, we agree that
these patterns have few implications for defining the roles of men and
women in contemporary society. We agree with Ruether that there is no
necessary relation "between reproductive complementarity and either
psychological or social role differentiation." Cultural roles for males and
females are for all practical purposes "rooted in culture and history
rather than in a relatively fixed 'nature.'"[35] Gestation and female proximity to childbearing warrant greater efforts to involve fathers and husbands in child care. Fathers have even more cause to provide bodily care
for children "precisely because that is less a physiological given."[36] They
must compensate proportionately for the time women spend gestating
and nursing. Transforming the sins of sexism demands a male conversion in which biological fathers provide "more than occasional supple-
mental help in this business of parenting children."[37]

Still, Ruether's goal is not the equality-as-sameness of liberal, humanist feminism but rather a "recognition of value, which at the same
time affirms genuine variety and particularity . . . a mutuality that allows
us to affirm different ways of being."[38] Gender is neither a mechanical
reflex of biology upon which an ideal of the family rests nor solely a male
or social construction with no biological referents. Roles and duties in
families and in sexual relations are arrangements women and men must
constantly renegotiate in face of both natural circumstance and historical contingency. Gender and sexual stereotypes signal an onerous
breakdown in this process with negative consequences for all involved.

Ruether uses historical resources to contest the religious right's claims
about the Christian view of the family. In a series of five articles published
in 1983 on the "church and family" from early Christianity to today, she
finds evidence of a radical countercultural egalitarianism. The "original
Christian vision of equality in Christ" contradicts, she argues, the
late–nineteenth-century patriarchal hardening of the Victorian ideal of
family.[39] She stresses Gospel and Acts passages subversive of the patriarchal family. In contrast to religions grounded in family traditions, as Judaism had been, early Christianity both subordinated and extended the
symbolism of blood kinship to the *ecclesia:* "Christian community is seen
as a new kind of family, a voluntary community gathered by personal
faith, which stands in tension with the natural family or kinship group"[40]

Historically, the household codes in the post-Pauline literature are a
conservative compromise of the gospel due to the social and political

pressures of the surrounding Roman state. The early Christian changes in relations between men and women effectively modify "traditional patriarchy by proposing a high ideal of husbandly benevolence toward dependents," as our own exploration of Christian alternatives to Greco-Roman honor-shame codes also suggested. She also agrees that this "love paternalism," although radical with reference to the surrounding culture, was incomplete when measured by the inner logic of Christian love.[41]

Ruether laments that Catholic and Reformed theologians took the household codes as a definitive Pauline statement on women's place under the husband's authority. Rather than interpreting these passages as signs of a revolution that needed to be completed, Christians for centuries have seen them as static truths to be defended.[42]

Ruether's historical grounding for egalitarianism in the Christian view of family is helpful. Yet she sometimes overlooks how later "conservative" reactions in Christian thinking on the family were also breakthroughs *of a kind*, especially when compared to the family ideology in the surrounding culture. This was the case in Ephesians with reference to the Greco-Roman world and the Reformation with reference to Catholic and Germanic precedents. A reading of New Testament passages that relativize the patriarchal clan leads her at times to disregard the analogical extension of kin preferences to the symbolism of the church. Membership in *ecclesia* and the kingdom subordinates, transforms, converts, and extends natural family ties but does not suppress or repudiate them.

Although Ruether does not denigrate intact families and biologically related parents and children, she does not work hard to give them a theological validation. This is partly because she is aware of the ways such appeals have been misused to exploit and further alienate women. Intact families and biological kin should be "committed communities of mutual service."[43] She emphasizes voluntary, mutual communities but does not deal in depth with the uniquely nonvoluntary relationship between parent and child and the conditions required to sustain them.

Ruether's practical theological response to current family dilemmas has implications for all kinds of families. She calls for a new social order that would alter the alignment between home and work, family and society. In an earlier text titled *New Woman/New Earth* (1975), Ruether concludes with descriptions of self-governing communities of families, such as the kibbutzim in Israel or communal groups in China, which would band together to help with parenting and other supports. Intact, nuclear families in her vision would be valued, but single-parent families and stepfamilies would also be included in these communities. Kin ties would be respected and supported, but elements of Plato's *Republic* or the African "village" would also be part of the vision. The entire community would be responsible for the children, not just biological or legal parents.[44]

Because such a broad revolution is unlikely, and because it requires the serious commitment of small groups with shared values, Ruether argues that changes will need to come gradually. Unlike Elshtain, she envisions a more interlocking, mutually supportive, and ecological society than we have at the moment. Parents in two-earner families should work individually no more than thirty or thirty-five hours a week; childcare must occur in institutions more proximate to work and home; and workplace, family, and neighborhood must have more organic relations to one another. Unlike Elshtain, she does not sacralize the private sphere; she preserves family life by bringing work and politics closer to the residential family. Like Okin, she wants women to participate more fully in the educational, cultural, political, and economic opportunities of the public world. She wants men to share in the responsibilities of home and parenting. In contrast to Okin, Ruether does not believe that this restructuring is simply a matter of adequate public policies and laws. It involves global structural and cultural shifts—new work patterns, new relationships between private and public spheres, ideological support for women in the public sphere, male parenting, and a recognition that all families raising children need help.

In contrast to Ruether, Christian ethicist Christine Gudorf gives specificity to a family ethic that evolves explicitly out of her mothering experiences and maternal thinking. Gudorf offers a nuanced discussion of sacrifice and self-regard in family obligation. She repudiates all theological and cultural views that blame family crises too simplistically on unfettered individualism and focuses on distorted views of selfless love and faulty understandings of parenting and sexuality.

Gudorf's work gets to the heart of what theological feminism has to offer the American family debate. Our analysis has elected individualism disconnected from the common good as a driving force alongside other causes of the family crisis. We argue, however, that individualism and ordinate self-regard are only destructive when disconnected from other restraints and guides. Furthermore, the excesses of individualism have played out differently for men than for women. Love as equal regard, as we envision it, finds a place for ordinate self-regard. Gudorf articulates this point of view with genuine clarity. Moreover, she develops her feminist view of love with an eye toward the dynamics of the human life cycle—a perspective mostly absent in secular feminists and even in Ruether. Gudorf gives us a theological perspective on the psychological aspects of the family crisis.

Gudorf makes these contributions around a theory of parenting. Contrary to others' assumptions that loving self-sacrifice buttressed her ability to care for her three children—two of whom were adopted, disabled, and, initially, very challenging—Gudorf discovered that disinterested love and disregard for self are poor foundations of parental love. Gudorf moves away from Protestant *agape* toward Aristotelian and Catholic views; she debunks self-sacrifice as the ideal of parent love and argues that love as mutuality is more central, even for parenting. But she adds a qualification:

> This is not to argue against the need for sacrifice. . . . But we need to be very clear that self-sacrificing love is always aimed at the establishment of mutual love. . . however far in the future. . . . Agape is valuable in the service of eros and does not exist otherwise.[45]

Mutuality is the more foundational love, as the theory of kin altruism suggests. Why would people all over the world—Christians and nonChristians, motivated by Christian love and not motivated by it—so willingly enter into parenthood if it were so inherently self-sacrificial, if they got nothing from it for themselves? Because, she asserts, "it is *not* essentially sacrificial. Parenthood is potentially enriching, life-enhancing, and joyous despite the real sacrificial elements within it."[46]

Gudorf is extremely sensitive to the dangers that exist when women in families make self-denial the primary criterion of their marital and maternal identity. For centuries the needs of children have prevailed over the needs of mothers and reduced women to a means to that end. The female problematic—the primordial willingness of mothers to raise children at the expense of their own needs with or without the father's involvement—may be a reality. Here Gudorf builds on Valerie Saiving's classic 1960 essay challenging traditional views of human sin associated with the male qualities of "pride" or the "will-to-power." Women and mothers are more likely to be tempted by the sins of "triviality, distractibility, and diffuseness; lack of organizing center or focus; dependence on others for one's own self-definition . . . in short, underdevelopment or negation of her self."[47] Or as one of us has written: "Hearing a child demands abandoning one's point of view or at least moving the self slightly off center to meet acute needs. Hence the different temptation for many women, particularly mothers: the temptation to lose oneself."[48]

Gudorf is among the first Christian ethicists to discuss love as mutuality from a developmental point of view. Gudorf tells us that "mutual love seldom begins mutually." Mutuality between parent and child requires a patience with the temporary imbalance and a gradual shift in the balance of giving and receiving. Children play a significant role in the reciprocity of family life, and theories of mutuality are inadequate until offspring and charges are taken into consideration as prospective peers of parents. They contribute to their parents' development into mature adulthood more than is commonly assumed or expected. Moreover, parents must grow and change along with their children, resolving their own early childhood idealization of their parents before they can regard their children as subjects in their own right. The latter is a central moral task of parenthood. Parenthood is a "process of relationship," specifically, "a mutual relationship, not merely a relation of parent to child."

> Under any circumstances, the parental role is a constantly diminishing one in the life of a child. For this reason, it is dangerous for adults to attempt to fill personal needs exclusively through parenting. We need to have other avenues for nurturing, for intimacy, for community involvement, for activity, outside of parenting, if we are to avoid using a child for our own ends.[49]

Parents also have a responsibility to model a fully embodied mutuality, even allowing their children to sense the shared warmth and openness of their own sexual relationships and parental responsibilities.

Gudorf, in *Body, Sex, and Pleasure* (1994), suggests a powerful, yet troubling ideal given contemporary reality: that *mutual* sexual pleasure, in which women are as active and receive as much pleasure as men, is a central criterion for healthy parental relationship. Indeed, the bodily pleasure derived from the intimate bonding of a sexual relationship is "one foundation for the individual's ability to nurture children well."[50] Instead of seeing sexuality exclusively in the service of procreation, it is time to emphasize the role of mutual sexual pleasure in sustaining and binding marital relationships.

However, when Gudorf in this later work talks about the importance of "bodyright"—the moral right to exercise control over one's body—as prerequisite to stopping sexual violence and to reaching personhood, she seems more focused on autonomy, separateness, and individual rights than on relationality, dependence, and mutuality, although the former values are absolutely necessary in situations of sexual violence. She sometimes breaks with her own concern with mutuality. Nevertheless, Gudorf's seminal article on parenting has been widely influential, certainly on the authors of this book.

Despite Gudorf's sensitivity to the importance of knowledge of the female and male physiology and Reuther's emphasis on the dialectic between mind and body, neither seems eager to define the ways in which biology might influence parental roles. Until the ways in which male and female physiology influence childrearing are adequately acknowledged, inequities between mothers and fathers cannot be fully resolved nor adequate parenting understood. We already have seen how male physiology influences the initial tentativeness of male commitments to offspring. For mothers, the intensity of a more immediate connection to infants and children can lead to overextension and difficulties in attending to other needs and relationships. Conflicts of contemporary mothers between caring for children and vocational commitments have become particularly acute.

Perhaps the most powerful insight of theological reflection on parenting is the realization that an overblown ideal of love as self-sacrifice distorts the reality of both children and mothers. A model of love that overemphasizes sacrifice requires serious rethinking not only for families but as a broader Christian teaching. There is little doubt that pregnancy, lactation, a mother's parental certainty, and other physiological changes give most women a head start over men in parental investment. This maternal energy helps children to thrive. But it is equally true that a mother's subjectivity, needs, joys, intentions, life plans, and personhood are also deeply important for the flourishing of children. As Jessica Benjamin argues so powerfully, children flourish not only because they are nurtured but because they are nourished by a mother with a self, intentions, a mission, indeed a vocation. Women's physiology and parental certainty may contribute to parental investment, but their personhood is the decisive factor in their children's growth. Yet the mother's biological investments, personhood, life projects, and public occupation can be held together only when husband, neighborhood, extended family, society, market, and government actively participate and make appropriate adjustments.[51]

As we have seen, among liberation feminists Ruether clearly sets the pace. She has the most systematically developed history of the family in theological feminism. Ruether, however, does not address the changing patterns of the family life cycle and what this means for the dynamics between husband and wife, parent and children, and parent and other dependents, relatives, neighbors, and so on. An ideal of the family as a cooperative interaction of interdependent and individuated men and women requires a psychological and ethical sophistication not required by the classical image of the male as corporate head of a household. At the time of the initial contributions of Ruether and other feminist theologians, the relation of mothers and fathers to children was not the salient issue. The plight of women in male-dominated families, societies, and religions most appropriately was. Hence Ruether created a theory more for adult mutuality than for family mutuality.

When children are introduced, the ethic of mutuality entails elements of parental investment, mutual recognition, appropriate self-assertion, transitional sacrifice, and the constant renegotiation of the conflicting premoral needs of the different family members at different levels of maturity. Love as mutuality and equal regard is expressed differently at different points in the human life cycle, as we will show in chapter 10. A life-cycle perspective on family mutuality is missing in Ruether and other feminist theologians. Introducing it, however, will solve important issues.

In light of the injustice experienced by many women in patriarchal families, it is understandable that much of feminist scholarship neglects the challenges of relating mutuality to both adults and children in two-parent families and to the value of two-parent families for children's welfare. However, theological feminism may be justified in now giving attention to the theory, practice, and ecology of the committed, equal-regard, public-private family. When the recent, slightly more gynocentric emphasis on mutuality and embodiment in theological feminism is filled out with a discussion of the biology and ethics of both female *and* male parenting, an even richer ecological approach results.[52] The ecology of fatherhood is less well stated by feminist theologians but is waiting to be added, as we attempt to do in this book.

Beyond Mainstream Theological Feminism: Conserving Christian Feminists and the Family

Early Christian feminists said much that was relevant to families, but they seldom concentrated on positive reconstructions of families. More gynocentric religious feminists turn to families more directly but generally omit careful consideration of men. Recently a conserving (or conservative) voice in religious feminism has addressed directly the religious and ethical ideals for family life. Although Catholic moral theologian Lisa Cahill and Calvinist psychologist Mary Stewart Van Leeuwen differ considerably by virtue of loyalty to distinct Christian traditions and audiences, two common themes emerge in their writings. Neither shies away from promoting the virtues of the intact, two-parent family and the value of children. Furthermore, both combine the strengths of particular religious traditions with the strengths of feminism.

Although conservative Catholics and evangelical Protestants might not consider either Cahill or Van Leeuwen to be "conserving," they do fit Judith Stacey's definition of conservative profamily feminists in giving sexual politics a backseat to religious loyalties. Both identify more with their religious traditions than they do with feminism as such.[53] Yet both have come to promote adamantly an egalitarian ethic of mutuality in family relationships and, on the basis of this ethic, to critique scriptures and earlier theological traditions. With insight and finesse, each risks a stance on the family that both religious conservatives and liberal feminists might find objectionable. The challenge, in Cahill's words, is "to reinstate full sexual-reproductive embodiment as part of the positive ideal of human sexuality, in a context of gender equality."[54]

Van Leeuwen's advocacy of the male-female relationship as normative for families is more direct. She is partly motivated by alarm over the chaos of unchecked sexual libertarianism. Her rationale for egalitarian coparenting as a norm that limits the acceptable range of family diversity combines a confessional Reformed theology and selected social science theories. She believes that her position offers a "middle way" between "traditionalism" and "mainstream feminism."[55] The former, she complains, has not given up on male authority and female domesticity, while the latter draws no line on the diversity of family forms that should replace these norms.

Van Leeuwen begins with certain elemental "truths" that follow from the basic Christian story of Creation and the Fall.[56] These include the classic Genesis affirmation that male and female are made in the image of God (Gen. 1:27), that a man should leave his parents to "cleave" and become "one flesh" with his wife (Gen. 2:24), and that together they should "be fruitful and multiply, and fill the earth" (Gen. 1:28). These are examples of Reformed theology's teachings on the "orders of creation"; in creation God willed certain human arrangements, of which the family is one.

Van Leeuwen takes the orders of creation on faith and as part of the specific church tradition that informs her thinking. But she does not end here. She uses psychology to refine, justify, and criticize Reformed theology, employing psychoanalytic object-relations theory much as Cahill uses the social sciences and evolutionary ecology to refine outdated formulations of Catholic natural law. The work of Nancy Chodorow and others, for example, shows how distortions in the development of both boys and girls and even misogyny result unless both mothers and fathers are invested and involved in the care of children.[57]

Hence, though she subordinates psychology to her Reformed theological beginning point, Van Leeuwen does not accept all teachings traditionally associated with Calvinist orders of creation. Careful reading of the Garden of Eden myth (Gen. 2:15–3:24) shows that the subordination of women is a consequence of the Fall and not the original will of God in creation, as traditional perspectives have sometimes held. The subjection of women is not part of God's created order. Men and women, although differentiated and complementary in their gifts of relationality and dominion, were created as partners. Male domination and female enmeshment in human caregiving are a result of sin. Salvation history brings an ever-widening inclusivity; in the end, all family commitments are secondary to the rule of God's kingdom.

In this mission, men and women are called to be servants to one another, which may entail sacrifices on both sides. This call to sacrifice, however, along with Van Leeuwen's sometimes abrupt dismissal of Enlightenment and "modernist" values of human freedom and self-determination, tends to jeopardize a model of mutual love that requires a certain amount of self-regard. Her understanding of equality is qualified by Calvinist premises and conventional family norms. In line with Calvinist theology, she believes that men and women are created as complementary and incomplete without each other and that Christ mandates mutual submission as much as equal regard, and she allows little place for the realities of circumstances that give rise to alternative family forms. Because she equates Christian feminism and biblical egalitarianism, she is more worried about the sins of inequity than the sins of sexism or oppression.

Nonetheless, it is important to recall her audience and the contributions Van Leeuwen has made in the evangelical sphere. Evangelical feminists represent an interesting division in conservative Christianity because they claim biblical equality between men and women and advocate for women in positions of Christian leadership, justice in the home, and paternal involvement in raising children. Precisely because they work inside the circles of evangelical Christianity, they pose an annoying threat to others within those circles. They disturb the notion that abiding by biblical standards implies only one outcome for gender and parental roles in families: the headship and spiritual leadership of the male.

Although Cahill argues for the significance (we call it the prima facie importance) of male-female, husband-wife, father-mother relationships for families, she does not pit this family form against others. Yet neither does she let go of its foundational importance for human flourishing. She is not satisfied with feminist efforts like Gudorf's to separate sex and reproduction, make pleasure the primary criterion for judging sexual activity, and define families as "collections of persons."

Complex epistemological and moral convictions lead to this position. Going against current feminist trends, Cahill rejects Foucauldianinspired interpretations of historic sexual mores as no more than social constructions of domination and control. This kind of deconstructionism, she argues, assumes Western values of liberty and individual rights that do not prevail in many other contexts. Such a position, for example, leaves feminists without grounds for assessing Asian prostitution or African genital mutilation.

In place of gender deconstructionism, Cahill outlines a historically nuanced, inductively reasoned naturalism that can arrive, she claims, at cross-cultural norms of equality, reciprocity, and respect. This approach opens the possibility of a shared truth about families—critical connections between love, sexual pleasure, and bearing children that are grounded in a common humanity and common human experience.

Cahill develops criteria for judging sexual activity that reflect a strong Catholic allegiance. Human sexual flourishing joins biological reproduction with intimacy and pleasure. She argues that parenthood, love, and pleasure together constitute the "complex and complete" human sexual experience, yet leaves open the question whether this constellation is the "richest, most excellent, or ideal." In other words, she wants a family ideal that is "humanly true and attractive for the circumstances for which it is appropriate" but does not disqualify as less virtuous other situations for which the ideal is not fitting.[58] She rejects, however, the excessive liberal Christian use of the language of relationality, its normless tolerance, its emphasis on personal autonomy, and its disassociation of sex from parenthood and social responsibility. In her mind, this form of liberalism has in effect handed moral leadership over to conservative authoritarian models of family that further oppress women. Emphasis on "free" choice in reproductive technologies, for example, has left a vacuum of ideals into which the effervescent appeals of market and patriarchy constantly flow. Furthermore, for many women in the poor countries of the world, the right to choose premarital sex, divorce, and careers by necessity remains secondary to the need to address gross economic inequities and the challenge of sheer survival in bearing and raising children.

Central for reclaiming the relation of parenthood to sexuality is, Cahill believes, a careful reading of early Christian scripture and Catholic moral theology. She reconstructs elements of the natural law tradition and also uses insights from evolutionary ecology. The strength of the Catholic tradition is "its strongly social vision." Cahill wants to reinstate the social and institutional functions of marriage and family within an interpretation of Christian discipleship oriented toward the common good. The personal sexual relationship is at the center of a series of concentric circles that emanate from the joy of sexual exchange to the parental relationship to the family and finally to the family's critical contribution to the common good. Parenthood is a "specifically sexual mode of social participation"; procreation is "the social side of sexual love."[59] Family choices are social and moral through and through.

Cahill reads Christian scripture against its own internal standard of community solidarity and inclusion of the dominated and marginalized. When read in the context of the family codes of the Greco-Roman world, even Paul destabilizes conventional hierarchies of sex, class, and culture. This allows for a more generous reading of the New Testament household codes. Rather than being scandalized at the restrictions of women's activity in 1 Corinthians 12–14 or 1 Timothy, readers might be encouraged that early Christianity introduced social changes that worked toward greater mutuality, respect, and solidarity, even if these ideals were actualized inconsistently.[60]

Cahill's important contributions would be even stronger if they contained one significant practical element: a concern with the psychological, interpersonal, and strategic dimensions of bringing about mutuality and equal regard. Her concern about the fixation in liberal sexual ethics on interpersonal fulfillment leads her to neglect the psychological complexities of enacting these ideals in real life. She gives little attention to what it takes in human relating to realize a socially responsible sexuality. It is one thing to argue for the correctness of an ethic of mutuality; it is another thing to understand the intricacies of communication and strategies of shared labor that go into it. To build a new critical culture of marriage, skills in the intersubjective negotiations of conflicts between work and family, guided by an ethic of equal regard, must find a place at the center of moral theologies of the family. Cahill, in the end, is more interested in how we ground our beliefs than with how we enact them. Both tasks are important.

Family Survivalist Womanists and the Family

In the past decade, under the rubric of "womanist theology," a new generation of African-American women has protested the exclusive definitions of "woman" by the white middle class. They have begun to define the concerns of family in ways that emphasize the importance of both biological and nonbiological mothers. Several womanists—Delores Williams, Cheryl Townsend Gilkes, and Toinette Eugene—have introduced new family themes.

Working toward a theology of survival and well-being, womanists focus on the threefold oppressions of sexism, racism, and classism as the proper context within which to understand family structures and dynamics. More specifically, in womanist theology we find a distinct ethic of familyhood that includes immense respect for mothers (broadly defined) *and* extended family systems. In contrast to the adversarial approach of some feminist theory on male-female and parent-child relationships, womanist ethics places strong emphasis on working together as men, women, and children to raise "the Race" in the midst of multiple social oppressions.

Although early feminists protested the ideals of the nineteenth-century family and the "cult of true womanhood," they did not challenge the ways these ideals depended upon and heightened racism.[61] Moreover, for most African-American women, the distinction between public and private as well as between productive and reproductive labor was not as sharply drawn as in the separate spheres of the Victorian ideal. Rather than functioning as prison and trap, the home and family were important springboards for political action, cultural resistance, community organization, and individual mobility.[62] And work for wages has seldom carried the same taboo and shame that it did for the white middle-class mother. Work outside the home was seen as "important and legitimate."[63]

More has been required of black women than white women in terms of sheer family sustenance. Delores Williams's, *Sisters in the Wilderness* (1993) begins by asserting that, in addition to liberation themes relevant to blacks, an equally relevant but unnoticed female-centered tradition can be found in the Bible. It has to do with survival and the quality of life.[64] While themes about the exodus of Israel from Egypt are widely appreciated in black churches, less recognized is the religious significance of the exploitation of Hagar, the surrogate mother who was enslaved, brutalized, impoverished, banished, and abandoned (Genesis 16 and 21). Hagar's story has analogies to African-American women who have struggled to care for children and families under the extraordinary circumstances of poverty, sexual and economic exploitation, surrogacy, homelessness, single-parenting, racism, and so forth.

As motherhood is a central theme in the Hagar story, Williams believes it is crucial in the stories of present-day African-American women. In contrast to the neglect of motherhood by much of feminist theology, Williams adamantly calls for the revaluing of black motherhood and its supporting ethic of familyhood: respect for mothers, sensitivity to children, the value of extended families, and the simultaneous importance of women's autonomy and female identities that do not derive from the status of husbands.

Not only are families valued as a source of resistance and survival, motherhood itself has a complex and positive valuation. Toinette Eugene chooses to ground her own liberation ethic of care in the mother as moral agent and in church seen as social system caring for kinfolk who are defined both biologically and symbolically. As she and others make clear, motherhood implies both a biological and a nonbiological function. While it certainly includes giving birth to children, the idea of motherhood also functions socially so that many women provide nurture and instruction to nonbiological offspring. Herein lie ideals that place the task of nurturing children within the wider community. White feminists have become concerned about the family because it is still central to many women's lives; womanist theologians do so because the very lives of children are at stake, especially in view of the high rates of homicide, unemployment, and imprisonment among black male children.

The womanist call for a social motherhood, is not, however, a call for greater sacrifice on the part of women. In fact, an essay by Gilkes on the multiple cultural humiliations and assaults suffered by black women ends with this claim: "Self-love is probably the most critical task we complete in establishing our commitment 'to survival and wholeness of entire people, male and female.'"[65] Part of the revolutionary power of novelist Alice Walker's definition of "womanist" is its demand that women love themselves "regardless." Womanists and white feminist theologians agree: the language of sacrificial love, unqualified by self-affirmation and mutuality, has outlived its theological usefulness. The only viable use of servanthood language, argues womanist Jacquelyn Grant, is in demanding that Christians become Christ's servants in the struggle against oppression. Since historically some have been "more servants than others," this means replacing traditional notions of servanthood with the language of empowering discipleship.[66]

Womanists have upheld an ethic and tradition of greater equity between genders and, if inclusion of children in worship is any indication, admiration for children. Some attribute this gender and family ethic to African traditions, others to the equally shared hardships of slavery and its aftermath. Although this ethic of gender equality offers an alternative to traditional family ethics, it stands on shaky ground, even in the black community, as our Gallup poll reveals. Womanist Frances Wood writes, "We must demythologize the notion that African American women and men working side by side in the cotton rows somehow automatically has translated into gender equality."[67] Black women, it seems, have supported black men far more than the reverse. As we will see in chapter 8, the message of male responsibility and servanthood is one of the most pervasively preached messages of the black church in America. Although

the rest of society can learn much from this message about male responsibility, it is also *monological* and latently patriarchal, that is, it remains
one-directional and hence unequally determined in relation to women.

Perhaps *at this point in history* womanist theologians and theology in
general need to delineate more carefully the different ethical requirements for men and for women. Many women need less emphasis on self-
sacrifice and more on self-love, whereas men may need the reverse. Our
love and marriage survey, as we noted, reveals differences in how men
and women respectively value mutuality and self-sacrifice. Furthermore, it shows that men *in general* prize self-sacrifice as a model of love
more than or nearly as much as mutuality. It also shows that these differences are magnified among African-American men and women.
Whereas 47.92 percent of African-American men preferred sacrifice as
a model of love to 33.33 percent preferring mutuality, African-American
women were quite different from both black men and white women.
Only 14.29 percent chose sacrifice, and 76.19 percent said a good marriage correlates with mutuality (see table 4).

Table 4. Comparison of African Americans' and European Americans'
Beliefs about Models of Love Correlating with Good Marriages

Beliefs	Total Percentage	African American*		European American*	
		Women	Men	Women	Men
Mutuality	55	76.19	33.33	63.68	49.53
Self-Sacrifice	38	14.29	47.92	31.72	44.31
Self-Fulfillment	5	9.52	10.42	3.22	4.03

Note: We are grateful to Christopher Browning, Ph.D. candidate in the sociology department at the
University of Chicago, for additional statistical analysis that provided the breakdowns in this table.
*Numbers represent percentages.

Although many reasons probably stand behind these differences, it
may be that black women, in light of hardships suffered and sacrifices
made by their foremothers in America, have the least desire to advocate
the importance of sacrifice for family relationships. What our survey
does not tell us is whose sacrifice, mutuality, and self-fulfillment are intended? When men choose self-sacrifice, do they mean their own or that
of others? Does the language of sacrifice mean something different to
men and women? When 10.42 percent of African-American men choose
self-fulfillment, whose fulfillment do they seek? And when women are
high on mutuality, who do they want to act mutually—themselves, their
husbands, or both?

Conclusion

Religious feminists have not solved all the problems of contemporary families, but they certainly advance the conversation beyond the reigning models and schisms in secular feminism and the wider public debate. They help resolve some of the dilemmas that secular feminists cannot resolve on secular grounds alone, and they suggest frameworks that women and men like Sarah Miles and Richard Good might use to reconstrue their personal, familial, and communal responsibilities and fulfillments. If the rules have changed midstream in people's lives, as Sarah says, new parameters of personal and family relationship must be determined.

Religious feminists point Sarah and Richard toward the many concentric circles of family connectedness—the first sacred covenants that bring husband and wife into mutual love, the embodied affections and investments of mother and father when children are born, the identification of the importance of extended families, the communities of tradition in church and synagogue which teach and support families, the more contractual duties and supports of state and market, and finally the deep grounding of individuals and families in the goodness of God, a goodness that makes us all worthy and deserving of care. Is it possible that if Sarah experienced this vision more profoundly, her life would be less anguished? And is it possible that if this vision were understood widely in our society, the new cultural swing toward love as mutuality would also yield more trusting and symmetrical understandings between men and women and the necessary changes in social structures and politices to secure its enactment?

7

Families and the Therapeutic

Powerful criticisms have recently been made of the so-called culture of psychotherapy, its individualistic tendencies, and its subversion of a viable marriage culture and familism. These criticisms are partially correct. But they should not be allowed to obscure the important new role, both remedial and educational, of the "therapeutic" for the construction of a critical marriage culture and a critical familism. Placed alongside needed religiocultural and economic reconstructions, the new therapies have much to contribute to one of the essentials of a critical marriage culture: the capacity for "communicative competence."

For several decades, many who have experienced problems in marital and familial relationships have turned to a relatively new source of help: individual, marital, and family therapy. Even Blondie and Dagwood Bumstead spent a week with Dr. Marjorie Squabble in 1995 when Dagwood could not handle Blondie's desire to move her catering business out of the home. Beyond the comic strips, in 1948 when the first Kinsey report (*Sexual Behavior in the Human Male*) appeared, the New York City Yellow Pages listed 3 marriage counselors, preceded by 16 marriage brokers. In 1991 the Yellow Pages listed more than 235 marriage counselors preceded by 3 marriage brokers.

Our interviews confirm this turn to therapy. Several people we talked to used therapy to help resolve family conflicts, with notably mixed results. Such social critics as Christopher Lasch, Philip Rieff, and Robert Bellah have viewed this phenomenon in a fundamentally negative light, and they are often quoted. The therapeutic climate of the late twentieth century, it is argued, promotes a psychologically grounded ethic of individualism, encouraging its many clients to pursue their own fulfillment, often to the exclusion of the good of family, community, or larger causes. Is this assessment of the therapeutic voice and the family entirely accurate?

Our interviews with families and our survey of the professional moral commitments of 1,035 marriage-family therapists suggest that this perception is limited. In addition, it is now necessary to distinguish therapy designed to uncover emotional difficulties from the use of therapeutic insights for education in communicative competence for marriages and families. The phrase "communicative competence" comes from the critical theory of Jürgen Habermas. It is used to speak of the communicative skills required for distortion-free dialogue to solve political conflicts without resort to force or manipulation.[1] The concept, however, applies equally well to communication in families. The big breakthrough in marriage therapy is the shift from attempting to solve the intrapsychic problems of troubled families to giving preparatory, preventative, and educational training in communicative competence or what we call *intersubjective dialogue.*

For the sake of convenience, we refer to the entire field—the psychodynamic and the new educative approaches—as therapy or the therapeutic. We do this because, in the present climate, the learnings from traditional therapy and the learnings relevant to good communication in marriage and family significantly overlap.

It is true that the psychotherapeutic culture of the twentieth century has had individualistic leanings and has reinforced individualistic social trends. But in marriage and family therapy, there is evidence that psychological intervention has moved from the older individualism toward a *relational ethic* or an ethic of *intersubjective dialogue.* The new psychologies of marriage and family may not command the moral language to express this ethic even if they increasingly have the expertise to help couples and families achieve it. In other words, we believe that the alleged therapeutic emphasis on individual needs does not exhaust the implications of psychological help for families. Moreover, among the multiple resources needed to sustain families in postmodern society, *the therapeutic has a limited but crucial role to play.*

Critics of the Therapeutic

Two prominent cultural studies, *Haven in a Heartless World* (1977), by Christopher Lasch, and *Habits of the Heart* (1985), by Robert Bellah, Richard Madsen, William Sullivan, Ann Swidler, and Steven Tipton, reflect disfavor, even antagonism, toward the therapeutic culture and its implications for family life.[2] With different methods and agendas, both books portray psychotherapeutic psychology as promoting an ethic of expressive individualism that leaves people unable to resolve family conflicts or enter into larger communities of moral discourse. But it is not only the individualistic therapeutic ethic that has hurt families; Lasch believes that the "so-called helping professions" have functioned to undermine the confidence of families.[3] These professions have unwittingly created a vicious cycle of dependency on external sources of expertise. They have declared families inept and invaded them with techniques and interventions that have eroded their capacity to help themselves. Most troubling, the interference of the "experts" vitiates parental authority and blocks moral development in children.

As a Marxist pleased with Freud's theory of personality but dismayed by its popular misuse, Lasch is something of a disenchanted modern elite. In both *Haven in a Heartless World* and *The Culture of Narcissism* (1983), he portrays popular psychology as one further mode of domination replacing parental, legal, and religious authority.[4] Indeed, the permissive society is more entrapping and dangerous than earlier forms of domination. Although Lasch only occasionally cites Philip Rieff's *Triumph of the Therapeutic* (1966), he is clearly influenced by his theory of the shift in moral authority from the medieval "religious man" to the nineteenth-century "economic man," and finally to the late–twentieth-century "psychological man."[5]

In Rieff's thinking, the restrained individualism of psychoanalysis vanquished the Protestant ethic of communal duty. But then, both Protestant and psychoanalytic forms of restraint were replaced by the regressive individualism of humanistic psychology. Lasch extends a Marxist version of Rieff's analysis to family life. He claims that consumerism plus a new class of educators, psychiatrists, and social workers have rendered families and private life passive, dependent, and sick—needful of the outside services of department stores, doctors, and therapists. The marketplace and the mental health professions have redefined and taken over problems formerly under the guidance of church and civil society. In the process, they have left families less able "to provide for their own needs without the supervision of trained experts."[6] Although Lasch wants new forms of authority and community, he sees institutional religion as having been co-opted by the therapeutic mentality and as mostly barren of resources. Therapists, he believes, do little more than perpetuate the values of consumption, personal fulfillment, and the "management" of interpersonal relationships—placing personal growth ahead of marital stability.

With much the same tone, the authors of *Habits of the Heart* undertake a cultural study of individualism and commitment, conducting qualitative interviews with approximately two hundred white middle-class Americans. They find self-fulfillment, autonomy, and self-reliance to be the "habits of the heart" permeating the lives of those they interview. They discover two closely related cultural types, the manager and the therapist. Both of these types pursue personal satisfaction, one in the utilitarian individualism of material success and the other in the expressive individualism of affective relationships.

They begin the book with portraits of four people. One is a therapist, Margaret Oldham. Margaret represents their central point: she puts "individual fulfillment higher than attachment to family and community" and believes the "most important thing in life is doing whatever you choose to do as well as you can." The good is that which yields the "most exciting challenge or the most good feeling" for oneself.[7] Both her portrait and the others illustrate a second point: people may possess values other than individualistic ones but lack the language to express the deeper commitments that drive their lives. Many people employ a mode of therapeutic reasoning that is "rooted in a nonsocial, noncultural conception of reality that provides remarkably little guidance beyond private life and intimate relations."[8]

With few exceptions, psychotherapy is portrayed as promoting individual self-involvement and self-sufficiency. The language of obligation and commitment are absent. Community is "something therapeutic language cannot really make sense of." Therapy's purpose is singular and narrow: to help people love themselves regardless of "anyone else's standards."[9]

This interpretation is both powerful and limited. It identifies a lack of language for broader relational and communal values that we also encountered in our interviews. Moreover, *Habits of the Heart* alerted the public to the moral dangers of a social model driven by the norm of self-satisfaction and gave words to something people were experiencing.

But the book's analysis of the culture of psychotherapy lacked sufficient nuance, concentrates too much on individual therapy, and may simply be somewhat out of date. The therapeutic model studied in *Habits of the Heart* is beholden to an older therapeutic theory associated with Carl Rogers and other so-called humanistic psychologists.[10] This framework was popular during the decades of the 1950s, 1960s, and 1970s, but it does not exhaust the range of contemporary therapeutic ideals. Furthermore, as we see below, Rogers's work was complex and had implications in several directions.

Moreover, even the interviews with Margaret Oldham and others require a more complicated analysis. Relationships, Margaret believes, require give-and-take; "not one person making all the sacrifice or one always giving—having a relative balance between what's the giving end and getting your own way." Similarly, in the portrait of Brian Palmer, the manager, we see that he is clearer than the authors seem willing to admit that his second marriage is better than his first precisely because it is "a totally reciprocal type of thing . . . founded on mutual respect, admiration, affection, the ability to give and receive freely."[11] Brian's language for love is limited to the language of reciprocity, but it does seem to go beyond simple individualism. He may be struggling to articulate a language of relationality and intersubjective equal regard that goes beyond the language of radical individualism.

From the perspective of our national survey of the professional ethics of marriage and family therapists, the argument of *Habits of the Heart* could be improved. Its reading of the culture of therapy is too narrow, its model of love gravitates toward strong *agape* with its overemphasis on self-sacrifice, and it overlooks how changes in gender roles and increased democratization in families require new capacities for communicative and dialogical competence as an adjunct of—not a substitute for—commitment.

The authors of *Habits of the Heart* write as though self-regard and regard for others are mutually exclusive. Christian norms of unselfish love and so-called therapeutic attitudes of self-love are placed on opposite ends of the moral spectrum.[12] They write as if the pursuit of one's own good always entails a denial of the good of the other and, inversely, as though commitment to the common good has within it no place for self-regard. While *Habits of the Heart* found its subjects groping for a better language to describe the relation between fulfillment and self-sacrifice in family and work, its authors provide a language that tilts moral obligation toward regard for the other with little room for an appropriate regard for self.

While Bellah and his colleagues are more optimistic than Lasch or Rieff about the resources of religion to subvert expressive individualism, the view of religion presented in *Habits of the Heart* associates it with the suppression of self-regard. The authors argue that America's churches and synagogues are its deepest religiocultural resource for repairing civic virtue, yet they are pessimistic that these institutions can perform the same service for the culture of therapy. Christian ethics has not influenced the therapies and probably will not do so. Because it denigrates therapeutic efforts to advance open communication and negotiation of love's duties within the family, some have seen in *Habits of the Heart* a nostalgia for bygone years when the family, especially women, modeled unselfishness, a time that disappeared when individualism entered family life. *Habits of the Heart* builds on Alexis de Tocqueville's concern that individualism might undermine democracy, but it obscures his concern with the evolution of equality *within* democracy.[13] While therapy has contributed to a heightened fascination with personal growth, it also has sought to enrich the communicative competence necessary for democracy within families.[14]

The egalitarian love between self-actualized persons critiqued in *Habits of the Heart* need not be "incompatible with self-sacrifice" merely because it seems so in certain psychological theories.[15] In our understanding of love as equal regard, a certain kind of self-assertion that therapy can sometimes inspire is absolutely essential to marital love. Furthermore, much of marital and family therapy encourages the expression of this self-assertion within the context of an intersubjective dialogue, a kind of dialogue that is now essential for marriages to hold within the context of fewer economic, social, and moral coercions—in short, within the context of the increasing democratization of marriages and families.

The Families

When asked in one of our interviews whether her marital therapy had a positive or negative influence on her family life, Tina Jones, a middle-aged mother of two living on the East Coast, cannot give a clear answer: "Kind of in between . . . not really . . . I mean hopefully positive. I guess it's been positive, it has been positive." She goes on to express her frustration with the neutrality of the counselor whom she and her husband had seen for almost a year. She wishes the counselor would "take more of a stand on things" and say, 'Look, you can't behave in this manner and expect . . .' Tina had hoped, it seems, that therapy would provide a moral environment capable of condemning or at least confronting both the physical assault and the sexual betrayal she had experienced because of her husband.

Tina Jones

On the other hand, Kate Knutsen, who a year prior to the interview was "really thinking about ending" her marriage, found therapy a "wonderful experience" that led her husband and her to "really rededicate ourselves to the marriage." Therapy enhanced conversation about shared family values and effectively became an arena of moral discourse. They had fought since the first years of marriage about money and raising their three children. Counseling "clarified our values." "Where we might have been more polarized with regard to our attitudes about things, we both moved closer to the middle and closer to each other."

Kate Knutsen

This was also true for Sarah Miles. Early on, a marital therapist had helped save her marriage. He gave Sarah and her husband basic skills: "He taught us how to negotiate with each other . . . how to talk to each other, how important it is for people to have a sense of gratitude to each other." The counselor modeled two essential values: care and hope. Although therapy involves extensive personal reflection, its implications need not remain simply individualistic. Here is how Sarah puts it: "It's improved my marriage unquestionably in that I work from a base of much more love and acceptance and I'm getting better and better and better at it and I see this as the goal—accepting myself and accepting Frank as he is and loving him." The language of "accepting Frank as he is" may not adequately capture the complexity of intersubjective equal regard, but it points to the importance of equal respect as one component. It raises the question, What is an adequate language for describing helpful marital education and therapy?

Sarah Miles

Our interviewees fell on a continuum from those who thought that therapy had little relevance to those who found it provided missing skills of intersubjective dialogue and understanding. At one extreme, one interviewer became almost unable to listen to a young man because of his "driving need to expound on therapeutic theories of family life." In his desperate exploitation of psychological language to fill the gaps in his empty moral and religious world, Tom Williams, a "househusband" with two children, fits well the character type captured by *Habits of the Heart*. Despite family messages he had received since childhood that only the sick seek therapy, in only three months of individual counseling Tom had been converted to new psychological norms for daily life, wishing that he could convert his workaholic wife from the values of professional success and consumerism. Alongside the imperative of emotional availability, the primary value therapy taught him was "a real honest inner sense of loving yourself regardless of what you are" and "a sense of independence."

Tom's endorsement of psychological advice goes hand-in-hand with his rejection of a strict Catholic upbringing where self-love was seldom "spoken about in my family" and guilt, fear, and corporal punishment reinforced rigid ideas about salvation and damnation. His desire to create a parental environment where anything goes is the inverse of his childhood experience of cold "barriers and . . . guilt and all that negative stuff." While he still has his seven-year-old and ten-year-old in Catholic catechism once a week, his rationale is vague. He dimly connects their religious education to "a part of the tradition," but his primary motive is simply his desire that they "believe in God" or a "power greater than us." When they are "old enough," they "don't need to go to church." All this is colored by his own negative memories of the presence of religion: "I don't want them to get crazy about it like I was, and my brothers and sisters were. We were just afraid to make a move because we were going to be struck down and go to hell. That was the fear that religion gave us back then."

Tom Williams

————————

The Turners, Mary Murphy, and Maria Taylor are closer to the opposite end of the spectrum from Tom Williams. Psychotherapeutic psychology becomes more peripheral, and reliance upon religious tradition comes to the forefront. Mary Murphy has never sought therapy, although one of her sons has. She isn't sure whether it has been a positive or negative influence on his marriage. The Turners know of counselors in only a secondhand way, including one story about a "primal scream" therapist who seems only to have helped a couple move toward divorce. Maria Taylor's closest experience of marriage counseling is her pastor, and that was "before I got married and that is all." As with other aspects of his life, Richard Good simply has never thought much about counseling, apart perhaps from his wife's work as an abortion counselor in the mid-1970s.

The National Survey of Therapists

Our national survey of 1,035 therapists, done in cooperation with Professor Thomas Needham of the Fuller Graduate School of Psychology, shows a more complicated self-perception of the ethical sensibilities of marital and family therapists than that suggested by *Habits of the Heart*.[16] They see themselves as far less individualistic in their philosophy of life than social critics have charged them with being. The partial truth, however, of the critic's view may be this: they are more divided in their professional ethics than in their general moral philosophy, and many focus on adult family relations and give less attention to the needs of children.

Our questionnaire included thirty basic questions, with several subitems for each question. It covered both general demographic information and attitudes about religion, morality, and family life. The latter included views about the moral life in general and about specific issues such as divorce, gender roles, and family forms. We mailed questionnaires to a random national sample of 2,500 therapists and we received 1,035 completed questionnaires representing seven professional organizations, with the largest number from members of the American Association of Marriage and Family Therapy. All respondents devote a significant portion of their time to marriage and family counseling. Their professional identifications were as follows: psychology (21.8 percent), social work (21 percent), pastoral counseling (20.9 percent), psychiatry (15.3 percent) and marriage and family therapy (13.8 percent). Forty percent identified themselves as mainline Protestant, 9.3 percent indicated no religious orientation, and the others were Catholic, Jewish, Evangelical, Quaker, Universalist, members of Eastern religions, or of New Age and other orientations. Respondents were 55.8 percent male and 43.2 percent female. Sixty-six percent had been married once, 26.2 percent two to four times. A majority (86.3 percent) had biological children, adopted children, or stepchildren.

Some of the questions presented classical options from the history of moral philosophy in an effort to measure the general moral attitudes of our respondents. The survey does not report how therapists themselves talk about their ethics; instead, it reveals the kinds of moral language they tend to affirm or reject.

One finding in particular surprised us. We went into the survey expecting to find in therapists' self-understanding the belief in self-actualization that had been critiqued by Rieff, Lasch, and Bellah. We found, instead, that only a small percentage (13.6) identified the good moral life with "being true to the unfolding potential of one's inner self." This view for the moral life was about as popular as "following the will of a higher power" (12.2 percent). Instead, two other markedly more "relational" positions won the majority of votes: the good life is either "creating and fostering loving and caring relations" (37.2 percent) or "acting toward others as you would ideally wish them to act toward you" (22.0 percent). These responses are "relational" in that they emphasize either the affective or the formal properties of intersubjectivity, the back-and-forth that takes place *between* individuals and binds them together. The fact that only a small percentage (2.1 percent) chose the utilitarian ethic of "doing the most for the largest number of people" might be due to the restriction of therapists' moral horizons to smaller groupings of people.

Marriage and family therapists seem to gravitate in their general philosophy toward an ethic that mediates between the two dominant moral viewpoints found in the literature of marriage and family therapy: an ethic of individual autonomy and an ethic that emphasizes the good of the entire family system. For convenience, we call their philosophy an *ethic of relationality*. This ethic emphasizes neither the good of individuals nor the good of the family as a whole. Rather it aims toward mutual, empathic, and caring bonds of relationship *between* family members. According to these data, the widespread charge that therapists are driven by an ethic of individualism seems overstated.

We saw this emphasis on relationality again when respondents were asked to rank five possible purposes of families. The therapists ranked lowest the contention that families are "for the individual members." Significantly, neither were "having and socializing children" or "affirming gender and sexuality" placed first. Instead 56 percent chose highly relational language, with "mutual support and practical helpfulness" ranked first. Thirty-one percent ranked "friendship and sharing" second. Finally, when asked how they handle divorce, only 2.4 percent "often recommend divorce when it is psychologically best for the individuals"—an answer that is surprisingly at odds with the portrait of therapists painted in much social criticism. A strikingly higher percent than often presumed are "committed to preserving marriage and avoiding divorce whenever possible" (33.3 percent). And 56 percent are more conservative about divorce when children are involved.

Our study suggests, however, that therapists experience some contradiction between their general philosophy and the ethics of their professional practice. Claims about the moral life in general do not have a one-to-one correspondence with professional priorities. When asked about the commitments informing their marriage and family counseling, the respondents were split between seeking the good of the individual and the good of the family. The highest percentage of therapists chose "to work for the greatest good for the family as a whole" (37.5 percent), with 31.6 percent choosing "to work for the good of the individuals of the family." This difference may be due to the fact that this group of questions did not contain a mediating option with the language of "loving and caring relations." Although therapists may emphasize individual values somewhat more in their practice than they do in their general philosophy of life, many of them emphasize the good of the whole family even more, once again suggesting that individualism as such is not dominant in either their general philosophy or their professional practice.

Another interesting split occurred between those who reported believing some family forms are better for children than others (58.6 percent) and those who do not (41.3 percent). Similarly, on the one hand only 3.6 percent of the respondents reported a belief in the need for a strong gender role differentiation between males and females, and 50.8 percent affirmed an "equality" and "flexibility" between men and women that still acknowledges that they are not "equally well suited for all roles." On the other hand, on a question that connected gender roles to childrearing, 43.3 percent ranked "traditional working fathers and stay-at-home mothers" as the best health-promoting form for children. Dual-income families came in a close second (31.2 percent). Both were rated higher than blended families, gay and lesbian couples, and single parents. It is important to remember here that the 41.3 percent who did not believe any particular family form is intrinsically superior did not respond to the question ranking family forms and likely includes those most supportive of two-income households, single parents, gay and lesbian parents, and blended families. Finally, when it comes to handling divorce in counseling, a majority of the therapists still fell back on an analytic attitude of impartiality. A majority (61.2 percent) said they are "neutral on divorce and do what is best from a therapeutic point of view." Yet, as we saw above, very few perceive themselves as actively promoting divorce.

These findings suggest that the thesis put forward by Rieff, Lasch, and Bellah about the individualism of therapists must be qualified. Therapists are primarily interested in an egalitarian "relationality" that balances meeting the needs of individuals with preserving the family, and they are working on building the communicative competence needed to promote this relationality. When we thought about these data in light of the therapeutic theories reviewed below, we concluded that our respondents were groping to express an ethic of *equal regard conceived intersubjectively.* This is probably what good marriage-family therapy and education are mainly about.

This ethic is a slender but very important part of a total ethic for marriage and family. It needs to be enriched by an ethic of commitment and self-giving and deepened by a theory of the determinate premoral goods of life that marriages and families help actualize, for example, the goods of procreation, parental certainty, sexual exchange, and mutual helpfulness. An ethic of intersubjective equal regard cannot adjudicate when conflicts arise between premoral goods that families organize. True, intersubjective dialogue helps couples arrive at more satisfactory ways of communicating about these goods, but we should not confuse the communicative process with these goods as such. Therapists may sometimes make this mistake. Communicative competence is a great human good, but it is not the *only* good at stake. Hence, an ethic of relationality and intersubjective dialogue cannot in itself provide complete answers to important issues about family form, the needs of children, and the responsibilities of parents. The liberal religious and political mind—partly under the influence of the therapies—may overemphasize the qualitative aspects of human communication at the exclusion of other important goods. Nonetheless, an ethic of intersubjective equal regard is an important part of the total picture.

Our Gallup survey also throws light on the goals of most therapists. Therapists may be intending to help people develop mutual communicative behaviors, not just beliefs that mutuality is good. In general, people tend to report relatively high degrees of satisfaction with their present intimate relations. Our survey shows that people who *believe* that mutuality correlates with a good marriage are in the majority, and they also tend to be highly satisfied with their intimate relationships. But those who value *behaving* with mutuality to solve conflicts have even higher satisfactions with their intimate relationships (see table 5). People who are predominantly "sacrificers" in their behavior are modestly more inclined to be extremely satisfied than those who chose one of the other models, but people who think they *behave* mutually are significantly more likely to report satisfaction than those who chose one of the other models (by 6.7 points). Therapists may be in the business of equipping their clients with communicative *behaviors* that make it more possible for them to implement their belief in mutuality. Those who solve conflicts to promote their individual good are significantly less likely to report satisfaction than those who chose one of the other models (by 6.1 percentage points).

But critics of therapy are partially correct. Marital and family therapists are adult-centered and tend to be neutral or individualistic on divorce.

Table 5. Correlation of Those Reporting Extreme Partner Satisfaction with Their Preferred Model of Love Measured as a Behavior and Belief*

Models of Love Correlating with Good Marriages	Behavioral Measure		Belief Measure	
	For All Respondents	For Those Exremely Satisfied	For All Respondents	For Those Extremely Satisfied
Mutuality	45.0	51.7	54.8	54.3
Self-Sacrifice	28.2	20.0	37.9	40.0
Individual Self-Fulfillment	13.4	7.3	4.7	4.3

Numbers represent percentages.

They are, however, more cautious about divorce when children are involved, especially female therapists, who are 3 to 12 percent more likely to be cautious in this situation than their male counterparts. Oddly, though, female pastoral counselors are 8 percent less likely to be cautious about divorce when children are involved than their male counterparts. It is also surprising to see that pastoral counselors are the least cautious of all the therapeutic professions about divorce when children are involved—nearly 25 percentage points less cautious than psychiatrists, who are the most cautious.[17] Although our survey does not explain these variations, they are worth noting as we explore the implications of religion for divorce.

Therapeutic Theory and the Family

When the authors of *Habits of the Heart* wrote about therapy, they had in mind primarily "neo-Freudian, Rogersian, Gestalt, interactionist and humanist therapists."[18] There is no doubt that psychological theories, particularly as shaped by such psychologists as Carl Rogers, contributed to a social milieu in which self-fulfillment became the guiding criteria for evaluating marriage, sexuality, divorce, and family life with children. In the 1960s and 1970s, many psychological theorists saw social institutions, like families and churches, establishing "conditions of worth," to use Rogers's term, that submerged personal emotions and self-knowledge under rigid, distorted, external demands that hampered self-development. When Rogers attempted an essay on the implications of client-centered therapy for family life in the early 1960s, he contended that family life should have the same goal as therapy—"facilitating each member of the family in the process of discovering, and becoming, himself."[19]

Nowhere does the ethic of individualism find clearer expression than in the American Psychological Association's (APA) official moral guidelines for therapists. The APA's 1981 *Ethical Principles of Psychologists* begins with this sentence: "Psychologists respect the dignity and worth of the individual and strive for the preservation and protection of fundamental human rights."[20] Other APA ethical guidelines offer similar language.[21] Few would dispute, of course, that individuals, even in family therapy, deserve respect for their personal needs and worth. The problem, however, is that the language of ethical individualism is too thin to express the commitments individuals have to the affective ties binding them together.

Psychotherapy, however, seldom had the kind of singularity of voice that its social critics portrayed. At least six movements in psychotherapy have modified the ethic of individualism operative in early therapeutic approaches. These six movements were (1) evidence in Rogers himself of an emphasis on intersubjective communication, (2) the advent of object-relations theory, (3) the turn toward marriage and family education, (4) the critique of therapy by feminist theorists, (5) the emergence of family systems theorists, and (6) the spreading influence of religiously oriented therapists.

Intersubjectivity and the "Reflection" in Therapy

There are two parts of Rogersian psychotherapy, its theory of personality and its theory of psychotherapeutic change. Its theory of personality contains an individualistic view of human fulfillment. But tucked away in its theory of psychotherapeutic change is a deep insight into the nature of intersubjective dialogue and communicative competence. This is its theory of the psychotherapeutic "reflection," a therapeutic response by the therapist designed to convey to the client that her or his words and emotions were being understood.[22]

The therapeutic reflection was the butt of thousands of jokes in comic strips and at coffee klatches and cocktail parties. "If I understand you," the therapist was depicted as saying, "you feel your husband constantly ignores you and this angers you." The therapeutic reflection communicated to the client that her words and feelings were being understood or, at least, that a genuine effort was being made to understand them. To advance understanding, the therapeutic reflection allowed the client to test and refine this understanding. For instance, the client might correct the therapist by saying, "No, not quite. That's close. But it is more that I *wish* that it angered me. I wonder why I simply *accept* the fact that he ignores me, especially when we're with other people." The therapist might say in turn, "Oh, what's disturbing you is that you *don't* get angry, yet you somehow think that you *should*." Within the boundaries of the therapeutic hour, the client experiences a *structured* attempt by another to understand her empathically, enjoys the right to correct that understanding, comes to understand herself better in relation to others, learns to formulate more clearly what she is trying to say, and experiences another person affirming both her *and* the communicative process that is going on.

The therapeutic reflection crystallized a part of what goes into intersubjective communicative competence. It permitted the development of a community of understanding between client and therapist. Gradually the client learned skills in expressing feelings and attitudes, learned to understand herself as she was being understood, learned to apply this understanding process to the feelings and attitudes of others, learned to communicate understanding in return to them, and gradually learned to communicate and understand better both self and other. In many types of therapy, she learned to do this with more *equal respect and regard* for self and other. But, and this is the real point, she learned to show equal respect and regard *communicatively or intersubjectively.* This means that clients go beyond abstractly espousing equal regard and learn to practice communicating this regard, understanding the claims of both other and self, testing that both actually experience being understood, and creating through this process a *lived reality* of love as equal regard.

For instance, if the therapy were ethically structured so that the client was led to treat the other (for instance, his wife) as he was being treated, a man could learn to say what he wanted to say, allow his wife to say what she wanted to say, learn to understand his wife's claims, learn to have this understanding corrected and deepened, learn to communicate this understanding to the other, learn to allow the other to communicate her understanding of him so that both could come to know that they can speak, be understood, and confirm that they are understood—all this concerning their most fundamental needs, hopes, and moral projects. This process then becomes an important part of what we mean by the love ethic of intersubjective equal regard, even though equal regard involves much more than adequate communication.

In individual therapy, however, this process could only be rehearsed. It happened incompletely between therapist and client and only implicitly between client and the absent partner. The other persons in the client's life—fiancé, spouse, parent, lover—were there only in imagination. In new approaches—couples, family therapy, educational—*the other partners in the dialogue are there. Hence work on real intersubjective dialogue and equal regard can take place.*

Object-Relations Theory
and Couples Therapy

We have claimed that human beings are embodied selves. They bring their species tendencies—including their asymmetrical reproductive strategies—into interaction with others and with the respective histories in which they all stand. This interaction process begins in infancy. Gradually an interaction process *between* infant and parents gets internalized in the psychological makeup of the growing infant. This process is highly pertinent for understanding how communication in marriage and families works and how skilled intersubjective communicative competence develops.

According to psychologists Jay R. Greenberg and Stephen Mitchell, with the growing importance of what is known as object relations in psychoanalytic theory, a major paradigm shift occurred in contemporary psychotherapeutic theory and practice. In place of Freud's model in which relations with others were understood as depending on how instinctual needs were satisfied or frustrated, a new model arose in which relations themselves, rather than the simple rise and fall of frustrated libidinal tensions, were understood as the fundamental building blocks of mental life.[23]

Melanie Klein, W. R. D. Fairbairn, Harry Guntrip, and D. W. Winnicott made important contributions to the new theory of object relations. We agree with Guntrip in seeing many of the values of object-relations thinking exemplified in the psychology of Erik Erikson.[24] Erikson believes that our inner psychological world is an internalization of our bodily *modes* (for example, incorporation, retention, elimination) and analogous interpersonal *modalities* of interacting with others (for example, receiving, getting, taking, intruding).[25] It is not instinctual satisfactions or frustrations alone that determine psychological meaning; it is more the interpersonal mode in which these satisfactions occur that creates psychological significance. Furthermore, these patterns of interaction can center on lower-order bodily needs, including what Erikson argues is our phylogenetically grounded need to be "recognized" by another.[26] The work of psychologists René Spitz and Robert White and Erikson's own work led him to believe that our need to be treated as an end, to be recognized, to be shown an affirming face, to be responded to, is not just a socially conditioned and historically relative construction; it is a evolutionarily grounded need. Theologians would say that this need is a consequence of the handiwork of God in the depths of creation.

Object-relations theory and evolutionary ecology come together around the concept of bodily modes and interpersonal modalities, which get abstracted from their immediate context, become internalized into our psychological structure, and then set up our fund of expectations about our interpersonal relations. This understanding of embodied relational selfhood has profound implications for our understanding of the selves that people bring to marriages and families. Our selves are internalizations of embodied patterns of interpersonal interaction. Humans are simultaneously social and biological creatures from the beginning. Communication is embodied speech. When we decide to trust a person in either business, marriage, or bed, we look to see how word and body interrelate—how the words of love and trust correspond to bodily gestures conveying relaxation, calmness, and steadiness. Intersubjective communication is made up of how our embodied speech and the other's embodied speech coordinate into a larger system of interaction and then become internalized into our respective psychological expectations and meanings.

The shift to object-relations theory has enhanced our understanding of the social nature of our embodied selfhood. In the past decade or so, several theorists have begun to emphasize a new model of human development. Psychologists as divergent as Heinz Kohut, John Bowlby, Daniel Stern, and Jean Baker Miller all adhere to the notion that human growth does not involve so much a movement from dependence to independence as a movement from immature dependencies to more mature dependencies and attachments. Development entails learning more and more sophisticated modes of relating. Stern, for example, combines both observation of children and object-relations theory to argue that early development "is not primarily devoted to . . . independence or autonomy or individuation—that is, getting away and free from the primary caregiver. It is equally devoted to the seeking and creating of intersubjective union with another."[27] This intersubjective union is built around the need for recognition and affirmation of the self. Authentic individual development, as Miller asserts, proceeds "*only* by means of affiliation."[28]

Even if the new object-relations theory still lacks a fully developed moral language of commitments beyond the self and leaves questions of social responsibilities vaguely defined, it does direct attention to interpersonal dynamics and questions individualistic views of the self. Moreover, public receptivity for the practical outcomes of a more relational theory has been high. Some of the popular couples and marriage therapies have made good use of both object-relations theory and the older Rogersian therapeutic reflection. They have brought the two together in a virtual training program in intersubjective communicative competence.

Several theorists could be reviewed in this context, particularly the work of Harville Hendrix, John Gottman, and Howard Markman,[29] but we confine ourselves primarily to the work of Harville Hendrix as an example of this trend. Hendrix, founder of the Institute for Relationship Therapy, has captured national attention with his proposals on strengthening marital relationships. It is not surprising, however, to discover that his eclectic approach essentially brings object-relational views of human development together with the Rogersian reflection. What is unique is that he brings these two sources to the concrete situation of couples in face-to-face communication. Although the title of his best-selling *Getting the Love You Want* (1988) seems to play on the lure of self-interest, the book actually protests psychology's individualism and attempts a step-by-step exploration of the intricacies of male-female marital relationships and communicative patterns.

Hendrix's book sprang from his need to understand the failure of his first marriage. Our selection of marriage partners, he discovered, is still determined by parents, although now in terms of unconscious needs rather than older customs of arranged marriages. The intensity of one's initial romantic attraction to another is complicated. It is a direct result of the unconscious need to recapitulate the positive and compensate for the negative aspects of one's relation to parents. In short, our inner psychological world is an internalization of these parental object relations, and we project them back on our marriages. Hendrix would not deny that mate selection evolves around some of the core values discussed above—reproductive interests, sexual exchange, mutual helpfulness, interpersonal affirmation, or friendship—but these needs are expressed through an unconscious search for someone who compensates for the predominant interpersonal flaws of those who raised us and who may have the potential to heal them. If this is true, then marriage is destined to reinjure sensitive childhood wounds, that is, old and inadequate object-relation patterns and modes of intersubjective communication. Hence divorce, under the uncoerced modern marital arrangements of today, is almost unavoidable: the disappointments are nearly inevitable, but there are today few internal tools available to manage them, and few external structures that support marriage.

This also means that marriage has unique healing potential. It has this potential precisely *because* it unites spouses with persons who resemble older patterns of interaction that each had with their parents. Ironically, the particular needs of the spouse are what attract, provoke, and potentially heal one's own childhood wounds. Marriage then becomes a crucible drawing together two people uniquely equipped to irritate yet spark growth in each other. There is no other way, therefore, to secure marital stability than to disentangle both individuals from the bonds of old disappointments and destructive expectations. Turning an unconscious marriage into a "conscious marriage" depends on gaining communicative competence in understanding and expressing not only one's own needs but the typical patterns used to communicate them. At the same time, one must understand not only what the needs of the other are but more specifically how the other communicates them. Divorce, Hendrix argues, is often a poor answer to marital conflict. Unless the unconscious desires and patterns that motivate dysfunctional communication are understood, a second marriage will repeat them.

Engaged couples often do not give careful consideration to the complex dynamics of their past and present relationships, waiting until marriage to take a closer look. If they like what they see, they stay; if they don't, they move on. Hendrix's training in communicative competence is designed to counter this tendency. But in the horizons of his educational and therapeutic model, we found more than techniques for learning communicative competence. We discovered at least two ideas with moral and religious roots: (1) an implicit ethic of equal regard, and

(2) the "old-fashioned idea, commitment" to one's partner in the hard work of marriage.

First, implicit in this communicative process, but seldom identified, is an ethic of equal regard modeled by the therapist-trainer. Mutual respect is the trainer's highest value; everywhere and always the leader is helping couples learn how to communicate respect for the selfhood and dignity of the other—indeed, an *equal* respect. Within this respect and only after it is secure (only after each partner feels "safe"), the workshops help couples gain the communicative competence to negotiate about more specific and sometimes conflicting goods and needs. The implicit message structured into the workshop is that each partner's individual needs are important. But even *more* important than the specific needs of each member of the couple is the deeper obligation to show respect for the selfhood of both other and self. Specific needs are subordinate to the dignity, respect, and safety of both partners.[30] This principle, as we will see in chapter 10, gets close to our understanding of love as equal regard that subordinates the *ordo bonorum* (the order of specific premoral goods and needs) to the *ordo caritatis* (the formal requirement to treat the other as an end and never as a means only).

Second, Hendrix *assumes* the importance of commitment in marriages and in successful work with couples. He writes that a "conscious" marriage requires a "commitment to healing our partners through unconditional giving."[31] John Gottman, whose model of intervention is simpler, more scientific, yet less imaginative, believes that following his steps requires "vigilance and commitment."[32] Howard Markman and his associates distinguish between forced commitments brought about by financial necessity or social pressure and "personal dedication, the intrinsic desire . . . not only to continue in the relationship but also to improve it, sacrifice for it, invest in it, link personal goals to it, and seek the partner's welfare, not simply one's own."[33] Our point is this: all of these programs, which hope to enhance the communicative competence of couples and families, *assume* a prior commitment that the therapies themselves cannot provide. They all assume a culture that takes marriage and families seriously. They assume culturally available ideas of commitment and self-giving needed to renew commitment. *All of these programs depend on religiocultural capital that they do not account for and that require a religious and theological examination to uncover and renew.*

The crux of Hendrix's contribution is his spelling out in small step-by-step exercises the constructive means to achieve genuine intersubjective dialogue. One might say that this combination of education and therapy creates in couples some of the habits of the heart, at least in families, that *Habits of the Heart* finds lacking. The total gestalt of Hendrix's work may illustrate why therapists ranked an ethic of relationality highly in our questionnaire. Good marriages require a committed practice of care that situates a depth of self-knowledge in constant dialogue with the other and sensitivity to the other's unresolved childhood needs. Hendrix's portrait of a good marriage begins with novelist Pearl Buck's rendition of the Golden Rule: "The answer is to be found . . . in the mutual discovery, by two who marry, of the deepest need of the other's personality, and the satisfaction of that need."[34]

Hendrix's therapeutic practice helps couples actualize this moral principle. His workshops are full of "structured" exercises designed to help couples learn "listening" and "reflecting" from the other's point of view. They give couples skills in "mirroring"—without interruption, challenge, or defensiveness—the claims, complaints, frustrations, and needs of the other. These exercises constitute training in the communication of empathic regard for the other as an end. The nuances of Hendrix's exercises reveal minute routines that enhance mutuality and equal regard as a background to meeting more specific interests of the respective partners. In essence, what Hendrix attempts to enhance through a series of practical communicative strategies is an intersubjective and dialogical expression of the Golden Rule and the principle of neighbor love as they work themselves out in premarital and marital relations. Hendrix, however, goes beyond a communicative ethic for the internal life of marriage and family. He believes that a central characteristic of a fully conscious marriage is the ability to reach out to others. The "capacity of love and healing that they have created within the marriage is now available for others." The "humble path of marriage" is one of the "surest routes" to an essential connection to the rest of the world.[35] The analogy of love works, as it did for Thomas Aquinas, from the intersubjective love within the marriage outward to the rest of the world. Key connections to the wider community are lost at times because of Hendrix's heightened focus on intrapsychic and interpersonal dynamics, but the family's contribution to the common good comes back into the picture. In Hendrix's move from youth evangelist in South Georgia to marital therapist in upper Manhattan, he has not completely lost his religious hopes. His therapy reflects not so much a secular replacement of religion by psychology as a transformation of key religious ideas into the intersubjective world of premarital and marital communicative competence.

The new educational-therapeutic communicative programs of leaders like Hendrix, Gottman, and Markham are a small but important part of reconstructing a critical marriage culture. Still, too much can be made of them. They can raise unrealistic expectations about the therapeutic or

emotional value of marriage. They probably will not help severely dysfunctional couples. They set aside issues of economics, work, race, gender, market, and government with their respective implications for
marriage and family. But they do illustrate a crucial resource for the
future—a way to envision the implementation of an intersubjective
love ethic of equal regard.

Feminist Theory
and the Therapeutic

When Lasch complains that post-Freudian theorists have lost sight
of Freud's insights into the connections between biology and culture,
he assumes that biology dictates certain forms of paternal authority,
specifically the authority of the father. Jessica Benjamin in *The Bonds of
Love* (1988) considers biology—at least the nature of human desire—
but arrives at different conclusions about the grounds of parental authority. Her work is of particular interest for one main reason: *it
provides one of the first attempts to understand the developmental and intersubjective foundations of mutuality*. It also provides a developmental
theory of why both parental self-regard and other regard are needed for
the development in the child of a rigorous capacity for mutuality. She
provides psychoanalytic warrants for parental partnership in place of
the ideal of an all-giving mother and an industrious, absent, and authoritative father.

Benjamin argues that mutuality is not a peaceful, easy-to-attain psychological state. Rather it demands sustaining a difficult balance between assertion of self and recognition of the other. The decisive
problem in early pre-oedipal development, she argues, is the paradox of
the infant's need to both assert herself and admit dependency on the
other (generally the mother) to recognize this self-assertion. The process
of differentiation is "necessarily contradictory" because the establishment of self as self-asserting necessarily requires the recognition of the
other. This, in turn, means that the self must finally "acknowledge the
other as existing for *him*self and not just for me." What Benjamin calls
"*mutual* recognition"—the need to recognize the other as well as be recognized by the other—"is what so many theories of the self have
missed."[36]

This psychodynamic is further complicated by social constructions of
parenting. Fathers adopt the assertive side of parenting while mothers
take the position of supporter, nurturer, and source of recognition. A
tension that occurs *within* persons is thus turned into a conflict *between*
men and women. When the mother functions as sole source of attach-

ment and the father as the primary source of agency and liberation, fundamental intrapsychic schisms between male independence and female sacrifice occur in early development. This makes it difficult, if not impossible, for girls and boys to develop the capacity for genuine mutuality. Moreover, the relegation of nurture to the private sphere and instrumental rationality to the public realm simply replicates this intrapsychic split on a social level. Hence current problems for families, Benjamin believes, are not in any simple sense the result of the loss of authority and privacy (Lasch) or individualism (Bellah, et al.). Instead, the "deep source of discontent in our culture is . . . gender polarity" and its consequences.[37]

Benjamin's solution includes but reaches beyond psychoanalytic insight and calls for a new vision of parenting. To reverse the domination of the self-assertive male and work toward mutuality, we must "get out of the antithesis between mother and father."[38] Specifically, to provide the recognition the child seeks, the mother must claim a "subjectivity," a sense of self, that is centered outside the child. The mother must have an identity that is not confined to the role of motherhood as such. For mothers to acquire this new selfhood, fathers must become active parental figures with whom girls can identify. They must also model for their sons a genuine respect for the subjectivity of their mothers. In essence, Benjamin creates a compelling argument for the developmental and intersubjective perspective on a love ethic of mutuality and equal regard. She writes,

> The problem of woman's desire has led us to the missing father. But to restore this father means to challenge the whole gender structure in which mother and father have mutually exclusive roles. Although I have stressed the girl's need for her father, this father can be used satisfactorily only by a girl who also draws a sense of self from her mother. . . . When mother and father (in reality and as cultural ideals) are not equal, the parental identifications will necessarily oppose each other.[39]

The split can be repaired only when each parent operates as a figure of both separation *and* attachment for the children, providing an example of integration rather than complementarity.

Benjamin's proposals reflect the momentous impact of two classic works of feminist theorists before her, Nancy Chodorow's *Reproduction of Mothering* (1978) and Carol Gilligan's *In a Different Voice* (1982). Although neither is immediately identified with creating a new family ethic, both develop psychological theories that—along with those of Benjamin, of other feminist theorists, and of family systems thinking noted briefly below— dramatically reshape thinking on the family on several counts. They (1) force psychological theory to consider the social construction of gender and sexual inequality, arguing for the importance of an equal division of power and labor for human development and family life, (2) identify how female relational thinking and acting has been labeled "immature" when judged by male norms of adulthood, thereby rendering parental activities less than fully "adult," (3) advance a woman-centered critique of individualism and a positive valuation of dependency, endurance, connection, affectivity, and relationality, leading to a reappraisal of the role of these values in responsible parenting, and (4) initiate woman- and mother-centered explorations of motherhood and fatherhood.

According to Chodorow, motherhood and fatherhood are not biologically or naturally determined roles. "Women come to mother because they have been mothered by women. By contrast, that men are mothered by women reduces their parenting capacities."[40] When only women mother, daughters identify with the same-sex parent and struggle to establish a sufficiently individuated and autonomous self, while sons engage in defensive assertion of ego boundaries, repress emotional needs, and struggle instead with attachment and intimacy. Intrapsychically and cross-culturally, the more father-absence and distance, the more severe the boy's conflicts concerning fear of women and assertion of masculinity. In turn, women and mothers are devalued, and the very requirements for good parenting are lost. Primary parenting must be shared. Although Chodorow underestimates the difficulty of bringing this about and mostly ignores the biological complications of pregnancy, birth, and nursing, her argument is convincing that parenting or mothering qualities can and must be created in men. Unless they are, families will continue to repeat patterns destructive to their very survival and the sustenance of community.

While Chodorow provides psychoanalytical and sociological grounding for the position that the sexes can and should parent equally, Gilligan's narrower focus on moral development reconfigures the internal ethic of care that ought to govern family life. Although she largely ignores social and political influences on morality, she uses empirical research on women's responses to moral dilemmas to propose a reconception of moral development that recognizes for both sexes the importance of the connection between self and other. Building on Chodorow, Gilligan identifies old conflicts between ideals of adulthood and womanhood that jeopardize sound models of parenthood. New ideals of mature parenthood mean enacting, by fathers *and* mothers, *both* care (the meeting of needs and the actualization of premoral goods) *and* justice (the fair ordering of these goods). This is close in meaning to our understanding of love as equal regard. The most advanced moral

self, Gilligan argues, is neither egoistically concerned for itself nor lost
in its concern for the other. Rather the moral imperative is "to act responsibly toward self and others and thus to sustain connection."[41] To
move to this more integrated stage of moral development that recognizes the mutual interdependency of self and other, women often require a powerful moment of choice such as meaningful productive work
or authority in reproductive decisions to offset their propensity toward
self-loss. Men, on the other hand, need pivotal experiences of intimacy
such as responsibility for the minutiae of daily childcare or acute sensitivity to a partner's needs to offset tendencies toward self-isolation.

Family Systems Theory

Alongside feminist and object-relations theory, family systems therapy also undermines the charge that therapy is incurably individualistic. Innovations in family therapy that modified the older individualism
began in the early 1960s. In the words of systems theorists Salvador
Minuchin and Charles Fishman, the goal of therapy shifted from realizing individual potential to helping "family members experience their belonging to an entity that is larger than the individual self."[42] In contrast
to giving psychological priority to the individual, the family system approach brings the processes, patterns, and interactions of larger systems
to the foreground. The individual is neither solely a member of a family
nor solely autonomous but a being-in-relation. Any view that individuals are constituted by and responsible to their systemic environments
can hardly be accused of fostering individualism. Because its basic
premise is the interconnection of all phenomena, systems-oriented family therapy has pushed beyond the boundaries of the therapeutic session
to consideration of the social systems that inevitably affect the family.

Some systems theorists have been inspired by their awareness of how
religious systems shape families. Evan Imber-Black begins her book
Families and Larger Systems (1988) by writing,

> My own fascination with families and larger systems reaches back
> to growing up in a family where the larger systems of synagogue
> and Jewish service organizations blended into the daily lives of my
> father . . . and my mother, . . . shaping our family's organization
> and relationships to the outside world.[43]

In reality her systems approach to family therapy carries her into what
we call the institutions of civil society. She wants to build a process by
which helping professionals can interact with families as members of a
common civil society with the goal of improving the well-being of individuals, families, and their supporting institutions. In fact, in her stance

as a family therapist, she is interested in remedying the very domination of the family by market and state that Alan Wolfe, Christopher Lasch, and Jürgen Habermas have exposed.

In a tenth-anniversary edition of *The Family Therapy Networker* it is observed that since its earliest inception the concepts of family systems have permeated public consciousness, influencing "hundreds of grass-roots programs based in schools, churches, hospitals and public and private agencies aimed at strengthening families by building stronger community networks."[44] From our perspective, the family systems approach has formulated at the level of therapeutic intervention much of what goes into an ecological perspective on the family.

A second instance of the inherent tendency in systems theory to stretch the boundaries of the therapeutic modality appears in *Ethnicity and Family Therapy* (1982), by Monica McGoldrick, John K. Pearce, and Joseph Giordan. In the introduction, McGoldrick makes a claim similar to Imber-Black's: "Just as family therapy itself grew out of the myopia of the intrapsychic view . . . family behavior also makes sense only in the larger cultural context in which it is embedded."[45] This time the expanding turn is not to public health care networks and policy but to cultural and ethnic context. Therapy must involve sociological and anthropological sensitivity to ethnic differences that determine what each cultural group defines as a problem and what they see as a solution. Therapists are urged to become "culture brokers," all the while maintaining the "relativity of all value systems." From our critical-realistic perspective on values, such positions should be corrected by an understanding of the cultural and value-laden character of all therapeutic work with families. Therapists need to acknowledge that pure value relativism will make it impossible to distinguish between cultural differences and social and cultural pathologies.

A third instance of family systems therapy pushing beyond customary limits is found in those theorists who make ethics central. McGoldrick, along with Carol M. Anderson and Froma Walsh, coedited a volume titled *Women in Families* (1989). They argue that family relationships cannot be separated from analysis of the power dynamics in the wider culture that define the ideals and parameters of families.[46] In this case, claims for the importance of a moral stance are put forth adamantly. In the preface to *Feminist Family Therapy* (1988), Rachel Hare-Mustin claims, "family therapy is a moral endeavor, one based on a vision of human life, and the moral questions should not be obscured," particularly when it comes to women's subordination, trivialization, and the harm of blaming women for family problems.[47] The authors define the values that undergird their approach: mutuality, reciprocity, and interdependence in nonhierarchical, democratic family structures. Power must be redefined in much the same way Gilligan defines the optimal stage of moral development—as "giving one's skills and influence towards the well-being of others just as one also does for one's own well-being."[48] In general, feminist therapists have presented one of the greatest challenges to family therapy's circumscribed worldview, making visible, for example, previously hidden patterns of domestic violence in many cases seen in the public health clinics of our country.

An explicit moral perspective can also be seen in one of the originators of the family therapy movement, Ivan Boszormenyi-Nagy. In fact, his perspective can function as a summary statement of the ethic of relationality—the ethic of intersubjective dialogue—that family therapists in our survey were struggling to articulate. His "contextual therapy" is characterized as "a cohesive approach based on an imperative of accountability" for the welfare of all those affected by the therapeutic intervention. His perspective has moved the family therapy movement toward an explicitly ethical middle ground between individualism and family obligation. Boszormenyi-Nagy locates his therapeutic investment within a context of broader political commitments to the disfranchised, commitments that stem from his earliest anti-Nazi actions in Hungary during World War II. He contends that the literature of family therapy "underrated its mission by omitting the ethical aspect or mandate of relationships." He argues for an "ethics of relating" guided by a norm of "interpersonal consequence," with consequences for children and future generations of particular relevance.[49]

In Boszormenyi-Nagy's relational ethics, therapy is governed by an ethic that explicitly tries to move beyond the tired options of egoism and altruism. Boszormenyi-Nagy does not state the obvious connections between this ethic and religious ethics such as the Golden Rule, the principle of neighbor love, or the norm of equal regard. But that he has in mind an intersubjective perspective on these very ideas is suggested by the importance for his ethic of Martin Buber's theory of the "I-Thou" relation. There is in his therapeutic ethic not only an implicit theory of mutuality but a life-cycle expression, an idea we develop in chapter 10. He writes that adults will find a "more peaceful resolve in their own lives if they can claim their own just due at the same time that they are actively involved and invested in caring for posterity." A valid therapeutic goal is no longer simply change but "self-sustaining continuity of relationship."[50] As family therapy has matured and begun to incorporate new ideas, its practitioners "do not do 'family' therapy as much as they do 'connection' therapy."[51]

William Doherty in his clinically nuanced *Soul Searching: Why Psychotherapy Must Promote Moral Responsibility* (1995) carries the discussion of the moral context of family therapy to new heights. He is more willing now than he was two decades ago to frame his family counseling in moral terms. The terms should recognize both the responsibilities of family members to each other and the responsibilities of therapists to families. Therapists, he argues, have a prima facie responsibility to preserve families within the limits of respect for the decision-making integrity of the individual family members involved.[52] When it comes to the needs of children, therapists must point out that children should count in the moral deliberations that go on in family counseling.

The Religiously Oriented Therapies

This discussion is not complete without a brief reference to the work of religiously oriented counselors, although they are often overlooked. As has been well documented by historian E. Brooks Holifield, the field of pastoral theology has an extended history of struggle with the therapeutic ethic of individual fulfillment.[53] While the profession of pastoral counseling flourished within the psychological climate of the 1950s and 1960s, many pastoral theologians recognized that an ethos of self-realization posed significant problems, especially for counseling or therapy involving family matters. One question that religiously oriented counselors cannot avoid is the relation between personal satisfaction and the larger good. Often this question emerges around the issue of family forms.

A prominent contribution in some secular psychotherapeutic psychologies has been the effort to destigmatize nonconventional family forms. This has influenced the movement in mainline Protestantism to endorse a relational morality unrestrained by efforts to identify determinate aspects of human nature that marital relations should promote. An example of the psychotherapeutic thinking that has influenced some liberal Protestants is found in Froma Walsh's edited collection *Normal Family Processes* (1993).[54] Her desire is to shift attention from so-called dysfunctional families to resources that can strengthen every family's well-being. This, she believes, requires an end to the "all happy families are alike" philosophy; healthy family functioning is not necessarily linked to a particular family form. Moreover, she dismisses monolithic family ideals, for they often compound rather than offset the sense of failure in the unconventional families that are now increasing in number.

Many therapists steer clear, as we saw in our survey, of endorsing one family form over another. They are sensitive to publicity about the negative consequences of single parenting that might jeopardize further the unstable balance of the families they serve. They believe that they should not be in the business of forming ideals that aggravate a sense of failure and guilt in those who are searching for help.

This fear of "ideals" *should* be less troubling for those representing religious communities. In many ways, theology stands at odds with so open an agenda for family well-being. Christianity has traditionally held up particular ideals and visions for human fulfillment, even as the role of families in their visions has fluctuated widely. Walsh makes an important point when she insists that family form and good family process are not identical. Her understanding of good family process, in fact, is close to our understanding of intersubjective equal regard.

Yet, much is theologically, philosophically, and culturally at stake in the prima facie ideal of the intact, equal-regard, mother-father partnership. This is true despite the entirely appropriate theological and commonsense concern not to use ideals to undermine a disrupted family's sense of self-worth and hope. We ourselves sound this cautionary note repeatedly in this book. But good families entail *not only* good processes but *high* investment, attachment, and commitment. When children are factored in, these features are most often held together in intact families that uphold an ethic of equal regard and in which the mother and father have joint access to responsibilities in both public and private spheres.

The claim in some secular therapies that family form is a neglible factor in family well-being has posed problems for those pastoral theologians who readily have appropriated secular psychotherapeutic approaches. Many pastoral theologians have avoided the challenging task of reinterpreting seemingly outmoded arguments based on natural law or orders of creation that attempt to hold form and process together. Many Protestant pastoral theologians state their theology in the most generic sense.

Indeed, some pastoral theologians, go to great lengths to incorporate a version of Walsh's view into their family counseling. The main family function is "caring for our generations," which is the subtitle of *Christian Marriage and Family* (1988), by John Patton and Brian Childs. Although they make important implicit claims for the resource of family structures in intergenerational care, function or process has little or no relation to family form. They do not ask whether some family structures of an extended family provide a wider range of resources for care of the generations than others. In the introduction to the book they repeatedly argue, "There is no ideal form for the Christian family toward which we should strive. There is, however, a normative function: care."[55]

In the third book in a five-book series on family living in pastoral perspective, *Regarding Children* (1994), Herbert Anderson and Susan Johnson articulate—better than do Patton and Childs—both the importance of having ideals for family life and the ambiguities that surround such ideals. They desire a vision of family sensitive to both individual and social good. Their intent is to wed "the vision of sacrifice for the greater good with a healthy commitment to individual freedom and creativity."[56] They seem more keenly aware than Patton and Childs that their reflections stand in a long tradition of carefully delineated prescriptions for ideal family life. They hope to "strike a middle way between families as they are and families as they ought to be." The concept of "the good enough family," they believe, serves to moderate the difficult tension between reality and ideals or between families as they are and families as they ought to be. A good enough family is "less than its own ideal and yet competent enough to raise reasonably adequate children." This does not eliminate the necessity of a normative vision. Ideals are important as a source of critical reflection and a map to living. However,

> We do not sketch maps in order to roll them up and beat ourselves with them. Rather we use maps to discover where we are and whether where we are is good enough. A Christian vision for family living should not add to the powerlessness or guilt people feel already for having failed to achieve their ideal picture. It should rather empower families to move toward a new future.[57]

Anderson and Johnson join other contemporary pastoral theologians in locating family struggles within the broader context of reforming cultural attitudes.[58]

Whereas the authors of *Habits of the Heart* collapse the manager and the therapist into two versions of radical individualism, investigation of recent marriage and family therapies reveals this to be an attractive oversimplification. Many therapies actually have a complex relationship to both market and state, and some actually promote civic discourse and responsibility, however weakly conceived. Therapies fall on a continuum of ethical commitments that range from valuing autonomy and self-actualization to valuing mutuality and agapic love. A therapeutic worldview need not always refer simply to a "psychology of me" or lead to the decline of accountability and responsibility. Unfortunately, by advancing this assumption, outspoken proponents of the family unnecessarily limit the use of essential psychological tools for the creation of communicative competence and intersubjective equal regard. To be sure, this slender ethic is not enough to sustain commitment to the common good, to assure the forgiveness and endurance needed to weather unavoidable bad times, or to elicit the transitional sacrifices needed to raise children, care for the elderly, and maintain families generally. But surely new therapeutic insights into intersubjective dialogue and equal regard have their place in a critical marriage culture and a critical familism.

8

Christian Profamily Movements

The Black Church, Roman Catholics, and the Christian Right

African-American churches, the Roman Catholic Church, and the Christian Right are all, in different ways, profamily. They all struggle to recreate a marriage and family culture. They are trying to renew commitment between husband and wife and between parents and children. They are familistic and want a marriage culture. It is not clear, however, that they are prepared to move toward what we call a *critical* marriage culture and a *critical* familism.

Therapy's contribution to communicative competence can be effective only if it is backed by a fund of commitment. But secular culture, including the secular therapies, cannot ground the commitment to spouses and children that a critical familism requires. In contrast, a renewed commitment to marriage and families is what most black churches, Roman Catholicism, and the Christian Right have in common, even though they connect it with different social philosophies.

Feminism, the therapeutic, and the Christian profamily movements each lack something that the other provides. Secular feminism celebrates equality between the sexes but generally lacks an intersubjective understanding of equality and a theory of commitment that bolsters relationships when they are strained. The therapeutic has insight into intersubjective dialogue but must borrow both its ethic of equal regard and its ideas about commitment from religiocultural sources beyond itself. The Christian profamily movements celebrate commitment but lack understandings of love as equal regard, lapse easily into "soft" patriarchy, and speak about justice between the sexes as a judgment made by males in isolation. A critical familism at this moment in history cannot be achieved without the contributions as well as critiques of each of these movements.

A convergence of black churches, Catholicism, and the Christian Right can be seen in a report from the *Chicago Tribune* that appeared two days after Louis Farrakhan's One Million Man March in October 1995.

Commenting on the central theme of the speeches delivered that day, the authors wrote,

> Most Americans have believed that political parties and individual politicians, from Franklin Roosevelt to Ronald Reagan, could represent their political interests.
>
> Few groups believed this more avidly than blacks, as they traditionally have offered all but monolithic support to Democrats. But as Monday's rally underscored, another view appears to be emerging.
>
> Much of the rhetoric at the march was *similar to what is heard at the religious rallies of predominantly white men called the Promise Keepers and in the homilies of William Bennett's best-selling "Book of Virtues."*
>
> Good marriages, good schools, safe streets, the message goes— all Americans have to do is reach out for it, commit to it, make it happen. The answer, those gathered at the Mall said, is not in America's institutions, but in themselves.
>
> That was the understanding Talmadge Hancock, 50, a lithographer from Washington, took away from the rally. "It was one central theme all the way through: Family," he said.[1]

Present in the march's rhetoric were also classic liberal themes: the need for "basic equity," the disadvantages blacks face "in securing jobs and housing, the prejudice against them, and their exclusion from society's benefits." "But justice," as theologian Anthony Tambasco said, includes "being responsible for one's own life."[2]

A convergence of liberal and conservative themes also was evident when Pope John Paul II came to the United States shortly before the Million Man March, emphasizing both traditional family values and the importance of government support for poor families. Reporters covering his visit were quick to notice this convergence of conservative and liberal emphases.[3]

A struggle to balance responsibility and justice within the context of Christian teachings brought blacks, Catholics, and evangelicals into the same conversational ballpark during the mid-1990s. Ralph Reed, until recently the executive director and chief theorist of the Christian Coalition, wanted to be the captain of the teams playing in the park. The most distinctive theme of his *Politically Incorrect* (1994) was his ambition to bring Catholics, blacks, evangelicals, and the more conservative elements of the Protestant mainstream into the Christian Coalition.[4]

The Shadow of
the 1960s Counterculture

How could Reed hope to unify these groups? According to Reed, it could happen because, beneath surface differences, all of them held the same mainstream American values and were reacting against the same countercultural movements of the 1960s. Journalist Myron Magnet in *The Dream and the Nightmare* (1993) argued that these movements—simultaneously celebrating individualism, expressivity, sensuality, and egalitarianism—contributed substantially to the creation of the black and the emerging white underclasses.[5] Cultural elites, he believed, were won over by countercultural values and for various reasons promulgated them. In movies, television, and journalism, for example, they celebrated these values, perhaps for profit. These values, Magnet claims, trickled down to and undermined large portions of the lower classes, aggravating the detrimental effects of discrimination, unemployment, a poorly designed welfare system, and an emerging drug culture. These movements precipitated defensive reactions from conservative Catholics and evangelicals and later the call by William Bennett and Gertrude Himmelfarb for the return of "virtue" to civic life.[6] In the fashion of Hegelian dialectics, some argue that the thesis of the counterculture gave rise to the antithesis of the religious and secular right.

Several of our interviews show the cultural effects of the 1960s and people's quest for an alternative vision—often a more conservative one.

> Take James Nelson, a black Baptist who, after years as a nightclub entertainer and then businessman, brought his family to a theological school in the South so that he could train for the Christian ministry. Although a conservative Christian as a youth in a church that prohibited instrumental music, he began performing in nightclubs at the age of fifteen. From then on, as he said, it was "sex, drugs, and rock 'n' roll." Before his adult "conversion" to Christianity, he had two children out of wedlock with Francis, the woman he later married. His Christianity, he thinks, saved him from the '60s.
>
> Although he has repudiated his counterculture days, he believes that much of that era lingers on in the society around him. For instance, even though he emphasized abstinence until marriage in the sex education of his sixteen-year-old son (something as a youth he did not follow), he instructed his son in the use of condoms just in case his teachings did not take.
>
> *James Nelson*

> Before John Schneider's conversion, he and his brother were deeply into drugs. Things were so out of control that he once planned to murder both his wife and her father for their money. His wife

knows this, but since his conversion she has come to trust him. John's repudiation of the '60s was deeper than James's. His video shop failed because he refused to sell X-rated tapes. He won't allow his children to participate in Halloween because it is a pagan holiday. He is dead set against the distribution of condoms at school. In spite of all this piety, cultural conservativism, and near fundamentalism, his marriage has been influenced by feminist equality.

John Schneider

The Christian Coalition and Myron Magnet would see the countercultural phase of Nelson and Schneider as displaying values that have infiltrated much of American life, undermining the lower classes who cannot afford them, and spreading the poverty of the black underclass into new sectors of society. They would say that Nelson and Schneider got saved from the 1960s; unfortunately, many were not so lucky.

Senator Moynihan, African Americans, and Catholic Social Philosophy

The activities of Senator Patrick Daniel Moynihan from 1965 to 1995 provide insight into the link between Catholics, evangelicals, and blacks on the family debate. Moynihan was one of the first to identify what is now called the black underclass. He did this in his famous 1965 report titled "The Negro Family: The Case for National Action," now referred to as the Moynihan Report. He wrote it while he was assistant secretary of labor under President Lyndon Johnson. Few reports written for the inner circles of government have sparked such widespread public furor. The report proclaimed that the "Negro" (the word then used) family was in trouble. For this pronouncement, many blacks and political liberals called Moynihan a racist. His message was seen by many as blaming the victim rather than the systematic racism that had produced the victim.[7]

Thirty years later, during the heat of the 1995 welfare debate, Moynihan, now older and more honored, still stood largely alone. He was angry at President Clinton for promising to "end welfare as we know it." This, he claimed, had opened the Pandora's box that led Republicans to end national government's guaranteed support of poor families and cede this responsibility to the states.[8] He derided the Republican Party's Contract with America, spearheaded by Speaker of the House Newt Gingrich, and the Christian Coalition's Contract with American Families, even though he agreed with their worries about rising rates of out-of-wedlock births and increasing male violence in inner cities.

During the 1960s, Moynihan was preoccupied with the increasing absence of fathers in black families, the proper role of government in helping families, the declining well-being of children, and the growing welfare dependency of both blacks and whites. A key to understanding Moynihan is remembering that he is a liberal Roman Catholic whose social vision has been deeply informed by Catholic social teachings.

Seen from this perspective, one must conclude that he has been sensitive to the plight of poor African-American families. But rhetorical problems plagued his report. The title was "The Negro Family," suggesting that he was talking about an average or standard condition of black families. Rather, he was talking about two types of black families: "a stable middle-class group that is steadily growing stronger and more successful, and an increasingly disorganized and disadvantaged lower-class group."[9]

Moynihan failed to celebrate the remarkable strengths of both types of African-American families—those overcoming centuries of discrimination and moving into the mainstream *and* those surviving even though on the margins of society. This was his big mistake. By failing to understand the cultural and religious assets of most black families, he moved too quickly to a characterization of the Negro family as a "tangle of pathology." What was this tangle? It was dramatically rising rates of divorce and out-of-wedlock births, father absence, increasing numbers of poor mothers and children, and increasing youth violence. His report documented trends that affected a portion of black families in 1965 but *did not affect them all.*

Moynihan made another mistake. His report was long on diagnosis and short on prescription. He thought that the solution was so self-evident that he needed only to hint at it. His point was this: The legal victories of the civil rights era would not automatically alter the results of centuries of discrimination and violence done against black families. These legal victories needed to be preserved and expanded, but even more needed to be done. Some of the necessary measures, he believed, were the rightful responsibility of government.

For instance, the effects of discrimination had gained a cumulative momentum; they were now affecting the culture of inner-city black communities. From 1948 to 1962, AFDC payments paralleled increases in unemployment in the black community. This made the disruption of the black family appear to be a result of economic deprivation. But Moynihan pointed out that in 1962, 1963, and 1964, though employment rates had improved in the black community, AFDC payments and indices of family disruption continued to rise.[10] A new dynamic was occurring among the more severely disadvantaged families of the black community, a dynamic that economic deprivation alone could not explain. African-American mothers and fathers were not marrying as they once did and were divorcing more. Fathers were not helping out as much, and this was true even during periods when employment and economic resources improved. Was this the added cultural factor that Magnet talked about?

The outlines of Moynihan's solution are clear even though not well developed. He wanted the government to invest in a major new family-centered initiative that would aim welfare at *families and not just individuals*. He wanted welfare to address the cultural factor by encouraging fathers to remain with their spouses and children. But even more, he wanted government to bring jobs to the inner city so that men could be employed and be financially able to marry and to support their families.[11] Moynihan was pleading for a view of justice that emphasized equality of results as much as equality of opportunity. He wanted disadvantaged blacks to have a genuine chance to catch up with the rest of society. Moynihan was suggesting government interventions similar to the ones sociologist William Julius Wilson recommended twenty years later in *The Truly Disadvantaged* (1987) and *When Work Disappears* (1996).[12]

In taking this stance, Moynihan was bucking the welfare patterns of his day, which emphasized helping individuals rather than families and which forced able-bodied husbands, fathers, and boyfriends to leave their families so that the mothers of their children could qualify for assistance. Furthermore, Moynihan was projecting into his welfare philosophy an appreciation for Catholic social teachings. Catholic social philosophy emphasized family interests as "the central objective of social welfare and social policy in general."[13]

Behind Moynihan's position is the Catholic doctrine of *subsidiarity*. It was applied to government's relation to families by Pope Leo XIII in his major statement on Catholic social philosophy in *Rerum Novarum* (1891). In this document, Leo limited state intrusion into the affairs of families while simultaneously encouraging appropriate state help for needy families. On the one hand, subsidiarity meant that government should help families to do what they do better than other agencies of society, that is, support and socialize their children. It also meant that the state should not disrupt family abilities and responsibilities. On the other hand, subsidiarity meant that governments should guarantee certain basic resources for families, such as requiring businesses to pay employees a wage that could support a family.[14]

Moynihan got his interpretation of what was happening to *some* black families from government statistics and the respected historical and sociological work of E. Franklin Frazier and Kenneth Clark. Even as Moynihan wrote in 1965, the out-of-wedlock birth rate was 23.6 percent in the black community—what it became among whites by 1995.[15] These trends, he thought, had their origins in the traumas of slavery. Frazier had painted a dismal portrait in *The Negro Family in the United States* (1939). He argued that slavery had completely deprived American blacks of their African family customs. Slave families were separated or sold at the whim of their masters, and marriage between blacks was illegal. Breeding and informal family formation were encouraged by masters but often disrupted by their lust or greed. Many stable family units existed at the time of emancipation, but many families were unstable. Large numbers of black males bolted from their families at the end of the Civil War, and many females gave birth and cared for their children outside of stable unions. Finally, the move of blacks into urban centers further disrupted many families.[16] In addition, Moynihan believed that Kenneth Clark's study of the deterioration of Harlem community life in his *Dark Ghetto* (1965) described a situation that was emerging in black inner-city communities throughout the nation.[17]

President Johnson in his famous June 1965 Howard University speech outlined a vision of governmental support of black families which drew on Moynihan's report. But then all hell broke loose. Reaction to the Moynihan Report was so vociferous that an announced White House conference on the black family was refocused to center on urban problems and nearly dropped the theme of the black family. In general, government rapidly retreated from the comprehensive programs for families in employment, income maintenance, and education that Moynihan had envisioned and hoped to implement.

The Strengths of African-American Families

Moynihan's failure to analyze carefully, celebrate, and build on the strengths of the African-American family was costly. More recent responses to his report have reversed the rhetorical order of Moynihan's concerns. They begin by emphasizing the strengths of black families and then set the disruption of black families into a new context. Because the plunder and misery inflicted by slavery and discrimination were so profound and had such lasting effects, one should ask the question, *What great secrets, spiritual or cultural, have made it possible for some of these families to survive and in many cases flourish? Rather than assuming there is little to be found in black families but disruption and ill health, why not be open to the possibility that there is something for the rest of society to learn from their experience?* This is the point of view of our book. Disruption, yes; but first of all, how do we account for the remarkable strengths?

This question dominates Wallace Charles Smith's *The Church in the Life of the Black Family* (1985).[18] Smith, pastor of the Shiloh Baptist Church of Washington, D.C., is not only critical of the Moynihan Report, but critical of all social science assessments of the black family written by white scholars. They all miss, he believes, the feel, the reality, and the beauty of the black family experience. Rather than speaking disparagingly of black matriarchy, we should first marvel at the survival skills of black mothers and their enduring love for their children. Rather than speaking about the weakness or absence of black fathers, we should first appreciate the many who have been faithful amid overwhelming difficulties. Rather than complaining about the fragmentation of so many black nuclear families, we should first celebrate the strengths of the black extended family. And most of all, we should not, as white social scientists are prone to do, ignore the importance of black religion to the health of the black family.

In fact, Smith sees a complex dialectical relation between family and church in the black community. This relation, from our standpoint, is much like the pattern of the early church outlined in chapter 5. Families in whatever form—intact, single-parent, stepfamilies, grandmother with daughter and grandchild, single males looking for families, and others—come to the black church. Smith argues that the black church from the beginning has been inclusive; in fact, it has functioned as a symbolic extended family. It has been nonjudgmental, supportive, encouraging, and full of practical helpfulness. The black church, according to Smith, works *as* an extended family, borrowing models of the extended family from Western African tribal patterns.[19] But it also builds on the models of church as spiritual family found in the New Testament.

The pattern of the black church is this: kinship energies from actual fathers, mothers, grandparents, and children are brought to the church in various fragmentary ways. In turn, the church and pastor become a new and larger metaphorical family, not so much replacing the old family but setting it in a new context of meaning and support and gently shaping it. In the church, all family members come gradually to develop a self-image that reflects their status as *imago Dei*.[20]

Smith follows theologians Karl Barth and Paul Jewett in interpreting the *imago Dei* as involving male and female in their fundamental relation to each other. Smith takes a modern rendition of Reformed theology's understanding of God's will for creation and uses it within the black church. Barth and Jewett interpret the words, "So God created man in his own image, in the image of God he created him; male and female he created them" (Gen. 1:27) to mean that the male-female relation is inextricably polar. As Barth states, "Man is directed to woman and woman to man. . . . This mutual orientation constitutes the being of each."[21] This polar relation for Barth is a consequence of the "divine command" for the created order.[22] Although Smith chides Moynihan for being preoccupied with the structure of the black family, in his own way he reinforces the intact, two-parent family and follows Barth in believing that "monogamy" is the will of God.

Like Moynihan, Smith is concerned about black family disruption[23] and wants African-American churches to reinforce the conjugal couple at the heart of the extended family. He writes,

> The image of God is rounded out as an image of male-female interrelatedness. Each of us individually is both male and female, but each is also specifically male or female. God's revelation clearly points to male-female monogamous relationships as the gift by God to humankind for the purposes of procreation and nurturing. Even for people of African descent, this concept of monogamy must be at the heart of even the extended family structure.[24]

However different their lines of approach, Smith's goals for the black family are similar to Moynihan's. They differ in their valuation of the black family's present strengths and of the black church's role as a source of renewal and a major buffer between family and state. But both Moynihan and Smith want government to help black families become more cohesive, as long as this happens with appreciation for their unique abilities, history, and culture.[25]

Smith has academic support in his attempt to enrich the black family by first recognizing its strengths. Historian Herbert Gutman and sociologist Andrew Billingsley have the same sensibility if not the same agenda. Gutman in his monumental study *The Black Family in Slavery and Freedom, 1750–1925* (1976) dismantled the Frazier-Clark-Moynihan thesis about the consequences of slavery on the African-American family. Both before and after the Civil War and into the twentieth century, there were many more intact families, cared-for children, and present fathers in black families, Gutman maintained, than this trio of scholars allowed. Throughout the South, slave sexual practices made nonmarital childbirth compatible with long-term unions and stable homes for children.[26] Even after the emancipation, census and birth records of black families in northern cities such as Buffalo and New York show high levels of family stability.[27]

Smith, however, is as skeptical of the positive picture that Gutman portrays as he is of Moynihan's use of Frazier's negative view. The ravages of slavery are deeper, he believes, than Gutman allows. Yet Smith agrees with Andrew Billingsley in *Climbing Jacob's Ladder: The Enduring*

Legacy of African-American Families (1992) that black families not only have strengths and enduring values, but, when rightly understood, have enormous lessons to teach middle-class and upper-class families, whatever their color. Billingsley wants to capture the "generative power" of black families and "use it in helping families realize their inherent potential."[28] We are highly sympathetic to Billingsley's claim that the African-American community contains the "best and the worst," the strongest and perhaps the weakest of American families. We also agree that the survival of both strong and weak families holds "*important keys to the regeneration of our families,* our communities, and our society." This is true not only for the benefit of families as such, "but for the enhancement of that larger sense of community that Martin Luther King, Jr., dreamed about."[29]

Billingsley agrees with Gutman, as opposed to Frazier and Moynihan, that blacks were remarkably committed to the two-parent family throughout slavery and the post-emancipation migrations, even after World War II. He agrees with social scientist William Cross, who wrote that "the evolution of the urban, poor black single-parent household is more a function of the unique stresses and supports these families face in urban areas" than an outgrowth of a matrilocal history or the culture of poverty.[30] But Billingsley joins Smith in holding that lingering African traditions among blacks have led them to value consanguineous family relations (especially the blood relations of mothers with their extended families) as much as, and sometimes more than, conjugal relations.[31] Nonetheless, in view of the obstacles, African Americans during and after slavery remained highly committed to mother-father partnerships. In addition, these partnerships were frequently quite egalitarian because of shared economic contributions required for families to survive.

Billingsley is critical of the Moynihan Report. There is evidence, however, that he never fully understood Moynihan's agenda. Billingsley ends his book by calling for a delicate balance of black family self-help and government supports. He believes that the reinvigoration of economic opportunities in inner-city communities is crucial for the renewal of black families. This is similar to the subsidiarity principle informing Moynihan's vision three decades earlier. Although Moynihan believed that the legal prohibition of racial discrimination needed to be broadened, he thought that government ought also to devise focused programs that support inner-city families in their totality: mothers, children, *and* husbands (fathers) as an integrated unit. Today, both Moynihan and Billingsley hold that state support for the whole family should come in ways that do not undermine what families can do for themselves.

What can the rest of society learn from African-American families? When tested against the standards of our view of love as equal regard, the black family displays four unique strengths: (1) a simultaneous high valuation of both the extended consanguineous family and the conjugal couple; (2) an enriching involvement with the black church; (3) a relative equality of sex roles; and (4) powerful symbolic and social procedures for overcoming male alienation from families.

We begin with the high valuation of both the consanguineous *and* the conjugal family. In lifting up the importance of blood relations in the black community, we are not suggesting that extended families are unimportant in middle-class white and ethnic communities—there is much evidence to the contrary.[32] But in the black experience, according to Melville Herskovitz and Andrew Billingsley, vestiges of the African heritage survived the discontinuities of the slave experience.[33] This heritage gave a priority to consanguineous relations; family identities were attached to bloodlines, especially on the mother's side, more than to the conjugal couple itself. This was partly associated with a polygynous West African marriage system in which the husband related to his wives as they continued to dwell in their original family compounds rather than in his place of residence.

Gutman, however, has shown the speed with which black American slave families moved to a high valuation of the conjugal system. It could be argued that African-American families brought together in the late nineteenth and early twentieth centuries a high evaluation of both systems, *conjugal* and *consanguineous*. These families illustrate the importance of an ecological perspective on families in which kin altruism functions as a source of premoral values connecting biological parents with their children but connecting children with grandparents, uncles, aunts, and cousins as well. When the conjugal black family became disrupted under the post–World War II pressures of urban isolation, discrimination, unemployment, and clumsy welfare practices, consanguineous ties became important for the survival of many families.

But as Smith pointed out, both Judaism and Christianity have been associated with the enhancement of the conjugal family and the subordination of the consanguineous family. The Genesis 2:24 passage, "Therefore a man leaves his father and his mother and cleaves to his wife, and they become one flesh" is precisely about this subordination. It elevated the free consent and covenant of the conjugal couple over the political-economic power of the Semitic tribe and clan. This "one flesh" commitment of the conjugal family was reaffirmed by Jesus in Matthew 19:5. But Smith believes that the relational *imago Dei* of Genesis 1:27 places the monogamous conjugal couple at the heart of "the extended family structure." He also understood that the consanguineous family must be valued as a significant source of strength, support, and natural fidelity. In the language of moral philosophy, the extended family is a powerful source of *premoral* goods and supports.

Second, the close, indeed dialectical, relation between black families and the black church probably captures one element of life in the early Christian church better than any aspect of contemporary social life. The early church showed that it understood the importance of extended families when it attempted to convert whole families (including the conjugal couple) to the kingdom of God. It also appropriated the language of extended and consanguineous families to speak of spiritual mothers, fathers, brothers, sisters, children, and grandparents in Christ. Many black churches project the intensity and investment of kin altruism into church life and an image of the universal family of God.

Third, society can learn from the black community some of the conditions for the egalitarian mother-father partnership. It is often argued that slave and post–Civil War black families were more egalitarian than the classic Victorian white family.[34] Historically, there have been more women in the breadwinner role in African-American families. We see this in the relation of Maria and Robert Taylor, who had one of the most egalitarian relationships of the couples we studied. Deprived of property and wages, black male slaves and tenant farmers had little economic power. Black women often had as much if not more earning ability than males. To survive, everyone in black families had to earn as much as possible and do whatever chores needed doing, regardless of gender. Women shared the breadwinning and had more power in the family. This was true despite the Freedmans Bureau's reinforcement of paternal power during the Reconstruction and despite the patriarchal language and structures of the black church.[35]

Finally, African-American families show how males, in the context of horrendous obstacles and temptations, can become integrated into families. We can speculate that some of the naturalistic conditions discussed in chapter 4 that brought *Homo sapien* males into the primordial mother-infant family may have functioned in the unstructured, unsanctioned situation of slave life, in spite of owners' involvement in the sexual life of slaves. These elemental conditions of family formation may have been part of what Gutman calls "the cumulative slave experience with its own standards and rules of conduct."[36]

But, as we saw in Thomas Aquinas's three-level analysis (naturalistic, moral, and theological), human inclinations need institutions, symbols, and narratives that pattern and further transform them. Smith gives us a sample of how Christian symbolism is used today in the black church to stabilize male inclinations.[37] Smith sees the black church as calling males to responsibility as husbands and fathers. In doing this, the church appeals to deep aspects of male human nature—aggressiveness and intrusiveness—by promoting a new model of male leadership. Christian leadership builds on yet redirects these archaic male energies. It must be a leadership that reflects the leadership of Christ. Smith believes that Ephesians 5:23, when placed in historical context, means, "The husband is head 'only' as Christ is head, and Christ's headship is not demonstrated by dominance but by subjection, both to others and to God."[38]

From our standpoint, Smith's representation of the black church has captured part of the creativity of early Christianity in inverting the honor-shame code of Greco-Roman culture and addressing the "male problematic" of that day. Black churches, in their many mentoring programs for boys, mass meetings for men of all ages, male retreats, father-son banquets, and Saturday men's breakfasts, are the leading institutions of our society helping males to attach themselves responsibly to families.

But Smith and much of the black church, in spite of their profound insights into Christianity and the male psyche, retain varying degrees of patriarchy and fail to carry their appeals for male servanthood and mutuality to a fully intersubjective point of view. It is not enough to idealize male leadership and servanthood: judgments about enacting love and justice cannot be solely the prerogative of husbands and fathers. A model of intersubjective equal regard, energized by the renewing capacities of servanthood and self-sacrifice, will permit both husband and wife, father and mother to move into full communicative exchange.

The Christian Right

The appeals to men in the black church have analogies to the largely white Christian Right family movement. Although their social philosophies diverge, both groups have identified a major problem: the issue of male responsibility to families in postindustrial societies. Not all the groups we discuss would feel comfortable with the label "Christian Right." When we use this phrase, we simply mean Christians whose thinking is to the right of center in the American family debate.

The Christian Right is a loose association of groups that are conservative Christian, mainly Protestant evangelical, and profamily.[39] We concentrate on the most respected and powerful expressions of the movement—primarily Focus on the Family, Promise Keepers, the Christian Coalition, and the Family Research Council. To concentrate on these groups is to ignore a vast landscape of evangelical Christianity that does not identify with them, but because we are interested in the American family debate, we limit ourselves in this discussion to voices making a public impact, and these groups clearly do. Four themes run through their public message: the problem of male authority, the autonomy of the family, the preservation of "Christian morality," and the proper relation of church and state.

First and foremost is the problem of defining male authority and responsibility in postmodern society. From the beginning of Christian fundamentalism in the last half of the nineteenth century, conservative Christianity wanted to reclaim a place for men in churches and families. As we saw in chapter 3, late–nineteenth-century evangelicals were aware of the "feminization" of American Christianity and the drift of men away from churches.

On the one hand, it was a healthy impulse for males to want to exercise responsibility and leadership in churches once again. On the other, it was lamentable that in doing this they reasserted patriarchy, reduced the presence of women as leaders of church organizations, further sacralized the Industrial Revolution's divided spheres of paid work and domestic life, and asserted a fundamentalist reading of the New Testament—generally the later pastoral epistles—to defend their claims.[40] Religion historian Margaret Bendroth shows how fundamentalism's effort to shore up male authority continued into the 1950s, 1960s, and 1970s. Groups such as Promise Keepers and Focus on the Family are continuations of these earlier Christian male initiatives to reclaim responsibility but also to reclaim power.

Both James Dobson's Focus on the Family and Bill McCartney's Promise Keepers have been influenced by feminism; they are also reacting against it. Neither Dobson in his books and radio talks nor McCartney in his huge football stadium rallies will baldly assert that women should not work outside the home or take part in public life. It is clear, however, that they value and idealize women as mothers at home. Furthermore, in reconstructing male responsibility they lapse into reasserting male authority, leadership, and headship. Although they quote the Bible to support their theories, it is astounding to see both how little and how noncontextually they use the scriptures.

Dobson, a clinical psychologist by training, has an informal theory of the asymmetrical reproductive strategies of males and females. However, he is not informed by recent evolutionary psychology on this matter and uses his homespun version in ways we reject.[41] He agrees that male sexual behavior is not easily organized into families and commitment to children—a point we recognize. But he then argues that women's sexual styles lead them to seek reliance on male strength and leadership—a point that contemporary evolutionary psychology does not make and that we repudiate. Females seek help from males but not necessarily *dependence* on males. Hence, Dobson, who champions men's help with household chores and parenting, makes the egregious mistake of reading Ephesians 5:22–28 and 1 Peter 3:1 as flat-footed endorsements of the view that "a Christian man is obligated to lead his family to the best of his ability. God apparently expects a man to be the ultimate decision-maker in his family." Furthermore, the man "bears heavier responsibility for the outcome of those decisions."[42] This is an excellent example of what we mean by a monological, in contrast to a dialogical, understanding of Christian love and justice.

Dobson, as with so many members of the profamily Christian Right, has little interest in reading the New Testament in the context of Greco-Roman culture. He has no understanding of the honor-shame model of family relations in that culture which the Gospels, Paul, and even the Epistle to the Ephesians, are undermining. Focus on the Family and Promise Keepers must be understood as half-right and half-wrong. Both are realistic about male alienation in the twentieth century. Both are aware that males have been sucked into the whirlwind of market forces, consumed by market values, deprived of a sense of direction from older males, and alienated from the duties of being a husband and father.[43] Nonetheless, their attempt to reclaim male responsibility has become overidentified with reasserting principled male leadership and authority.

Listen to prominent Promise Keeper Tony Evans tell men how to overcome alienation from the home and reclaim responsibility. He suggests that men sit down with their wives and say, "Honey, I've made a terrible mistake. I've given you my role. I gave up leading the family, and I forced you to take my place. Now I must reclaim that role."[44] He goes on to say to men, "Don't misunderstand what I'm saying here. I'm not suggesting that you *ask* for your role back, I'm urging you to *take it back*." If the husband simply asks for it, the wife will say, "Look, for the last ten years, I've had to raise these kids, look after the house, and pay the bills. I've had to get a job and still keep up my duties in the home. I've had to do my job *and* yours. You think I'm just going to turn everything back over to you?"[45] Evans concludes this imaginary dialogue with these decisive words:

> Your wife's concerns may be justified. Unfortunately, however, there can be no compromise here. If you're going to lead, you must lead. Be sensitive. Listen. Treat the lady gently and lovingly. But lead.
>
> Having said that, let me direct some carefully chosen words to you ladies who may be reading this: Give it *back*. For the sake of

your family and the survival of our culture, let your man be a man if he's willing. Protect yourselves, if you must, by handing the reins back slowly; take it one step at a time. But if your husband tells you he wants to reclaim his role, let him! God never meant for you to bear the load you're carrying.[46]

The remarkable thing about this imagined dialogue is that it is *not* a dialogue. It is a monologue where Evans fills in both sides of the conversation. The conversation is *about* higher levels of responsibility by males. This is good. We don't disparage it. But its monological character excludes women from helping to develop the meaning of responsibility and justice in the family and from administering it. The ideology of masculinity in Focus on the Family and Promise Keepers must be seen as simultaneously a step forward and a step backward. It is a step forward in its recognition of the "male problematic" and the call for male responsibility; it is a step backward in its failure to place its calls for responsibility within an *intersubjective* view of love as equal regard.

The second common theme in these groups is the concern to preserve the relative autonomy of the family from governmental intrusions. It is a part of their political theory. In *Children at Risk* (1990), Dobson and Gary Bauer, president of the Family Research Council, complain bitterly about how a "13 and 14 year-old girl—who is still a child in many ways" can today be provided contraceptives and even given an abortion "without parental knowledge."[47] The problem is not with state programs as such, it is that "the philosophy which governs them is out of harmony with the immutable laws of the universe!"[48] The Christian Right envisions a positive role for government, and that role is different from the one that has been dominant over the past forty years.

Ralph Reed, when executive director of the Christian Coalition, was more articulate about the rights of parents. In his first book, Reed's statement of his case is amazingly similar to the Catholic concept of subsidiarity. "Where the family meets a need better than government, let government step out of the way."[49] Conservative Christians "are far less interested in legislating against the sins of others, and far more interested in protecting their own right to practice their religion and raise their children in a manner consistent with their values."[50] The Christian Coalition's attempt to influence school boards, as they did with regard to New York City's sex education programs in 1992 and 1993, had more to do with protecting family rights, according to Reed, than controlling the values of others. Reed quotes Congressman Richard Armey of Texas: "Millions of evangelicals and orthodox Roman Catholics in the 1970s felt their way of life to be under subtle but determined attack by federal policies." They sought to reenter public life, according to Armey, "not to impose their beliefs on others, but because the federal government was imposing its values on them."[51]

We were surprised to find this latent concept of subsidiarity in Reed's writings. He states it explicitly in *Active Faith* (1996), writing, "We have heeded the church doctrine that Roman Catholics refer to as subsidiarity, the idea that charity is best practiced by those closest to the problem."[52] This, of course, is just part of the meaning of subsidiarity. The corresponding part is that government should help support grassroots communities, including families, when they genuinely need help. Furthermore, Reed overlooks the fact that subsidiarity resists government subversion of families because it contains an implicit theory of kin altruism that accounts for why families are more invested in their children than in more remote groups. When Reed invokes subsidiarity, he doesn't really explain it.

Evangelical that he is, Reed might well have used the Protestant "orders of creation" to support family autonomy from government. This is what evangelicals informed by the Reformation generally have used to assert the autonomy of family, state, church, and market and the respective covenantal responsibilities of these spheres to God. Indeed, sociologist of religion John Coleman has discovered that the "spheres of creation thinking of the late nineteenth century Dutch theologian and statesman Abraham Kuyper has indeed had influence on the state organizations loosely affiliated with Focus on the Family."[53]

Individuals affiliated with Calvin College, a conservative intellectual school in the Reformed tradition, imported Kuyper to the Michigan Family Forum, which is associated with Focus on the Family. His theory then became almost normative for defining the relation between family and state for the other thirty-one state organizations associated (but not legally linked) with Focus on the Family. Most operatives at the state level have never heard of Kuyper and certainly do not have a firm grasp of the intricacies of Calvinist thinking on orders of creation. Coleman summarizes his research by writing,

> Most of those we interviewed, however, believed in at least three divinely ordained spheres of authority—family, church, government. Adherents to this view note that the Bible reveals (and thus, God intended) each of these spheres to have distinct functions and that each has its own authority structure which is not the province of the other sphere. Problems arise in society when the government, for example, begins to encroach upon the functions that properly belong to family and church by, for instance, usurping social welfare.[54]

The Christian Right oscillates in an effort to defend theologically and philosophically its intuitions about the rights of parents to raise their children according to their traditions and the need of government to respect these prerogatives. Sometimes they lean toward the Reformed orders of creation; sometimes they advance arguments that have more in common with Catholic subsidiarity. If anything, subsidiarity has the more weight. If this is true, the Christian Right will need to face the fact that this concept is difficult to ground biblically. Referring to Jesus' words, "Render therefore to Caesar the things that are Caesar's, and to God the things that are God's" may give scriptural warrant for the separation of church and state, but it hardly addresses the details of family autonomy or government responsibility. This scripture does not provide for subsidiarity in its full meaning.

It is clear that Catholics and the Christian Coalition share something like a theory of subsidiarity. This is why Richard John Neuhaus, editor of the conservative journal *First Things,* and former Nixon aide Charles Colson, now a born-again evangelical, envision a new Catholic-evangelical alliance on family matters called Evangelicals and Catholics Together.[55] This is why Reed envisions what he calls a "new ecumenism" that would include not only Catholics but blacks and Jews as well—all directed by the Christian Coalition.[56] Indeed, 16 percent of the membership of the Coalition is Catholic, and appeals to Catholics by the Christian Coalition are mounting.[57] Furthermore, Reed has quoted surveys showing that 87 percent of African Americans rank family as their most important concern.[58] Reed believed he had a chance to bring blacks into the Christian Coalition as well.

This leads to the third theme: their view of Christian morality, which they feel is profoundly under threat. Covenanted, heterosexual, lifelong marriage and gender complementarity are at the core of their moral message. Marriage is about children, although it is also about intimacy, friendship, and sexual pleasure between husband and wife. Christian Right groups are more open to talking about intimacy and sexual pleasure than are Catholic encyclicals on marriage and family. Furthermore, marriage for these groups entails equal respect between husband and wife, but it also involves significant role differentiations as well, with males taking the leadership. Sex outside of marriage is ruled out, and although homosexual persons are affirmed as persons, their sexual activity is rejected, as is all sex outside of marriage. Abortion is seen as un-Christian. Dobson, Bauer, and Reed did not want this moral code undercut by the public institutions influencing their children. Sexual and family morality are at the heart of what must be defended against interference by government, public schools, or public policies, including welfare policies.[59] Family morality should be under the control of families and the free institutions of civil society with which families associate.

This leads to the fourth theme: the relation of church and state. How does the Christian Right defend its family morality without dictating the morality of the public institutions? All Christian Right leaders deny that they want to dictate public policy. To preserve their moral integrity, they try first to limit government influence and resort to influencing it only when government intrusion becomes oppressive. As Harvey Cox points out in his 1995 *Atlantic Monthly* review of evangelicals in politics, the Christian Coalition does not perceive itself as pursuing a "dominion" theology of direct Christian control of public institutions. At least, that is what they say. Cox argues that its public theology is not logically different from that of Latin American liberation theology,[60] a point Stephen Carter makes as well in his *Culture of Disbelief* (1993).[61]

Reed explicitly asserts that "religious conservatives do not want a 'Christian' nation."[62] He argues that Christians have a right to influence public policy because their heritage has a special place in the formation of American culture, is time honored, and has a wider cultural and social validity beyond the special confessional boundaries of believing individuals and churches. Hence, it is civil religion—indeed, civil religion with a "Christian face"—that Reed invokes in arguing that evangelicals have a right to influence public polity.[63] Assumptions about the reality of a divine being and about the relevance of Judeo-Christian sexual morality were once accepted parts of America's political culture and discourse. Reed thinks that day is gone, but he wants to bring it back, and Dobson and Bauer make similar points.

But Reed's arguments are much more sophisticated; Dobson often avoids giving reasons for his public policy positions, saying that they are simply a matter of "faith." Reed, however, says that Christians must explain their positions, not just assert their faith: He admonishes his followers to "persuade rather than preach." Fellow Christians may be convinced by the use of scripture in defending their positions, but "it is likely to fall on deaf ears in the larger society." He quotes the Bible: Speak in public debate "only such a word as is good for edification according to the need of the moment, that it may give grace to those who hear . . . (Ephesians 4:29)."[64]

Reed seems not to understand the ramifications of using a double language for the Christian influence of public policy. Nor is it clear he is supported on this by Dobson, Bauer, and Robertson. Such a stance drives one into the depths of the relation of Christian ethics to moral philosophy, politics, and even metaphysics. The movement has made little headway with any of these issues of public ethics. Reed's position about the need for a double language shows the movement is maturing. But has it grown up?

Catholic Synthesis—Catholic Truth

If something like the Catholic theory of subsidiarity is buried in the thought of the Christian Right, they have a point of contact with Patrick Moynihan. The Catholic theory of subsidiarity has guided Moynihan throughout his career. In 1991, writing in the journal *America,* Moynihan quoted words by Judith Gueron, President of the Manpower Demonstration Research Corporation, about the 1988 Family Support Act, a piece of legislation that Moynihan helped write and pass. The subsidiarity principle is evident throughout.

> The vision of welfare reform that we see reflected in the F.S.A. (Family Support Act) is of a "social contract" between poor parents and government, in which each party has responsibilities. Parents—both mothers and fathers—have the responsibility to contribute to the support of their children to the best of their abilities and to engage in activities designed to improve their self-sufficiency. The responsibilities of government are to provide the means for poor parents to become self-sufficient—such as employment services and supports—and to provide income when their best efforts fall short.[65]

In this statement, both fathers and mothers are seen to have abilities and responsibilities: the state must stand ready to help, but its help should enable families to exercise their responsibilities "to the best of their abilities." Even in the best circumstances, families should not stand totally outside the web of supporting relations. Throughout his article, Moynihan credits Pope Leo XIII's social encyclical *Rerum Novarum* as the dominant source of his vision.

Leo XIII was an avid Thomist, and one sees the imprint of Aristotle and Thomas Aquinas in *Rerum Novarum* and in his earlier *Arcanum* (1870), his major encyclical on marriage. John Paul II uses Thomas Aquinas and Aristotle as well, but he wraps them with the softer cloth of European phenomenology and Kantian personalism. One sees this personalism in his *Love and Responsibility* (1960).[66] The person, the young Karol Wojtyla tells us, is an end in herself that should never be treated as a means. In contrast to Kant, however, young Karol grounded the person as end in the *imago Dei* rather than the fact of human rationality.

In spite of these personalistic motifs, the older Thomistic naturalism, indeed its prototheory of kin altruism, is still found in John Paul II. Throughout his writings, the pope tries to unite the sacred, the personalistic, and the bodily aspects of marriage and family by moving downward from the first to the last. God's love is the origin of personhood, gives personhood its dignity, makes it free, leads a man and a woman to become attracted to one another and "consent" to form a "one flesh union," and gives them from this union the gift of children. These children are simultaneously "like" (that is, partial copies) of their parents and manifestations of God's love. This is the logic of the following words from John Paul's "Letter to Families" written for the United Nations International Year of the Family. The marital

> union of male and female, rather than closing them up in themselves, opens them toward a new life, toward a new person. As parents, they will be capable of giving life to a being like themselves, not only bone of their bones and flesh of their flesh (cf. Gen. 2:23), but an image and likeness of God—a person.[67]

We have in this passage a juxtaposition of three lines of thought: the child is simultaneously a person (as the parents are persons), flesh of their flesh (the element of kin altruism), and yet made in the "image and likeness of God." All three levels, as we saw earlier, were in Aquinas. Furthermore, the logic of the relations is more consistently from the top, from God, downward. The love of the couple is a result of the downpouring love of God for creation and the church; this love spills over into the procreation of life—of children. Both the child's personhood and natural substance—flesh, genes—come from God as well. Aquinas, as we saw in chapter 4, sometimes went from the bottom up, from the naturalistic motivations that stimulate family formation, and gradually added the personalistic and supernatural to this. Karol Wojtyla's personalism is not fundamentally different from the thought of Aquinas; it simply keeps the person more consistently in the center.

This helps us understand more profoundly what modern Catholic teachings on subsidiarity are all about. The naturalistic element of the Catholic theory of family and society is crucial to a correct understanding of the concept. Leo XIII, the most Thomistic of the popes, states it clearly in his *Rerum Novarum*.

The idea of subsidiarity is based on an argument about human nature; it brings together a philosophy of the person, labor, and the moral significance of the biological relation of parents and children with a threefold view of the person as having needs, rationality, and selfhood. A human is a rational being who is "aware of his needs and has foresight." Needs and rational awareness give humans the right not only to labor but to think ahead, plan, store, conserve, and own the fruits of their labor. In short, humans have the right to private property.[68] But as a right it does not trump all other rights.

The argument is not based alone on the two poles of natural need and rationality; there is also the factor of the self-involvement of the rational laborer in his or her work. The rational laborer is also a self who leaves an "imprint of himself" on the product of his labor and, indeed, "becomes so completely mingled with it as to . . . become to a large extent utterly inseparable from it."[69] Here Leo is offering a critique of socialism: no one, including the state, has a right unjustly to separate a rational worker from the property that satisfies her needs and with which she has become self-identified. Starting from the same point, the early Marx made much the same critique of capitalism. Capitalism, where owners claim profits for themselves, also alienates the self-involved worker from the fruits of his labor.[70] But Leo believes socialism is even worse on this score than capitalism. The right to property, he taught, does not mean that workers should not share their fruits with others. Sharing is the Christian's duty, but to have something to share *is a human right*.

Claims about the natural abilities, rights, and responsibilities of families link a theory of private property and the concept of subsidiarity. Leo's androcentric and paternalistic version of this connection served to perpetuate paternal authority and ownership. Despite this limitation, much can still be learned from him. His argument is implicit in much of the Christian Right's profamily argument, even though they are largely unaware of it. The family is for Leo, as it was for Aristotle, "older than any state." It is a society in itself with its own "rights and duties which depend not at all upon the state." These rights reside with the parents—in fact, with the "father." He tells us that a "most sacred law of nature ordains" that the "head" of a family should provide for the children he has begotten.

Then comes the key passage, which merits close analysis. Providing for children is not only a law of nature but an *inclination* embedded in human nature.

That same nature leads a father to want to provide for his

> children—who recall and in some sense extend his personality—a reasonable degree of protection against ill-fortune in life's uncertain course. This he can do only by leaving income yielding property to his children as his heirs. As we have said, the family is a true society equally with the state and like the state, it possesses its own source of government, the authority of the father. Provided that it stays within the bounds set for it by its own special purpose, the family has for this reason at least equal rights with the state to choose and employ whatever is necessary for its rightful life and liberty.[71]

This paragraph condenses huge chunks of Western religious, political, and ethical thought. How should we understand it?

Let's drop the word "father"; what is said can apply equally to biological mothers or fathers. Leo underscores (as do Aristotle, Thomas Aquinas, John Locke, and evolutionary psychologists) that both mothers and fathers are not just "ordained" to provide for their children; they are *inclined* to provide because their children, as Leo follows Aquinas in saying, "extend" their "personality."[72] Furthermore, the rights and responsibilities of parents to care for their children are partially based on this inclination; on the whole, no one else will have the same energies, investments, and degree of self-involvement. Finally, the inclination and duty of parents to labor and earn wealth that will support their children should not be impeded by government or any other institution. This, according to Leo, is part of the justification for the institution of private property and some method of inheritance.

Has Leo refuted socialism and communism only to end in the defense of unbridled capitalism? Not quite. He is aware that capitalism has its own dangerous consequences for families. And he is conscious of the need for the state to support needy families in the exercise of their capacities and duties. It is, therefore, the task of the state to keep its eye on the "whole system of laws and institutions" and mediate between its various parts. This includes requiring employers to pay a family wage, establishing the rights of workers to assemble and organize for just wages, regulating work conditions so that they enhance psychological and physical health, and assisting poor families to move toward an appropriate degree of self-sufficiency.[73] Leo concludes, "public authority ought to take proper care to safeguard the lives and well-being of the unpropertied class." Furthermore, he says: "not the least . . . of duties which fall to rulers in their regard for the common good . . . is to keep inviolate the justice which is called distributive by caring impartially for each and every class of citizen."[74]

A hundred years later, Pope John Paul II in his *Centisimus Annus* affirmed the teachings of *Rerum Novarum*. He does this, however, with his characteristic personalism. His affirmations included the right to private property, the right and obligation of parents to provide for their children, the necessity of government not to interfere in these parental prerogatives, but at the same time, the obligation of the state to help poor families and guarantee that employers treat workers justly.[75]

It is remarkable how utterly philosophical this line of argument is, how reliant it is on Aristotle's and Aquinas's philosophical anthropology, and how independent it is of biblical grounding. The same is true of the analogous arguments found in Ralph Reed and James Dobson. To this extent, Reed's assumption that there is common ground between evangelical and Catholic profamily strategies is correct. But it has as much to do with their shared Aristotelianism as with their shared Christianity. Parallel

anthropological arguments for the right to private property and the capacities and rights of families (and the relation between the two) can be
easily found in Aristotle.[76]

Catholics and Evangelicals
in Dialogue

In the end, however, the Protestant orders of creation and Catholic
subsidiarity are not completely antithetical. Karl Barth thought that they
were and saw creation solely as a "command of God" viewed from the
perspective of the revelation of Jesus Christ.[77] The doctrine of creation
for him had nothing to do with our natural observations of different
kinds of human action. But his contemporary Emil Brunner showed the
overlap between the orders of creation and the naturalistic observations
involved in the idea of subsidiarity. Brunner's thinking is a meeting
point between Catholic and Reformed thinking. He also offers a correc-
tive to any perspective that addresses all family issues with a *thin* theory
of mutuality alone. Brunner wrote that the principle of neighbor love is
not enough to order marriage and family: "For how can we possibly argue that union between the sexes must be limited to union with one person, and that such a union should be lifelong, on the basis of the general
idea of love of our neighbor?"[78] Our view of mutuality and neighbor is
thick: it brings equal regard together with concern for the different kinds
of premoral goods to be actualized in different spheres of life. Hence, it
is consistent with the thrust of Brunner's concerns.

We see the similarities when Brunner asks, what is the origin of the
mono in monogamy? His answer depends on a substructure of life dis-
coverable by human reason but completed by God's will for creation.
Reason, he tells us, shows us that there are different kinds of human
community—community built on work for a living (markets), community built on the desire for stability (government), and community built
on erotic attraction, the desire for children, and a need to educate them
(family).[79] The spheres of market, state, and family are "recognized by
means of reason . . . by means of the purely natural power of cognition."
They are built on the "psychophysical nature of man."[80] The meaning of
neighbor love is somewhat different, depending on which of these orders of human action and community it is applied to. In the sphere of
the family, it must order the long-term relation of husband and wife,
which provides not just for procreation but for the education of the
child. He writes, "the unity and permanence of the family . . . is the presupposition for the necessary continuity and uniformity of education."[81]

It is God's will in creation that further orders the raw natural inclinations that create families. *Eros,* intercourse, birth, growth—they do not alone dictate the long-term love of the other as a self and child of God. This comes from the command of God. Sacrificial love, the willingness to love the other in adversity, does not arise alone from these natural inclinations. The "orders" commanded by God complete nature's inclinations. Brunner provides a model, then, for current dialogue between Catholics and evangelicals by showing that the natural regularities assumed by subsidiarity and the natural regularities assumed by the Reformed doctrine of orders have points of contact.

In Catholic theology, the philosophical anthropology undergirding subsidiarity is blended with the theology of the *imago Dei.* In this view, all humans, in contrast to animals, are created at conception in the image of God. It is the image of God in humans that makes humans rational. As rational animals, humans project their selfhood into their labor and both their selfhood and genes into their children. But subsidiarity's philosophical anthropology can be extracted, or at least gain distance, from the doctrine of *imago Dei.* This accounts for its elasticity as both a theological concept and a public-philosophical concept that believers and unbelievers can understand. This explains why Catholics enter public discourse more easily and with a surer compass. They have a more differentiated double language that is both theological and philosophical, both confessional and public. The Christian Right enters public discourse with more confusion because its confessional and public languages are deeply entangled.

Catholicism's Lingering Patriarchy

Catholics historically have been sensitive to the male problematic, that is, the male alienation from families that has worried blacks and evangelicals. Aquinas's concern about this issue appears again in the writings of Leo XIII. Various quotations from Ephesians 5 were employed time and again in both his *Arcanum* and *Rerum Novarum* to sanction male servanthood, fidelity, and responsibility—all modeled after the love of Christ for the church. Yet this servanthood model of fatherhood was mixed by Leo with the idea that the father—as the head of the house, the principal breadwinner, and the moral leader of the family—needed a family wage to fulfill his responsibilities. Male responsibility was emphasized, but the distinction we have argued for that cuts the link between male responsibility and male monological headship was not applied by Leo.

Some progress has been made, however, in the encyclicals and statements of John Paul II. Mutual love between husband and wife has become more central in Catholic teaching than was the case as recently as Pius XI's *Casti Connubii* (1930). It is now coequal with procreation, although certainly not separated from it.[82] With sacramental love as its general context, mutual love, service to life, the development of society, and the mission of the church are the purposes of marriage that both Vatican II and John Paul affirm.[83] Even sexual pleasure receives a more positive vote in these later writings. But the unitive aspects of sexual pleasure never gain much distance, as Catholic moral theologians Lisa Cahill and Christine Gudorf lament, from the purposes of procreation.[84]

A slightly more flexible understanding of the roles of women can be detected in these later papal writings. Women have rights to enter the wage markets and public life, but never at the expense of denigrating motherhood or seeing employment as a substitute. Although later encyclicals speak less of a family wage earned by the husband, they still insist that it is necessary; they fail to say, however, what it means when both husband and wife are working.

In recent papal writings, the Ephesians analogy of Christ and church has been applied to both husbands and wives rather than only to husbands. In the Vatican II document "Pastoral Constitution on the Church in the Modern Word (*Gaudium et Spes,* 1965), we read the words, "just as He loved the Church and handed Himself over on her behalf, the spouses may love each other with perpetual fidelity through mutual self-bestowal."[85] In John Paul's "Letter to Families," he extends the identification with the self-giving of Christ to both husband and wife: "Only if husbands and wives share in that love and in that great mystery can they love 'to the end.'"[86]

But there is no clear renunciation of male headship in spite of the growing prominence of love as mutuality and equal regard. Nor is there an admission that if a wife can represent Jesus in marriage, a woman should be permitted to do the same in the priesthood, something that John Paul II has explicitly rejected. Nor is there any direct admission of the importance of intersubjectivity in implementing the justice and goods of love as mutuality and equal regard. In the end, in spite of these modifications of its patriarchy, there is no real dialogical understanding of married love, fully inclusive of women, present in the Catholic church.

Conclusion

The Christian profamily voices in the American family debate must be taken seriously. Their shared principle of subsidiarity, their appeals to family responsibility, their realism about male responsibility, their concern with children, their skepticism about the sexual liberation of the 1960s, and their growing willingness to emphasize the themes of mutuality and equal regard as core realities of family love—these elements must be respected.

But there is much that is incomplete. We can affirm the values of subsidiarity but recognize that its theological grounds are vague. Furthermore, there is a considerable distance between its abstract formulation and how it works in practice. Witness the disagreements in 1995 over welfare reform that existed between the National Conference of Catholic Bishops on the one hand and the Christian Coalition and Family Research Council on the other. All could hold to something like subsidiarity, but the bishops opposed cutting support for the poor, and the Coalition wanted to sacrifice these supports as part of cuts designed to guarantee a viable economic future for the next generation.

Finally, as we have said repeatedly, male responsibility and leadership must be a *shared* responsibility and leadership. It must be arrived at through an ethic of communicative discourse, an intersubjective understanding of equal regard. The conservative voices—whether African American, evangelical, or Catholic—have all fallen short of a full understanding of this ethic.

A dialogical understanding of mutual love must be part of the conscious ideological formulations of these movements. At the moment, this is not the case. This does not deny that in many instances, the lived reality of some conservative Christian families may be vastly better than the official rhetoric of certain conservative Christian groups would indicate. There is a great deal of intersubjective communication between Jim and Sally Turner, Maria and Robert Taylor, James and Francis Nelson, and Mary and Patrick Murphy—four of our conservative Christian families.

It was John Schneider, the man who once nearly murdered his wife before his conversion, who tried the hardest to give a genuine, although confused, dialogical understanding of the ethics of Ephesians 5. He admitted that these passages suggest that "wives should submit to their husbands. Sounds really harsh." But he continues:

> But also it says that husbands should love their wives as Christ loved the church. Okay, kind of interesting you know, you really have to be reading the Bible and understand what this is. Christ really loved the church 'cause he died for it.' You know what I'm saying? So it's a two-way street. What the Bible's saying is it's a two-way street.

What does it mean to say family authority is a two-way street? Is this really the implication of Ephesians? Our answer is that it is the *direction* of Ephesians. But it requires philosophical and theological reflection on Ephesians, and many other passages—especially those dealing with neighbor love—to come to this conclusion. It requires a critique of all monological ways of understanding mutuality and friendship between spouses. All this is required before John Schneider can arrive at the full meaning of "two-way street."

Has John, an admirable example of the evangelical profamily mind, arrived at this point? Not quite. For soon after stating his "two-way street" theory of the meaning of submission, he added "but wives should submit to their husbands, you know, in certain areas." In saying this, John Schneider becomes an apt example of the strengths and weaknesses—indeed, the double-mindedness—of much of the Christian profamily movement.

9

Economic Voices

State Family, Market Family, and Civil Society

Societies should be organized to help couples assume the responsibility of raising their children unless parental illness or incompetence requires other arrangements. Parents should have the support of churches, local communities, the market, and the state—in that order. Market and state must never be permitted to crowd out local communities and churches. But churches and local communities as parts of civil society are often undermined by market and state.

Markets and state have expanded in recent decades, and their cost-benefit determinations and bureaucratic functions have begun to take over the face-to-face and tradition-based interactions of civil society. As we saw in chapter 2, Jürgen Habermas and Alan Wolfe have called this process the "colonization of the life-world." Whether we call it civil society or the life-world, the point is the same: when this sector of society declines, families suffer.

Such strange bedfellows as Pope John Paul II and Ralph Reed are worried about this phenomenon. Reed is more concerned about the state than the market. John Paul II, like Habermas and Wolfe, and like his predecessors Leo XIII and Pius XI, is worried about *both* state and market usurping the initiatives of families. The Pope, Reed, Habermas, and Wolfe share a concern about the decline of civil society and the influence of state and market on its deterioration. Long before Harvard sociologist Robert Putnam's famous article titled "Bowling Alone" (1995)[1] called attention to "the strange disappearance of civic America,"[2] this issue had been the concern of a variety of commentators.

In the American family debate, popular rhetoric about the respective impact of market, state, and civil society on families can be volatile. At one extreme are those who bewail the intrusion of government bureaucrats and meddling judges in the "private" matters of family life. In this view, the troubles of families are produced by the ideology of liberal secular humanism that is promoted by government power and used to undermine spiritual and parental authority. At the other extreme are those who decry the takeover of families by corporate forces, the absorption of fathers *and* mothers into the demands of the market, and the reduction of family needs to the cost-benefit logic of economic competition. In this view, government should protect families from the dislocations of the market—a message seldom heard from political and social conservatives.[3] Between these extremes are those who defend civil society as the best support for families, including those (like Putnam) who lament its decline and those (like sociologists Nancy Ammerman and Robert Wuthnow) who portray more complex and hopeful assessments of its present well-being.[4] *We argue that church and synagogue as parts of civil society, whether they are declining or holding their own, are essential for the strength of civil society and the support of families.*

In this chapter, we listen to the voices of some who believe that the state is the answer to family problems. We also listen to those holding that the market—at least the *theory* of the market—is the answer. Both positions point to something important, but neither in itself is satisfactory. Rather, we hold that both market and state are important for strengthening families and that civil society (churches, neighborhoods, and voluntary associations) must itself be reinvigorated if market and state are to be contained and thereby enabled to make their proper contributions. Furthermore, we contend that both the Protestant "orders of creation" and Catholic subsidiarity, when held in tension and interpreted in light of the ethic of equal regard, provide important resources for the renewal of civil society.

The Political Economy of the Family: An Anthropological Perspective

An evolutionary-ecological view of parenting provides an important perspective on several dilemmas in the contemporary family debate. Vital biological tendencies—infant dependency, kin altruism, parental certainty, paternal investment, sexual exchange, mutual helpfulness with basic needs—provide bonds between mother, father, and child. These natural tendencies in self-transcending humans are quite fragile and need powerful supports to be sustained. Throughout this book we have avoided isolating parents and children from the wider social networks. We now extend this ecological perspective to include the importance of community networks that support family formation and the vulnerable process of having and raising children.

Anthropologist A. F. Robertson argues in his *Beyond the Family* (1991) that the processes of human reproduction are much more complex than we usually think.

> Reproduction is the process in which mature organisms exercise
> their physical capacity to produce other organisms, thereby regen-
> erating their species. . . . [H]uman reproduction transcends the
> lifespan of a single individual: the process involves a minimum of
> three persons, and exponentially larger numbers as one cycle of re-
> generation follows another. Organizing reproduction involves life-
> times of complicated relationships among many people. . . . It is,
> after all, the process by which society itself is recreated. Organiz-
> ing it demands extensive cooperation, not just among family mem-
> bers but in the wider context of community and state.[5]

The reproductive process, as Robertson sees it, refers not simply to biological procreation but to the entire range of activities that makes possible the continuation of the human species.

The procreating couple contributes to but does not exhaust the activity of human reproduction. Although central for providing energy, investment, and stability for reproduction and socialization, human
parents never were sufficient to themselves and are far less so today. The
economic system, state, schools, banks, neighborhood associations,
churches, and friendships all contribute. Robertson observes,

> The problem is that while we still make the prime assumption that
> organizing reproduction is properly and exclusively a family affair,
> it is very evident that in the kinds of society in which we now live,
> "families" have much less to do with the social organization of re-
> production than they ever did in the past.[6]

No family, in other words, is an island unto itself.

The risks incurred by the reproductive process are large. While some
biological tendencies shape the natural inclinations that undergird it, the
institutions developed by humans to manage these risks are not prede-
termined. Human natural tendencies are flexible and need to be guided
by society and culture. In recognizing how institutions legitimate power
and what counts for knowledge, "social constructivists" like Michel Foucault and Thomas Laqueur are partially correct.[7] Our central sexual tendencies are multiple, are somewhat contradictory, and are always further
organized by institutional and cultural contexts. Although Robertson may
overstate his case, he writes, "Nature seduces us with the pleasures of sex
but leaves the ensuing burdens of reproduction to the powers of organization and invention."[8] The plasticity of these biological tendencies, while
a great benefit to humans as they adapt to various ecological situations,
also places a premium on our abilities to construct forms of social relatedness that can genuinely support and express human flourishing.

According to Robertson, humans bear the risks of reproduction by
creating a panoply of social and economic networks: "Faced with this

instability at the reproductive nucleus, it is fortunate that human beings have the capacity . . . to form larger, durable associations: households, corporations, communities, states."[9] Forming stable relationships beyond the mother-father-child nucleus is itself an evolutionary strategy to secure the reproductive process.

Market, State, and the
Decline of Civil Society

Alan Wolfe helped us see how both state and market, as expressions of technical rationality, can undermine families and voluntary organizations even while they function as networks of support. State bureaucracies can do this by creating a climate of dependency, thereby undermining what the subsidiarity doctrine calls the right and capacity of individuals, families, and small communities to exercise their natural inclinations to initiate care for themselves. Markets do this by influencing us to think of family and neighborhood in cost-benefit and instrumental terms, thereby undermining more generous forms of voluntary care. State and the market, Wolfe continues, are designed to regulate relations between people who are more or less "strangers." "The paradox of modernity," he writes, "is that the more people depend on one another owing to an ever-widening circle of obligations, the fewer are the agreed-upon guidelines for organizing the moral rules that can account for those obligations."[10] Why are there fewer guidelines? The answer: the market and the state often undercut the capacity of the institutions of civil society to create, sustain, and revise these rules.

State Familism American-Style

In spite of these warnings, some strongly advocate greater roles for government in solving family problems. Conservatives pin the label of "big government" on liberals, a designation that Bill Clinton learned to deny and even disparage. Even though he announced the end of big government, some serious political theorists still argue for expansive government involvement in family problems.

The State and
Expressive Individualism

We saw in chapter 2 how Dizard and Gadlin in *Minimal Family* argue that the rise of "expressive individualism" is the dominant cultural trend producing family disruption. Expressive individualism encourages persons "to have a robust sense of entitlement and a dramatically reduced inclination to defer gratification."[11] "The expressive self," they observe, "is one eager for challenge, for change, for new experience."[12] In contrast to Bellah, who first introduced but did not like the expressive individualist, Dizard and Gadlin believe there are few ways to stem the cultural tide in this direction.

What is their solution to the family problems that expressive individualism has helped create? Their answer is a new kind of state or *public familism,* a "shift in the locus of responsibility for well-being, one's own as well as that of others, from the family to the broader community."[13] Society needs more comprehensive public programs to relieve burdens that families can no longer bear. Expressive individualism is more suited to family forms where there are "minimal obligations and enlarged scope for self-actualization."[14] "At the extreme," they note, "expressive individualism dissolves the emotional basis upon which crucial aspects of social life rest, precisely because it disparages all forms of constraint."[15]

Dizard and Gadlin have some reservations about expressive individualism. They are open to expressive individualism in the areas of sexual experimentation, career decisions, consumer choice, and emotional satisfaction but not regarding certain collective obligations to the state. For them, the dilemma is this: although left to itself, expressive individualism is a dead end, returning to traditional familism is both impossible and undesirable. Their idea of public familism is an effort to give public support to expressive individualism yet provide means by which persons can be connected to "a larger social purpose." They do not completely bemoan expressive individualism as do neoconservatives like Bellah, Lasch, or Rieff. For them it is not the demise of the family that is the problem but rather the loss of connection and community. By community, they mean state supports to individuals and familylike groups who have not flourished in the society created by expressive individualism. They write, "What we experience as a crisis of the family is less a family problem than it is a breakdown in the means by which individuals feel connected to their milieu."[16] What will provide that sense of connection?

Dizard and Gadlin propose that we shift the center of our obligations from family and kin to wider aggregates, largely through the instruments of government legislation. We hear in this proposal shades of Plato's thought experiment in the *Republic,* in which the state assumes obligations formerly thought to belong to individuals. They urge parents to participate in the formation of public policies that lessen the burdens of reproduction (day care, child allowances, welfare for single mothers, state-financed foster and elder care, orphanages) and give it to the whole community, through state instruments. They write, "we must put a premium on citizenship, on making involvement a central feature of adulthood."[17]

Note the twist: the cure for the excesses of expressive individualism is for citizens to participate together in getting the state to assume responsibility for what they no longer can or want to care for themselves. They admit the need for greater connections between individuals, but the only way they see to achieve this is through public policies of the state. Through this form of citizenship, expressive individualism may retain its newly won freedoms and be saved from collapsing on itself.

Political Culture
and State Beneficence

A second theory of state familism is proposed by University of Minnesota social scientist Shirley Zimmerman. She is a strong advocate of the positive role of government in family life. Based on an array of empirical studies, she argues that government programs, rather than hurting families, actually strengthen them, even the so-called nuclear family.

Zimmerman has argued that family well-being varies by political culture. There are three types of political culture: individualistic, which minimizes government intervention; moralistic, which emphasizes the public good over the private; and traditionalistic, which values government intervention but only when aimed at preserving traditional forms of relatedness.[18] Zimmerman is interested in how these different political cultures promote social integration, which she defines as the strength of individual ties to the normative institutions of society.

Her research indicates that the more a state's political culture legitimates government intervention, the greater the social integration and the higher the well-being of families. Among our fifty states, those "that were more individualistic did *less* to mediate connections among people, and had *lower* levels of individual and family well-being; by the same token, states that were *less* individualistic did more to mediate connections among people and had *higher* levels of individual and family well-being."[19]

It is not true, she concludes, that the "government that governs least, or does the least, is best." She believes that there is no evidence that government programs produce family breakup, illegitimacy, and poverty.[20] Although Zimmerman does not discuss expressive individualism, she joins Dizard and Gadlin in rejecting a political culture that appears coercively to require individual responsibility. For all three scholars, it is a mutual care mediated through government—care at one remove—that is effective.

A Critique of State Familism

These two arguments for state familism have strengths that should not be neglected. Surely, as Robertson has argued and as the doctrine of subsidiarity suggests, more inclusive orders of organization like governments have a role in assisting, protecting, enhancing, and mediating between local communities and families. So long as neighborhoods remain broken, churches overburdened, and private charities stretched thin, there will be a need for state intervention to secure the reproductive process against its inherent vulnerability.

But these two positions present difficulties. First, both completely ignore civil society—the mediating institutions of civic organizations, churches, boys' and girls' clubs, neighborhood support groups, and labor unions. Both positions consider only the state and families—*nothing between*. Second, there is something disturbing about Dizard and Gadlin's passive acceptance of expressive individualism as a *fait accompli* from which there is no retreat. Once again, they fail to consider the relevance of civil society. They see no points of leverage from which social and cultural transformations can take place, such as have been provided by the voluntary organizations of civil society. Hence, Dizard and Gadlin conclude too quickly that our only recourse is to have public policy take up the slack of our self-preoccupations.

Furthermore, it is unrealistic to think that if expressive individualism leads us to exercise *less* care for our close kin, we will, somehow, exercise *more* care in designing remote government programs to exercise this care in our place. Our love ethic of equal regard takes the claims and needs of the self and other with equal seriousness. Love as equal regard affirms individual self-regard, but it does not collapse into an expressive individualism that thrives at the expense of family obligations.

Finally, Zimmerman's argument about the importance of political culture should be taken seriously. She neglects, however, documented cases by liberal social scientists Mary Jo Bane and David Ellwood in *Welfare Realities* (1994) that show how some patterns of government intervention do contribute to the culture of dependency.[21] Neither does Zimmerman fully account for the deeper sources of "political culture." Are not the culture-carrying and culture-creating institutions of civil society a major source of political culture, as Wolfe and Putnam would argue? If civil society is declining, won't the hopes and dreams guiding political culture wane as well? Political scientist David Held says it well: the "current structure of civil society does not create conditions for effective participation, proper political understanding and equal control of the political agenda."[22] Is successful government support of families a matter of what the state does by itself, or is it more how government orchestrates its interventions *in relation to* evolving institutions of civil society?

Market Voices and Market Theories

Just as the state has spread into family life, so have market forces. We see it first in the culture of consumerism that appeared in the late 1800s with the emergence of large department stores and mass-market advertising. Historian William Leach has referred to this process as the "democratization of desire," by which he means the equal rights of everyone "to desire the same goods and to enter the same world of comfort and luxury."[23] This highly individualistic understanding of democracy emphasized "self-pleasure and self-fulfillment over community or civic well-being."[24]

By the 1920s, popular culture was permeated with images of the "consumer family" as the ideal family: parents and children surrounded by automobiles, gas stoves, and other icons of mass consumption. Women were the linchpin of this imagery. On the one hand, they were to be in charge of the domestic sphere and were, therefore, the chief consumers. On the other hand, as historian Alan Dawley has observed, "the very advertising imagery that portrayed consumption as the route to freedom lured housewives into the job market."[25] The culture of consumerism both disrupted and intensified the patriarchal character of family life. It disrupted patriarchy by encouraging women to enter the paid labor force; it intensified patriarchy because women still had the primary responsibility in the domestic sphere. Consumerism, some believe, cripples the ability to delay gratification and to evaluate life's ends beyond the satisfaction of immediate impulses. Consumer products become the "drug" that families use to hide from themselves the disappointments and frustrations that are rooted in impoverished relationships, both in the family and in civil society at large.[26]

Although consumerism summarizes the felt-experience of a market society, the theory of the market has cultural implications for the family as well, especially for those who turn to the market both to understand family changes and to find solutions. The Chicago school of economics describes the influence of markets on families, but it also uses the theory of markets to explain how families *should* function. The Chicago school goes beyond economic analysis and addresses, as Alan Wolfe points out, "issues in moral philosophy" that pertain to families.[27] Wolfe charges this school with legitimating the culturewide drift toward viewing families in analogy to the cost-benefit logic of the market.[28] Long-term commitments, parental obligations, and intimate relations between husband and wife are being shaped increasingly by the market values of short-term satisfactions, utilitarian individualism, and technical rationality. The Chicago school, Wolfe claims, gives aid and comfort to this process.

Through its many Nobel prize winners, this school of economics is one of the most powerful voices of the social sciences in America and the world. Both church and the general public should take this voice as seriously as the voice of state familism. The two preeminent theorists are Gary Becker, winner of the 1993 Nobel prize in economics, and Judge Richard Posner, rumored to become a possible candidate for the U.S. Supreme Court.

Becker is the leading Chicago economist writing on the family. In his *Treatise on the Family* (1991), he applied economic theory to an analysis of human activities such as families.[29] In his earlier *Human Capital* (1975) and *The Economic Approach to Human Behavior* (1976), Becker expanded the concept of wealth beyond money and property to include such things as human learning and skill, the wise use of time, the value of children, and the worth of domestic or household work.[30] These, he argues, are forms of capital—what he calls "human capital" in contrast to material capital or wealth.

Posner follows Becker in this expansive concept of economic wealth and brings these insights to the theory of law and jurisprudence. Posner, once a law professor at the University of Chicago and now judge of the U.S. Seventh Circuit Court of Appeals, is a leading figure in the so-called law and economics movement, a movement that defines law in relation to its economic functions. Posner's most relevant book for our purposes is his major contribution to the legal theory of sex and family titled *Sex and Reason* (1992).[31]

Becker and the Efficient Family

Gary Becker is a neoclassical economic theorist. The basic theory of neoclassical economics is easy enough: humans always act rationally to maximize individual satisfactions or utility in economic environments, as they perceive them.[32] They do this, in other words, within the context of the opportunities for satisfaction provided by various markets. A market is a context of exchange where an individual uses his or her money or property to purchase commodities that satisfy enduring desires. Rational action is means-end and cost-benefit action; the rational individual balances the satisfactions of a commodity with the costs of obtaining it.

Classical economic theory assumes that humans are driven by a relatively small but stable set of desires. Becker describes these desires as underlying preferences that inform a variety of more specific interests.

They include inclinations toward "health, prestige, sensual pleasure, benevolence, or envy."[33] Benevolence refers to parents' concern for their own children. Both Becker and Posner agree with sociobiologists that this is an inborn human tendency. We love our natural children— as well as our blood-related brothers, sisters, nieces, and nephews— because they carry our genes and are, for that reason, partially us.[34] This is the theory of kin altruism that we also use but in quite different ways.

Thomas Aquinas said that we love our children for two reasons: because they are part of us and because they are gifts—veritable manifestations—of the goodness of God. By contrast, Becker and Posner are stark naturalists and realists—reductionists, one might say. They do not inhabit a world in which God gives good gifts. Love of our children is for them simply and completely one of the stable desires that humans want their various markets to satisfy.

Becker applies rational-choice theory to nonmaterial aspects of life by metaphorically extending its language. For instance, a home is a little "factory" that both "produces" and "consumes" wealth. Children are both "consumer" and "producer durables."[35] Children give "satisfaction" to their parents just as does food, clothing, or a night at the movies. Children are like "commodities," and parents can be said to "consume" their children as they do other commodities. People bring "cost-benefit" calculations to the selection of their mates just as they do to decisions about cars and even their decisions to have children. That is why we have fewer children today: their costs in relation to the benefits they afford have gone up.

Becker's expansion of the concept of wealth has the advantage of helping us perceive the importance of other forms of utility besides property and money. Domestic labor—meal preparation, house cleaning, childcare, house and automobile maintenance—produces wealth. To show how this is true, we can assign monetary values to these activities. Because wealth refers to total produced and consumed satisfactions, Becker demonstrates how two-person households with differentiated functions (especially men and women in marriages) produce more wealth than single-person households.[36] In expanding the concept of wealth, Becker makes it nearly equivalent to the *ordo bonorum* (the order of the premoral or nonmoral good) as this concept functions in the thought of neo-Thomist Louis Janssens and, before that, in classical Aristotelian and Thomistic ethical traditions. What is different is the centrality that Becker gives to individual cost-benefit satisfactions within the constraints of existing market environments.

We saw in chapter 2 how rational-choice theory analyzes the situation of families today. Men left the farm and went into the wage market. In the twentieth century women followed. Women became less dependent on men, more dependent on the wage market, and in some cases more dependent on welfare and the government. Divorce and nonmarriage became more manageable. The Chicago school of economics explains everything, even the emergence of feminism, as a consequence of the interaction between rational choice and new market opportunities. Cultural explanations such as Bellah's and Lasch's are rejected.

Posner and the
Bioeconomic Theory of Families

For Richard Posner, the function of law is to maximize society's utility—its wealth, in Becker's broad sense of the term.[37] Posner refers to his position as "consequentialist" and "morally neutral." In reality, it is "utilitarian" in ethical orientation and "libertarian" in its social philosophy.[38] Posner is sophisticated enough to know that utilitarianism is not a morally neutral philosophy. What does he have in mind? His answer is that the utilitarian can be dispassionate—can analyze the consequences of legal and economic arrangements without prior religious or philosophical biases.

Posner brings a "bioeconomic" theory of sexuality to his utilitarian theory of family law. It is a synthesis of evolutionary psychology and the rational-choice theory of markets. He holds that males and females follow asymmetrical patterns to maximize their inclusive fitness and do this within the possibilities of various environments or markets.[39] Given these tendencies, Posner thinks that rational choice has led humans in most ancient societies to be polygynous. This was due not to the inequality between men and women but to the disparity of wealth and power among men themselves. This disparity gave some men, especially in agricultural societies, more resources to attract women and meet their needs for protection during their vulnerable childbearing years.[40]

Because modern societies are built around capital and wages, men and women can earn separate incomes. Such societies are also wealthy enough for governments to support poor women and their children, a form of "state polygyny" where many women in effect marry the state.[41] In such markets, men and women increasingly choose to work out their satisfactions and inclusive fitness independently of each other—hence, the high divorce rate, late marriages, large numbers of out-of-wedlock births, and increased use of artificial insemination by unmarried women.

Posner believes that the law can and should do little to change these trends and that *the companionate mother-father partnership raising children may be passing into a minority position in modern societies.* He believes that protecting and enhancing the companionate family can no longer be the central commitment of the law, as it has been under the impact of Christianity and the incorporation of Catholic canon law into secular law.[42] Sweden, where family instability is extremely high, has shown that the mother-father family is not essential for the well-being of children and mothers. There family instability has not translated into poverty for mothers and their offspring as it has in the United States.

The only issue remaining for Posner is whether absent fathers are costly for children. If it can be proved that the presence of fathers in families is required for the well-being (read "wealth") of children independent of their economic support, then Posner would lend the force of law to the defense of the mother-father family. But after a rather cursory review of the social science literature existing in the early 1990s, he saw no solid evidence supporting such a vaunted role for the male half of the race.[43]

Clearly, Posner did his research on this issue too quickly and too soon. He ignored evidence we have presented showing that fathers are important for both sons and daughters, neglected recent evolutionary arguments for the importance of paternal investment, and entirely missed other health and personal benefits to children of long-term committed relationships. Nor did Posner acknowledge the many ways that families benefit men, as social scientist James Q. Wilson has argued, in channeling their sexuality and aggression, overcoming their tendency to drift into isolation and self-indulgence, and maintaining their health.[44] Sociologist Linda Waite has brought together definitive demographic evidence that both men and women, but especially men, profit immensely from marriage as measured by mental and physical health, wealth, sexual fulfillment, and general life satisfaction.[45]

Because Posner feels that fathers are not needed, he does something that most Chicago economists would never imagine. His solution to fatherlessness is Sweden's form of a welfare state with its extensive state-sponsored provisions for day care, medical insurance, paid pregnancy leaves, unemployment compensation, and other such supports necessary to remedy the current situation that has caused the feminization of kinship to become the feminization of poverty. Posner agrees with Dizard and Gadlin: rather than trying to change behaviors that lead to divorce and fatherlessness, we should learn to support those who suffer from the consequences. Although Posner moves toward state familism, he does not affirm socialism: in fact, he claims it takes the superior power of capitalism to support the state family he envisions.

Posner's Challenge to
the Moral View of Families

In spite of Posner's belief that his utilitarian-libertarian theory of family law will eventually replace Jewish and Christian influence on the law, he holds a somewhat positive view of their accomplishments. Christianity helped create the companionate family, proclaimed that men and women were made in the image of God, limited arbitrary patriarchal divorce, rejected the Greco-Roman double standard in sexual ethics, and made fathers important for the spiritual education of their children.[46] These trends were visible, he admits, in primitive Christianity but became synthesized with Roman family law in the creation of Catholic canon law. After some amendments of Catholic canon law by the leaders of the Reformation, this tradition flowed into the secular law of most modern societies.

But Posner is consistent in his rational-choice utilitarianism. When faced with the worldwide drift toward the feminization of kinship and the declining role of fathers, he calculates in rational-choice terms the consequences of these trends. Christianity, he believes, with its foundations in natural law, has overestimated the natural need for fathers to provide for and protect their children in companionate families. He writes, "Under the social and economic conditions prevailing in modern societies such as that of Sweden, an insistence on compliance with the traditional marriage-centered Christian morality may no longer be necessary for the protection of women and children."[47]

A Critique of the
Rational-Choice Family

Posner can hold this position because, in the end, he holds that humans are rational egos and not selves. Humans are for him reality-oriented rational maximizers and not selves with identities, self-images, anxieties, self-fragmentations, self-deceptions, and profound needs for self-regard and self-cohesion. He sees humans as pervasively satisfaction seeking; they readily sacrifice dignity, self-esteem, self-justification, and a sense of equal regard for increased utility.

It seems simplistic to say that humans need both dignity and wealth, regard and material resources. Such a simple statement points to the basic difference separating the world of Christian anthropology from the view of humans found in market-oriented rational-choice theory.

Because Becker and Posner live in a world of egos without selves, they also live in a world of selves without narratives and stories. They are blind to the narratives—even quasi-religious narratives—that are implicit in their own economic theories. Because their thought contains such narratives, they are fit candidates for theological analysis.

Recent analyses of various social science disciplines have shown that, in spite of their alleged moral and metaphysical neutrality, they are riddled with deep metaphors and narratives possessing religious significance.[48] Economist Donald McCloskey in his engaging *If You're So Smart: The Narrative of Economic Expertise* (1990) argues that like other arts and sciences, economics uses what he calls "the whole rhetorical tetrad: fact, logic, metaphor, and story."[49] Although he claims neoclassical economists such as Becker are aware that they use metaphors when they self-consciously extend the terminology of markets into nonmarket spheres such as families, they are unaware of the ethical stories that they implicitly advocate, such as the inevitability and moral permissibility of greed.[50] To their credit, McCloskey thinks economists advocate a prudent greed aimed toward the production and not just the consumption of wealth. What McCloskey writes about neoclassical theory as a whole applies to Becker's economic theory of the family. "The ethical effect of paying close attention to economic behavior . . . is not entirely bad."[51] It helps us think ahead, make revisions, be methodical. From this angle, Becker's economics is not unlike the "Protestant ethic" of families that sociologists have described.[52] The good family is the hardworking and somewhat ascetic economic unit that produces more than it consumes.

Posner tells a different moral story. Becker would restore not just the companionate family but even the traditional (or industrial) family—the breadwinning husband and the mother producing material and human capital at home. Posner's story, however, points to an ethics of consumption more than production. He tells a story of how both market and state will replace the father and between them produce the wealth necessary to keep the feminization of kinship from becoming the feminization of poverty.

Evaluating these stories is not McCloskey's main aim. His point, and a very good one, is that *societies need more than one story to make them work.*[53] McCloskey believes that the neoclassical story of honest, hardworking, and prudent self-interest is not bad as far as the sphere of economics is concerned. He agrees that this story and ethic are relevant to the economic dimensions of families. Indeed, *we tend to agree:* societies—even families—need multiple and complementary stories. To that extent, there is a place—a limited one—for something like the Chicago school's economic story of families. But this is true only if countervailing stories keep it in check.

People need to understand the bioeconomic dimensions of families. Young people, as a part of marriage preparation, need to understand that families are in part about high-stake bioeconomic goods and huge investments of resources. Properly guided by a larger moral framework, people should make their investments wisely. Indeed, this is the level of family life that is properly governed by public contracts. Sexual exchange, childbirth, and childrearing are not matters of private predilections and tastes like choosing between cappuccino or mocha. The stakes are much higher. These are big-ticket items that affect the material health and wealth of all concerned. Some single mothers, publicly harassed deadbeat fathers, and teenagers with sexually transmitted diseases learn this truth *too late.* If people really understood the material costs at stake, they might be far more cautious, prudent, and deliberate in making sexual and procreative choices than modern romantic, individualistic, and privatistic views of sexuality lead them to be.

Other Stories, Alternative Ethics

The bioeconomic understanding of families, however, cannot stand alone. It needs to be bounded and organized within more explicit ethical and narrative understandings. Amitai Etzioni in *The Moral Dimension* (1988) demonstrates how economic decisions must not, and generally do not, rest solely on cost-benefit calculations, as important as these are in a limited sense.[54] The Chicago school neglects, he believes, the broader "deontological" logic of justice that surrounds the utilitarianism that appears, at first glance, to dominate market and sometimes family decisions.

Etzioni believes that humans have multiple selves, including both moral selves and selves that perform rational calculations. Our calculating selves are bounded and guided by our moral selves. The moral self, according to Etzioni, operates by using deontological principles of duty or reversible obligation. It treats other people as ends and not as means only, and it regards others equally as seriously as it does itself. In keeping with his view of the moral self, he recommends a "mixed deontological" ethic for both markets and families, an ethic that finds a place for judgments about costs and benefits but places them within a wider moral field defined by the fundamental moral idea of equal respect for persons. This kind of moral thinking should even guide and constrain economic transactions about costs and benefits.

Within this ethic, there is room for "teleological" judgments about maximizing mutual advantage. Indeed, at the teleological level, Etzioni argues for the importance of fathers in the well-being of children, reading the costs and benefits of absent fathers in complete opposition to Posner.[55] His mixed deontological ethic, which subordinates calculations about the good to respect for persons, has similarities to our love ethic of equal regard. Both bring together a formal theory of equal respect (the *ordo caritatis*) with a concern to maximize life's satisfaction (the *ordo bonorum*), subsuming the latter to the demands and constraints of the former.

Although Posner flirts with the deontological constraints of an equal-regard ideal of the companionate marriage, with admirable consistency he is willing to sacrifice it to the vision of utility that he believes the law should serve. Becker, on the other hand, speaks unwittingly in several places of "equality" in family relationships without fully realizing that this is generally thought to be a deontological concept based on a judgment about the equal dignity of persons. To invoke the concept of equality without careful explanation compromises the purity of his rational-choice model, an inconsistency one finds sooner or later in all rational-choice thinking.[56] Christian family theory is based on judgments about the equal good of all selves before God. Starting with this, Christians will do well to follow Aquinas in allowing for subordinate judgments based on the infant's needs, paternal certainty, and kin altruism. Aquinas could have absorbed Becker's and Posner's bioeconomics, but Becker and Posner cannot absorb the ethic and narrative of Aquinas without forsaking their reductionist epistemology.

The narrative and ethic surrounding rational-choice economics are a fit subject for theological critique. From a Christian perspective, they are not adequate. Although moral philosophers have shown for centuries that moral commitment cannot be grounded on ethical egoist assumptions, this is nonetheless the kind of moral thinking basic to rational-choice theory. Commitments dissolve in an ethical-egoist morality when costs exceed benefits. Societies in their public policies should seek to maximize the benefits of marriage and family over their costs, but *they cannot stabilize families through these incentives alone.* Posner's story is even more unsatisfactory than Becker's because it fits so poorly the facts about parental and paternal investment that ancients knew and that moderns are now reclaiming. If fathers are needed, Posner has no moral story that might inspire them to accept their responsibilities.

From a theological perspective, rational-choice theory makes a profound mistake. In almost all religions, and particularly Judeo-Christian traditions, it is considered a tragic mistake, even the essence of human sinfulness, to measure all the goods of life by their market or exchange value. No more powerful statement of this can be found than the biblical parable of the rich man who built new barns to store his wealth and then measured his "soul"—the essence of his self or personhood—by the abundance of his possessions. Then God said to him, "You fool! This very night your life is being demanded of you. And the things you have prepared, whose will they be?" The parable concludes with the words, "So it is with those who store up treasures for themselves but are not rich toward God" (Luke 12:19–21).

This parable does not say that there is no place for the rational-choice narratives of Becker and Posner. Indeed, the parables abound in references to landlords who hire and fire, who expect an honest day's work from their employees, and who hope for returns on their investments. These religious stories did not totally displace the economic stories of their day; they instead constituted a countervailing narrative that balanced and relativized them. In the same way, the Gospel parables should not totally displace the material aspects of marriage and families; they instead should relativize and balance them with other stories that have primarily to do with the anxiety-driven excesses of the will, the inevitability of loss, and the possibilities of recovery and renewal—both material and spiritual.

The Demise of Civil Society

Our final criticism concerns Becker's and Posner's neglect of civil society. Dizard, Gadlin, and Zimmerman mostly ignore it, speaking only of state and individuals. Becker and Posner either ignore the institutions of civil society or reduce them to their market value. Although they discuss schools, clubs, and churches, they do so mainly in terms of their need-satisfying and wealth-producing functions. Voluntary civil institutions as the arena of tradition, moral discourse, and the ethical reconstruction of society are not their central concern.

As we have seen, there is new public interest in civil society. Politicians now admit that government cannot solve all problems and that help from civil institutions is needed. Catholic subsidiarity values civil society as a source of basic initiatives. Neo-Reformed theology speaks of the relatively autonomous institutions of civil society: family, market, and church, all covenantally responsible to God. Many civic leaders now see voluntary institutions as the basic source of character formation.

We agree that civil society is the carrier of the fundamental narratives, ethics, and social networks that support families. The religious narratives that balance economic narratives are carried by the institutions of civil society, with churches and synagogues chief among them. The failure to address civil society as a support for families was a shortcoming of theorists of state familism; it is equally a shortcoming for those who find the family's salvation in the logic of the market.

The institutions of civil society are crucial resources for all families—intact, two-parent families, single-parent families, stepfamilies, and gays and lesbians who bear responsibilities for children. In spite of the prominence given in this book to supporting the intact and egalitarian mother-father partnership, trends toward family disruption will not be immediately reversed. Even if trends toward disruption are slowed, alternative families will continue to exist. They too need appropriate supports from state and market, but they need support even more from the institutions of civil society. But that is the problem. *The crisis of the family is paralleled by an analogous crisis in other parts of civil society.* In order to support and renew families, we must renew as well all other aspects of civil society.

Civil Society and
Help for *All* Families

In his controversial "Bowling Alone" article and elsewhere, Robert Putnam documents the retreat of Americans from their voluntary organizations. Ever since Alexis de Tocqueville's report of his visit to our shores, the United States has been known as an unusually civic-minded country, a nation of joiners. The evidence warranting such a reputation appears to be declining, especially since World War II. Putnam's research indicates that membership and participation is declining in such men's organizations as Lions, Elks, Moose, Eagles, Jaycees; women's groups such as the League of Women Voters, the Federation of Women's Clubs; churches, Red Cross, Boy Scouts, labor unions, parent-teacher associations, choral clubs, neighborhood athletic associations, and indeed bowling leagues.[57] More people are bowling today than ever before, but bowling in leagues is down 40 percent since 1980. Organizations such as the Sierra Club and the American Association of Retired Persons have increased their membership. But Putnam notices that these are generally single-cause, low-participation organizations in which the chief act of membership is writing a check for dues.

Some have accused Putnam of exaggerating. For instance, people not bowling in leagues may be bowling with friends. Furthermore, churches and synagogues may not be declining even though their general attendance is still sinking. Sociologist Nancy Ammerman's study of 449 congregations found some that were dying, some thriving, and many new congregations.[58] Robert Wuthnow argues that Putnam's thesis only partly holds with congregations. His studies show that church membership means less to people, that churches have less influence on public life (with the exception of the new political involvement of evangelicals), but that there is remarkable vitality in the "small group" movement in churches.[59] Putnam's thesis may have merit when applied to civil society as a whole, but congregations are still centers of vitality.

But if Putnam is partly right, what have we lost with the deterioration of civic participation? We have lost networks of mutual helpfulness, social dialogues that create local norms, friendships that keep us from loneliness, community guidance of our children, funds of successful family traditions, valuable skills learned from one another, adult mentors for our children, neighborly interest, baby-sitting exchanges, mutual protection, reciprocal material help—the list goes on. Many of these "dense networks" of mutual assistance are clearly beneficial to families— to all families but especially those that need extra amounts of support from the outside, *such as single-parent families and stepfamilies.*

As we discussed in chapter 2, the networks of a healthy civil society constitute "social capital"—a favorite new phrase of the social sciences. Sociologist James Coleman introduced the term by extending the idea of "human capital" (education, skills, health) invented by economist Gary Becker. Social capital refers to the resources of social networks, especially the many ways the interactions and traditions of civil society define and guide our daily lives, including the action of our children.[60] If the institutions of civil society are numerous and healthy, they constitute social capital for the guidance of individual action. This is another form of wealth. Material capital, human capital, social capital—every society needs all three to be successful.

But we should ask, why all this obsession with the economic metaphor "capital"? Why extend it to the human capacities and the social networks of civil society? The answer is that this is the only way that rational-choice social scientists can admit *that money and material wealth alone will not solve the problems of the family.* Those supporting public familism are tempted to believe that the material wealth of the state will solve all family problems. Market family theorists such as Robert Dole and other economic conservatives are inclined to think that the material wealth of the market will solve all problems. Now comes a message from economic social scientists themselves that *money won't do the job all by itself.* We need social capital to help form human capital. Coleman became famous for his research showing that wealthy public schools do not in themselves provide good education. Parental support and involvement in their children's education, he found, is the more crucial factor.[61] Strong families are in this case social capital that create human capital—educated kids. Do we now hear economists delivering the biblical message that we cannot live by bread alone?

The message, however, *is* distorted. Underneath the language of capital is the rational-choice model of human action so pervasive in the social sciences. If all human action is guided by calculations that maximize individual satisfactions, then indeed the word "capital" is appropriate. We have argued, however, that although there is in human action a place for concern about the calculation of premoral goods, this is morally acceptable only within a framework of equal regard that sees humans as ends and never as means only. More pointedly stated, some of the social norms carried by what Coleman calls social capital cannot be justified on rational-choice grounds. They must be grounded in other ways—deontologically, or by tradition, or by revelation. If that is the case, then why call these social norms "capital"?

Social Capital, Disrupted Families, and the Church

When a theory of social capital is placed within a broader ethic of equal regard, it can help illustrate some contributions churches make to families. If the institutions of civil society constitute social capital, then churches are by far, at least in the United States, the most important aspect of civil society to consider. Concepts of social capital help the secular mind understand why churches can contribute to the norms fostering intact, egalitarian families as well as the norms that help disrupted families to work better.

After presenting evidence that, on average, single parents and stepparents do less well with children than do families with two biological parents, McLanahan and Sandefur shift gears in the last chapter of *Growing Up with a Single Parent*. They show what it takes to help disrupted families do better.[62] Biological relatedness does, on average, increase parental investment, *but it is not the whole story*. They use Coleman to show how parental investment has a related consequence; it brings children into contact with the social capital of their parents—with the networks of community relatedness in neighbors, friends, extended family members (doting grandparents, uncles, aunts, cousins), schools, clubs, and churches. According to them, a major reason that the children of divorce and out-of-wedlock births do more poorly is this: the social capital for these children is dramatically reduced. For children of divorce, especially in the days of no-fault divorce, the family home is frequently sold or left behind; mother and children move to a different neighborhood; contact with the father and the father's networks goes down; contact with paternal grandparents and extended family may decline; the mother may spend less time with children because she must now work; the mother has less time to take children to clubs, friends, and churches; old friends are lost because of changes in residence and because single parenthood itself forces realignments in friendships.

The child born out of wedlock may never know the father well and have no contact with the father's social networks. Many single parents live in isolated inner cities bereft of community organizations and networks. Low income and scarcity of time make it difficult to afford alternative social resources. Grandmothers, often thought to be great resources, are increasingly young themselves, may still have their own children to care for, or may need employment outside the home and therefore have little time to help single-parent daughters with their children. Churches in such neighborhoods may be few and far between. Groups such as Boy Scouts and Girl Scouts may not exist in many inner-city communities. Even the regrouping of family patterns connected with establishing stepfamilies may end in removing much customary social capital from easy grasp of these parents and their children.

These deficits in social capital may be as important as the more immediate day-to-day love, attention, and guidance of a biological father or mother, as important as that is. When family disruption occurs, McLanahan and Sandefur recommend that parents and the wider community do everything possible to control the diminution of social capital.[63] If parents and children must change residences, it's good to try not to move far away. Other recommendations: Try to find an area with strong community resources. Stay close to the extended family—one's own and that of the nonresidential parent. Stay close to the nonresidential parent if at all possible. Find a good church with excellent programs for families, both parents and children. We would recommend, from the perspective of this book, finding a church with a love ethic of equal regard that tries to create a critical marriage culture supportive of intact families but supportive of disrupted families as well. Churches do exist, we have discovered, that energetically do *both* and without a sense of contradiction. Good schools are important, and for most people they must be financed by government—hence a role for the state. Government-financed welfare programs that do not create dependency are important for the basic reason that some social capital and all material capital (food, clothing, lodging) require money. Although the market, and especially its cost-benefit logic, can be an enemy of social capital, it could be much more supportive than it presently is. Good jobs are the result of healthy markets and constitute a crucial source of financial capital which, in turn, supports human and social capital. But the market should go beyond providing jobs in helping families.

It is dangerous to think of churches in terms of social capital. Churches are carriers of religious stories that reveal God's will and grace. Salvation, not the increase of social capital, is the primary purpose of churches and their narratives. Christianity tells the story of how God's creation, love, and grace empower us not only to live an ethic of equal regard but to risk moments of self-sacrifice with a sense that God's grace will sustain us. Salvation is having the trust to risk sacrificial love and self-giving, even though the mutuality of equal regard is its ultimate goal. Christians do not live the Christian life to produce social capital, but it appears that increased social capital is a long-term, secondary consequence of the Christian life.

Hence, churches that are true to their calling constitute immense resources for the construction of social capital for families. Many families know this. This is why parents with small children return to churches after years of absence. They want practical assistance and basic norms to support their fragile equilibria. This is also why alert single parents and stepfamilies do the same. There is little doubt that behind much of this "coming home to the church" on the part of many families lies a rational-choice survival instinct.

But conversion is always possible and often happens. Churches must permit themselves to be *used* as social capital; they must become good social capital themselves. They can do this because they have a deeper faith in the possibility of conversion. Families turning to the church may first seek only to survive but later learn how to transcend narrow self-preoccupations and minister to others. Churches should have the faith that through "meeting the needs of families," these families will learn to generalize to others the social capital—the love and grace—first given to them through acts of charity done in the name of Christ.

As the early church modeled a love ethic of equal regard in its communion celebrations and as Christian households were supported and taught to consider other members as brothers and sisters, so this happens even now to countless families in churches. It should happen much more than it does. Ministry to all kinds of families must become a higher goal of all churches. In turn, churches must become newly appreciated as a major part of what civil society offers families. Most important of all, churches should be the major carriers of countervailing narratives that balance the stories undergirding the imposed justice of states and the cost-benefit logic of markets.

PART 4

Directions

10

A Practical Theology
of Families

If there is a cultural shift toward defining love as mutuality in marriage and family as our national survey suggests, what precisely does mutuality mean? Our survey questions defined mutuality as treating both self and other with equal seriousness. We cannot be certain, however, that respondents who value mutuality understood our question as it was asked. For some people, it may have meant reciprocity—doing to others *as* they do to us or treating others well *if* they treat us well. Furthermore, we do not know precisely how respondents related mutuality to self-sacrifice.

At best, our survey tells us that our culture is valuing the language of mutuality more and the language of sacrificial love less than older generations. This means that there is much to be done to give precision to the meaning of mutuality, determine its compatibility with Christian love, and discover how it can be lived in families.

We address these issues in light of the wider concerns of the Christian faith. At the end of chapter 5, we mentioned four themes that can inform a practical theology of the family: (1) the centrality of equal regard in a Christian view of love, (2) the legitimate place of self-sacrifice in the service of mutuality, (3) the need for a life-cycle perspective on discerning the meaning of equal regard in families, and (4) the subordination of families to the larger common good, whether seen as the common good of civil society or the kingdom or reign of God.

These themes emerged from our study of tradition and scripture. They come out of the confessing tradition of Christianity. We also present them as ideals that can command philosophical support and be consistent with experience and reason. Because that is true, we found perspectives on these same themes in both the secular and religious voices reviewed in the preceding chapters. Only one major concept, the nature of sacrificial love, requires a distinctively Christian defense. Even this can be shown to have philosophical plausibility. Hence, principles for families that are informed by a Christian perspective are not just confessional and therefore meaningful only to the faithful but are also arguable in public discourse.

An Ideal of the Family
and Christian Irony

Ideals guide human flourishing, but they can be dangerous. Ideals can crush with moralistic harshness; they can be used to attack others and can be infused with spiritual pride—a constant theme of Protestantism from Luther to Reinhold Niebuhr.[1] We saw in chapter 3 how the ideal of the middle-class family of the nineteenth century, whatever its value in that historical context, placed harsh burdens and judgments on those who could not match them. Authentic Christian ideals, however, should not crush; they should uplift and liberate.

The genius of authentic Christianity has been its capacity to project commanding ideals and point toward perfection but admit that sin leads us to fall short of that which is expected. On the one hand, in the Sermon on the Mount Jesus tells his disciples, "Be perfect, therefore, as your heavenly Father is perfect" (Matt. 5:48). On the other hand, when the rich young ruler called Jesus "Good Teacher," he replied, "Why do you call me good? No one is good but God alone" (Luke 18:18–19). There runs throughout the New Testament a dialectical—indeed, an ironic—relation between the ideals to which we are called and our finitude, sin, and pervasive inability to conform to them. The stricture on divorce uttered by Jesus is one of the best illustrations of this tension. On the one hand divorce was prohibited except for adultery; on the other it was acknowledged as a concession to reality "because you were so hardhearted," as Jesus put it (Matt. 19:8).

This is why, in the end, we affirm the Pauline teaching that we are redeemed not by our own perfections and merits but by our trust, faith, and openness to manifestations of God's love, forgiveness, and grace. It is precisely the trusting self that is free to grow morally. Undergirding good communication in families are moments of unmerited respect, listening, and forgiveness—moments experienced as grace. Irony in the Christian faith is the tension between our positive visions and our human frailty, a tension that is sustained by a sense of forgiveness, grace, and hope.

Although we are not saved by the degree of health in our families, Christians should be interested in the health of families as a *highly important proximate good*. The secular mind that does not understand the language of forgiveness and grace is far more likely to fall into moralistic and condemning attitudes than a truly Christian sensibility. Moralism abounds on all sides of the American family debate. The secular mind—indeed, secular public policy—oscillates between permissiveness and condemnation. The Christian sensibility is better able simultaneously to project ideals and handle shortcomings with charity and forgiveness. No part of the Christian scriptures gives testimony to the ironic character of the Christian faith more strikingly than the Gospel of Mark. There the pretensions to perfection of the Pharisees are relentlessly exposed by the measuring stick of the "rule of God"—the command to love the neighbor.[2] It is the concrete love of the neighbor that is both the rule of God and the final measure of our pretensions and moralistic condemnations.

Marital Love as
First Mutuality, Not Self-Sacrifice

We turn to our first theme. If in our day mutuality is popular and self-sacrifice less valued, we must ask: is it possible to give a faithful definition of mutuality from a Christian perspective that is also valid for non-Christians? We begin by boldly asserting that *love as mutuality or equal regard, rather than love as self-sacrifice, is the core of Christian love in both life in general and in families.* Furthermore, love as mutuality and equal regard is not uniquely Christian. Love as mutuality becomes explicitly Christian when it is grounded on the *imago Dei* in humans and renewed by the capacity for sacrificial love, a love that recapitulates the Christic drama and the passion of God.

We already have seen how Christian feminists promote the idea that Christian love is primarily a matter of mutuality. Christine Gudorf says it succinctly: "Much love is mutual; all is directed at mutuality."[3] As we have seen, a host of contemporary Christian ethicists—Andolsen, Harrison, Outka, and Farley—have formulated love in this way.[4] We believe that this is the way love should be interpreted in the second half of Jesus' Great Commandment, "You shall love your neighbor *as yourself*" (Matt. 22:39, our italics). The principle of neighbor love is older than Christianity. First stated in Leviticus 19:18 and 19:34, it serves there primarily as an injunction restraining revenge and applies only to members of one's own group, "the people of Israel."[5] In the New Testament, the love commandment is more universal and is frequently combined with Deuteronomy 6:5, on the love of God, and formulated as the double commandment to love both God and neighbor (Matt. 22:37–39; Mark 12:30–31; Luke 10:27).

Love of neighbor is grounded in the love of God for the neighbor. Aquinas taught that we must love the neighbor because God does. Loving

God means we should love what God loves.[6] But when neighbor love is applied to family members, Aquinas tells us to love for two reasons. First, we love our family members because God loves them, gives them as gifts, and indeed manifests God's love in them. Second, we love them as finite goods. For instance, we should love our children because they are part of us, and we should care for them as we care for ourselves. Similarly, Christians love their spouses first because they are manifestations of the goodness of God but secondarily because they may be beautiful, handsome, dependable, healthy, or good parents.

Jesus made the love commandment the interpretive key to both the Old and New Testaments by asserting, "On these two commandments hang all the law and the prophets" (Matt. 22:40). Paul too used it as an adequate summary of the law in Galatians 5:14 and Romans 13:9. We saw love as equal regard implicit in the early "discipleship of equals" described by Elisabeth Schüssler Fiorenza and the many status reversals of Jesus' parables, some dealing with the household. Even more deeply, and with special reference to marriage, the love command is implicit in the passage in Ephesians that says, "In the same way, husbands should love their wives as they do their own bodies. He who loves his wife loves himself. For no one ever hates his own body, but he nourishes and tenderly cares for it" (5:28–29). The mutuality of the love commandment is visible even at the beginning of the passage when it says, in ways we would not say today, "Be subject to one another out of reverence for Christ" (5:21).

The logic of the love commandment does not require a life of perpetual self-sacrifice, self-abnegation, or self-denial. Strong agapic views of Christian love such as those associated with Anders Nygren are now thought to be overstated. The structure of neighbor love is analogous to the form of the Golden Rule. The Golden Rule reads, "In everything do to others as you would have them do to you" (Matt. 7:12). Neither the Golden Rule nor the principle of neighbor love expressly commands self-sacrifice.

The logic of these commands has been analyzed rigorously by the neo-Thomist moral theologian Louis Janssens. He writes, "Love of neighbor is impartial. It is fundamentally an equal regard for every person, because it applies to each neighbor qua human existent."[7] When Janssens uses the word *impartial* in this context, he is not saying that love is unfeeling or has no concern with the good of others—with what humans want, need, or find satisfying. He is simply saying that, to follow the requirements of neighbor love, we must treat the personhood, claims, and needs of the other as seriousnessly as we treat our own. This is the formal character of love as equal regard; it is a rigorous and demanding ethic.

Love as equal regard is not primarily what ethicists call "other regard," an exclusive regard for the other. The love command exhibits a reversible logic of the kind written about by neo-Kantians such as Lawrence Kohlberg and John Rawls.[8] Every right or need that I ask another to recognize is one that I must allow the other to make on me, and the reverse is also true. As Janssens writes, in the principle of neighbor love, "Valuing the self as well as other remains a manifest obligation."[9] Love as equal regard does not exclude self-love, self-regard, or an ordinate concern with one's own self-fulfillment. It simply requires that we take the other's self-fulfillment as seriously as our own, just as it requires the other to give equal consideration to our fulfillment. Janssens's understanding of neighbor love gives a place for individual fulfillment— the hallmark of modern individualism—but puts it at the very heart of love as equal regard, a love that rigorously balances self-regard with regard for the other.

In the technical language of moral theology and philosophy, Janssens places the teleological ethics of Aquinas within the wider neo-Kantian framework of the influential Protestant theologian Gene Outka. It is a creative reconstruction of the more attractive features of Aquinas. As Janssens understands it, love as equal regard brings together the formal character of reversible regard (the *ordo caritatis*) with the search for the *good* for both self and other (the *ordo bonorum*). In fact, the latter is subsumed under the former; love as equal regard organizes the search for the good within a more encompassing commitment to the formal character of equal respect for self and other.[10]

Applied to the realm of the husband-wife relationship, it means that the wife and husband should *regard* or *respect* the other as a self or person just as one regards oneself as a self or person. It means, as Kant once said, that we must treat both self and other "always as an end and never as a means only."[11] But it also means that one should *will the good* for the other as earnestly as one does for oneself.

Love as Intersubjective:
Not Deciding for the Other

We have discussed the meaning of equal regard as an intersubjective and dialogical concept. It entails a discourse where all speak, listen, attempt to see from the other's perspective, empathize, test to determine whether we understand correctly, remain open to correction, support each other through this process, and stay *committed to the covenant of dialogue*.

In applying Jürgen Habermas's theory of intersubjective discourse to family relations, we extend his theory by taking feelings and affect into consideration in ways he fails to do. Habermas sees discourse in politics as concerned with three validity claims: truth, rightness, and integrity of expression.[12] These validity claims are relevant to family discourse as well; couples must speak the truth about facts, make moral claims that all agree are just, and speak honestly about what they are thinking. But communicative competence in families also entails empathic identification with the deep needs, emotions, and narrative histories of the family members.

Habermas's critique of Kant's understanding of morality also applies to Janssens's theory of equal regard; Janssens also states his understanding of moral obligation *too* monologically. Equal regard for Janssens is presented as an act and judgment that a single person—the individual husband, wife, lover, boyfriend, or girlfriend—makes with regard to the other. Love as equal regard is not something that one individual expresses unilaterally toward another. It is something that people *create* together. It is, as we learned in the chapter on the therapeutic, created through successive attempts to communicate needs and desires, to listen and understand, to empathize with, hold, and accept, and then to live their mutual agreements.

That love and justice are intersubjective is a point that moral philosophers such as Kant, Outka, and Janssens tend to overlook. Describing love as a dialogical phenomenon adds something crucial to the normative understanding of love. Love is not simply a psychological dessert that tops off the main philosophical meal. Either we experience love intersubjectively or we don't experience it at all. Love as equal regard can be a dead externality, an inauthentic foreign object, a fraud, unless it is experienced dialogically as a felt unity of thought and emotion. The ancient teaching that in marriage husband and wife become *one flesh* can receive new meaning if enriched by the idea that marriage is a *covenant of intersubjective dialogue* that enacts love as equal regard.

The new marital therapies, in their best moments, are engaged in the moral task of teaching couples the intersubjective meaning of love and helping them move from its hoped-for possibility to its experienced reality. Until love as intersubjective is thoroughly internalized, the great men's movements of our day—Robert Bly's wild men's weekends, Promise Keepers, the Million Man March—will never move beyond a vision of love as responsible paternalism.

Love as Promoter of the Good Things of Life

The French philosopher Paul Ricoeur formulates the meaning of love in much the same way as Janssens. For both thinkers, love entails not only respect for the other but a proactive commitment to do good to the beloved. Ricoeur develops his position by restating the Golden Rule. To do to others as we would have others do to us really means doing *good* to others as we would have others do *good* to us. Ricoeur believes Rabbi Hillel's formulation of the rule caught what philosophy today calls the "teleological" elements of love—its concern to promote good for the other as well as communicate respect. His version reads, "Do not do to your fellow what you hate to have done to you."[13] Ricoeur believes that this "refers to *goods* which we would love being done to us, and to *evils* which we would hate being done to us."[14]

This formulation of love is clearly relevant to married life. When both members of a couple respect each other *and* work for each other's welfare, they are actively helping the partner pursue a range of vital values and goods, what Janssens calls *premoral* values and goods. These goods are important for the living of life; they contribute to the *moral* good but are not themselves moral goods unless pursued within a moral framework of equality and fairness. These premoral values include such needs and satisfactions as food, clothing, housing, pleasant friendships, sexual pleasure, rest, recuperation, and many more. We should not forget the importance of these goods for families, as evolutionary ecologists and economists are right to point out.

Education for our children is a premoral good. Premoral values include higher goods such as the exercise of one's talents, a sense of self-esteem, the need for interpersonal regard, and affirmation by others. Among our interviewees, James Nelson worried that his marriage to Francis had deprived her of self-actualization—the exercise of her skills as a professional dancer. Sarah Miles resented that marriage had brought the premoral good of her musical talent into conflict with the premoral good of maintaining a nice home and having children. Maria and Robert Taylor didn't speak much about the goods of self-actualization but did worry about the good of being able to pay the rent.

The premoral values that love as mutuality seeks to realize *can also include children and the continuation of oneself in one's progeny or in the offspring of sisters, brothers, or other close kin.* Premoral values include the goods that one associates with the concept of inclusive fitness and kin altruism. In fact, if evolutionary psychologists are right, these are very abiding premoral goods that motivate behavior more profoundly than moderns think. These premoral goods are part of what most humans appear to desire.

Human beings, however, desire many things beyond what goes into inclusive fitness, an important point that some evolutionary psychologists forget. Humans, as philosophers William James and Mary Midgley have put it,

are creatures of "multiple" desires.[15] Although we have desires that
make up our asymmetrical reproductive strategies, we have *other* desires
that sometimes conflict with these strategies. That is why on occasion
we appear to go against our pervasive reproductive tendencies.

Desires, of course, are more than raw instincts even though all desires
have instinctual foundations. As many philosophers of language have
argued, we know our desires partially through the symbols of our language systems and cultures.[16] This does not mean, however, that our
culturally mediated language systems, as Michel Foucault would insist,
create or "construct" our desires. It means that these language traditions
color our desires and influence our valuations of them. We learn how to
interpret our desires partially from what our bodies tell us but partially
from how our cultures teach us to interpret our desires.

Since the premoral goods and values of life can conflict with and
override one another, they have to be evaluated by criteria applied in the
following order: first, by the formal principle of equal respect (fairness);
second, by their contribution to the human flourishing of both other(s)
and self; and third, by their long-range consequences for both fairness
and human flourishing. Within love as equal regard, we should not just
seek to maximize good consequences; we must maximize good within
a framework of equality. *More* is not always morally *better*.

Here are examples of how premoral goods can conflict—examples
that a family theory informed by Christianity should keep in mind. Premoral goods of health can conflict with the goods of wealth. Our work
for material wealth (a good) can make us sick, even to death. Maria Taylor feels Robert, like her own father, would do this if they still lived under the old single-breadwinner system. The good of exercising one's
talents can conflict with the good of the spouse to do the same and even
the good of raising children. The goods of pleasure can conflict with the
goods of wealth and health, as growing numbers of youth afflicted with
sexually transmitted diseases have learned.[17] Sexual pleasure is a human
good; it feels good and helps humans bond. It is one of life's great
sources of delight, whether experienced by a teenager or a mature, married adult. But sex for a teenager can lead to a variety of premoral disvalues: pregnancy and the birth of an infant before either mother or
father are educationally and financially equipped to raise it. Sex and babies, clearly wonderful goods, can conflict with the premoral values of
education, wealth, and the health of all involved, mother, father, and
baby. Since premoral values can conflict, humans should pursue them
in such a way as to permit the realization of the widest range of compatible values and do this within the boundaries of justice, fairness, and
equality.

Monogamy and the
Ordo Caritatis et Bonorum

Using a pattern of moral thinking similar to the one described above, Aquinas justified his belief in monogamous matrimony. Monogamy, his logic went, realizes a wide range of premoral goods. Restating his argument with the help of contemporary insights, we arrive at an extensive list of premoral goods. Monogamy provides a secure environment for dependent infants, protection for the mother during a period of vulnerability, increased paternal certainty, the secure grounds for the exercise of kin altruism, sexual exchange, mutual helpfulness, the good of intimacy, the intrinsic joy of children, and the sense that one's life is being extended beyond the finite years of one's days on this earth.

In contrast to Aquinas, we believe that these goods should be pursued within a relationship of friendship that is equal in the strictly reversible and intersubjective sense of that word. Aquinas's understanding of marital friendship as *proportional* does not hold up to either theological or philosophical scrutiny. Whether one grounds personhood on moral rationality, possession of the image of God, or identification with Christ, the abiding evidence of moral psychology, philosophy, and theology is that women and men are fundamentally equal and therefore deserving of friendship and love marked by equal regard.

Furthermore, monogamy brings about moral goods (in contrast to premoral goods) which Aquinas implied but did not articulate fully. Monogamy offers the possibility of commensurable household structures. Polygyny, polyandry, and single parenthood invariably leave large numbers of adults outside of marital relationships and parenthood. In polygynous societies, wealthy men may hoard young and attractive women. In polyandrous societies, landed brothers may conserve wealth by marrying a single woman, leaving many females out of the marriage system. As single motherhood increases in modern societies, many males are left out of families. Because of its emphasis on individual dignity before God, wherever Christianity spread, the number of monogamous households increased, and the poor and marginalized found mates.[18] Love as equal regard demands equal treatment *between* families just as it does within families.

Searching for a
Language of Mutuality

Mutuality is what Sarah Miles wants in her marriage and family but cannot actualize. Part of the problem is a lack of language by which to understand what she desires. Her moral language goes back and forth between an individualistic language of self-fulfillment ("There's totally a place for it. There's not only a place, that's what it's all about") and a language that only grudgingly admits the role of sacrificial love ("self-sacrifice is the pits, a necessary evil"). Sarah needs an intermediate language of love that understands sacrificial love not as an end in itself but as derived from and in the service of mutuality.

Sarah Miles

———————

At first glance, love as mutuality seems close to the moral language of Richard Good. He defined the Golden Rule as a "mutual sense of giving each other freedom to be what you want to be." For Ricoeur and Janssens, however, neighbor love and the Golden Rule go beyond giving the same freedom to the other as one wishes for oneself. These principles also entail esteeming the other and actively working for the well-being of the other in the same way one wishes these things for oneself. Furthermore, Richard, like Sarah, has difficulties with the idea of sacrificial love. Richard says sacrifice "is too strong a word. Compromise is a better word." For both Sarah and Richard, self-sacrifice is a threat to mutuality.

Richard Good

Mutuality and the Secular Mind

It is a mistake to think that only Christians understand dimensions of love as equal regard. The liberal Enlightenment theory of loving relations—from Locke, Kant, Marx, and secular humanistic feminism—has captured parts of the idea of love as equal regard. This may explain why, in our national survey, the better educated—those most influenced by Enlightenment values—are higher in valuing mutuality than those with less education. This may also explain why some of the liberal, mainstream denominations (like the Episcopalian and Presbyterian) support mutuality more than the general population does, and why they match more nearly the profiles of the highly educated than do the profiles of more conservative Christian groups. The percentages in table 6 report people's view of their preferred behavior, in contrast to beliefs, in solving conflicts with loved ones. The percentage of Southern Baptists valuing the behavior of self-sacrifice is approximately twice as high as the percentage for Episcopalians and Presbyterians. The percentage of Episcopalians valuing mutuality in conflict resolution is fifteen points higher than the national total and nearly twenty points higher than the figures for Southern Baptists. The percentage of Episcopalians and Presbyterians valuing the language of self-sacrifice is approximately ten points lower than the national total and more than twenty points lower than Southern Baptists.

Table 6. Preferred Behavior in Conflict Situations*

Model of Behavior	All	High School Educated (and under)	College Educated (and under)	Episcopalian	Presbyterian	Southern Baptist
Mutuality	45	41	51	60	48	42
Self-Sacrifice	28	30	26	17	18	39
Self-Fulfillment	13	12	12	13	15	12

*Numbers represent percentages.

It is possible that Enlightenment philosophical perspectives articulated secular versions of the Jewish and Christian principle of neighbor love. Proving this, however, is beyond our scope. What can be argued is this: the philosophical theories generally base equality in love on appeals to the shared rationality of both men and women, husbands and wives. The believing Jew and Christian, however, base equality on the shared image and goodness of God in both male and female. This is an increasingly accepted interpretation of Genesis 1:27—"So God created humankind in his image, in the image of God he created them; *male and female he created them*"—which Jesus reaffirmed in Matthew 19:4. Sometimes in the Christian scriptures, equal regard is grounded on a variation of this idea—all Christians's equal identification with Christ: "There is no longer male and female; for all of you are one in Christ Jesus" (Gal. 3:28). Or "Be subject (*hypotassomai*) to one another out of reverence (*phobos*) for Christ" (Eph. 5:21). Although the Christian and some secular perspectives emphasize the formal character of equality as reversible regard and good will, they vary in how they ground or justify their respective views.

The important question is, which ground or justification provides the more profound reasons for husband and wife to respect each other: (1) respect based on the spouse's rationality or (2) respect based on the spouse's equal status in the eyes of God? We believe that equality in God's eyes provides the greater weight and seriousness.[19] Furthermore, the Christian narrative that surrounds equal regard—the narrative that God identifies with a suffering humanity through the life of Jesus—affirms human dignity *even more*. These are the Christian grounds for commitment in marriage which secular perspectives lack. But whether these deeper reasons energize Episcopalians' and Presbyterians' high valuation of mutuality is a question that our survey does not answer.

Mutuality and Narrative Identity

If love as mutuality means regarding the other's selfhood as you would want your own to be regarded, the question emerges, What is the nature of the self? Our discussion of why family therapies often work should give us a clue. Learning how to communicate intersubjective equal regard for the other is really learning to express respect for the life history or narrative of the other's self. The self *is* a self because, as Alasdair MacIntyre and Paul Ricoeur have argued, it can tell a story about itself, that is, it can locate itself in a narrative history.[20] The idea of selfhood, according to MacIntyre, requires two concepts. First, "My selfhood—my identity—is a synthesis of what I and others take to be the story (or stories) which give my life coherence." Second, "I am the *subject* of a narrative history that is my own and no one else's."[21] Narrative selfhood is a combination of the stories we are born into and the stories we create as we live our lives.[22]

Hence, *to love the other as oneself means to regard and empathize with the narrative identity of the other just as one regards and empathizes with one's own.* The theological affirmation that personhood reflects the goodness of God means that in and through all particular narrative identities, Christians find traces of people's relation to the goodness of God. Being a child of God is constitutive of one's story. Seeing a person's ultimate worth within the context of that person's personal histories is extremely important for understanding the *concrete* meaning of equal regard and for understanding, as we will soon see, not only how families are formed but, more important, how they are sustained.

The Role of Self-Sacrifice in Love?

This leads to our second point—the role of self-sacrifice in love. Is there a role for self-sacrifice, for the drama of the cross, in Christian love defined as mutuality or equal regard? And does the element of self-sacrifice or self-giving add something to the permanence and renewal of the inner core of families?

Both Richard Good and Sarah Miles were justifiably nervous about the language of sacrifice. We believe, however, that there is a way of talking about self-sacrifice in love that addresses their concerns. The formula reads: *self-sacrifice is needed to renew the true goal of love, which is mutuality. Self-sacrificial love is not an end in itself.*

The Complaint against Sacrificial Love

Some feminists have rejected a role for self-sacrifice in love, whether within or outside of families. But feminist theologian Rosemary Radford Ruether makes a point similar to ours when she argues that the sacrifice of Christ was a subversion of the patriarchal patterns of the ancient world—patterns we have interpreted with the categories of honor and shame. Christ manifests "the *kenosis* of patriarchy, the announcement of a new humanity that discards hierarchical caste privilege and speaks on behalf of the lowly."[23] The *"kenosis* of patriarchy" meant the self-emptying of the agency, domination, and hierarchy that was part of the male code of the ancient world. Ruether argues that the modalities of servanthood and sacrifice must now be disconnected from their customary association with masculinity and seen as modalities of the Christian life applicable equally to men *and* women. Harvard theologian Sarah Coakley joins Ruether in asking feminist theology to reinterpret, not discard, the role of self-sacrifice in Christian love. In a recent essay she offers "a defence of some version of *kenosis* as not only compatible with feminism, but vital to a distinctively Christian manifestation of it."[24]

Several Christian feminists agree with Coakley and Ruether and articulate a limited role for sacrifice. Gudorf writes, "All love both involves sacrifice and aims at mutuality."[25] She questions whether *agape* is essentially self-sacrificial and approvingly quotes Outka, who does not think that self-sacrifice should be appraised as "the purest and most perfect manifestation of agape." Self-sacrifice, writes Outka, "must always be purposive in promoting the welfare of others and never simply expressive of something resident in the agent."[26] Andolsen, following Beverly Harrison, writes this about the sacrifice of Jesus on the cross: "Jesus did not desire death on the Cross as a manifestation of total self-surrender. Rather he accepted death as the consequence of his unswerving commitment to mutual love."[27]

Janssens also argues that self-sacrifice is, in fact, *not* the ideal of the Christian life. Furthermore, he reminds us, as does Beverly Harrison,[28] that love as genuine equal regard is a strenuous ethic. It is not easy to take others as seriously as we do ourselves and, indeed, ourselves as seriously as we do others. Some people find this a very threatening, almost impossible ethic. Most humanistic psychologists who prefer ideals of self-actualization would find this ethic too demanding. Economists of the rational-choice persuasion would find it inconceivable. Humans, they argue, even in their intimate family relations are ethical egoists, always calculating individual satisfactions and fulfillments.[29]

If love as equal regard captures the heart of the Christian idea of neighbor love, it follows that sacrificial love, as important as it is, is *derived* from equal regard. For Janssens, self-sacrifice is "justified derivatively" from the other regard built into love as equal regard.[30] We should sacrifice for the other and go the second mile in order to restore our relations to the more ideal state of equal regard and mutuality.

We saw the close relation between self-sacrifice and equal regard in Ephesians. Husbands were asked to love their wives as "Christ loved the church and gave himself up for her" (Eph. 5:25). Then came the appeal to love as equal regard: "Even so husbands should love their wives as their own bodies" (5:28). This is a consequence of marriage, of becoming "one flesh," as Genesis 2:24 indicates. Furthermore, Ephesians finds a place for natural self regard in its view of love as equal regard. "He who loves his wife loves himself. For no man ever hates his own flesh." In contrast to the views of Christian love which make self-sacrifice its end, the Ephesians passage seems to see love as mutuality as the goal, with sacrificial love working to maintain Christ's relation to the church and the husband's relation to the wife.

What is important, here, is the logic of the connection between relatedness and sacrifice. But, as we have argued, if Ephesians has validity for today, it must be interpreted reversibly in all respects—as applying to the wife as profoundly as it does the husband. Paul imagines in one place the possibility of wives being to their husbands as Christ was to the church. In his first letter to the Corinthians, Paul advises Christians facing marital conflict to remain in their present state due to his eschatological expectations that this world was ending and the new creation was beginning.

> if any believer has a wife who is an unbeliever, and she consents to live with him, he should not divorce her. And if any woman has a husband who is an unbeliever, and he consents to live with her, she should not divorce him. For the unbelieving husband *is made holy through his wife,* and the unbelieving wife is made holy through her husband. (1 Cor. 7:12–14, italics added)

This passage communicates the revolutionary idea that the wife can "make holy" (some translations say "sanctify") the unbelieving husband. This suggests that Paul could imagine how women can mediate Christ's transforming and self-giving love to the family. Women too can participate in the Christic drama, not as subservient recipients but as active leaders performing the work of Christ.

The logic of this trend toward elevated roles for women must be decisively asserted in any reappropriation of Ephesians. The wife should love the husband in the same way, as a part of her body because of her participation in the Christic drama. It follows that she too should have access to the power, financial capacity, and social respect required to make certain that this sacrificial love is not exploited. Both wife and husband should be willing to go the second mile, extend themselves, take a chance, endure in the relation when at times it is not completely mutual. Both should do this, however, not in the name of sacrificial love itself, but as a means—as a transitional ethic—designed to maintain or reinstate love as mutuality.

Even in this Ephesians passage, it is assumed that humans have a natural inclination and right to cherish and nourish their own bodies. Even in these verses, considered to be the great passage in the Christian heritage that calls for sacrificial love in marriage, we have a full legitimation of the right of self-regard. Hence, self-regard is intrinsic to the logic of equal regard, and it applies to both the husband and the wife as humans made in the image of God.

Christian Realism
and the Need for Grace

Christian realism, as we said earlier, holds that humans live in a world of finitude and sin. Because of this profound and pervasive aspect of the human condition, perfect mutuality and equal regard never prevail completely in any human relation inside or outside of families. The capacity for self-sacrifice is required to maintain relationships even though self-sacrifice is not the goal of life.

Because of the challenge, the strain, the near impossibility of this sacrificial moment, the Christian tradition has offered an additional resource: the belief that this sacrificial moment in marriage (with all of its attendant features of forgiveness, patience, and renewal) can participate in a deeper drama rooted in the divine life and manifested in Christ's love for the church. The sacrificial moment within the love ethic of equal regard does not call for couples to stand alone, unaided and unassisted. When Jim Turner said, "You have got to learn to love the one you marry," it sounds as though he is placing great emphasis on will and determination. Actually, both he and Sophie believe that grace plays a role in empowering this determination—not the special sacramental grace that Mary Murphy believes in but the power of God's love witnessed to by church and scripture. Either way, the Christian believes that expansive and enduring marital love is finally a reflection of the outpouring and overflowing of God's love, indeed, the divine passion. *This additional capacity for sacrificial self-giving inspired by the suffering and grace of God is what turns love as equal regard into a distinctively Christian reality.*

Sacrificial Love and
the Passion of God

In an incomplete way, those who step into the Christic drama identify with God. The Christic narrative portrayed in Ephesians suggests that God's uniqueness is God's capacity for relationality, endurance, and faithfulness. The philosophies of religion of Alfred North Whitehead and Charles Hartshorne are relevant to understanding a view of the divine consistent with a self-giving God working through the love of Christ.[31] These philosophers rejected the classic scholastic idea of a perfect and unchanging God who was unaffected by human experience and suffering. They argued that God undergoes change as a consequence of God's effort to enjoy and maintain a loving relation with the world in its transient and suffering condition.

God's drive for relationality makes God, as Hartshorne once said, "a sympathetic being" who "delights in our enjoyment."[32] God's sacrificial love is derived from a more fundamental thrust toward enjoyment. This is clearly analogous to Janssens's belief that self-sacrifice is *derived* from the drive to maintain mutuality. This view, once associated mainly with process theology (a view of theology that emphasizes the changing nature of God and reality), can now be found in the trinitarian theologies of a new generation of Christian feminist theologians, principally the work of Elizabeth Johnson and Catherine LaCugna.[33] The Trinity, for these thinkers, no longer expresses God's relation to God's own self; it expresses instead the relation of God to God's world in the history of creation and salvation. God is a God *who can be moved and who can suffer* out of empathic identification with the suffering of the created world.

The secular mind has difficulty believing that the sacrificial element of marital commitment is grounded in the love of God and the metaphysical foundations of the world. But we can show, we believe, that this belief is *at least plausible*. Take the proposition, all love requires the capacity for modifications of experience, and the openness to undergo such modifications. Does this make sense? We think that it does. Love, even at the most elemental levels of life, entails attachments with other beings who are growing, changing, becoming sick, and even dying. *To love is to delight and endure in experiencing these modifications in the object of our love.* All this is done to maintain the joy of the relation.

If this is a describable aspect of all finite loving relations—if the core of love is the capacity to endure modifications of experience as philosophers from William James to Charles Hartshorne have argued—isn't it reasonable to believe that this feature of human experience is crucial to all that holds the world together?[34] If it is, then it is plausible to think that the modifiable, sensitive, and empathic nature of experience is a fundamental characteristic that can reasonably be thought to describe the nature of God. Perfect love is perfectly constant in its capacity to endure modifications—to maintain relationality—with the beloved; imperfect love handles the sufferings and modifications of relations imperfectly but still measures itself by the perfect. Human love is imperfect but contains signals of the divine perfection within its every manifestation. The Ephesians drama is a concrete illustration of this truth about God, applied to God's relation to the church and to the foundations of marriage.

Mutuality and the Marital Covenant

Men and women *get married* and form families, as we have seen, for various natural reasons. But people *stay married* because these fragile natural tendencies and communicative needs are shaped and renewed by powerful religiocultural symbols that evoke commitment. The idea of covenant is one of these symbols.

Love as mutuality and equal regard has had the character of covenant in the history of Christianity. Covenant is not a limited contract, although all marriages should have their contractual, legal, and public dimensions. The marital contract, within a Judeo-Christian context, should be subordinate to an idea of covenant. This marital covenant is analogous to, is modeled after, and enacts God's ongoing covenant love with humanity (the insight of Genesis), with Israel (the insight of the prophets Hosea and Malachi), with the church (the testimony of Ephesians), and finally with the family. The formation of a family involves natural tendencies that are given further form by God's intentions for creation. But God's sacrificial love for the church is a model for the steadfastness and permanence of marriage and family. This is the teleological understanding of Christian marriage—an understanding that transforms the natural foundations of marriage into a covenantal commitment, as insightfully argued by Aquinas and later by Reformed thinkers like Emil Brunner. In Christian family theory love as equal regard must take the form of covenant between husband, wife, God, and other affirming communities.

3. Mutuality in a Life-Cycle Perspective

Third, we claim that *a love ethic of mutuality is more intelligible when stated within a theory of the marital and human life cycles.* How does love as equal regard and mutuality look when we acknowledge that everyone— parents, children, neighbor, stranger—lives within a cycle of birth, growth, middle age, aging, and death? This is a question that moral theologians and philosophers usually fail to ask explicitly. Yet many of the dilemmas of love as equal regard in marriage cannot be solved unless situated within a life-cycle context of the relation between husband and wife.[35] Then there is the issue of how children and adults, who are at different places in the human life cycle, participate in an ethic of mutuality.

Mutuality and Dialogue in the Human Life Cycle

The human life cycle is not a simple unfolding of the natural processes of growth and decay, although this is part of the story. It is useful to see life cycles as combining natural processes with historically situated narratives; this is something we can observe in the process of marital couples uniting.

We have spoken of four forms of democratization that the postmodern context of families has brought about: the democratization of *intimacy, work, value formation, and parental authority*. In the future, the rhythms and nuances of making love, earning a family income, establishing the values of the family, and exercising parental authority increasingly will be shared equally by husband and wife *or* the marriage will collapse. Family patterns governing all of these areas will need to entail a mutual and critical dialogue between husband and wife about what their respective family traditions have to offer. In addition to the natural exchanges identified by evolutionary ecologists and the emotional exchanges identified by the new marital therapies, family formation must also be a matter of critical dialogue about what is viable from the family's past traditions and the narratives of both husband and wife. These narratives contain their respective images of birth, growth, maturity, and aging.

The psychoanalyst Erik Erikson showed that when children identify with their parents, they internalize their parents's superegos, ego ideals, and identities.[36] By identities, Erikson had in mind something close to what MacIntyre and Ricoeur call "narrative identities." Superegos, ego ideals, and identities are not simply psychological realities; they are cultural and historical realities as well—indeed, narrative realities. When children identify with their parents, not only do they internalize their parents's narrative history, they take in their parents's conflicts about this history. They then mix their parents's conflicted stories with their own conflicts with parents. People bring these conflicted narrative identities to their efforts to form a life with another person.

Family formation is a process of biological, psychological, historical, and religiocultural negotiation. This negotiation, however, should be subordinate to *a covenantal commitment to the process of dialogue*. To invent a phrase, this covenant is a commitment to a "psychohistorical dialogue," a "dialogue between diverse narrative identities." This is a complex covenant that should include not only wife and husband but families of origin, the wider community, historical traditions, children as they are born, and finally God—but a God apprehended through these multiple communities and traditions. This covenant of mutual dialogue should also include, redirect, and give stability to the natural dimensions of family formation. It takes an open dialogue to achieve some degree of "oneness" between husband and wife. To regard positively and to empathize with the narrative identity of both self and other does not, however, mean uncritically affirming all aspects of these identities.

Helping couples create interpersonal environments that support their respective sense of self in the midst of these dialogues is the major contribution of marriage counseling, premarital counseling, and early marital education with young adults and teenagers. Most people, however, learn to create these holding environments in their families of origin, their churches, or their religious traditions.

Hermeneutics, Spirituality, and the Covenant of Dialogue

Contemporary hermeneutic theory helps to clarify aspects of how stable marriages are formed. Hermeneutic theory concerns how humans gain understanding of texts, but it can also clarify the process of achieving understanding in marriage and family. The philosopher Hans-Georg Gadamer claims that all understanding comes through dialogue.[37] Some therapeutic theories also see communication as a dialogue, a play of question and response that proceeds out of the psychohistorical traditions of husband and wife.

Furthermore, hermeneutic theory adds the idea that the questions and responses of a marital dialogue reflect the largely *unconscious* historical starting points of the parties involved.[38] When applied to family formation, it means that a dialogue must begin, and perpetually rework, the psychohistorical inheritance of the husband and wife. The democratization of family formation means that value formation and parental authority must become a complex psychohistorical dialogue. This requires a *covenant* of dialogue.

Hermeneutic theory also suggests how ideals or positive visions function in our dialogues. Our dialogues are laden with ideals: images of the good, the right, and the obligatory taken over naively from our family traditions and deeply embedded in our psychological makeup. The ideals carried by our dominant family traditions and by many people arise from long religiocultural dialogues that can be traced through American history and backward to the Reformation, Aquinas, medieval Catholicism, early Christianity, and its Jewish and Greco-Roman contexts. The history of family theory in the Western world, which we have spent much time in this volume uncovering, is not just an external history, old, distant, and long forgotten. It is a history of our own identities that gets grafted on to our childhood experiences, even if we come from different non-western traditions.

Couples forming families should give equal regard to each other's narrative selves, including how ideals of the family are entangled with images of the divine. Ideals of the family and images of the divine always become mixed in our inner psychological worlds. As Ana Maria Rizzuto so brilliantly argues in *The Birth of the Living God* (1979), our God-images at one level are complex unconscious syntheses of our images of our parents.[39] Since all of us have some kind of parental imago, we all carry images of the divine in our unconscious, even if we conceive of ourselves as atheists. Rizzuto did not emphasize sufficiently, however, that our parental images are themselves shaped by historical narratives that originate in religiocultural traditions. Images of the divine mediated by tradition and parent-shaped images of the divine interact and modify each other to varying degrees, depending on our patterns of socialization. Therefore, because God-images inherited from tradition help us reconstruct images of our human parents, who are experienced as divine, it makes a big difference what our traditions tell us about the nature of God's love, trustworthiness, forgiveness, or suffering.

Every married couple should participate in an empathic yet critical dialogue about the images of the divine in the narrative identities of each partner. A spirituality of marriage can be enriched by a God-image that depicts God as so concerned to enjoy friendship with humans that God is willing to suffer and endure to maintain those relations. God's love becomes a model for a marital commitment that endures the pain of hard times but endures for the joy of mutuality.

In our national survey on love, we found that people who have had spiritual experiences are more likely to value the role of self-sacrifice in loving relations. *This finding is ambiguous.* Throughout we have argued that self-sacrifice should empower equal regard and not stand as an end in itself. Nonetheless, the capacity for self-sacrifice—a self-giving that endures even when an immediate return is not in sight—is important for marital commitment and covenant. Table 7 shows how people correlate their preferred *behavior* for resolving conflicts with types of spiritual experience. Table 8 does the same for the kind of love people *believe* is associated with a good marriage.

Table 7. Types of Conflict-Resolving Behavior
Correlated with Spirituality*

	Mutuality	Self-Sacrifice	Self-Fulfillment
Importance of religion	40	32	13
Most important thing in life	44	33	9
Born again	42	34	12
Presence of God	45	30	12
Mystical experience	45	30	33
Religious beliefs	44	33	10
All respondents	45	28	13

*Numbers represent percentages. The types of religious experience measured are (1) the importance of religion ranked from "extremely" to "not at all" (we report here only the percentages for "extremely," (2) religion as the most important thing in life (we report here those saying "yes"), (3) religion as a "born again" experience (we report "yes"), (4) religion experienced as the presence of God (we report "yes"), (5) religion as a mystical experience (we report "yes"), and (6) a religious experience that has reinforced a person's religious beliefs (we report "yes").

Table 8. Beliefs about Love Correlated with Spirituality*

	Mutality	Self-Sacrifice	Self-Fulfillment
Importance of religion	50.3	42.7	3.5
Most important thing in life	44.4	47.6	4.2
Born again	46.6	47.4	4.3
Presence of God	54.2	39.6	3.8
Mystical experience	52.0	42.8	3.7
Religious beliefs	53.5	40.8	3.2
All respondents	54.8	37.9	4.7

*Numbers represent percentages. The types of religious experience measured are (1) the importance of religion ranked from "extremely" to "not at all" (we report here only the percentages for "extremely," (2) religion as the most important thing in life (we report here those saying "yes"), (3) religion as a "born again" experience (we report "yes"), (4) religion experienced as the presence of God (we report "yes"), (5) religion as a mystical experience (we report "yes"), and (6) a religious experience that has reinforced a person's religious beliefs (we report "yes").

In our survey 34 percent of people who have had "born-again" experiences and 33 percent of those who believe that religion is the "most important thing in their lives were more inclined than the average (28 percent) to use self-sacrifice to solve conflicts with loved ones. The exception are those who only have mystical experiences and diffuse experiences of the "presence of God," who seem less willing to sacrifice. These proportions are even more pronounced when looked at from the perspective of beliefs and spirituality (table 8).

Our study does not tell us whether those who hold a positive view of self-sacrifice use it to serve mutuality. Nor does it tell us whether those who value sacrificial love have capacities for intersubjective dialogue. It suggests, however, that people who have had experiences of transcendence see themselves as more open to the risk of sacrificial love. One of the great tasks of our time is to create a spirituality of marriage which links sacrificial love and the experience of the transcendent in ways that reinforce a steadfast love in the service of equal regard and mutuality.

Equal Regard and the Birth of the Child

Even if a husband and wife do create a democratic dialogue in the early stages of their marriage, the birth of children dramatically changes the rhythm and meaning of equal regard between husband and wife. Mutuality must take different forms depending on the presence and the age of children. In past societies, a birth circumscribed the mother's more than the father's life. Yet the birth of the child is deemed so important that most societies have modeled their ideals of adulthood for both men and women around images of parenthood (though sometimes the women's more than the men's).

Psychologist David Gutman believes that in most human groups there is a "clear identity between mature adulthood and parenthood."[40] Gutman has studied adulthood and aging in Navajo, Mayan, and Druze societies and found the near equation of adulthood and parenthood to be particularly important for men. Time after time men told him that "they had been wild in their youth, but that marriage had shifted their character dramatically toward greater responsibility, selflessness, and moderation." What made the difference? A regular response was, "I got married; I had kids."[41]

Gutman argues that in traditional societies, having children marks the beginning of a dramatic alteration and eventual exchange in the roles of husbands as well as wives. The birth of a child creates a temporary narrowing of roles for both parents. Gutman calls this the "parental emergency." In most societies there is general agreement that "parents will . . . accept deep restrictions on their own needs and deep revisions of their own psychological makeup, in order to meet their children's essential needs."[42] In simpler societies, this narrowing of roles demanded by the parental emergency meant that men moderated their indulgences, redirected their aggressiveness, searched for protein for spouse and child, and protected the perimeter around the vulnerable mother-infant dyad. The mother, in turn, accepted the restrictions of nursing and staying close to the infant.

Both roles entailed sacrifice; both entailed the renunciation of a wide range of roles and powers exercised in youth—what Gutman calls the "omnipotentiality" of youth.[43] In fact, according to Gutman, the entire socialization of men and women prepared them to limit the full exercise of their powers for the benefit of the transitional renunciations involved in parenting.

By omnipotentiality Gutman means that even in traditional societies, "young men and women are allowed . . . to indulge a wide range of psychological potentials." He continues,

> Thus prematernal women are often tomboys, flirtatious one day, actively competing with men the next, while young men, including prepaternal husbands, may live out the extremes of their nature toward violence on the one hand and tenderness on the other. . . . After children come, dedicated parents can never completely relax into self-absorption or self-indulgence.[44]

Gutman makes the interesting point that parenthood in these societies involves one of the "most potent transformations of narcissism in the entire life cycle," competitive with the transformations that occur in infancy when the infant learns to live for longer periods without its mother. In parenting, narcissism is redistributed to include the life and well-being of the infant.

Gutman sees parenthood in traditional societies as going through a transformation, one quite relevant for a life-cycle theory of love as equal regard, even in modern societies. After the parental emergency subsides, married couples begin to shift roles. More specifically, *they begin to reclaim potentialities that they suppressed during the parental emergency:*

> Having raised the next generation of viable and procreant children, the parents have earned the right to be again . . . omnipotential. As a consequence, postparental men and women can reclaim the sexual bimodality that was hitherto repressed and parceled out between husband and wife . . . (or) lived out externally, vicariously, through the spouse. They can afford the luxury of elaborating the potential and pleasure that they had to relinquish early on, in service of their particular parental task.[45]

Men in traditional societies become more spiritual, passive, receptive, and contemplative. Women begin to investigate the external world, become more active, executive, and managerial. This reversal of roles shows that traditional societies approximated equal regard between men and women, not moment by moment, but through elaborate procedures of taking turns and exchanging roles over the entire life cycle.

This analysis suggests that love as equal regard shifts in its meaning when a child is born. Bonnie Miller-McLemore writes about contemporary parenting:

> Before our first son, I could compartmentalize work and love, expecting equal treatment at work and establishing an egalitarian partnership in private life. . . . Upon becoming parents, a personal commitment to fairness . . . could no longer remain private.[46] . . .
>
> Almost immediately . . . the physiological disparities of bearing and nursing children necessitated a reappraisal of the mutuality internal to our relationship. However, these differences did not lessen our commitment to a mutuality and partnership. . . . We discovered that the mutuality we wanted to maintain could not be spelled out as easily as kitchen duty, but required a measured and steady response to the continually emerging, evolving needs of our children for love, and our needs to love ourselves as parents.[47]

In a sense Gutman is right: equality in marriage takes different forms at different points in the human life cycle. But Gutman's perspective is limited when applied to modern societies. The demand for greater participation of fathers, not just on the perimeter of the family but in the inner domestic circle, is based on a recognition of the change in the economic environment of modern societies. The threats on the perimeter have lessened, and the domestic demands of child care and household duties have increased. Furthermore, women are now able to participate on the perimeter in wage earning and in political life. Finally, if men are to develop nurturant, receptive, and caring potentials in postmodern societies they must not wait until the parental emergency subsides to exercise them.

Nonetheless, it is wise to recognize the demands of childbearing and the changes it brings in mutuality between parents. The physical demands of infant care are huge. The fact that mothers, as sociologist Alice Rossi has pointed out, carry children for nine months, undergo hormonal changes that attune them to their infants, know definitely that the infant is theirs, and increasingly acknowledge nursing as a boost to the infant's health, means that it is difficult to achieve fully a perfect exchangeability of roles between mother and father during birth and immediately thereafter.[48] Furthermore, research suggests that although men can learn the skills of parenting very young children, they are in fact easily distracted, less sensitive to the needs of the infant, and more inclined when caring for infants to divide their attention between the child and other endeavors.[49] Full involvement in childcare, on a footing equal to the mother, probably comes more naturally for men, according to Rossi and others, when children are between one year to eighteen months in age.[50] After that, differences between fathers and mothers are decisively less important. Nonetheless, as one of us has written,

> A mother's physiological investments in her offspring should never be used to deny the attainability of an emotional and cognitive equity between women and men in the care of offspring. It suggests instead that if attachment is more attained than given for men, and if it is more given than attained for women, then men must make more efforts to learn the practice of caring for others, and women may need to make efforts to tip the scale the other way.[51]

For life-cycle equal regard to work in our day, fathers must *learn* the skills needed to express direct parenting for infants in the early months.[52] For this to happen, society must go beyond what fathers can do alone. There must be new efforts to help mothers exercise their wider potentials *throughout* the parental emergency and not just after it subsides. This *requires a more flexible restructuring of society as a whole in addition to broadening the roles of fathers.* Day care for children is often mentioned as the main solution. But we will propose in the last chapter a more radical social reorganization of the patterns of paid work—what we call the "sixty-hour work week"—and a closer relation between work outside the home and the rhythms of child care and the domestic economy.

What does this mean for a mutual marital love formed by openness to the Christic moment? Although the demands for self-sacrifice created by the parental emergency have lessened in postmodern societies for both parents, reciprocity in parental roles is not likely ever to be perfect, given life's anticipated and unanticipated challenges. Rhythms of equality and self-sacrifice are necessarily *spread out over time,* although ideally the intervals of self-sacrifice should be brief. Moments of self-sacrifice are a necessary part of any durable relation. But whether the time of sacrifice is long or short, or in some cases unavoidably permanent because the loved one becomes handicapped or terminally ill, its ultimate goal is the restoration of mutuality and equal regard, a message especially important for the inevitable challenges of the parental emergency.

Mutuality and Raising Children?

What sense does it make to talk about mutuality and equal regard with children, especially infants? To answer this, we must bring the logic of mutuality into contact with developmental psychology, especially advances in psychoanalytic theory. A strong analogy can be made between love as equal regard and the late Erik Erikson's definition of *generativity:* "the concern in establishing and guiding the next generation."[53] Generativity is an adult virtue that can apply equally to fathers and mothers, even though Erikson's theory of generative work followed the gender roles of the 1950s. Although presented as a model of mental health, the concept of generativity contains within it an ethical principle. In one place Erikson offered a redefinition of the Golden Rule in light of his understanding of generativity. To "do unto others as you would have them do unto you" means from the perspective of generativity that "truly worthwhile acts enhance a mutuality between doer and the other—mutuality which strengthens the doer even as it strengthens the other."[54] In advancing this interpretation of the Golden Rule, Erikson came close to an understanding of love that blends the *ordo caritatis* (the formal character of equal regard) with the *ordo bonorum* (the premoral developmental needs that love meets and actualizes), as do Janssens and Ricoeur.

There is a big difference, however, between Erikson and these two ethicists. In contrast to them, Erikson's view of mutuality is built on a generationally based life-cycle theory of the premoral good; he held that there is a series of developmental needs emerging at different times throughout the life cycle, needs functioning in children and parents. Children and parents *need each other* to meet these needs. Under optimal conditions, when they are met, there is a deepening experience of mutuality between parent and child.

We gave examples of goods that integrate males and females into families: sexual pleasure, parental recognition, and practical aid with the necessities of life. Other such values undergird the mutuality of parents and infants. For instance, there is the need for mutual recognition. Generative mutuality between parents and infants begins early in life with mutual recognition between them. Amid infant dependency of feeding, wiping, cleaning, keeping warm, there are important moments of face-to-face mutual recognition between parent and infant that are fundamental for the creation of basic trust.

Erikson describes this mutual recognition: "While the baby initially smiles at a mere configuration resembling the human face, the adult cannot help smiling back, filled with expectations of a 'recognition' which he needs to secure from the new being as surely as it needs him."[55] Psychoanalyst Jessica Benjamin makes the same observation, with special reference to the mother-infant relation, when she writes,

> As she cradles her newborn child and looks into its eyes, the first-time mother says, "I believe she knows me. You do know me, don't you? Yes you do." . . . For the mother, this peaceful moment after

a feeding—(the) baby's alert, attentive, yet enigmatic look—this moment is indeed one of recognition.[56]

Benjamin points to the importance of the two-way exchange, even at this early stage: "Later, as baby is able to demonstrate ever more clearly that he does know and prefer her to all others, she will accept this glimmer of recognition as a sign of the mutuality that persists in spite of the tremendous inequality of the parent-child relationship."[57]

The mutual recognition of adult equal regard has its developmental foundations in the mutual recognition of parent and infant. In the early days, the mother may have a slightly grander role to play, but the father by nature and training needs to be involved in this mutual recognition from the beginning, not only for the child but for himself. It is in infancy that humans first learn to recognize, in rudimentary ways, their parents as ends-in-themselves—as having desires, needs, and the right to take initiatives—a point well stated by Gudorf, Benjamin, and Erikson, all three.[58]

Equal regard, when given a life-cycle interpretation, is an important guide for raising children. Raising children takes extreme effort and some self-sacrifice. But it is important, even for the health of children, to realize that self-sacrifice should not be the single foundation of their care. Erikson gave one of the first statements in social science about how parents love their children because they get something out of it. They receive pleasure from holding and from the physical acts of nursing and feeding.[59] In caring for their children, parents get some sense that they are enriching their own lives.

In this view, parental self-sacrifices are transitional moments in parent-child relations designed to help offspring grow toward capacities for equal regard, even with their own parents. Elements of equal regard must inform parental relations with their children from the beginning, and acts of sacrifice should be moderated constantly in the course of the life cycle as children's capacities for mutuality develop. Children from the beginning need to sense that they are enriching the lives of their parents and contributing to the wider community as they gradually grow toward adult mutuality. Families exemplifying an ethic of equal regard require more, not less, of children as they gradually become capable of assuming household chores and commitments; they require from children even more than families modeled on self-sacrificing parents. Equal-regard families are "pitch-in" families and need children, at appropriate ages, to contribute to the work and welfare of the house.[60]

Parents with religious sensibilities have felt through the ages that in the face of the infant—in the child's recognition of them—they come into contact with the divine. Both mother and father frequently describe

the birth of a child as a religious experience. When Jim and Sophie
Turner described their children "as a gift of God," they echoed the words
of other parents we interviewed and what Aquinas and Luther said centuries ago. In the mutual recognition between parent and infant, parents
gain the recognition of their child, but they sense as well that the face of
their child reflects the foundations of all creativity and life—indeed, the
face of God.[61]

Parental Authority as Dialogue
with Tradition and Community

We cannot provide a detailed account of a life-cycle ethic. We should,
however, say more about parental authority and the move of children
toward mutual authority with their parents. Clearly parents have to exercise authority with their young. They must trust that their values, view
of life, and commitments are worthy grounds for the guidance of their
children.

But this settled sense of authority is best anchored when it reflects not
only the convictions of a father and mother but those of a community
of interpretation to which the parents belong. At their best, religious
communities are communities of interpretation which also model love
and care. The sacred texts and traditions of these religious communities
should be constantly interpreted and reinterpreted in light of contemporary challenges. Parental authority is best established when it comes
out of such communities of interpretation from which parents learn and
which they use to model their convictions. As one set of parents told us,
they too were subject "to a higher authority." Gradually the children
themselves become involved in the interpretive task, becoming eventually equals in clarifying the narrative identities of the "communities of
memory" to which they belong.

Families as Communities
of Interpretation

Family life as an interpretive process involving both parents and children was seen in several families we interviewed. But it took different
forms and evidenced different degrees of democratization.

Francis Nelson bore two children of James's before they got married. Since their marriage, the sense of forming a family out of an
intentional respect for each other's history and family narratives

has been high. This might have come, in part, from James's own sense of history. His theological education has contributed to this. But when asked what he wanted most to teach his two children, he said, "Connection to a larger sense of history and self . . . " He continued, "I am just now beginning to claim that for myself. I remember fondly the times at my grandmother's house, and I miss the times when my family was close. I'm remembering how good it felt when I heard either my mother or her brothers and sisters talking about something that happened when they were growing up. And to be able to connect to that is important and I am trying to convey that to my children, a sense of connection with something more than just who they are as individuals in a society. They are part of a larger family unit that has a history, part of a people that has a history."

James Nelson

Jim and Sophie Turner see their marriage as a dialogue with scripture and their evangelical tradition. They are constantly in dialogue with the Bible, both within and outside the boundaries of their home life. The Turners freely admit that they back up their parental authority with the wider authority of church and Bible. But do they indoctrinate their children? That is not their understanding of the process. Jim said, "You can't indoctrinate children. I don't think that is right." The Turners try to avoid two extremes—either the principle of "do what I say" *or* it's "totally your decision." They seem to say to their children that the whole family, even the parents, are subject to a higher truth and that they should grow together to discover it and build their lives around it. What appears, at first glance, to be authoritarian may not work that way. The entire family seems to pursue the will of God, this higher truth, together. Parents simply set the pace. Jim and Sophie Turner, in spite of their conservativism, have one of the most open dialogues with their children of all the families interviewed. This dialogue took place within a larger, intensely respected community of faith. When the Turners read scripture, they ask their children to help with the interpretation. When they pray, they ask their children to share their concerns and offer their own prayers.

Jim and Sophie Turner

Although equally serious about her faith, Mary Murphy describes a very different relation with her children. Although devout Catholics, the Murphys had little inquiry and dialogue about their religious faith at home. The family piety was expressed through attending mass. Faith was not a matter of inquiry and dialogue that involved children as well. Authority was not something a family could inquire into together and establish in conjunction with a wider community. Is this the reason why none of her sons, as Mary says, "are following our lead"?

Mary Murphy

Sarah Miles had yet another image of parental authority. Her goal for her children was that they should grow up "to be self-sufficient." This goal leads Sarah and her husband to give their children much freedom of decision, even as young children. This includes the freedom to choose what clothes to wear, when to go to school, when and if to go to synagogue. With regard to family and religious values, she says that her children have "no obligation, just whatever they take with them is who they are and what they have." Sarah's therapeutic view of religion leads her to see it as either supportive or oppressive—there is little in between. Her synagogue was not portrayed as a community of interpretation helping to support and reconstruct her family's view of the world.

Sarah Miles

It would be difficult to say that Richard Good and his wife had involved their children in a hermeneutic dialogue. The church, for him and his children, was mainly a place to internalize the Golden Rule. It was not a place for serious dialogue and interpretive inquiry. Richard, even though a liberal, saw family authority resting on simple, rather self-evident, moral rules. Ideally, his children should have maximum freedom within those rules. When discipline broke down, he would first try "logic." When that did not work, his wife would say that if the children did not do the right thing, "Your father will take care of it." At those points, in response to his children's question, "Why should I?" he would say, "because I am your father." There was little sense in Richard's family of parents and children growing together in an interpretive dialogue attempting to discern the lasting elements of a deep and complex Christian tradition. Their sense of authority oscillated between individual freedom and arbitrary parental authority.

Richard Good

4. The Family and the Reign of God

The fourth point of a practical theology of families is this: *As important as families are, they must be seen as subordinate to both the reign of God and the common good.* This is the essential meaning, and essential rightness, of such biblical passages as "Whoever loves father or mother more than me is not worthy of me; and whoever loves son or daughter more than me is not worthy of me" (Matt. 10:37). In spite of the fact that such passages applied more to clans and their religiopolitical insularity than to modern conjugal couples and children in all their fragility, it rejects any form of family idolatry, ancient or contemporary.[62]

Such passages, as we pointed out in chapter 4, have given rise to two competing interpretations. The repressive view holds that for fidelity to the reign of God to be supreme, family affections must be repressed if not completely rejected. The transformative view says that for loyalty to the reign of God to be uppermost, family affections should be transformed, extended, and analogically applied to the wider community—indeed, extended all the way to the universal community or family of God.

The transformative strategy is more consistent with the biblical witness; it is also far more philosophically defensible. Thomas Aquinas stated the matter well: Jesus "commanded us to hate, in our kindred, not their kinship, but only the fact of their being an obstacle between us and God."[63] In stating the matter this way, Aquinas was siding with Aristotle and against the Plato of the *Republic* in working out the proper relation between families and the larger common good.

Ancient clans were religiopolitical units competitive with other kin groups and resistant to national states, central religious shrines, religious administrations, and even socially transcendent ideas such as the kingdom of God. It was Plato's awareness of how family preferences can undermine communal harmony that led him to propose in the *Republic* an ideal society in which children would be raised by the state. There natural parents and children would be unaware of their biological ties with one another. Under these conditions, Plato thought that natural kinship preferences would be extinguished—indeed, repressed—so that a new social harmony could arise.[64]

By the time that Plato wrote *The Laws,* he offered an alternative vision.

It entailed keeping natural parents and children together but addressed tribalism by proposing that conjugal couples and their children be organized into larger, nonkin neighborhoods, that is, twelve artificial tribes in cities of 5,040 people. Even then he prohibited private domestic shrines because they would intensify prejudicial kin solidarity and undermine loyalty to the state and the common good.[65]

Aristotle joined Plato in being concerned with how kin preference (evolutionary ecologists' kin altruism) can compete with the larger community good. Although he held that families preceded states historically and developmentally, Aristotle also taught that the state is finally the higher good since it is concerned with the good of the whole social body—with the economy, education, and defense as families.[66] Christians, of course, have resisted this part of the Aristotelian view; the state was necessary, they conceded, but not necessarily higher than families and certainly not higher than the reign of God.

Nonetheless, Aristotle tried to heal the tension between family and state by developing in children the virtues of citizenship, principally the virtue of justice.[67] Aristotle was clear that natural biological parents have a proclivity to love their own children. If this tendency were suppressed, as Plato recommended, one of the fundamental glues of society would come unstuck. Adults, he believed, would not care as much for the young, nor would the restraints of kin affection work to deter violence.[68] Citizenship, for Aristotle, was clearly an extension of the affections of family ties to wider and wider circles of society. Family ties must be transcended, but this should be done not by suppressing such affinities but by building on them and extending them outward to others. We follow Aristotle's lead, as do those who uphold the principle of subsidiarity. Families must be subject to the common good but not in ways that permit the state to undermine kin affections.

The strategy of early Christianity was similar to Aristotle's extension of family affections to the wider community. This strategy applied to the *ecclesia* and the reign of God and not to the state as such. Although some Christians may have left their families to become involved in the Christian movement, on the whole marital relations were not renounced, husbands and wives did not leave each other, and parents did not leave their children for others to raise. Rather, the *ecclesia* included families, families were converted en masse when possible (Acts 11:14; 16:15), and family affections were extended to the wider house church and the kingdom of God. Members of the *ecclesia* became one another's spiritual brothers and sisters, fathers and mothers, parents and children in Christ (1 Thess. 4:9–10; 1 John 3:17). The energies of kin altruism were not extinguished but used both to invest in kin and to fuel, with the help of God's grace, the wider loyalties of *ecclesia* and God's kingdom.

Part of the attractiveness of early Christianity must have been its in-
genious use and analogical extension of what such evolutionary theorists as James Q. Wilson are now calling the seat of our "moral sense":
our fundamental affective attachments to our kin.[69] To love our distant
neighbor, we must first love our mother and father, brother and sister,
which, under normal circumstances, we are profoundly inclined to do.
But to learn to love our distant neighbor, as citizen of the state or a member of the reign of God, we must have a new definition of the neighbor
which kin altruism itself does not provide. To capture the energies of kin altruism, there must be a symbolic representation of the distant other, a
way of designating the neighbor as in some way kin and basically similar to and united with us. The symbols of Christianity—the image of
God in the neighbor, the mutual identification of husband and wife with
Christ, the self-giving love of Christ poured out for both other and self,
the goodness of God manifest in all humans—all these symbols can
function for the faithful to transform their primitive "archaeologies"
(their biologically grounded kin affections) and extend them teleologi-
cally and analogically to wider circles.

One's spouse was included in this extended covenantal circle. Part of
the ancient meaning of covenant was the idea of sharing or mixing blood
with the person, clan, tribe, or political entity with which one was
covenanting. In marking a covenant with the symbolic or actual sharing
of blood, the parties entering the covenant became *as if* they were actual
blood-related kin to one another.[70] This is part of the meaning of "one
flesh" in Genesis 2:24 that was repeated in the idea that the "two shall become one" in the great marriage passage of Ephesians 5:31. When applied to one's spouse, who is not blood kin and not literally "bone of my
bones and flesh of my flesh" (Gen. 2:23), the marriage covenant is a symbolic way of extending kin altruism to the marital partner. It says, "I will
treat you with the same affection and sense of obligation that I formerly
extended to members of my family or kin." The symbolic family relation
or covenant—whether it is between husband and wife, between members of the *ecclesia*, or between participants in the kingdom—is built by
analogically extending and redefining the basic energies of kin partiality.

Covenant, Equal Regard, and Subsidiarity

Love as mutuality or equal regard, the principle of subsidiarity, and the
Reformed doctrine of covenant can all be clarified by stating their relation
to kin altruism. Equal regard, when applied to relations between families,
means that each family should respect and support the inclinations of

other families to care for their kin. Love as *ordo caritatis et bonorum* applies to relations between families as well as to relations between individuals. This means that no family has the right to become so engrossed in the welfare of its own members as to damage or neglect the welfare of other families. Furthermore, it means that each family should support a public policy that works for the justice and welfare of all families *as* families and not just the welfare of individuals in abstraction from family ties.

This brings us again to the principle of subsidiarity. Subsidiarity, because of its Aristotelian and Thomistic backgrounds, grants natural parents the prima facie responsibility for raising their children because of their deep inclinations for this task. Although the state has the general responsibility of guaranteeing the welfare of the social whole, it must not interfere with the integrity of families or their responsibility to care for their own, unless incompetence, abuse, or neglect are discovered. Not only does the principle of subsidiarity assume the reality of kin altruism, it requires a *social ethic* of equal regard. Governments must try to guarantee the basic justice needed for families to flourish. They must protect families from injustice perpetrated by other families, from the disruptions of an ever-expanding market, and from the undue interference of the state itself. Finally, when families falter in their responsibilities because of accident or neglect, government must provide forms of assistance.

The principle of subsidiarity implies a principle of social interdependence. As Pam Couture has written with special reference to the situation of single mothers, "The care of single mothers and their children, and therefore, the possibility of their equality and their flourishing, can only be insured through the interdependencies of the government, the local community, the family and the individual." [71] We also include the church in this list of needed communal supports. In cases of radical family breakdown, government may need to find and support surrogate parents.

Subsidiarity, kin altruism, and love as equal regard—these three concepts are intimately connected. When associated with secular assumptions that ground personhood on rationality, they give us the meaning of the common good. When grounded in God's love for each person and each family, they point to a theory of divine covenant and the reign of God. From a Christian perspective, equal regard, subsidiarity, and kin altruism stand within the context of God's covenant relation to the world in creation and the new covenant in redemption.

Christians should bring these foundational beliefs into their family thinking in both church and secular society. But in secular life, the Christian should work to create approximations to the reign of God by making alliances with those whose basic beliefs have *analogies*[72] to those of Christians. Christians and non-Christians can often agree at the level of practical reason on an analysis of the premoral and moral goods needed for mundane family life. There will be less agreement between Christians and non-Christians at the level of foundational beliefs, but there may be sufficient analogies to permit cooperation.

Families and kin altruism should become the new intervening variable, one which often is left out of more individualistic understandings of the reign of God or the common good typical of liberal social and religious philosophies. We must create a new day when equality and justice apply not only to individuals but to families and their deep inclinations to care for one another.

11

Critical Familism:

New Directions for Church and Society

The central message of this chapter, as one member of our team expressed it, is that "there *really are* ideas out there." This is a quick way of saying that sprinkled around in church, society, government, and market are both ideas and functioning models for helping families and creating a new critical familism. This chapter identifies some of these ideas and models, though there are many that we have missed. Our purpose is not to find *the solutions* but to suggest that new directions and initiatives are possible. Our purpose is to show the grounds for hope.

In this chapter, we address first what churches can do within their congregations and in their communities. Then we turn to what churches can do in the realm of public policy. The first is the more important, but the two sides of the churches' witness should be coordinated. Although the local witness and the public stand of churches should be related, they should not be identical. Failure to appreciate this has often led Christian conservatives to impose their ideals for Christian families on public policy, and Christian liberals to think that good public policy for families defines Christian ideals as well. Neither is right.

To move beyond these alternatives, we carry forward our central ideas: the Reformed idea of God's covenant with the different spheres of life, Catholic subsidiarity, and love as equal regard with its implications for justice both within and between families. We ground both subsidiarity and love as equal regard in God's covenant love for creation (the *imago Dei*). Both subsidiarity and equal regard, however, can be distanced (not removed) from this theistic beginning point for effective discourse in public debate.

Churches and a Critical Marriage Culture

We address first the local witness of churches with their own members and immediate communities. The following guidelines identify ministries and strategies that can be initiated from the locus of congregations and parishes.

The Critical Retrieval of
a Marriage and Family Culture

1. *More than anything else, churches must retrieve their marriage and family traditions, even though they must do so critically.* As we attempted to do in these pages, churches on a smaller scale should examine their heritages, enter into dialogue with other denominations, survey the human sciences, and articulate a fresh vision of marriage and family. No longer should these topics be seen as private, individual, unheroic, and unimportant for church concern. Just as the early church quickly addressed marriage and family after the first burst of its missionary zeal, churches today must do the same.

Churches should go beyond Focus on the Family, the Christian Coalition, the Family Research Council, and the recent familism of the Republican and Democratic parties in promoting a *critical* familism and a *critical* culture of marriage. Churches should not just promote getting married and staying married; *they should themselves be sensitive to the power distortions, inequalities, convoluted communications, and failures in intersubjectivity characteristic of families since the beginning of human history.* Churches should proclaim a critical family culture guided by the ethics of equal regard, realistically attuned to the energies of kin altruism, and appropriately compensating for the asymmetrical ways males and females tend to work out their parental investments.

One caveat immediately must be added: This critical culture should not obscure what theologian Margaret Mills calls "connected aloneness," a personal identity founded on the love of God that grounds both dignified singleness or individual integrity in marriage.[1] Nor should we forget its importance for vulnerable mothers who are tempted to identify their self-worth with the regard of their husbands because they need their financial help and assistance with child care. Connected aloneness may constitute the final grounds for resistance to exploitation or the grounds for survival when someone is faced with abandonment.

We urge that the churches' critical familism rest on a differentiated theological language. By this we mean something like the three levels of language used in this book: (1) a language about the natural conditions of family formation, (2) an ethical language of equal regard grounded in the *imago Dei,* and (3) a narrative-religious language that undergirds the first two and tells the Christian story. When Christians use these languages in preaching and worship, the language listed third is always first. This narrative shapes and grounds everything else. In public discourse, the second and third levels are sometimes "distanced" from the first; that is, the narrative is *temporarily* set in the background. In public debate, Christians should be responsible for presenting arguments supporting all of these levels. Cooperation between churches and other parts of society depends on finding analogies between the churches' own arguments at any of these levels and the arguments of other sectors of society. But a differentiated theological language is also important *within* the church. Increasingly, people in the pews are like the public— they need to hear both a powerful witness and a good argument.

Reclaiming Family as "First Church" and "Little Church"

2. *One of the most important learnings from our interviews was just how crucial home-based worship is for the transmission of faith and family traditions.* The Turners, Taylors, and Nelsons prayed with their children, read scripture, and discussed their faith, their moral commitments, and their views of sexuality, marriage, and family. They did this at home— at the dinner table, before bed, and on trips. The Murphys, as deeply religious as they were, did not do these things at home with their four sons, and the sons are currently not following their parents in making a religious commitment.

The continuity between the gathered *ecclesia* and the church at home has been a constant theme throughout Christian history and, as seen in chapter 3, American history as well. Because the early church met in homes, sacred actions around rituals and common meals in the gathered *ecclesia* spilled into home life. The dominant-subordinate, male-female role patterns of the honor-shame culture of antiquity were fractured because of this overlap between house church and home life. Home in such contexts became a little church.

When home and public worship became differentiated, special efforts were needed to make home the scene of the little church. In New England, home was seen as a "little church" and a "little commonwealth" that had authority directly from the family's covenant with God. Parents (mainly the father) modeled at home the family's obligations to church and state without deriving their final authority from either.[2] Catholics have had their idea of the church at home—a "domestic church." It has its authority through the sacraments of the church rather than in a direct relation to God, as Protestant parents claim to enjoy. The intimacies of home life are the first arena for living out the sacrament of baptism, a sacrament conferred by the priests and magistrates of the church.[3]

We propose a more Protestant, dialogical, and nonpatriarchal model of the domestic church. Our model grounds parental authority in a *dialogue* between parents' own covenant with God and the church's covenant. This assumes that God has a covenant with both church and family. Parental authority, therefore, should evolve from a dialogue with a church that itself is dedicated to an appreciative yet critical inquiry into its traditions. As it becomes possible, authoritative parents introduce their children into this dialogue as well. Whether Protestant or Catholic, both traditions understand the importance of spiritual life in the home. As Protestants, we authors confess having drifted away in varying degrees from the tradition of the little or domestic church in our own home lives. Our research, and especially our case studies, convinces us of its profound importance.

Ecumenicity and Critical Familism

3. *Churches must join with other churches and synagogues to create a new critical marriage and family culture.* This guideline follows our vision of church as the primary carrier of the interplay between mutual and sacrificial love needed to humanize our natural inclinations. It is also based on the sociological fact that churches and synagogues perform 75 percent of all marriages, even today. Hence, strong arguments support the idea that churches must work together in proclaiming and implementing a marriage and family culture.

But how can this happen? Evangelical journalist Michael McManus in his widely read *Marriage Savers* (1993) makes an interesting admission for a conservative Protestant. He tells his readers that for the most part Roman Catholic churches in America are doing a significantly better job of preparing and supporting individuals for marriage and family commitments than Protestant churches, whether evangelical or mainline. This is because they have a coordinated program of premarital and marital support that they call the "Common Marriage Policy."[4] Of 142 dioceses in the United States, 124 implement this policy. In other words, Catholic churches have a common front. Young Catholic couples considering marriage confront a common set of expectations and a common culture about marriage and family, and what it takes to prepare and endure in family relations.

This common policy has five components: (1) a six-month minimum preparation period, (2) the administration of a premarital questionnaire (PREPARE, the Pre-Marital Inventory, or FOCUS), (3) the use of lay leadership and "mentoring couples" with the engaged and newly married, (4) the use of marriage instruction classes (Pre-Cana workshops or weekends, evenings for the engaged in the homes of mentor couples, and the use of Engaged Encounter and Marriage Encounter—all premarital and marital programs that Catholics have pioneered), and (5) engagement ceremonies held before the entire congregation. McManus proposes bringing together Catholic, evangelical, and mainline churches to create a "Community Marriage Policy,"[5] an ecumenical common marriage policy that would help churches across denominations develop a united front on marriage and family.

This united front helps churches counter the individualism and impatience of couples and parents who expect ministers to perform marriages on demand without careful preparation. Several cities, he reports, have tried it: Modesto, Fresno, and Tracy in California; Peoria, Quincy, and Moline in Illinois; Fairbanks, Alaska; Austin, Texas; Louisville, Kentucky; and others. The common elements look much like the Catholic model but often with shorter waiting periods to accommodate Protestant customs.

This suggestion has genuine possibilities. But McManus's glowing reports of early success need to be verified.[6] He admits that each community is different and that pastors have difficulties deciding on the "minimum" elements of a common policy. Furthermore, it is clear that his vision falls far short of being a *critical* common policy concerned with critiquing gender inequality, overly strong doctrines of self-sacrificial love, and male headship.

Even if a common community marriage policy is a good idea, it needs refinement. It should be seen as the beginning of a process rather than an idea that needs only to be implemented. Churches will not create local marriage and family cultures successfully without simultaneously beginning a new task of critical reflection about the marriage traditions of Christianity and Judaism. In spite of the energy of McManus's suggestions, the biblical, historical, and philosophical basis of his arguments are effective primarily with those already sympathetic with his cause.

The Churches, Civil Society, and the State

4. *Churches should join with other parts of civil society in their local communities to create a critical marriage and family culture.* In some instances, this will entail partnerships with the state. Christians can respect the differentiation of church and state and still believe that God has implicit covenants with the state that Christians should help fulfill. The state too should be guided by an ethic of equal regard for individuals and families. It also should abide by the principle of subsidiarity that respects the initiative and responsibility of families yet supports them when they need help. Some of this cooperation between churches, state, and institutions of civil society already exists: witness the cooperation between churches and public health institutions or churches and the Red Cross.

Churches should not permit public institutions to become isolated from the energies and positive cultures of specific religiocultural traditions. For example, sociologist James Coleman argued that Catholic high schools provide better education than public schools because Catholic students receive more support from parents and church.[7] As societies organized around clan and extended family have disappeared, Coleman believes that market, corporations, and government have organized more of society, including schools. Public schools now represent the impersonal forces of government and market more than the values and energies of families, churches, and neighborhoods. Catholic schools are succeeding because they are an exception to this trend; they represent the values of families and their churches. Coleman urges us to abandon the idea that schools are agents of the state. Rather, Coleman writes,

> the school is properly an extension of the family and the social community or value community of which that family is a part. . . . [W]hatever the basis for community, the role of the school is, according to this alternative, to foster that community.[8]

Our view is sympathetic to Coleman's but is somewhat different. We believe that family and church should not simply dominate public schools. If there is a divine covenant with different spheres of life, whether this covenant is acknowledged or not, a differentiated field of authority must bear on schools. Because of this, families, religious institutions, and the state need to conduct an intense dialogue about the direction of public schools. Clearly, public schools should be closer to families, neighborhoods, and communities than they have been. Furthermore, there is a place in our society for critically reflective private schools working out of a variety of important traditions, even though they sometimes divide neighborhoods and communities. Our point, however, is this: *Part of this dialogue between local church, family, and public school should result in developing new educational approaches to marriage and family life, approaches that have continuity with, but may not be identical to, the basic values of families and churches.*

But the cooperation between church, civil society, and the state can take other forms. At the time of this writing, William Bennett and Indiana Senator Dan Coats's Project for American Renewal constitutes the most ambitious proposal to date for government's efforts to revive civil society. This initiative will raise important issues that churches should address *actively*. Coats and Bennett, Republicans themselves, are mildly critical of Republican proposals to turn welfare for poor families over to the fifty individual states—proposals that became law in late summer of 1996. But they also reject liberal Democratic proposals to center power and social programs mainly in the federal government.

Project for American Renewal calls for government stimulation and support directly to the voluntary institutions of civil society, including the churches. Bennett and Coats argue that these institutions are the conveyors of civic virtue, do most of society's moral education, and need to be revived.

How can government help revive churches and other institutions of civil society? Should churches cooperate in this? The idea has possibilities but only if churches take control and direct this alliance rather than being passive clients. Churches must have a clear understanding of their primary role in proclaiming a gospel of salvation and liberation; once this is foremost, they can cooperate with government and other institutions of civil society in moral guidance and the enrichment of the common good.

The Coats-Bennett plan allows individuals to give $500 of their tax liability ($1,000 for married couples) to worthwhile nongovernmental charities, including churches and their charities, that help poor families.[9] It recommends demonstration grants for programs that match welfare recipients and nonviolent criminals with religious communities offering moral guidance and help. Schools would receive demonstration grants to enlist community groups to connect children with mentors and other role models, some doubtless found in churches. To encourage savings by poor families, demonstration grants would be provided for family deposits to be matched by churches, foundations, and corporations. Some proposals would apply directly to families. Funds would be made available for predivorce counseling. Tax credits of up to $5,000 would be offered to adopting parents with an income of less than $60,000. To make marriage more profitable for poor people, $1,000 tax credits would be given to married couples who make at least $8,500 and receive the Earned Income Tax Credit. And there is much more.

Many of these proposals seem in keeping with our basic theological principles: the relative autonomy of, yet cooperation between, the social spheres of family, church, market, and state; the principle of subsidiarity; and an ethic of equal regard between poor and rich families. But there are many twists and turns to such proposals. Sheer workability is an issue. Furthermore, there is more to reviving civil society than providing money, especially money from external forces such as central governments. Gertrude Himmelfarb, generally supportive of these proposals, warns that civil society is itself "de-moralized." Many churches, voluntary organizations, and schools (both private and public) have lost their moral direction. There may be energy at local levels, as kin altruism and the principle of subsidiarity predict, but this energy often may be morally confused. Himmelfarb, a well-known neoconservative intellectual, surprises us by suggesting a role for government in taking the moral leadership.[10] Because the principle of subsidiarity means that both wholes and parts have their proper place, we too admit that moral wisdom may come from a variety of places, not always from the grass roots. This is why the dialogical model of the relation of church, state, civil society, and market is so important.

Youth and a
Critical Marriage Culture

5. *Churches should take the lead in preparing youth for a critical familism.* Large portions of society have retreated from guiding and inspiring youth in the areas of marriage and family. Many churches do not do adequate marriage preparation with engaged couples; they do even less with youth and teenagers. Churches have yielded leadership to public education, at the college level and below.

As churches have retreated from sex, marriage, and family education, secular courses, primarily at the college level, have taken their place. A recent authoritative review of college textbooks by Professor Norval Glenn of the University of Texas has revealed that most of these texts are devoid of historical knowledge of the family, overly optimistic about the successes of alternative family forms, neglectful of children, and uninformed about new research on the benefits of marriage.[11] They tend to ignore evidence, recently summarized by Professor Linda Waite of the University of Chicago, showing that married people are mentally and physically healthier, have more wealth, have much more sex, and are generally far more content with life than those who are not married; this is true for both wives and husbands, though more so for husbands.[12] College texts seem to give neither good preparation for marriage nor good information about it. Should churches be concerned about this?

What about high school and junior high curricula? Most of what is said systematically about marriage and family in secondary schools is within sex education courses whose value for the prevention of disease and out-of-wedlock births is now being questioned.[13] Setting aside the question of their effectiveness for the control of unwanted pregnancies and disease, they tend to handle sexuality independently of careful discussions of what we call a critical marriage culture.[14] The so-called comprehensive approach, which mentions abstinence but primarily emphasizes individual decision and knowledge about birth control, says little about marriage or families except to promote an attitude of respect for family pluralism. Sex Respect, a conservative Christian program, emphasizes abstinence until marriage but spends little time talking about preparations necessary to meet the demands of an equal-regard, public-private marriage.[15] The most competent sex education program is Postponing Sexual Involvement, designed by Marian Howard of the medical school at Emory University. It takes a clear stand that sex should be postponed and equips students through role-playing exercises with the communicative skills to say no in situations of social pressure.[16] This program, however, is not about education for marriage and family but about the delay of sexual activity until "maturity."

Three programs for youth do discuss positive images of marriage and family. The secular Teen Aid uses Aristotle, Erich Fromm, and Kahlil Gibran to project images of marriage around mutuality and friendship within a sex education and AIDS prevention program.[17] An American Bar Association program called Partners features a video designed to acquaint high school students with "the realities" of the legal, economic, and communicative aspects of marriage.[18] The marriage problems of a young couple are enacted, and two professionals, a lawyer and a marital communications expert, provide commentary. The communications expert uses PREPARE (Premarital Personal and Relationship Evaluation), a program developed by psychologist David Olson but similar to the methods of Harville Hendrix, Markham, and John Gottman. Its appeals, however, are based on self-interest and a contractual view of marriage. Religion is noticeably absent, and deeper dimensions of love as equal regard renewed by sacrificial love are also absent. But the program is an important step in the right direction; it needs to be enriched, not dismissed. Perhaps a third professional resource from religion should be added. True Love Waits is an extensive, multivolume, age-graded Southern Baptist program designed for youth. As one would expect, it presents conservative views on abortion and premarital sex. Its images of marriage and family are theologically grounded and emphasize mutuality, forgiveness, and good communication. Relatively free of gender stereotypes, it is a program worth studying and adapting because of its range, age sensitivity, theological grounding, and appreciation of most of the elements of love as mutuality.[19]

The Catholic Church has developed a successful version of its Marriage Encounter called Engaged Encounter for couples who are contemplating marriage.[20] These two important programs, in addition to their instructional and mentoring features, are now including insights from the therapies teaching communicative skills to couples. Our proposal, however, recommends something that would come *much earlier*—something that helps youth before engagement to understand the institutions of marriage and family; gain a grasp of the moral, religious, economic, and legal components of marriage; and do this with a critical understanding of the intersubjective communication required for the equal-regard family. *As it appears now, such programs must be created anew.* We argue that they should be created first by churches and then spread into the institutions of secular society.

Bilingual Theology and Bifocal Programs

6. *Churches should develop a bilingual theology and a bifocal program that supports intact families and addresses the realities of other family forms.* The cultural and social forces that are disrupting families are relentless, as we have seen. In addition, the frailty of the human spirit that touches all individuals and families should be readily acknowledged by the Christian faith.

Churches must recognize that family disruption is a fact of life. Family dissolution is often necessary in cases of violence, abuse, and addiction, even if churches rightly aspire to lessen the extent of it. Furthermore, there is much to be done to mitigate the strains on disrupted families, be they never-married single parents, the divorced, or stepfamilies. Finally, we must recognize the advent of families with gay and lesbian parents and families consisting of heterosexual parents with gay or lesbian children. New programs such as COLAGE (Children of Lesbians and Gays Everywhere) help the children of gay and lesbian parents discuss marriage and family life. Although there is a range of positions in the churches about the nature and moral status of homosexual orientation and practice, almost all churches, fundamentalistic to progressive, wish to minister in different ways to these families. And they should; the people in these families are *children of God.*

We should study in detail those churches that can simultaneously and aggressively prepare people for stable and fulfilling marriages yet affirm and assist those people in alternative family forms. For example, we discovered a burgeoning white Pentecostal church in the western suburbs of Chicago that has, in addition to its strong emphasis on marriage and a general opposition to divorce, a highly popular twelve-week post-divorce support program.[21] It has been our experience that African-American and evangelistic churches have made more progress on such bifocal ministries than Catholic or mainline Protestant churches. Megachurches, both black and white, are particularly worth studying.

For instance, we studied Shiloh Baptist Church, located in the poorer black section of Washington, D.C. Its minister is Wallace Charles Smith, whose book we discussed in chapter 8. Shiloh's twofold theology and bifocal programs are facilitated by having the Family Life Center adjacent to the church. The Family Life Center addresses needs of the entire surrounding community, not just the members of the church. Its programs include the Male Youth Health Enhancement Project, which brings together sixty African-American boys every weekday afternoon from 3:00 to 6:30. They are involved with older mentors and participate in tutoring sessions; workshops on sex, drugs, and communication skills; discussions about the difficulties and responsibilities of early fatherhood; lessons on African-American history; and recreation. The program combines an emphasis on abstinence and knowledge-based approaches to matters of sexuality. The leaders of Male Youth Health Enhancement stay in contact with the schools, monitor the students' school performance, and involve parents (most of whom are single) in the life of the Family Life Center. A similar program for young women called the Debutante program emphasizes not only preparation for marriage, as the name suggests, but the attainment of skills relevant to a career. These programs are accompanied by a day-care center and the Human Service Center, which provides counseling and services for single parents and stepfamilies, and vocational counseling for people with alcohol- and drug-abuse problems.

The language of the center is more public, less confessional, less freighted with the specifics of Reverend Smith's theology, which emphasizes simultaneously, as we saw, the power of the extended family, church as symbolic extended family, *and* the importance of intact two-parent families. There is little evidence of moralism and shame at Shiloh even though it is patently clear what the family standards are. Although no participant in the programs of the center is forced to come to church on Sunday morning, many do. Furthermore, the ethics and ethos of the worshiping church pervade the work of the center as a whole.

Shiloh is an excellent example of a cooperative relation between civil society, government, foundations, and the market. Shiloh gets grants to run these programs from a variety of sources, yet its programs bear the distinctive character of Shiloh's religious and ethical commitments. Does it violate the separation of church and state? No, because it does not coerce and it does not proselytize. Nor does it hide its convictions or bar individuals from moving into its confessing ranks if they elect this path. Isn't this the bargain we have to accept to renew civil society and families in a society where both have been buffeted by the forces of technical rationality in state and market?

Churches and the
Balance of Work and Family

7. *Churches should address one of the major sources of strain on families: the tensions between family needs and the demands of paid work.* Mothers have joined fathers in the workforce, the average workweek has been extended, parents spend less time with children (the "parenting deficit"), and marital couples spend less time with each other. Clearly, it *takes time*

and energy to create an equal-regard family with parents guiding children into an ever-deepening dialogue with them and their faith traditions. If local churches are serious about helping families develop the communication patterns needed to fulfill their covenants of equal regard, they should challenge families to work less and balance employment and family life better. We propose a model not exceeding a sixty-hour workweek for a mother and father that could be divided between the partners as thirty–thirty or forty–twenty. Churches should discuss this concrete image of work with their families and advocate it as a national policy, as we do later in this chapter.

There is evidence that the happiest families are those in which both husband and wife have some paid employment, share household chores and childcare,[22] and work less than two full-time positions. There is arresting new evidence that fathers are happier and healthier if involved in childcare, just as mothers are happier and healthier if they participate in paid work.[23] A small but provocative study done in the department of psychiatry of Harvard University is worth contemplating. It found that there was more intimacy between husband and wife, more optimism about the future, a higher sense of bonding between husband and wife after the birth of a child, more involvement of husbands in childcare, and slightly less depression for wives among couples where the wife worked part-time in contrast to those with wife at home or with both husband and wife working full-time.[24] This kind of marriage had more time for children, more time for the couple to relate to each other, and more excitement because both made new contacts and learned new things from their employment. This suggests a dialectical relation between more investment of time in the marriage and higher marital commitment. It takes commitment to create an equal-regard relation, but an equal-regard relation, in turn, enhances commitment.

This study, however, investigates only cases where the part-time worker is the wife rather than the husband. It does not study those existing cases where both are employed only thirty hours a week, an idea we explore shortly. Although suggestive, this study gives rise to the idea that the sixty-hour workweek should be divided only one way, forty–twenty, and that the woman should always take the twenty-hour job. *This implication, we think, should be challenged. The proportion could be reversed, and it certainly could be thirty–thirty.* Even today, according to one poll, 62 percent of mothers say that they would prefer to work part-time, although only 28 percent were actually doing it, indicating that a significant number were not doing what they want.[25]

Churches must address the issue of the family workweek at the local level in their preaching, teaching, programming, and community work.

From the beginning, we have emphasized the potential disruptive forces of market rationality and demands on families. The spirituality of the equal-regard marriage must rescue families from being devoured by the demands of the market, and a theology of Sabbath rest should be applied to the strains of overworked families. Mainline Protestant churches were early in supporting the idea of women entering the labor market. Now the demands of a prophetic ministry are more subtle; all churches, including progressive mainliners, must *protect the family from the ravages of the market*. Mothers and fathers should have equal access to the benefits of paid work, but this should be tempered by respect for individual circumstances and a philosophy that protects families from materialism and market idolatry.

If the equal-regard family is to become a reality, couples will need help in gaining the intersubjective communication needed to *work out* what is just and equitable in light of the demands of shared housework, their respective skills, personal inclinations, and the needs of children. Church-sponsored day-care centers, support groups for working parents, church-sponsored baby-sitting networks, church-sponsored nursing support for parents of sick children—dozens of programs are possible. But more fundamental than any of these is a new theology that sanctions the balance of work and parenting and helps establish a new social system requiring no more than sixty hours of paid employment for parents.

The Churches and Divorce

8. *Churches should do more to address the reality of divorce.* From the teachings of Jesus and Paul, through the sacramental theologies of the Catholic church, and into a freer yet restrictive attitude toward divorce in the Reformation, Christianity has taken a conservative attitude toward divorce. In spite of the trends in secular society and church toward easy acceptance of divorce, the church should continue to be conservative on this issue. But this does not mean an absolute prohibition of divorce. Theologian Helmut Thielicke is helpful in his interpretation of Jesus' words: "It was because you were so hard-hearted that Moses allowed you to divorce your wives, but from the beginning it was not so" (Matt. 19:8). Rather than seeing this as an absolute prohibition against divorce, it is more likely a call for repentance in view of the contradiction between God's will in creation and the realities of a fallen world.[26]

We recommend four strategies that local churches can use to address the reality of divorce. First, prevention is the best cure. The best prevention is extensive marital preparation of the kind envisioned by Mc-

Manus's Community Marriage Policy (qualified by instructions on the complexity of the equal-regard marriage) and our proposals on early church-based and school-based education for marriage and family.

The second strategy would have church-based marriage counseling begin with a humane bias toward preserving marriages as, indeed, much of secular marriage counseling is starting to do. As we saw in chapter 7, William Doherty has set the tone of the new trends in marriage and family counseling. His words can apply to the counseling pastor as well as the secular psychotherapist: "As therapists, we are moral consultants, not just psychosocial consultants. We should not try to impose our beliefs on undecided clients, but we can advocate in an open manner when appropriate."[27] Counseling that presents theological and naturalistic reasons for the importance of preserving marriage is entirely justifiable *as long* as it is not coercive, does not override the decision-making integrity of the individuals involved, does not suppress important dynamic and communication issues that the couple should face, and does not ignore abuse, violence, and addiction. The idea that divorce is generally not good for children and that couples not involved in physical and mental violence may be able to learn to communicate and love one another again must be taken seriously in the counseling of churches.[28]

The third strategy calls for churches to love, minister to, and sustain the divorced. In spite of what churches do to discourage them, *divorces will occur,* although we hope they will become increasingly less common. But how can churches simultaneously promote a marriage culture, discourage a divorce culture, and yet promote a culture of care for divorced and remarried persons?[29] Our research suggests that some churches are successful at this for two reasons. First, such churches have a commanding and differentiated theology for addressing the "ironies" of the Christian life, that is, a theology that holds up marital ideals yet confesses the faults of us all—married, divorced, single, or remarried. Second, these churches develop a *culture of openness* in talking about marriage and family. The churches who have not developed this culture of openness talk about neither marriage nor divorce. In short, they are embarrassed to talk about the intimate aspects of life. The churches that have this culture of openness can address both family ideals and family frailties. Hence, these churches can promote intact families, develop support groups for the divorced, help them with the single life, help them remarry, and help them as stepfamilies. Furthermore, they help disrupted families create the networks—what sociologists call social capital—necessary for all families, especially those undergoing transitions.

The final strategy calls for churches even at the local level to join the national discussion about our divorce laws. Many believe that the great revisions of family law called no-fault divorce contributed to the creation of a divorce culture. Whether or not this is true, local church leaders should get involved in the national dialogue over whether these laws should be amended. This is a topic we return to below.

Churches and Fathers

9. *Churches should do more to address what we have called "the male problematic."* In saying this, we do not mean to ignore the issues facing women, especially single mothers and their children. But the issue of fathers is especially acute, and addressing this issue also helps women and mothers.

It is time for churches to acknowledge that a key consequence of family change has been the growing absence of fathers from families and their children. We must face this issue squarely: if the movement toward father absence is to be abated, nearly every aspect of civil society must address it, and churches must do so first of all.

As we saw in chapter 8, there is much to learn from black churches about restoring responsible fatherhood. Different strategies are taken by these churches, but they are often equally effective. The ten-thousand-member Pentecostal Church of God in Christ on Chicago's south side routinely and vigorously addresses father absence and discusses the positive contributions to children that fathers make. Many people in this huge church hardly knew their fathers when growing up. One man from the "projects" who is now a bank vice president said, "I saw my father three times—once when I was five, once when I was twelve, and once at his funeral." His relation to the same church for thirty years "had made the difference" in his life. What had he heard? He heard in countless sermons and talks a message that named and addressed the problem of father absence, promoted a model of male servanthood reversing the honor-shame codes of the streets, respected marriage, confined sexual expression to marriage, connected young men to older male mentors, supported their education, taught them to honor their wives, and challenged them to care for their children. He heard these messages at countless men's breakfasts, father-and-son banquets, outings, conferences, and Bible studies.[30] As we have noted, the model of love in many of these churches fails at the symbolic level, and often at the practical level, to project a fully intersubjective and democratic understanding of love. The strong wives of the marriages in this particular church however, helped enact that model. Furthermore, this church and its pastor were aware that the black male problematic is aggravated by discrimination, poverty, and job flight. But this church first appealed to what men could do to change their own actions; individual change (they called it conversion) should precede social change, however important the latter is thought to be.

Another nearby church does all these things but with more consciousness of African themes. They too use the phrase "it takes a village to raise a child," A saying that critiques the individualism of middle-class white culture. This church holds a monthly service that recognizes the "father of the month" and brings all men and young boys into a huge circle where they hold hands and bond in Christian solidarity. It holds plays and skits that role-play how young girls should defend themselves against the sexual advances of boys, especially older young men in their twenties.[31] This church has rites-of-passage ceremonies for both teenage boys and girls that combine African themes and Christian meanings in defining adult male-female relations. The conjugal couple as the core of the family is celebrated but set within the importance of the extended family and larger church community. Furthermore, this church is part of an "adopt a school" program in which adult mentors relate to a neighborhood school, give courses on "responsible living," and help guide students away from gangs and toward their studies.

Other worthy programs address the situation of men and families, some relating churches and government in creative ways. Indianapolis has launched a citywide initiative called *Rebuilding Families* that establishes a wide range of cooperative ventures between churches and the city government to discourage teen pregnancies, promote marriage, and help young fathers support their children. It also reaches out to single mothers and their children. A cornerstone of the Indianapolis program is a Mississippi-based initiative known as *Faith and Families. Faith and Families* pairs congregations with two types of families: vulnerable families (teen mothers, their babies, and the fathers of those babies) *and* intact families that are underemployed or on public assistance. For the first group, they help fathers to find employment and support their children; they help the teen mothers to complete school and not get pregnant again; for the second group, the church helps them find and keep employment or upgrade the employment they already have.

The dangers and opportunities of such programs are obvious. Can government and the public allow churches to bring their morality and religious convictions to these situations as long as they do not seek coercively to convert? Can churches cooperate with government without becoming the tool of government and losing their identity and transcendent goals? We think such experiments are worth trying. Such programs may give churches new opportunities to be simultaneously truly confessing and truly public. Furthermore, such programs may transform the moral sensibility of church members themselves; to help others is also to be a model and a mentor.

Public Policy:
What Churches Can Do

Strengthening the inner life of churches and their relation to their immediate communities should be our first priority. Churches have a covenant responsibility to help people form and sustain strong families. They have an obligation to nourish, order, and renew that which is close at hand. Nonetheless, wider social realities, including government policy, must be addressed. From the perspective of Christian ethics, this is a task of social outreach, a task of *diakonia*—the ministry of social service to the wider community.

Critical Familism and
Public Policy: Beyond Value Neutrality

1. *Churches must help society understand that public policy should not and cannot maintain "value neutrality" on family matters.* But neither can public policy be guided solely by the uncritically asserted dictates of any one religious tradition. To say this, however, does not mean that religious traditions, including Christianity, cannot enter into the public conversation about the moral values guiding public policy. Instead, we argue that public policy should be guided by a critical familism and that Judaism, Christianity, and other traditions have much to contribute to its formulation.

Public policy must be willing to project and implement positive ideals for families created through democratic dialogue. The conversing parties should not only be in dialogue with one another but also respect and appropriate critically their respective family traditions.[32] Christians and Jews, Protestants and Catholics, and increasingly Muslims, Hindus, and those groups shaped by Confucianism should bring their family traditions into the public policy debate. As we pointed out above, we interpret Christianity as having a language that functions at three levels: the level of premoral goods, the level of the ethics of equal regard, and the level of a language of commitment built on the metaphors of covenant, fidelity, and mutual and self-giving love. The first two levels can function easily in public debate as parties dispute about the goods at stake in families and the best principles of obligation to order them. The language of covenantal love can be used in public debate as well, not to convert people but to ground Christianity's ethic of *commitment*, a commitment that even public policy on families requires but has difficulty articulating.

A public policy guided by a critical familism should affirm the naturalistic conditions of family formation—the premoral values of parental investment (especially paternal investment because of its fragility), mutual helpfulness, uncoerced sexual exchange between bonded husband and wife, and monogamy. Furthermore, public policy should help these values to be realized with high levels of physical and mental health for conjugal couples and their children; hence, it should be concerned that jobs, education, and medical resources exist. Second, public policy should support the realization of these values within an ethic of equal regard between husband and wife: equal power, equal respect, and equal access to the goods and responsibilities of both public and private realms. Third, public policy should take an open and accommodating attitude toward the various languages of commitment that come from specific religious traditions, including the Christian tradition with its massive influence on Western thinking about marriage and families. Public policy on families that does not nourish a language of marital commitment from outside itself will surely fail.

From the standpoint of public policy, commitments applying to sexual relations that can end in pregnancies, births, and sometimes disease and poverty must take the form of *public* commitments. The language used in both secular and church discourse of "committed relations" for sexual relations that involve no public or legal contract and no witnessed covenant with wider extended families, communities, histories, or "gods" is essentially secret or privatistic and contrary to the common good. The goods at stake in sexual relations are enormous—pleasure, yes, but health, wealth, and birth of irreplaceable infants. Hence, society has great investment in wanting the language of marital commitment, however inspired, to be public and responsible to both the contracting partners and the wider society. The private language of "committed relations" undercuts the great accomplishment of the Reformation, which made marriage "public," thereby gradually bringing to an end the turmoil of the "secret" marriage of the Middle Ages.[33] In these types of marriages, a private consent between male and female, which one or the other later disputed, was all that was needed to effect a marital union. Churches should remember this tradition and help society resist the drift toward what Australians call de facto marriage or what American legal theorists call the deinstitutionalization of marriage and families.[34]

The Economic Support of Families

2. *Although both ecclesial and public commitment to a critical familism is our central resource for coping with mounting family disruption, these commitments need economic supports.* This follows from equal regard as *caritatis et bonorum*—love as equal respect ordering the more proximate goods of life and in turn receiving reinforcements from those goods. Economic supports help couples achieve the proximate goods of marriage. Such supports should include improved earning power for families, tax supports, and the kind of welfare supports that strengthen families rather than undermine them.

One of the most complicated economic trends affecting families is the globalization of the market economy—the meshing of national markets with worldwide systems of production, banking, labor, and communication. Globalization has the potential of raising the standard of living of poor countries and keeping prices lower throughout the world. It threatens, however, to depress wages in advanced industrial societies and subject working people everywhere to new uncertainties as corporations roam the world in search of cheap labor and profitable markets.[35] These trends affect first-world families by lowering salaries, making two or more incomes a necessity for some families, reducing parental time that should be spent in childcare, and frequently throwing parents out of work because of corporate downsizing and business failures.

Proposed solutions to this state of affairs were heatedly debated during the 1996 elections. They included combinations of the following: a new protectionism, tax cuts to stimulate business, job training for the unemployed, new enterprise zones in inner cities, education for universal computer literacy, minimum-wage increases, penalties for companies that transfer production to foreign countries, radical reductions in executive salaries, reductions in immigration to reduce job competition for resident citizens, and reductions in corporate red tape so that profits and salaries can be higher. Public policy should encourage any combination of these proposals that will be effective and consistent with the ethic of equal regard, that is, that actualizes the premoral goods needed for families but does so with justice between and within families of the world.

But an additional point must be made: *If harder economic times are coming, a critical familism is all the more important if mothers, fathers, children, grandparents, and extended families are to survive, flourish, and relate with justice to other families.* In tough times, we need a viable ethic all the more. We need to be even better prepared for marriage, more skilled as parents, and more committed than we were during good economic times. And families need to find meaning in simpler lifestyles and connections between families of different socioeconomic levels.

There are other economic strategies for helping families. For instance, our tax structure could be far more family-friendly than it is. If the child exemption had kept pace with its value in 1948 when it was first enacted, it would today be equivalent to $8,200 rather than the $2,500 that it is currently.[36] Proposals were made to give tax credits of $500 per child in the Republican Contract with America,[37] $1,000 per child in the report of the Presidential Commission titled *Beyond Rhetoric*,[38] and $1,500 by William Mattox of the Family Research Council.[39] Earned income tax credits for poor families are generally believed to have contributed to the stability of low-income working parents. The so-called marriage tax penalty—the fact that married couples often pay considerably more in taxes than they would if single—is both a real and symbolic assault on the social value of marriage and should be removed.[40]

Then there is the issue of welfare, the grand political issue on which Americans have projected their conflicts about families as people project fantasies on inkblots. We are sympathetic to Princeton social scientist John DiIulio's comparison of government welfare programs to a bull in a china shop; the bull has created damage, but unless it is removed with great care the destruction will be all the more catastrophic.[41] DiIulio, a Catholic and neoliberal in political philosophy, is the first to admit that the metaphor of bull-in-china-shop has limitations. He acknowledges that welfare over the past thirty years has fed and clothed poor people, given them shelter, immunized their children, provided Medicaid, and in some cases provided job training, counseling, and encouragement. But DiIulio also holds the widely shared belief that many programs have created dependencies, hurt families in some instances, and undermined the supporting institutions of civil society by replacing them with state bureaucracies.

Hence, DiIulio would join the conservative Dan Coats in saying that government's first obligation at this moment in history is to stimulate the institutions of civil society—churches, clubs, community organizations, voluntary service organizations—and then gradually build its welfare supports around them. "Help civil society," DiIulio said, "but don't drop government supports at a time when we are already overwhelmed." To be realistic, he believes that government must always be involved in welfare to assure consistency, sufficient funding, and universality of some fundamental programs. But it is now time, he argues, for a new cooperation between government and civil society, with the balance of power, energy, and initiative tilted toward the side of civil society.[42] We detect a doctrine of subsidiarity in the Catholic DiIulio not unlike the one we detected in Daniel Moynihan.

A stronger role for civil society in welfare is needed. Much was correct about welfare reform as it developed from 1994 to 1996, but it *went too far*. First, what was correct about it? If one takes a bird's-eye view of welfare proposals ranging from President Clinton's early 1993 plans to those implemented in Wisconsin, Michigan, Indiana, and New Jersey in 1994 and 1995, the following common features emerge. Welfare was turning into job placement and job training for able-bodied people, whether they were parents or not. The harsher points of the Republican Contract with America, which would deny medical and childcare assistance for working single mothers, were rejected. Various programs designed to reward marriage and make it more attractive to marry and stay married were discussed and tried.[43] Some of these programs encouraged intact families by allowing both parents to receive some welfare benefits while earning salaries up to certain levels.

Such programs cost more in the beginning.[44] In fact, the Republican-devised Wisconsin plan provides single mothers help with childcare and medical benefits and will be at first more expensive than the plan it replaced. When the national welfare reform bill finally passed, food stamps were continued but at reduced levels. Employment was required for recipients in two years, and the years of AFDC payments were limited to a lifetime total of five years.[45] This was the most controversial feature of the new proposal. Truly radical programs such as those recommended by Charles Murray were rejected.

But welfare reform took a final turn in the wrong direction. *Passing welfare to the states was a bad idea.*[46] State experiments of the kind seen in Wisconsin, Indiana, and New Jersey taught the nation new things. As Senator Moynihan pointed out, experiments could have continued and the better features could have been packaged into national programs without going so far as to fragment the system as we contend devolution will sooner or later do.[47] We agree with Moynihan when he pronounced a plague on both liberals who resisted reform and conservatives who went too far. The promising neoliberal-neoconservative alliance that appeared in the early 1990s, died in 1994, and rose again in 1996 lost its balance in the end. In an effort to do something with welfare reform, this alliance for all practical purposes passed the buck to the states. Systematic welfare reform was aborted. Ultimately, devolution corrupts the principle of subsidiarity by undercutting government's capacity systematically and evenhandedly to give help if it is truly needed.

Furthermore, we are compelled to inject a little-discussed recommendation for welfare mothers that was omitted from the recent welfare reform.[48] We have argued that a couple should work in paid employment no longer than a combined sixty-hour week. If this is true for a wife and husband partnership, this arrangement has implications for single parent on welfare. Their paid employment should not exceed thirty hours, roughly six hours a day. This should be undergirded with state-supported child and medical care. Six hours each day in daycare, although long for an infant, still may be manageable, and six hours roughly corresponds with the length of a school day for the later years. Finally, we should be reminded that for two decades, from 1930 to 1950, W. K. Kellogg ran his cornflake plant in Battle Creek, Michigan, on a six-hour day. Historian Benjamin Hunnicutt's recent book, based on interviews with older employees, reveals a high level of satisfaction with the arrangement, even though post–World War II consumer-oriented male workers and unions finally demanded a return to the eight-hour day.[49]

New welfare reform efforts should begin again. They should be guided by a critical familism that rewards family formation, encourages paternal responsibility, discourages family dependency, equips people for work, supports them with childcare and medical care, and makes these items a national policy as we continue to encourage new state experiments. Our new effort should bring government, civil society, religious institutions, and market into dialogue and practical cooperation for the enhancement and practical support of family commitments.

A Family-Friendly Workplace

3. *Churches should encourage a public policy that promotes a family-friendly workplace.* In advancing proposals for a family-friendly workplace during the 1996 presidential campaign, the Democrats got the upper hand. Dole and Kemp wanted to solve work strains with tax reductions that would lower the need for two-income families and give parents more time with their families—a proposal seen as supporting the nineteenth-century industrial family. Clinton and Gore made gestures toward middle-class tax reductions but primarily emphasized smaller proposals such as more hospitable job conditions for parents, more flextime, an extension of the Family and Medical Leave Act, twenty-four hours a year for parents to keep school appointments and take children to doctors, on-site childcare at workplaces, modest steps toward paid paternity and maternity leaves, insurance benefits for part-time workers, and compensatory time off in lieu of overtime.[50] These proposals seemed to acknowledge women's desire to work and the realities of the postmodern family.

But none of these things proposals went far enough. We already have introduced the idea of the sixty-hour workweek as a goal for dual-income families. Churches should help create the cultural climate supporting such a move, but they should also concretely lobby industry and government to bring it into existence. The equivalent of a job-and-a-half—this is what millions of families with young children want and need. Business must be willing to provide the new twenty- and thirty-hour-a-week positions that make it possible for families to piece together the right combination.

These jobs must provide retirement and medical benefits. State and market must band together to provide them. This raises again the idea of a basic universal health plan. We do not presume to settle here the best way to provide universal, cheap, and equitable health coverage for all workers, whether employed twenty, thirty, or forty hours a week. But to create flexible work arrangements that give parents sufficient time with their children, some such system of health care also must be designed. None of the proposals debated during the 1996 political season pushed the idea of the sixty-hour family workweek with supporting health care. Nor did we see churches discuss this issue.

We believe, however, that its time will come and that churches and synagogues should take the lead in promoting it. Why? Family commitments, even when viewed theologically, *take time and energy*. If love as equal regard requires, among other things, that fathers and mothers have in principle equal access to the responsibilities and privileges of both the public and domestic realms, something like the sixty-hour week with appropriate benefits and without penalties in promotion must become a widespread social reality.

Is There a Place for
State-Supported Marriage Education?

4. *Public policy should provide for marriage and family education.* As we saw above, the state through public education is already participating in marriage education, mainly through university-level courses on the family and public elementary and high school sex-education classes. Much of this instruction is deficient if not directly misleading. Yet if family life is an ecological reality and if the public has a right to shape natural inclinations toward safer and more productive arrangements as it does in other fields of ecology, it can be argued that the state should promote marriage and family education and also use it to enhance family ecological environments.

The philosophy of such courses should be based on both ancient and modern knowledge about the benefits of intact and extended families to children, adults, and society. They should be based on a love ethic of equal regard, which can be defended, as we have shown, on philosophical as well as religious grounds. They should deal with the basics of marriage and family, leaving room for special traditions to add their unique Christian, Jewish, Hindu, Confucian, or secular perspectives.

Other countries sponsor such state-supported marriage and education courses. Australia has a modest system of state-supported premarital education which uses existing, mainly church-supported, programs. Australia already is experimenting with state and civil society cooperation in the area of marriage education. Margaret Andrews, a marriage education expert, has proposed a national strategy of marriage education for Australia.[51] Andrews makes the new distinction between marriage education and marriage counseling; her proposal deals primarily with marriage education that teaches communication skills, conflict management, and parenting skills.

Andrews's far-reaching proposal entails a vast state-civil society venture. Not only would it entail premarital education with engaged couples, it would experiment with relationship education for high school youth, marriage education for those who have been married for several years, and even education for aging couples. It would have a *life-cycle* character consistent with our views in chapter 10. It would understand that marital commitment evolves, is constantly faces new challenges, must move through various stages, and therefore needs fine-tuning and renewed commitment. As theologian and family expert Herbert Anderson says, marriage is a process of "promising again" time and time again.[52] Andrews's marriage education would be voluntary, but incentives for engaged couples would be offered, such as money vouchers at the time of applying for marriage licenses. Education at the high school level would not be directed to couples as such but would emphasize general skills of intersubjective communication, conflict management, and awareness of the demands of parenting—skills good for life in general but relevant as well to the later demands of marriage.

Working through the institutions of civil society would make it possible for specific traditions to communicate their unique language of commitment. But not all marriage education, according to Andrews, would be done in voluntary associations. In Australia, 42 percent of all marriages are done by civil authorities; such officials too should be trained in marriage education.

Are such proposals realistic and transferable to the United States? Such ideas need careful evaluation, but isn't it time to discuss them? Isn't it time for churches and synagogues to consider them and possibly take the lead in proposing them?

Mothers, Fathers, and Public Policy

5. *Churches should influence public policy to help both mothers and fathers with the new challenges they face.* In developing this point, we go beyond present public preoccupation with deadbeat fathers and ways to force them to support their children. Measures to garnish wages, use federal and state income taxes to collect delinquent payments, and compel responsibility by canceling auto or professional licenses should be supported. But such policies, although necessary, are basically punitive. Fatherhood education can be a part of publicly supported relationship and marital education, but additional programs will be necessary.

The state should become a moral and financial partner of the initiatives of civil society. Take, for instance, Charles Ballard's widely recognized National Institute for Responsible Fatherhood and Family Development, which receives some state support. Ballard's program is designed to reunite fathers with their children and to create in these men an attitude of respect for former girlfriends or wives. Counselor-educators (called Sages) visit alienated fathers in their homes, help establish paternity, and model responsible fatherhood themselves. Sages urge a "no-risk life style" that discourages "alcohol, tobacco, other drugs, abusive behavior, sex outside of marriage, obesity or other high-risk behaviors."[53] Sages try to reunite fathers with their children's mother; this sometimes leads to marriage. When this is impossible, fathers are taught to relate to their children, support them financially, and create an atmosphere of respect for their children's mothers. Mothers themselves are helped, when fathers are absent, to find positive male models for their children. There are early programs for high school boys which take a "proactive stance against alcohol and drug use, domestic violence, gang involvement, criminal activity, and out-of-wedlock pregnancies."[54] Programs that help guide the lives of young men also indirectly help protect young women.

Other programs receive moral support from government even though they get no direct financial help. The National Fatherhood Initiative was founded by Don Eberly and Wade Horn during the autumn of 1994 with bipartisan support from Democrats Al Gore and William Galston as well as Republican William Bennett. The National Fatherhood Initiative attempts to address the problem of the growing absence of fathers from their children at all levels of our society. It distributes information on the costs of father absence and the importance of fatherhood, sets up speakers' bureaus, introduces a fatherhood agenda to service clubs and churches, creates father-friendly workplaces and government policies, and generally promotes a positive attitude among men toward the responsibilities of marriage and family life.[55] Ken Canfield's National Center for Fathering is an older hands-on program with considerable grassroots impact.[56] Both organizations have more general audiences than Promise Keepers, and their messages are less laden with the language of evangelical Christianity.

We have here four kinds of organizations with different relations to public policy. Ballard's group receives some government support, the National Fatherhood Initiative gets government moral support, and the National Center for Fathering and Promise Keepers receive neither of these directly. Since the passage of the Religious Freedom Restoration Act (1993) however, such religious organizations as Promise Keepers were viewed more favorably by government: William Galston called this a policy of "maximum feasible accommodation between church and state."[57] It is too early to tell whether the Supreme Court's invalidation of this act in 1997 will damage productive church-state relations.

The situation of mothers in contemporary society has been very different, partially because of the asymmetrical reproductive patterns of the human species. Mothers have not so much fled families as been trapped by them. Because a mother has always known that the infant she gives birth to is hers and because she has carried it for nine months before it was born, mothers have had a head start on sensing their parental investment, a fact that men have exploited throughout the ages. Even today many women feel that they must choose between paid employment or time spent with their infants, a choice that often leads mothers to leave the workforce and fall behind in job and career advancement. This predicament has led economists Richard and Grandon Gill to propose what they call a Parental Bill of Rights.[58] Just as American men were given the GI Bill to help them make up for lost career time after serving in the armed forces during World War II, so should parents (in most cases this will continue to be mothers) receive childcare payments, job training, education, and other protections so that a few years spent in attending to their infants will not constitute long-term financial, job, and career penalties. Annual childcare payments of $1,500 a child would be given whether a parent was employed or stayed home. For those who stay home, as much as $15,000 in parent educational benefits would be allotted after a child reaches the age of five. Parents could use these educational grants to retool for the market. The Parental Bill of Rights would cost citizens no more than $200 annually per capita in 1990 dollars. Such a program would help parents (increasingly fathers as well) to be parents while later being helped to catch up with job and career.

This proposal should be evaluated and discussed. It might have specific benefits for mothers who, for whatever reason, often experience the tension between employment and childcare with piercing intensity. But it might create a cultural climate that encourages fathers to stay home more often as well.

Divorce and Public Policy

6. *Divorce laws should be revised and the churches should lend a helping hand with the task.* Since the advent of no-fault divorce in the late 1960s and early 1970s, the marriage contract has become weaker than most business contracts. It can be broken unilaterally, and the dissenting partner has little recourse. From a philosophical and theological perspective, marriage agreements should be more like covenants. In reality, they should be both contracts and covenants. Because of this, Michigan and other states are considering instituting a modified "fault" divorce law.[59] William Galston, in a variety of articles, also has campaigned to put the issue of divorce law back on the American agenda.[60] Most of the serious proposals would permit no-fault divorce to remain on the books for couples without children.

The fault proposals concern couples *with* children. Here the recommendations tend to go as follows: In cases of mutual consent, there would still be no fault. But couples, during a waiting period would undergo required education and counseling on marriage, parenting, substance abuse, the potential impact of the divorce on the children, and on possible grounds for reconciliation. If reconciliation was deemed impossible, then the couple would be required to develop a long-term financial plan to cover the needs of children until they are eighteen and in some cases older. This plan would have to be final before the divorcing couple turned to the task of dividing property between them.[61] In cases where there is no mutual consent and one partner wants to maintain the marriage, many experts propose that courts establish fault on the basis of various types of desertion, physical abuse, substance abuse, or infidelity.[62] In such cases, damages would be assessed against the offending party and the divorce delayed for two to five years, depending on the proposal.

These proposals should be taken seriously, and churches should debate them. From our perspective, the assignment of fault may not be really necessary if waiting periods, required counseling, and plans for long-term child support are part of the proposal. However this is decided, marriage should be acknowledged as simultaneously a natural, moral, and public good of vital interest to society. Law and government, therefore, should be interested in stabilization of marriage as an institution. Divorce law is one of the many factors that shapes our understanding of the gravity of marital commitments. As the churches once shaped the marriage codes of Catholic canon law of the Middle Ages, made amendments to that law during the Protestant Reformation, later made further changes in Geneva, Holland, England, and finally the United States, so too should churches today be active players in reshaping divorce law.[63]

Some believe that churches and society should not waste time supporting families by making divorces slower and more deliberate. Instead, they believe churches and society should promote premarital and marital education, tax breaks, or an improved economy. We have advocated a multidimensional approach that advocates such measures but also sees that divorce reform is *part of the total picture* and should not be neglected. We also believe that there are humane and inhumane ways to get a divorce and that an intersubjective ethic of equal regard is relevant to the entire process of divorce when it does come about.

The Media, Public Policy, and Civil Society

7. *The churches should join with government, the market, and other institutions of civil society to launch a critique of media images of marriage and family.* The emphasis here should be on providing criticism and well-grounded evaluations, not censorship. Nor should criticism be voiced in ways that obscure the good that educational television can do and the positive images that some programs and movies convey. But critiques of the unhealthy aspects of the media should be relentless, should come from many different voices, and should be heard.

As we said in chapter 2, the media is just one expression of the overflow of cost-benefit, ethical-egoistic, and consumption-oriented patterns of the market which increasingly pervade our society. We are not against the market; we are for its placement in a wider ethic, as outlined in chapter 9. All this applies as well to our critique of the family images of movies, television, popular music, and popular journalism.

Rather than portraying the media as uniquely and single-mindedly seditious, as movie critic Michael Medved does in *Hollywood vs. America*,[64] it is better to follow cultural analyst Kay Hymowitz's more dialectical analysis.[65] She points out that marriage and family patterns have changed because of the cultural, economic, legal, and psychological factors we outlined in earlier chapters. The media do not create these changes in any simple sense, but they address, exploit, and feed off these changes. Furthermore, in order to sell movies, television series, and consumer products, they use shock and excitement to create interest and viewing addiction to the more titillating aspects of these changes. They give a stamp of normality to behavior and conditions once thought to be immoral and still deserving of analysis and moral criticism.

Censorship is not the answer. A new critical familism is the answer. But this familism—this new critical culture of marriage and family—should give rise to multiple voices critiquing and sometimes boycotting the media, voices no longer afraid of the charge of moralism. So far, few groups are willing to do this. Often the topic of criticism is limited to the important topic of violence; addressing family issues seems more difficult.[66] More needs to be done on both. Catholics and some evangelicals have taken the lead. The kind of criticism we have in mind is found in a long critical document by Roger Cardinal Mahony, archbishop of Los Angeles, in which he publicly urged the entertainment industry to "adopt general guidelines for the depiction of violence, sex, family, and the treatment of women."[67] Recent steps taken to adopt an industry-administered rating system that will later be reinforced by the parent-controlled V-chip may help.[68] But until a new artistic sensibility informed by a critical familism emerges, these will inevitably be partial measures. As Secretary of Health and Human Services Donna Shalala challenged Hollywood to live up to its creative potential by inventing stories not featuring people smoking cigarettes, so too should multiple voices challenge the media to tell better stories about human love, sexuality, marriage, and families.

Conclusion

There is no single cure for the family crisis. There is no magic bullet. We have listed sixteen strategies that churches can take, some coming directly out of the depths of their own life and some involving the shaping of public policy. They follow from our analysis of the four causes of the crisis and offer solutions that address our cultural values, our economy, our psychologies of gender and communication, and the continuing need to critique patriarchy. We could have listed many more proposals and discussed the ones listed in more detail. The power of these strategies will come not one at a time but in how they are orchestrated into a powerful new gestalt—a powerful new and critical familistic culture.

To make a difference in the national debate over the family, churches and synagogues need first to admit that there is a crisis—a significant point of vulnerability, change, struggle, and new possibilities. We have worked to show that Christianity, when properly interpreted and firmly appreciative of its Jewish background, can be a genuine resource for addressing both the problems and the possibilities. Christianity, it must be understood, has purposes beyond service to families, but its understanding of families and its placement of them in a larger scheme of the reign of God and the common good are relevant to contemporary family concerns.

Appendix: Hermeneutic Social Science and Practical Theology

From Culture Wars to Common Ground has its subject matter—the American debate over the family, especially as it is informed by religion. But it also makes strong implicit claims about the nature of methodology in both theology and the social sciences. By methodology we mean the steps and procedures that make for faithful theology and accurate social science. These claims were not directly argued on the pages of the first edition. We decided simply to enact our methodological commitments in the way we wrote the book and made our arguments rather than burden the reader with the technical matters that methodology entails. Several readers have asked that we add this technical appendix for teaching purposes in colleges, seminaries, and graduate schools. We happily accommodate.

Our claims go like this. When done rightly, good theology will look a lot more like good social science; that is, it will describe the world it is addressing with much more care and nuance than theology generally does. The converse is also true. When done rightly, good social science will look a lot more like good theology; that is, it will take more responsibility for revealing and critically defending the implicit norms and ideals that unwittingly guide its descriptions of the social world. It is now time to explain these propositions that silently informed almost every page of *From Culture Wars to Common Ground*.

In the preface of the first edition, we wrote that from one perspective our book could be understood as an "exercise in hermeneutic social science" similar to the method of the well-known *Habits of the Heart* (1985). We also contended that our book has a far more "explicit argument for its normative religious and ethical" claims than does *Habits*. From another perspective, we said that our book could be seen as a "project in practical theology." These statements raise the following questions: What is hermeneutic social science? What is practical theology? Why are they, or at least why can they be, similar?

We follow Hans-Georg Gadamer and the authors of *Habits of the Heart* in seeing all social science as seeking understanding, not just objective description and explanation. It is an understanding, however, that resembles a conversation or dialogue. In fact, social science from these perspectives is a conversation or dialogue, as all attempts to understand anything must necessarily be.[1] The authors of *Habits* write in one of its footnotes, "Hans-Georg Gadamer has provided us with valuable guidance in our understanding of our work as always involving a dialogue with the tradition out of which we come."[2] By dialogue with tradition they mean dialogue with some of the classics or basic monuments that provide the ideals and norms of a tradition. In *Habits,* this was accomplished by describing and interpreting much of contemporary American life *in light of* the norms and ideals (indeed classics) of two overlapping but distinguishable traditions that shaped our democracy—the civic Republican tradition and the biblical covenantal tradition.[3] One of the central methodological claims of *Habits* is that social science must inevitably locate itself within some historical tradition, and its descriptions and explanations of contemporary trends must always to some extent be influenced by the ideals informing that tradition. Social science, according to *Habits,* should acknowledge this truth and be more accountable for its implicit norms.

In his monumental *Truth and Method* (1982), Gadamer tells us that all dialogues or conversations have something of a circular character, but it is a circle that is not necessarily a vicious one.[4] It can be open, make progress, and actually deepen understanding. Viewed as a conversation, the process of understanding entails an exchange of questions and answers. The purpose of the conversation is practical—to produce a working understanding between parties, to resolve conflicts, and to discover orientations to action. The questions that we bring to any dialogue comes out of our own history, and all the histories before us, that have shaped who we are. The history that has shaped us also *affects* the very way that we ask our questions; this history, including its implicit *ideals,* shapes how we interpret the world before us and evaluate its tensions and conflicts. To even understand our own questions and our initial interpretation of what is happening in the situations surrounding us, we must deepen our understanding of the ideals that have colored what Gadamer called our "effective history."[5] To describe something responsibly, we must also do history.

These insights inform a book by Browning titled *A Fundamental Practical Theology* (1991), which in turn shapes much, but not all, of the methodological steps of *From Culture Wars to Common Ground.*[6] We say *not all* of the steps because each author brings his or her own sensibilities and nuances that either complicate or go beyond the practical-theology method described in that book. *A Fundamental Practical Theology* converts Gadamer's and *Habits'* hermeneutic circle, described in the paragraphs above, into a comprehensive theological method. This same hermeneutic circle is the key to understanding the social-science method that Robert Bellah and his colleagues describe. This method turns all theology into practical theology and makes what we generally call practical theology—religious education, pastoral care, liturgics, etc.—into the culmination or the last step of theology. According to this model, the steps or stages of theological reflection are: (1) descriptive theology, (2) historical theology, (3) systematic theology, and (4) strategic practical theology.

Good theology, especially good practical theology, should address problems and conflicts in contemporary social practices. It should try to describe these conflicts and, to some extent, explain what is producing them. All of this is part of *descriptive theology*. Because it should describe contemporary situations partially in light of the ideals and norms that shape present experience, theology should then go backward from the present into the past to determine whether it understands its ideals rightly and in their proper context. This is the task of *historical theology*. Third, theology should then try to gain a more systematic or comprehensive understanding of these ideals—ideals generally conveyed in narratives and metaphors. It should also test these ideals in various ways. This is the task of what is often called *systematic theology*. But when systematic theology is seen as a part of a more inclusive practical theology, the original practical questions that first stimulated theological reflection will organize and give direction to the systematic moment. Finally, the theologian (in our case, theologians) should return to the original situation with these ideals—now better understood and tested—to determine what practical light they can throw on the original context of action. Obviously, deeper interpretations of this situation should now be possible. And certainly, part of the test of these norms and ideals comes from their capacity to order, heal, and nurture the persons and groups in the original conflict. This is the task of *strategic practical theology*.[7]

From Culture Wars to Common Ground is organized in four parts reflecting these four steps of a fundamental practical theology. Part 1 is titled "The Issues" and is aimed at accomplishing the tasks of descriptive theology. It describes the contemporary debate and the situation of today's families from several perspectives. It is, we hope, a "thick description" of the contemporary situation of families. We listened to real families—a technique used by *Habits* and employed by our colleague Miller-McLemore in her work on motherhood.[8] We also tried to listen to each other, even reveal some of our tensions as a team; this helped locate us in our individual histories and allowed our own voices to shine forth to some extent—a principle consistent with hermeneutic social science and used within the methods of practical theology as exemplified by the writings of Miller-McLemore, Couture, Lyon, and Franklin.[9] We also tried to set forth the demographic facts that help explain marriage and family trends—cultural individualism, the absorption of both men and women into the wage economy, poverty, racism, and a myriad of new psychological stresses. In tracing these causal factors, we wanted to accomplish something of the rhythm of understanding-explanation-understanding that philosopher Paul Ricoeur thinks is so important for any interpretive endeavor, be it social science, philosophy, or theology.[10] But we also contextualized these explanatory efforts in the following chapter by Couture on the narrative history of diverse eighteenth- and nineteenth-century family traditions in the United States. This history is often missed by strictly social-science perspectives, yet it is crucial for understanding the larger struggles surrounding social-systemic and economic trends, which are often the only factors studied by sociology and economics. Much of this history was shaped by very different interpretations, in very different sections of the country, of the Western biblical and theological tradition. Even today, our controversies over the family are significantly shaped by these different interpretations of the ideals and norms of the Jewish and Christian scriptures and theologies. This raises the question, how should we *really* interpret Genesis, Jesus, Paul, Augustine, Aquinas, Luther, Calvin, and others on family? And did our ancestors sometimes interpret them inadequately?

Part 2 is titled "Traditions" but begins by addressing the questions developed in Part 1. It is an exercise in historical theology. Even there, we gradually move backward in history from the near past to distant past—from the nineteenth century to late Roman Catholic and early Protestant sources (Aquinas, canon law, and Luther) and then still further back to early Christianity understood within its Greco-Roman context. We carried with us our initial practical questions each step of the way as we moved back into history to understand, and sometimes criticize, that which had shaped us. We advance a different reading of early Christianity than is usually put forth by either progressive or conservative interpreters. Although early Christianity is still embedded in the patriarchy of antiquity, when interpreted against the background of Greco-Roman honor-shame codes and their celebration of male dominance and agency, the earliest strands of Christianity can be seen to have moved in the direction of what we call the equal-regard family and marriage. We conclude that interpreters today are entitled to extend and further clarify that trend.

Part 3 is titled "The Voices." It is primarily a dialogue between our emerging position on family issues—what we call "critical familism"—and other contemporary voices in the family debate such as feminist, the therapeutic, conservative pro-family movements, and certain economic points of view. This part also accomplishes some of the critical tasks of systematic theology. We deepen our understanding of the tradition and test it in light of other contemporary perspectives. This section shows that *From Culture Wars to Common Ground* practices what David Tracy calls a "critical correlational" view of practical theology; we not only assert our position but we try to correlate it (find analogies and differences) with other perspectives, critically test it in light of these alternatives, and give reasons in defense of our point of view.

Finally, Part 4 is titled "Directions." Here we return to the contemporary American family situation and develop a more comprehensive practical theology for families that builds on the foregoing questions and investigations. This section also contains nearly a score of concrete suggestions for both the family life of churches and their efforts to influence public policy and the common good. In this section, we develop, with the help of psychoanalysis, our life-cycle theory of love as equal regard—an ethic we think is a usable guide to both families in churches and families in the wider society. Our practical theology is also a public theology, as Kyle Pasewark and Garrett Paul grasped in the insightful interpretation of our family theory in their recent book.[11]

There is another strand of methodological steps that runs through *From Culture Wars to Common Ground*. It has to do with how practical theology invariably will require explicit theological-ethical arguments for which its practitioners should take responsibility. Because of this, the five dimensions of practical-moral reason developed in *A Fundamental Practical Theology* are also employed in this book on the family. What are these dimensions? *A Fundamental Practical Theology* argues that all moral thinking contains five levels or dimensions: (1) a visional level generally conveyed through narrative and metaphor, (2) an obligational level guided by some implicit or explicit moral principle, (3) a theory of premoral goods (goods that are satisfying but not directly moral, such as health, pleasure, or economic power), (4) some theory of the social, economic, and environment pressures that constrain and limit our wants, and finally, (5) specific practices guided by very concrete but often changing rules.[12] Morality is thick, and to describe moral action requires description at all of these levels.

Where do these dimensions show up in *From Culture Wars to Common Ground*? We illustrate this primarily for professors and students in theological ethics, where both books—the practical theology book and the family book—are now sometimes being read side by side. The first three of the five dimensions show up in chapter 4, where we analyze Thomas Aquinas's explanation of, and moral-theological argument for, matrimony, which we use as something of a model for our own ethical position and our understanding of love as equal regard.[13] We will briefly identify the argument so that the interested reader can pursue it further. First, let's mention the level of premoral goods—dimension three of the five levels. Aquinas was perceptive in identifying some of the naturalistic goods that pair bonding between male and female satisfy, i.e., the joint care of highly dependent human infants, paternal recognition and investment in the child (more difficult to achieve for the male), mutual helpfulness between male and female, and mutual sexual satisfaction.[14] Aquinas tells us that pair bonding between mother and father helps actualize these premoral goods. But these goods and their realization do not alone dictate the overall moral character of the bonding, i.e., whether the bonding should be one of equal regard, aristocratic rule by the husband, or perhaps even polygynous. At the ethical or obligation level—level two—Aquinas argues that the bonding of husband and wife should be a matter of equity and friendship—close to, but not identical with, our love ethic of equal regard. Why for Aquinas should a relation between husband and wife be one of friendship? His answer is this: because both female and male are made in the image of God, although, as we point out, Aquinas never fully moved beyond Aristotle's proportionate, and hence still patriarchal, understanding of this friendship and equity. Yet his move of placing the premoral goods of matrimony within a more inclusive principle of obligation involving mutual friendship and equity is instructive.

Aquinas places these two levels within an overarching theological narrative; it helps illustrate the function and importance of the visional level of practical-moral thinking. First, the biblical story about God's creation of the world gives him his understanding of the *imago dei* in both male and female—the grounds for marriage as friendship and mutuality. But second, his understanding of the love of husband for wife as modeled after the unbreakable love of Christ for the church gave him his argument for the permanence of marriage. We, in contrast to Aquinas, extend the Christ-church analogy to both husband *and* wife, not just the husband; both can and sometimes should play the Christic role in marriage. Furthermore, we use this analogy to explain the role of the cross in restoring relations to mutuality and not to argue for the absolute permanence of marriage, as was the case with Aquinas. The sacrificial or self-giving love of the cross functions for us to revitalize and restore love as equal regard and mutuality and is not simply an end in itself nor an absolute impediment to divorce.

The point of this far-too-technical discussion is this: a full understanding of our love ethic of equal regard exhibits the top three of the five dimensions of practical moral thinking—the level of premoral goods, the principled level of moral obligation (in our case, love as equal regard), and the narrative level that surrounds, gives meaning to, and actually informs the first two dimensions. The last two of the five dimensions—the social-ecological constraints and the concrete rules of marital practices—were constantly examined in both our descriptions of the contemporary situation and our historical work on the past. The main point of these analyses is this: the contexts surrounding marriage and family have drastically changed; therefore, *the concrete rules must also change.* These changes are primarily due to the enormously different economic situation that has developed from the fact that today both men and women participate in the wage economy. This change is one of many important factors that went into the formulation of the idea of critical familism, which we define as the "theory, practice, and ecology of the new family ideal, what we call the 'committed, intact, equal regard, public-private family.'"[15] *From Culture Wars to Common Ground* gave a gentle boost to this religiocultural ideal, but did so, we hope, with genuine concern for the welfare and dignity of all families.

Finally, near as our book is to the methodology of *Habits of the Heart,* it tries to be much more self-conscious about the obligations that hermeneutic social science should accept in arguing for, and not simply asserting, the normative horizon that it brings from the past. *Habits* invokes the republican and biblical traditions (classics) and uses them as perspectives from which to interpret twentieth-century individualism. In a similar manner, we uncover some of the classics of the Christian family and marriage tradition, use them to help interpret the present, but also try to defend them—give reasons for their continuing power and efficacy. If hermeneutic social science of the kind found in *Habits* actually accepted the responsibility of giving reasons for the continued relevance of the classics it assumes, it would take a step toward moving into the arena of a hermeneutically oriented practical theology. In the end, our book is an attempt to overcome the marginalization of theology in public discourse and the social sciences by showing what more responsible understanding and explanation actually entails. The complexity of this task takes insights from various disciplines and probably requires multiple authors, as was the case with this book. But such collaborative work is needed for good practical theology and is, we believe, a sign of what theology must become in the future.

Notes

Notes to the Introduction

1. David Herlihy, *Medieval Households* (Cambridge, Mass.: Harvard Univ. Press, 1985).
2. Although theological reasons motivated the church's respect for women's decision in marriage, this move also helped the church break the power of wealthy families who used arranged marriages as a way of consolidating family power, sometimes in opposition to the church. See Jack Goody, *The Development of the Family and Marriage in Europe* (Cambridge: Cambridge Univ. Press, 1983).
3. In the constructivism versus realism debate that occupies so much of the time of academics, we are "critical realists." Language and culture shape humans in highly significant ways, but we still hear the promptings of our archaic bodily tendencies. For a good statement on the nature of critical realism and a refutation of the use of constructivism in family and gender studies, see Lisa Sowle Cahill, *Sex, Gender, and Christian Ethics* (Cambridge: Cambridge Univ. Press, 1997).
4. Paul Ricoeur, *Freud and Philosophy* (New Haven, Conn.: Yale Univ. Press, 1970).
5. *Webster's Ninth New Collegiate Dictionary* (Springfield, Mass.: Merriam-Webster, 1991), 934.
6. This study was a pilot project under the direction of Ben Zablocki, professor of sociology at Rutgers University, New Brunswick, New Jersey. It consisted of five modules lasting approximately two hours each. The interviews, conducted during the autumn of 1992, generated nearly four thousand pages of material. Advisers to the study were David Popenoe, also of Rutgers, and Norval Glenn, Department of Sociology, University of Texas. The five authors of this study were part of a larger team of interviewers.
7. The *Love and Marriage Survey* was done with the gracious help of Corinne Kyle of the George H. Gallup International Institute. The tabulations and the transcripts of the twenty-seven interviews are on file with Don Browning, Divinity School, University of Chicago, Chicago, Illinois 60637.
8. In most cases, we interviewed only one informant from a family, the husband or wife. In those cases, we gave brief questionnaires to the spouse not interviewed to determine the extent to which husband and wife agreed in

their views about the family. The general extent of agreement was surprising. Maybe this is one reason these families are intact. In the case of the Turners, we interviewed both husband and wife.

9. Robert Bellah, Richard Madsen, William Sullivan, Ann Swidler, and Steven Tipton, *Habits of the Heart: Individualism and Commitment in American Life* (Berkeley, Calif.: Univ. of California Press, 1985), 68–69.

10. Frank Furstenberg and Andrew Cherlin, *Divided Families* (Cambridge, Mass.: Harvard Univ. Press, 1991).

Part 1. The Issues

Notes to Chapter 1. The Family (1990–1996):
From a Conservative to a Liberal Issue

1. *Families First: Report of the National Commission on America's Urban Families,* John Ashcroft, chair (Washington, D.C.: U.S. Government Printing Office, 1993).

2. Nancy Ammerman and Wade Clark Roof, *Work, Family, and Religion in Contemporary Society* (New York: Routledge & Kegan Paul, 1995).

3. William Neikirk, "Family Values Returns to Political Scene," *Chicago Tribune,* Sept. 11, 1994; Michael Wines, "Clinton Speech Stresses Issues of Morality," *New York Times,* Sept. 9, 1994; "Excerpts from Clinton's Speech to Baptist Group," *Chicago Tribune,* Sept. 11, 1994.

4. B. Drummon Ayres, "Quayle, Defending 1992 Speech, Returns to Family Values Theme," *New York Times,* Sept. 9, 1994; E. J. Dionne, "Bill and Dan and Murphy Brown," *Washington Post National Weekly Edition,* Sept. 19–25, 1994.

5. Hillary Rodham Clinton, *It Takes a Village: And Other Lessons Children Teach Us* (New York: Simon & Schuster, 1996); Dan Quayle and Diane Medved, *The American Family: Discovering the Values That Make Us Strong* (New York: HarperCollins, 1996).

6. Barbara Dafoe Whitehead, "Dan Quayle Was Right," *Atlantic Monthly* (April 1993): 47–84.

7. Sara McLanahan and Gary Sandefur, *Growing Up with a Single Parent* (Cambridge, Mass.: Harvard Univ. Press, 1994).

8. Charles Murray, "The Coming White Underclass," *Wall Street Journal,* Oct. 29, 1993.

9. Daniel Patrick Moynihan, *"The Negro Family: The Case for National Action,"* in *The Moynihan Report and the Politics of Controversy,* ed. Lee Rainwater and William L. Yancey (Cambridge, Mass.: MIT Press, 1967).

10. Joan Beck, "Teenage Pregnancy Is an Issue That Crosses Party Lines," *Chicago Tribune,* March 27, 1994, sec. 4; William Raspberry, "That Disturbing Charles Murray," *Washington Post National Weekly Edition,* Dec. 6–12, 1994; Clarence Page, "Wrong Target for Welfare Reform," *Chicago Tribune,* May 11, 1994.

11. David Broder, "Family Values: Stop Arguing about Them and Start Changing Them," *Chicago Tribune,* Feb. 16, 1993, sec. 1.

12. Barbara Dafoe Whitehead, "The Experts' Story of Marriage," Institute for American Values Working Paper, 1992. See also Jessie Bernard, *The Future of Marriage* (New York: World Publishing, 1972). In this book, Bernard, a leading sociologist of the family for her day, predicted that in the future there will be "many families," even "polygynous ones." People will not speak of being married but rather as being "pair-bonded." People, she continues, will tailor their relationships to their "circumstances and preferences." See also Brigitte and Peter Berger's *The War over the Family* (Garden City, N.Y.: Doubleday, 1984) for a discussion of the politics behind the change from the original title "White House Conference on the Family" to "White House Conference on Families." Ira Hutchinson's working paper argued that because families *were* changing, the conference *should* give normative recognition of the new diversity.

13. Charles Murray, "Keeping Priorities Straight on Welfare," *Society* 33:5 (July/August 1996): 10–12. Fifteen responses from leading social scientists and ethicists are given to his proposals in this journal.

14. Murray, "Coming White Underclass."

15. For his report on England, see Charles Murray's "The Next British Revolution," *The Public Interest* (Winter 1995): 3–29.

16. Charles Murray, "Does Welfare Bring More Babies?" *Public Interest* (Spring 1994): 17–30.

17. Ayres, "Quayle, Defending 1992 Speech." Here Quayle said, "What I was talking about then, and what I am reiterating today, is the importance of fathers. Raising children is not just a mother's responsibility."

18. Nancy Gibbs, "Bringing up Father," *Time* (June 28, 1993): 53–61; William Raspberry, "Society Must Face the Bottom Line: Kids Need Fathers," *Chicago Tribune,* May 17, 1993, sec. 1; Pepper Schwartz, "When Dads Participate, Families Benefit," *The New York Times,* August 18, 1994; Steve Johnson, "Some Young Dads Have to Grow into Fatherhood," *Chicago Tribune,* May 23, 1994. For a good summary of the social science research about the decline of father support after divorce, see Frank Furstenberg and Andrew J. Cherlin, *Divided Families* (Cambridge, Mass.: Harvard Univ. Press, 1991), 34–44.

19. David Blankenhorn, *Fatherless America* (New York: Free Press, 1995).

20. James Coleman, "Social Capital and the Creation of Human Capital," *American Journal of Sociology* 94 (1988):95–120.

21. McLanahan and Sandefur, *Growing Up,* 38.

22. Martin Daly and Margo Wilson, *Homicide* (Hawthorne, N.Y.: Aldine de Gruyter, 1988).

23. David Popenoe, *Life without Father* (New York: Free Press, 1996), 164–88.

24. Stephanie Coontz, *The Way We Never Were: American Families and the Nostalgia Trap* (New York: Basic Books, 1992); Judith Stacey, "The New Family Values Crusaders," *Nation* (July 25–August 1, 1994): 119–22; Iris Young, "Making Single Motherhood Normal," *Dissent* (Winter 1994): 88–93; Arlene Skolnick and Stacey Rosencrantz, "The New Crusade for the Old Family," *American Prospect* (Summer, 1994):59–65.

25. In addition to Popenoe's writings that we have listed, see Jean Bethke

Elshtain, *Public Man, Private Woman: Women in Social and Political Thought* (Princeton, N.J.: Princeton Univ. Press, 1981); Amitai Etzioni, *The Spirit of Community: Rights, Responsibilities, and the Communitarian Agenda* (New York: Crown Publishers, 1993); Norval Glenn, "The Recent Trend in Marital Success in the United States," *Journal of Marriage and the Family* 53 (May 1991):261–70; William Galston and Elaine Kamarck, "Putting Children First: A Progressive Family Policy," (Washington, D.C.: Progressive Policy Institute, 1990).

26. William Galston, "The Liberal-Democratic Case for the Two-Parent Family," *Responsive Community* (Winter 1990/91):14–26.

27. *Marriage in America: A Report to the Nation* (New York: Council on Families in America of the Institute for American Values, 1995).

28. *Beyond Rhetoric: A New American Agenda for Children and Families* (Washington: National Commission on Children, 1991); see also *Families First.*

29. *Beyond Rhetoric*, xix, 15–37.

30. Young, "Making Single Motherhood Normal," 89–93.

31. Ibid., 88.

32. Ibid., 90.

33. Ibid., 91.

34. Stacey, "New Family Values Crusaders," 119.

35. Ibid., 121.

36. Ibid., 122.

37. Ibid.

38. Pamela Couture, "Single Parents and Poverty," in *Pastoral Care and Social Conflict,* ed. Pamela Couture and Rodney Hunter (Nashville: Abingdon Press, 1995), 57–70; Bonnie Miller-McLemore, "Will the Real Pro-Family Contestant Please Stand Up," *Journal of Pastoral Care* 49:1 (Spring 1995):61–72.

39. James Davison Hunter, *Culture Wars: The Struggle to Define America* (New York: Basic Books, 1991), 42–49.

40. James Davison Hunter, *Before the Shooting Begins: Searching for Democracy in America's Culture War* (New York: Free Press, 1994), 45–67.

41. This was a common theme of interviews conducted with Susan Hirshman of Eagle Forum, Beverly La Haye of Concerned Women of America, and Bill Maddox of Family Research Council of America. The interviews were conducted Nov. 18, 1993, in Washington, D.C.

42. Joe H. Leonard, "Strengthening Families in a Changing World," *Church and Society* 84 (December 1993):7–15; see also the strong emphasis on economic analysis and a de-emphasis on the importance of intact families for children in Janet Fishburn, "Family Values and Family Ministry," in the same issue of *Church and Society,* 39–55.

43. See the position of the conservative Family Research Council in *Free to Be Family* (Washington, D.C.: Family Research Council, 1992), 34–43: Also see Wade Horn, "Government Can't Buy You Love," *Policy Review* (Spring 1993):75–76.

44. Michael Vlahos, "The New Wave," *National Review* (Sept. 26, 1994):

38–46. For the mixed composition of the Christian right, see "Christian Right Defies Categories: Survey Discloses Diversity of Politics and Doctrine," *New York Times*, Aug. 22, 1994.

45. Cary Henrie, "Is Fundamentalism Fundamentally Changing Society?" *University of Chicago Magazine* (April 1993): 16–22.

46. Judith Stacey, *Brave New Families* (New York: Basic Books, 1990).

47. Ralph Reed, "Casting a Wider Net: Religious Conservatives Move beyond Abortion and Homosexuality," *Policy Review* (Summer 1993): 31–35; see also David Von Drehle and Thomas B. Edsall, "The Religious Right Returns: 1992 Wasn't the End—It's Back, with a Moderate Message," *Washington Post National Weekly Edition*, Aug. 29–Sept. 4, 1994, 6–8.

48. Thomas Edsall, "The Christian Right Calls Due a Debt: It Wants the GOP to Make Good on a 'Contract with the Family,'" *Washington Post National Weekly Edition*, May 22–28, 1995, p. 13.

49. Michael McManus, "Veil of Tears: The Church Is Part of Our Divorce Problem—and Solution," *Policy Review* (Winter 1994):50–54.

50. Henry Hyde, "A Mom and Pop Manifesto," *Policy Review* (Spring 1994):29–33.

51. Richard Berke, "Two Top Republicans Soften Their Tone," *New York Times*, Sept. 17, 1994.

52. Martin Mawyer, "A Rift in the Ranks of the Christian Right," *Washington Post National Weekly Edition*, October 4–10, 1993, p. 24.

53. Peter Steinfels, "Some Catholics and Evangelicals Seek Ties," *New York Times*, April 30, 1994.

54. Sam Howe Verhovek, "Abortion Barely Mentioned, Its Opponents Are Offended," *New York Times*, Aug. 15, 1996.

55. Barbara Vobejda, "Going Down without a Fight?" *Washington Post National Weekly Edition*, June 12, 1996, 8–9.

56. William Galston, "Beyond the Murphy Brown Debate: Ideas for Family Policy" (New York: Institute for American Values, 1993).

57. Clinton, *It Takes a Village*, 41.

58. Todd Purdum, "Clinton's Use of Incumbency: The Little Plans Loom Large," *New York Times*, July 24, 1996.

59. Steve Kloehu, "Gore Urges Active Role for Dads in Kids' Lives," *Chicago Tribune*, May 5, 1996, sec. 4.

60. Michael Harrington, *The Other America* (New York: Macmillan, 1960).

61. Benton Johnson, "From Old to New Agenda: Presbyterians and Social Issues in the Twentieth Century," *The Confessional Mosaic: Presbyterians and Twentieth-Century Theology*, ed. J. Coalter, John Mulder, and Louis Weeks (Louisville, Ky.: Westminster/John Knox Press, 1990), 208–35.

62. John Witte, "From Sacrament to Contract: The Legal Transformations of the Western Family," *Criterion* 34 (3):3–11.

63. *Keeping Body and Soul Together: Report to the 203rd General Assembly*, Presbyterian Church, U.S.A., 1991, pp. 39–40. This report was prepared by an appointed committee. Defeated at the 1992 General Synod, the report is still a topic of debate.

64. Ibid., 53.

65. Lenore Weitzman, *The Divorce Revolution* (London: Free Press, 1985).

66. *The Church and Human Sexuality: A Lutheran Perspective* (Chicago: Division of Church in Society, 1993), 11.

67. Ibid., 15–16.

68. Joanna Gillespie, "Episcopal: Family as the Nursery of Church and Society," in *Faith Traditions and the Family*, Phyllis Airhart and Margaret Bendroth (Louisville, Ky.: Westminster John Knox Press, 1996), 148–49.

69. Ibid., 150.

70. Daphne and Terence Anderson, "United Church of Canada: Kingdom Symbol or Lifestyle Choice," in *Faith Traditions and the Family*, 126–42.

71. Ibid., 131–34.

72. Ibid., 134.

73. Jean Miller Schmidt and Gail E. Murphy-Geiss, "Methodist: Tis Grace Will Lead Us Home," in *Faith Traditions and the Family*, 85–99.

74. For documents pertaining to these initiatives, refer to World Wide Web at http://www.umc.org/bishops.

75. These statistics must be handled with caution. Out of the 1,019 respondents there were 22 Episcopalians and 42 Presbyterians. Yet for 62 Southern Baptists, 39.2 percent valued self-sacrifice and only 42.6 percent valued mutuality. Ninety-four Methodists were in the middle, with 31.1 percent valuing self-sacrifice and 49.8 valuing mutuality.

76. William R. Garrett, "Presbyterian: Home Life as Christian Vocation in the Reformed Tradition," in *Faith Traditions and the Family*, 114–25.

77. See James Levine and Edward Pitt, *New Expectations: Community Strategies for Responsible Fatherhood* (New York: Work and Family Institute, 1995), 35. These authors hope to produce more responsible care for children by nonresident fathers. Encouraging marriage, discouraging out-of-wedlock births, or discouraging divorce is not a part of their strategy for producing responsible fatherhood.

78. "Excerpts from Clinton's Speech to Black Ministers," *New York Times*, Nov. 14, 1993.

Notes to Chapter 2.
The Family Crisis: Who Understands It?

1. Martin Castro and Larry Bumpass, "Recent Trends in Marital Disruption," *Demography* 26 (February 1989):37–51.

2. *Marriage in America: A Report to the Nation by the Council on Families in America* (New York: Institute for American Values, 1995), 7.

3. Carol Lawson, "When Baby Makes Two: More Women Choose Single Motherhood," *New York Times*, Aug. 5, 1993; "More Unmarried U.S. Women Are Becoming Mothers, Census Says," *Chicago Tribune*, July 14, 1993; Amara Bachu, *Fertility of American Women* (Washington, D.C.: Bureau of the Census, Current Population Reports, P20–470), xix.

4. Tamar Lewin, "Births to Young Teen-Agers Decline, Agency Says," *New York Times*, Oct. 26, 1994, sec. A.

5. *Marriage in America,* 4.
6. Sara McLanahan and Gary Sandefur, *Growing Up with a Single Parent: What Hurts, What Helps* (Cambridge, Mass.: Harvard Univ. Press, 1994), p. 81.
7. Lenore J. Weitzman, *The Divorce Revolution* (London: Free Press, 1985), 323; Frank F. Furstenberg and Andrew Cherlin, *Divided Families: What Happens to Children When Parents Part* (Cambridge, Mass.: Harvard University Press, 1991), 50.
8. "Census Reports a Sharp Increase Among Never-Married Mothers," *New York Times,* July 14, 1993, sec. A.
9. Donald Hernandez, *America's Children* (New York: Russell Sage Foundation, 1993), 65.
10. Larry Bumpass and James Sweet, "Children's Experience in Single-Parent Families: Implications of Cohabitation and Marital Transitions," *Family Planning Perspectives* 21 (November/December 1989):256–60.
11 *Kids Count Data Book: State Profiles of Child Well-Being* (Washington, D.C.: Annie E. Casey Foundation, 1993), 14.
12. McLanahan and Sandefur, *Growing Up,* 25.
13. *Kids Count Data Book,* 14.
14. As reported in Furstenberg and Cherlin, *Divided Families,* 35–36.
15. Ibid., 36.
16. McLanahan and Sandefur, *Growing Up,* 26. Sociologist James Coleman is the author of the concept of social capital. The development of this concept can be found in "Social Capital and the Creation of Human Capital," *American Journal of Sociology* 94 (1988):95–120. See also his *Foundations of Social Theory* (Cambridge, Mass.: Harvard Univ. Press, 1990).
17. Bureau of Labor Statistics; Lynda Richardson, "No Cookie-Cutter Answers in the 'Mommy Wars,'" *New York Times,* Sept. 2, 1992, sec. B.
18. Sylvia Nasar, "Woman's Progress Stalled? Just Not So," *New York Times,* Oct. 18, 1992, sec. 3. See research by Goldin, Blau, and O'Neill quoted in this article.
19. Judith Schor, *The Overworked American: The Unexpected Decline of Leisure* (New York: Basic Books, 1991).
20. Amitai Etzioni, *The Spirit of Community: Rights, Responsibilities, and the Communitarian Agenda* (New York: Crown Publishers, 1993), 64; for similar statistics see also Sylvia Hewlett, *When the Bough Breaks: The Cost of Neglecting Our Children* (New York: Basic Books, 1991), 15.
21. David Popenoe, *Disturbing the Nest* (New York: Walter de Gruyter, 1988).
22. Judith Wallerstein and Joan Kelly, *Surviving the Breakup: How Children and Parents Cope with Divorce* (New York: Basic Books, 1980); Judith Wallerstein and Sandra Blakeslee, *Second Chances: Men, Women, and Children a Decade after Divorce—Who Wins, Who Loses and Why* (New York: Ticknor & Fields, 1989); and E. Mavis Hetherington, "Family Relations Six Years after Divorce," in *Remarriage and Stepparenting: Current Research and Theory,* ed. Kay Pasley and Marily Ihinger-Tallman (New York: Guilford Press, 1987), 185–205.
23. Nicholas Zill and Charlotte A. Schoenborn, "Developmental, Learning, and Emotional Problems: Health of Our Nation's Children, United States,

1988," *Advance Data* 190 (Nov. 16, 1990):8–9. The authors report an extensive national survey of the emotional, learning, and developmental problems of American youth. In their conclusions they write: "Overall, nearly 20 percent of young people ages 3–17 years were found to have had one or more of these conditions. By the time they reached ages 12–17 years, 1 in 4 adolescents, and nearly 3 in 10 male adolescents, had experienced one of these disorders." Although they admit that this condition could be due to a variety of causes, they report that "young people from single-parent families or stepfamilies were 2 to 3 times more likely to have had emotional or behavioral problems than those who had both of their biological parents present in the home. . . . The alarmingly high prevalence of emotional and behavioral problems among today's children and the observed relationship between family disruption and youthful problem behavior reinforce public concern about the increasing number of U.S. children who are being raised in something other than harmonious two-parent families."

24. McLanahan and Sandefur, *Growing Up,* 157. The four studies are the Panel Study of Income Dynamics (PSID), the National Longitudinal Survey of Young Men and Women (NLSY), the High School and Beyond Study (HSB), and the National Survey of Families and Households (NSFH). The first three are longitudinal studies.

25. Ibid., 1.

26. Ibid., 10.

27. Ibid., 44.

28. Ibid., 50–51.

29. Ibid., 59, italics in original.

30. Ibid., 60.

31. Ibid., 78–94.

32. Ibid., 94.

33. Robert Bellah, Richard Madsen, William Sullivan, Ann Swidler, and Steven Tipton, *Habits of the Heart: Individualism and Commitment in American Life* (New York: Harper & Row, 1985), 32–35, 46, 47, 142, 311.

34. Jan Dizard and Howard Gadlin, *The Minimal Family* (Amherst, Mass.: Univ. of Massachusetts Press, 1990), 11–13.

35. Edward Shorter, *The Making of the Modern Family* (New York: Basic Books, 1977); Lawrence Stone, *The Family, Sex and Marriage: In England 1500–1800* (New York: Harper & Row, 1977); Lawrence Stone, *Road to Divorce: England 1530–1987* (Oxford: Oxford Univ. Press, 1990).

36. Philippe Ariès, *Centuries of Childhood: A Social History of Family Life* (New York: Vintage Books, 1962). For a refutation of the idea that only moderns have had affection for their infants and children, read Richard Saller, *Patriarchy, Property, and Death* (Cambridge: Cambridge Univ. Press, 1994), 5–8.

37. Alexis de Tocqueville, *Democracy in America* (Garden City, N.Y.: Anchor Books, 1969).

38. Max Weber, *The Protestant Ethic and the Spirit of Capitalism* (New York: Charles Scribner's Sons, 1958).

39. Jürgen Habermas, *Theory of Communicative Action,* vols. 1 and 2 (Boston: Beacon Press, 1984, 1987).

40. Ibid., 2:182–96.

41. Alan Wolfe, *Whose Keeper? Social Science and Moral Obligation* (Berkeley, Calif.: Univ. of California Press, 1989), 52–60, 133–41.

42. Mary Jo Bane and David T. Ellwood, *Welfare Realities: From Rhetoric to Reform* (Cambridge, Mass.: Harvard Univ. Press, 1994), 68, 78–81, 95, 116, 120–23.

43. Charles Murray, "Does Welfare Bring More Babies?" *Public Interest* 115 (Spring 1994):17–30.

44. Frederick Engels, *The Origins of the Family, Private Property, and the State* (New York: International Publications, 1972 [1884]).

45. Gary Becker, *A Treatise on the Family* (Cambridge, Mass.: Harvard Univ. Press, 1991), 356, 359.

46. Murray, "Does Welfare Bring More Babies?" 17–30.

47. Ron Lesthaeghe, "A Century of Demographic and Cultural Change in Western Europe: An Exploration of Underlying Dimensions," *Population and Development Review* 9:3 (September 1983):429.

48. Ibid., 430.

49. Victor Fuchs and Diane Reklis, "America's Children: Economic Perspectives and Policy Options," *Science* 255 (Jan. 3, 1992), 42.

50. McLanahan and Sandefur, *Growing Up*, 85–88.

51. William Julius Wilson, *The Truly Disadvantaged* (Chicago: Univ. of Chicago Press, 1987).

52. Susan Okin, *Justice, Gender, and the Family* (New York: Basic Books, 1989), 17–24.

53. Nancy J. Chodorow, *Feminism and Psychoanalytic Theory* (New Haven: Yale Univ. Press, 1989); Jessica Benjamin, *The Bonds of Love: Psychoanalysis, Feminism, and the Problem of Domination* (New York: Pantheon Books, 1989).

54. Judith Bruce, et al., *Families in Focus* (New York: Population Council, 1995), 14–21, 25, 34.

55. Daniel Moynihan quoted in Carol Jouzzitus, "Welfare Debate Begins with 'I told you so,'" *New York Times*, August 8, 1995.

56. For a discussion of the role of anxiety in sin, see Reinhold Niebuhr, *The Nature and Destiny of Man*, vol. 1 (New York: Charles Scribner's Sons, 1941), 168.

57. Valerie Saiving Goldstein, "The Human Situation: A Feminine View," *Journal of Religion* (April 1960):100–112; reprinted in *Womanspirit Rising*, ed. Carol Christ and Judith Plaskow (New York: Harper & Row, 1980), 25–42.

58. McLanahan and Sandefur, *Growing Up*, 38.

Notes to Chapter 3.
Religion and the Ideal Family

1. Peter Laslett, *Family Life and Illicit Love in Earlier Generations* (Cambridge: Cambridge Univ. Press, 1977), 13.

2. John Demos, *A Little Commonwealth: Family Life in Plymouth Colony* (Oxford: Oxford Univ. Press, 1970), 64.

3. John Demos, *Past, Present, and Personal: The Family and the Life Course in American History* (Oxford: Oxford Univ. Press, 1986), 7–10.
4. Kari Børreson, *Subordination and Equivalence* (Washington, D.C.: University Press of America, 1981).
5. Demos, *A Little Commonwealth,* 96–97.
6. Ibid., 84.
7. Philip Greven, *Four Generations: Population, Land, and Family in Colonial Andover, Massachusetts* (Ithaca, N.Y.: Cornell Univ. Press, 1970).
8. Demos, *A Little Commonwealth,* 71.
9. Ibid., 100–101.
10. Ibid., 79–81.
11. Ibid., 77–78.
12. Elizabeth Fox-Genovese, *Within the Plantation Household* (Chapel Hill, N.C.: Univ. of North Carolina Press, 1988), 31–32.
13. Ibid. 63–64.
14. Herbert Gutman, *The Black Family in Slavery and Freedom* (New York: Pantheon Books, 1976), xxii.
15. Bertram Wyatt-Brown, *Southern Honor* (Oxford: Oxford Univ. Press, 1982), 4.
16. Fox-Genovese, *Within the Plantation Household,* 6–7, 200–201.
17. Compare, for example, interpretation in Charles Elliott, D.D., *The Sinfulness of American Slavery . . . its contrariety to many scriptural commands, prohibitions, and principles, and to the Christian spirit* (Cincinnati: L. Swormstedt & J. H. Power, 1851), and Albert Taylor Bledsoe, *An Essay on Liberty and Slavery* (Philadelphia: J. B. Lippincott, 1857).
18. Gutman, *Black Family in Slavery and Freedom,* xxii.
19. Ibid., xxii–xxiii, 9.
20. Ibid., 96–98, 123–38.
21. Ibid., 9–14.
22. Ramon Gutiérrez, *When Jesus Came, the Corn Mothers Went Away: Marriage, Sexuality, and Power in New Mexico, 1694–1875* (Palo Alto, Calif.: Stanford Univ. Press, 1991), 15–17.
23. Ibid., 12; David M. Brugge, *Navahos in the Catholic Church Records of New Mexico* (Tsaile, Ariz.: Navajo Community College Press, 1985), 109–14.
24. Ibid., 47, 50, 55.
25. Gutiérrez, *When Jesus Came,* 78–79.
26. Linda Kerber, *Women of the Republic: Intellect and Ideology in Revolutionary America* (New York: W. W. Norton & Co., 1980), 15–23.
27. Ibid., 17–18.
28. John Locke, *Two Treatises of Government,* ed. Peter Laslett (Cambridge: Cambridge Univ. Press, 1967), par. 60; Michael Walzer, *The Revolution of the Saints: A Study in the Origins of Radical Politics* (Cambridge, Mass.: Harvard Univ. Press, 1965), 185–86; see also Robert Filmer, *Patriarcha: Or the Natural Power of Kings,* in *Two Treatises of Government, with a Supplement, Patriarcha, by Robert Filmer,* ed. Thomas I. Cook (New York: Hafner Publishing Co., 1947).
29. Locke, *Two Treatises,* par. 47. Kerber argues that Locke more fully integrated women into the political order than his contemporaries, especially

Robert Filmer as seen in his views stated in *Patriarcha* (Kerber, *Women of the Republic,* 17–19). Michael Walzer has shown that the Puritans also repudiated Filmer's attempt to justify the patriarchal rule of monarchy by seeing it as a natural extension of the patriarchal rule of fathers in families.

30. Kerber, *Women of the Republic,* 16–17.
31. Ibid., 33–114.
32. Ibid., 228.
33. Ibid., 229–31.
34. William McLoughlin, *Cherokees and Missionaries, 1789–1839* (New Haven, Conn.: Yale Univ. Press, 1984), 16–18.
35. Ibid., 25–26.
36. Mary Ryan, *Cradle of the Middle Class: The Family in Oneida County* (Cambridge: Cambridge Univ. Press, 1981).
37. Ibid., 67–68.
38. David Hackett, "Gender and Religion in American Culture, 1870–1930," *Religion and American Culture: A Journal of Interpretation* 5 (Summer 1995):127–57.
39. Colleen McDannell, *The Christian Home in Victorian America, 1840–1900* (Bloomington: Indiana Univ. Press, 1986).
40. Ibid., 77–91.
41. Ibid., 121–23.
42. A. Gregory Schneider, *The Way of the Cross Leads Home: The Domestication of American Methodism* (Bloomington: Indiana Univ. Press, 1993), 51.
43. Ibid., 76–77, 97, 116.
44. Janet Fishburn, *Confronting the Idolatry of Family* (Nashville: Abingdon Press, 1991), 19–36.
45. Fox-Genovese, *Within the Plantation Household,* 39.
46. Donald G. Matthews, *Slavery and Methodism: A Chapter in American Morality, 1780–1845* (Princeton, N.J.: Princeton Univ. Press, 1965), 166.
47. Ibid., 62–87.
48. Andrew's antebellum essays from the *Southern Christian Advocate* were republished as James O. Andrew, *Family Government, A Treatise on Conjugal, Filial, and Family Duties* (Nashville: Southern Methodist Publishing House, 1882). In 1859 the Southern Methodist Publishing House republished Rev. David Hay, *Home: Or, the Way to Make Home Happy* (Nashville: Southern Methodist Publishing House, 1859). Hay was a member of the British Wesleyan Methodist Conference. See also *The Beneficial Effects of the Christian Temper on Domestic Happiness* (London, 1812), printed for J. Hatchard by his wife, who modestly withheld her name. See also H. A. Boardman, *The Bible in the Family, or Hints on Domestic Happiness* (Philadelphia: Lippincott, Grambo & Co., 1852). This book includes chapters on single women, masters, and servants and a sermon delivered to the Philadelphia Bar. For a discussion of strangers, masters, servants, widows, and singles, see Rev. W. K. Tweedie, *Home: A Book for the Family Circle* (Springfield, Mass.: Holland, 1872). W. B. Mackenzie's *Married Life: Its Duties, Trials, and Joys* (London: Seeley, Jackson, & Halliday, 1860) reflects only on marriage and not on broader family issues.

49. Andrew, *Family Government,* 152.
50. Lillian Schlissel, *Women's Diaries of the Westward Journey* (New York: Schocken Books, 1982), 19.
51. Ibid., 25.
52. Ibid., 13, 15, 77–78.
53. Ibid., 36.
54. Laurie Maffly-Kipp, *Religion and Society in Frontier California* (New Haven, Conn.: Yale Univ. Press, 1992), 4.
55. Ibid., 161, 169.
56. Ibid., 169.
57. Robert C. Ostergren, *A Community Transplanted: The Trans-Atlantic Experience of a Swedish Immigrant Settlement in the Upper Middle West, 1835–1915* (Madison, Wis.: Univ. of Wisconsin Press, 1988). See also Kristian Hvidt, *Flight to America: The Social Background of 300,000 Danish Immigrants* (New York: Academic Press, 1975), 100–102, 146–55 and Harold Runblom and Hans Norman, eds., *From Sweden to America: A History of the Migration* (Minneapolis: Univ. of Minnesota Press, 1976), 37, 126, 130–32.
58. A fuller accounting of this story can be found in a chapter in another volume in the series. See Pamela D. Couture, "Rethinking Public and Private Patriarchy," in *Religion, Feminism, and the Family,* ed. Anne Carr and Mary Stewart Van Leeuwen (Louisville, Ky.: Westminster John Knox Press, 1996), 249–273.
59. Theda Skocpol, *Protecting Soldiers and Women* (Cambridge, Mass.: Harvard Univ. Press, 1992).
60. Frances Willard, *Glimpses of Fifty Years: The Autobiography of an American Woman* (Chicago: Woman's Temperance Publication Association, 1887), 609–13.

Part 2. Traditions

Notes to Chapter 4.
Love, Christian Family Theory, and Evolutionary Psychology

1. Anders Nygren, *Agape and Eros* (Philadelphia: Westminster Press, 1953).
2. Garth Hallet, *Christian Neighbor-Love: An Assessment of Six Rival Versions* (Washington, D.C.: Georgetown Univ. Press, 1989).
3. Alan Soble, *The Structure of Love* (New Haven, Conn: Yale Univ. Press, 1990), 4.
4. For discussions of the various meanings of *caritas,* see Nygren, *Agape and Eros,* 55–56, 449–562; see also Louis Janssens, "Norms and Priorities of a Love Ethics," *Louvain Studies* 6 (1977):207–38.
5. Immanuel Kant, *Foundations of the Metaphysics of Morals* (Indianapolis: Bobbs-Merrill, 1959), 39. Although Kant does not explicitly discuss love in this book, the model of obligation developed in the categorical imperative has frequently influenced various modern formulations of the meaning of love.

6. Aaron Sachs, "Men, Sex, and Parenthood in an Overpopulating World," *World Watch* (March–April 1994): 12–19.

7. Sara McLanahan and Gary Sandefur, *Growing Up with a Single Parent* (Cambridge, Mass.: Harvard Univ. Press, 1994), 38.

8. Charles Darwin, *On the Origin of the Species by Means of Natural Selection* (London: Murray, 1959), and idem, *The Descent of Man and Selection in Relation to Sex* (London: Murray, 1871).

9. E. O. Wilson, *Sociobiology: The New Synthesis* (Cambridge, Mass.: Harvard Univ. Press, 1975).

10. For a discussion of William James as an evolutionary psychologist, see Don Browning, *Pluralism and Personality* (Lewisburg, Pa.: Bucknell Univ. Press, 1980), 52–58, 156–77.

11. Mary Midgley, *Beast and Man* (Ithaca, N.Y.: Cornell Univ. Press, 1978); Peter Singer, *The Expanding Circle: Ethics and Sociobiology* (New York: Farrar, Straus & Giroux, 1981); Richard Alexander, *The Biology of Moral Systems* (Hawthorne, N.Y.: Aldine de Gruyter, 1987); Robert Wright, *The Moral Animal: The New Science of Evolutionary Psychology* (New York: Pantheon Books, 1994).

12. Aristotle, *The History of Animals,* Book. 9, chap. 1, and *On the Generation of Animals,* Book 1, chaps. 20–23, in *The Basic Works of Aristotle,* ed. Richard McKeon (New York: Random House, 1941).

13. Pierre Van den Berghe, *Human Family Systems* (New York: Elsevier, 1979), 14; William D. Hamilton, "The Genetical Evolution of Social Behavior, II," *Journal of Theoretical Biology* 7 (1964):17–52.

14. Hamilton, "Genetical Evolution," 17.

15. James Levine and Edward Pitt, *New Expectations: Community Strategies for Responsible Fatherhood* (New York: Families and Work Institute, 1995), 20.

16. Martin Daly and Margo Wilson, *Sex, Evolution and Behavior* (Belmont, Calif.: Wadsworth Publishing Co., 1978), 56; Robert Trivers, "Parental Investment and Sexual Selection," in *Sexual Selection and the Descent of Man,* ed. B. Campbell (Chicago: Aldine Publishing Co., 1972), 139.

17. Stephen Post, *Spheres of Love: Toward a New Ethics of the Family* (Dallas: Southern Methodist Univ. Press, 1994), 63–66. For an explicit grounding of ethics in kin altruism, see James Q. Wilson, *The Moral Sense* (New York: Free Press, 1993).

18. Van den Berghe, *Human Family Systems,* 20–21; Helen Fisher, *Anatomy of Love* (New York: W. W. Norton & Co., 1992), 63.

19. David Buss, *The Evolution of Desire: Strategies of Human Mating* (New York: Basic Books, 1994).

20. The theory and evidence of evolutionary psychology indicates that women's desire for sexual variety, on the whole, is more associated with maximizing material benefits for themselves or present and future offspring. Variation is less likely to be pursued as an end in itself, as it appears to be for most men. See Buss, *Evolution of Desire,* 86–91.

21. Ibid., 76–79.

22. Donald Symons, *The Evolution of Human Sexuality* (Oxford: Oxford Univ. Press, 1979), 131–36.

23. Van den Berghe, *Human Family Systems*, 131–40; see also David Popenoe, *Living without Father: Compelling New Evidence that Fatherhood and Marriage are Indispensable for the Good of Children and Society* (New York: Free Press, 1996), 139–90.

24. Daly and Wilson, *Sex, Evolution, and Behavior,* 124–29; Van den Berghe, *Human Family Systems,* 25–26.

25. Symons, *Evolution of Human Sexuality,* 31.

26. Female activity in resisting manipulation within the context of asymmetrical or "antagonistic" male-female reproductive patterns is a recent subject of investigation by feminist evolutionary psychologists. Address by Patricia Gowaty, Human Behavior and Evolution Society (June 26–30, 1996).

27. Barry Hewlett, ed., *Father-Child Relations: Cultural and Biosocial Contexts* (Hawthorne, N.Y.: Aldine De Gruyter, 1992); Robert Trivers, *Social Evolution* (Menlo Park, Calif.: Benjamin/Cummings Publishing, 1985), 203–38.

28. Trivers, "Parental Investment and Sexual Selection," 139–41.

29. S. Gaulin and A. Schlegel, "Paternal Confidence and Paternal Investment: A Cross Cultural Text of a Sociobiological Hypothesis," *Ethology and Sociobiology* 1:4 (December 1980):301–09.

30. Hewlett, *Father-Child Relations,* 21; Barry Hewlett, *Intimate Fathers* (Ann Arbor: Univ. of Michigan Press, 1991).

31. John Snarey, *How Fathers Care for the Next Generation* (Cambridge, Mass.: Harvard Univ. Press, 1993), 311–60; Hewlett, *Intimate Fathers,* 151–66.

32. Snarey, *How Fathers Care,* 149–91.

33. Erik Erikson, *Childhood and Society* (New York: W.W. Norton, 1963). For a summary of Erikson's concept of generativity and an extension of the concept into moral psychology and philosophy, see Don Browning, *Generative Man* (New York: Dell Publishing, 1993).

34. McLanahan and Sandefur, *Growing Up,* 19–38.

35. David Popenoe, "The Fatherhood Problem" (New York: Institute for American Values, 1994), 38. See David Bakan, *The Duality of Human Existence* (Chicago: Rand McNally, 1966), and idem, *And They Took Themselves Wives: The Emergence of Patriarchy in Western Civilization* (New York: Harper & Row, 1979). See also James Q. Wilson, *Moral Sense,* and idem, "The Family-Values Debate," *Commentary* (April 1993):24–31.

36. J. Weisheipl, *Albertus Magnus and the Sciences* (Toronto: Pontifical Institute of Medieval Studies, 1980).

37. James Brundage, *Law, Sex, and Christian Society in Medieval Europe* (Chicago: Univ. of Chicago Press, 1987), 421.

38. Thomas Aquinas, *Summa contra Gentiles,* English trans. Dominican Fathers (London: Burns, Oates & Washbourne, 1928), 3, ii, p. 115 (hereafter referred to as *SCG*).

39. Thomas Aquinas, *Summa Theologica* (London: R. & T. Washbourne, 1917), 1, i, q.92, a.1 (hereafter referred to as *ST*).

40. *ST,* I, i, q.92.

41. See Kari Børresen, *Subordination and Equivalence: The Nature and Role of Women in Augustine and Thomas Aquinas* (Washington, D.C.: University Press of America, 1981).

42. Paul Ricoeur, *Freud and Philosophy* (New Haven, Conn.: Yale Univ. Press, 1971), 12–26.

43. For a useful discussion of the importance of naturalism for family theory, even from a feminist perspective, see Lisa Sowle Cahill, *Sex, Gender, and Christian Ethics* (Cambridge, N.Y.: Cambridge Univ. Press, 1996).

44. Thomas Aquinas, *Summa Theologica*, 3, "Supplement," trans. Fathers of the English Dominican Province (New York: Benziger Brothers, 1948), q.41.1. We also want to express our thanks to Professor Stephen Pope of Boston College for his many excellent articles on the biological dimensions of Aquinas's thought and its analogues to modern biological theory. See particularly his "The Order of Love and Recent Catholic Ethics," *Theological Studies* 52 (1991): 255–88. Although his unpublished essay titled "Sociobiology and Family: Toward a Thomistic Assessment and Appropriation" came into our hands after this chapter was complete, it was encouraging to see how closely our interpretation of Aquinas was converging, since he is the leading Aquinas scholar on these matters.

45. Thomas Aquinas, *SCG*, 3, ii, p. 112.

46. Ibid.

47. Ibid.

48. William James, *The Principles of Psychology*, vol. 2 (New York: Dover Publications, 1951), 383–441; Midgley, *Beast and Man*.

49. *SCG*, 3, ii, p. 117.

50. Ibid., 118.

51. Ibid., 114.

52. Aristotle, *Politics*, in *The Basic Works of Aristotle*, ed. Richard McKeon (New York: Random House, 1941).

53. Ibid., 1, i.

54. Plato, *The Republic*.

55. Aristotle, *Politics*, 1, iii.

56. Ibid., iv.

57. *SCG*, 3, ii, p. 118.

58. So argues Professor William Irons, Department of Anthropology, Northwestern University, a leading anthropologist using the evolutionary ecological approach (oral communication).

59. *ST*, 3, q.41, a.1.

60. 1 Cor. 7:3–4; Augustine, "The Good of Marriage," in *The Fathers of the Church*, ed. Roy J. Deferrari (New York: Fathers of the Church, 1955), 13, 16.

61. *ST*, 3, q.64.

62. Ibid., q.41, a.3.

63. Don Browning, *Religious Thought and the Modern Psychologies* (Minneapolis: Fortress Press, 1987), 17; idem, *A Fundamental Practical Theology* (Minneapolis: Fortress Press, 1991), 105–09; idem, *Religious Ethics and Pastoral Care* (Minneapolis: Fortress Press, 1983), 53–71.

64. *SCG*, chap. 124.

65. *SCG*, 3, p. 118.

66. Ibid., 119.

67. *SCG*, chap. 124.

68. See also Matt. 19:5; Mark 10:7; 1 Cor. 6:16; 7:10, 11; Eph. 5:31.
69. *ST*, 3, q.41, 1.
70. Aristotle was an important source for Aquinas's thinking on friendship. He distinguished three kinds of friendship: friendship based on utility, pleasure, and virtue. Christian friendship for Aquinas adapts friendship based on shared virtue to the belief that the good of each human is first of all the good of God in that person. For Aristotle's discussion, see *Nicomachean Ethics* in *The Basic Works of Aristotle*, Book 8, chap. 3, and Book 9.
71. *ST*, 2, ii, q.26.
72. *ST*, 2, ii, q.26, a.3.
73. *SCG*, 115.
74. Ibid., 114.
75. Ibid., 115.
76. Ibid.
77. Ibid., 115–16.
78. Ibid., 115.
79. For an excellent summary of the debate on the moral psychology of the sexes, especially the Kohlberg-Gilligan debate, see Owen Flanagan, *The Variety of Moral Psychologies* (Cambridge, Mass.: Harvard Univ. Press, 1991), 196–247.
80. *SCG*, p. 116.
81. Ibid.
82. Augustine, "Good of Marriage," 4. Aquinas's doctrine of marriage as sacrament is based on a great confusion. He followed the Vulgate in rendering the Greek word *mysterion* as the Latin word *sacramentum* rather than the more accurate *mysterium*, which should be translated as "mystery." This led him to amend Augustine's three purposes of marriage: procreation and education of children, mutual exchanges in sex and domestic affairs, and *sacramentum*. He affirmed the first two but interpreted *sacramentum* to mean supernatural grace rather than marital permanence, as Augustine taught. See *Fathers of the Church*, 12–20.
83. *ST*, 3, q.42, 1.
84. Quoted in Popenoe, *Living without Father*, 5.
85. Mircea Eliade, *The Sacred and the Profane* (New York: Harper & Row, 1961).
86. Ricoeur, *Freud and Philosophy*, 462–68.
87. "Casti Connubii: Encyclical of Pope Pius XI," in *The Papal Encyclicals*, ed. Claudia Carlen (Wilmington, N.C.: McGrath, 1981), par. 23.
88. For Catholic documents accentuating the theme of mutuality in husband-wife relations, see *Follow the Way of Love: A Pastoral Message of the U.S. Catholic Bishops to Families* (Washington, D.C.: National Conference of Catholic Bishops, 1993); H. Richard McCord, Jr., "Viewing Families from Three Perspectives," *Origins: CNS Documentary Service* 24:17 (Oct. 6, 1994):294.
89. Stephen Ozment, *The Protestants* (New York: Doubleday, 1992). Furthermore, it must be noted that much of Catholic canon law on marriage was taken over by the Protestant Reformation, but now administered by the

state more or less as civil law rather than by the church itself and its courts, as it had been under Catholicism. See J. Brundage, *Law, Sex, and Christian Society in Medieval Europe* (Chicago: Univ. of Chicago Press, 1989).

90. Martin Luther, "The Estate of Marriage," in *Luther's Works* 45 (Philadelphia: Muhlenberg Press, 1959), 18.

91. Calvin's view of the family was similar to Luther's, although he built a larger place for the idea of covenant than did Luther and used it to order not only the family but other institutions such as government, law, and church. For an excellent discussion of Calvin's theology of family, state, and law, see. chapter 3 of John Witte, Jr., *From Sacrament to Contract: Marriage, Religion, and Law in the Western Tradition* (Louisville, Ky.: Westminster John Knox Press, 1997).

92. Ibid.

93. Martin Luther, "Order of Marriage for Common Pastors," in *Luther's Works* 53 (Philadelphia: Fortress Press, 1965), 115.

94. Martin Luther, *Luther: Lectures on Romans,* The Library of Christian Classics, vol. 15 (Philadelphia: Westminster Press, 1961), 366.

95. Ibid.

96. For feminist theologians who have criticized distorted ideas of the cross, see Christine E. Gudorf, "Parenting, Mutual Love and Sacrifice," in *Woman's Consciousness, Woman's Conscience: A Reader in Feminist Ethics,* ed. Barbara Hilkert Andolsen, Christine E. Gudorf, and Mary D. Pellauer (New York: Harper & Row, 1985), 182–85; Barbara Andolsen, "Agape in the Feminist Ethics," *Journal of Religious Ethics* 9 (Spring 1981):64–83; Judith Vaughn, *Sociality, Ethics, and Social Change: A Critical Appraisal of Reinhold Niebuhr's Ethics in the Light of Rosemary Radford Ruether's Works* (Lanham, Md.: University Press of America, 1983); Judith Plaskow, *Sex, Sin and Grace: Women's Experience and the Theologies of Reinhold Niebuhr and Paul Tillich* (Lanham, Md.: University Press of America, 1980).

Notes to Chapter 5. Honor, Shame, and Equality in Early Christian Families

1. Jürgen Habermas's reformulation of Kantian ethics from the perspective of an intersubjective point of view can be found in *Moral Consciousness and Communicative Action* (Cambridge, Mass.: MIT Press, 1990), 62–74; and idem, *Justification and Application* (Cambridge, Mass.: MIT Press, 1993), 43, 131.

2. Raphael Sealey, *Women and Law in Classical Greece* (Chapel Hill: Univ. of North Carolina Press, 1990), 107, 181.

3. *Oxford Latin Dictionary* (Oxford: Oxford Univ. Press, 1968), 674–75.

4. Leo Perdue, Joseph Blenkinsopp, John Collins, and Carol Meyers, *Families in Ancient Israel* (Louisville, Ky.: Westminster John Knox Press, 1997).

5. There was not only a conflict between the household and clan and the kingdom of God, there was conflict between family and state as another kind of superordinate whole, as Plato shows in his *Laws* (London: Penguin Books, 1975), 446–47.

6. Bruce Malina, *The New Testament World: Insights from Cultural Anthropology* (Louisville, Ky.: Westminster/John Knox Press, 1993), 117–48.
7. Ibid., 134–41.
8. Stephen C. Barton, *Discipleship and Family Ties in Mark and Matthew* (Cambridge: Cambridge Univ. Press, 1994), 112–20.
9. Peter Brown, *The Body and Society: Men, Women and Sexual Renunciation in Early Christianity* (New York: Columbia Univ. Press, 1988), 83–84, 272–73.
10. Malina, *New Testament World,* 134–35.
11. Elisabeth Schüssler Fiorenza, *In Memory of Her: A Feminist Theological Reconstruction of Christian Origins* (New York: Crossroad, 1983).
12. Ibid., 143. Q and pre-Q refer to documents about Jesus that biblical scholars believe existed before the writing of the Gospels.
13. Warren Carter, *Households and Discipleship: A Study of Matthew 19–20* (Sheffield, England: Sheffield Academic Press, 1994).
14. Aristotle, *Nicomachean Ethics* (New York: Random House, 1941), Books 8–9, chap. 10.
15. Carter, *Households and Discipleship,* 31, 46, 49–55.
16. Stephen Barton, "Paul's Sense of Place: An Anthropological Approach to Community Formation in Corinth," *New Testament Studies* 32 (1986):74.
17. Ibid., 122.
18. David Balch, "Theses about the Early Christian Family," prepared for Annual Seminar of the Religion, Culture, and Family Project.
19. Turid Karlsen Seim, *The Double Message: Patterns of Gender in Luke and Acts* (Nashville: Abingdon Press, 1994).
20. Ibid., 255.
21. Ibid., 253.
22. Ibid., 259.
23. Ibid., 260.
24. Halvor Moxnes, "Honor and Shame," *Biblical Theology Bulletin* 23:4 (Winter 1993):167–76; see also idem, "Honor and Righteousness in Romans," *Journal for the Study of the New Testament* 32 (February 1988):61–77.
25. For a discussion of how to place Paul's view of sexuality within the controversies between Stoic and Cynic points of view, see Will Deming, *Paul on Marriage and Celibacy* (Cambridge: Cambridge Univ. Press, 1995).
26. Balch, "Theses about the Early Christian Family," 2.
27. Ibid., 3.
28. Aristotle, *Nicomachean Ethics,* Book 8, chap. 7.
29. Carolyn Osiek and David L. Balch, *Families in the New Testament World* (Louisville, Ky.: Westminster John Knox Press, 1997), 5–89.
30. David Hunter, ed., *Marriage in the Early Church* (Minneapolis: Fortress Press, 1995), 8–9.
31. John Milbank, *Theology and Social Theory* (Oxford: Basil Blackwell Publisher, 1990), 368.
32. J. H. Neyrey, *The Social World of Luke-Acts* (Peabody, Mass.: Hendrickson Publishers, 1991), 32. For an application of the honor-shame concepts to classical Greece, see David Cohen, *Law, Sexuality and Society* (Cambridge: Cambridge Univ. Press, 1991).

33. Neyrey, *Social World of Luke-Acts,* 29.

34. Eva Cantarella, *Bisexuality in the Ancient World* (New Haven, Conn.: Yale Univ. Press, 1992); for the controversial character of male bisexuality in Athenian society, see Cohen, *Law, Sexuality, and Society,* 171–201.

35. Osiek and Balch, *Families in the New Testament World,* 39–41.

36. David Cohen and Richard Saller warn against reading the totality of Greek and Roman society in family and sexual matters from the perspective of what is permitted by the law. For Saller's view, see his *Patriarchy, Property, and Death in the Roman Family* (Cambridge: Cambridge Univ. Press, 1994), 74–101.

37. Malina, *New Testament World,* 49–50; see also Tom Sapp, "The Birth of a Daughter Is a Loss: The Ethos of Honor and Shame in the Wisdom of Ben Sira," seminar paper, Divinity School, University of Chicago, 1995.

38. It should be admitted that often Christianity has been absorbed into honor-shame patterns with little tension. Latin Christianity in southern Italy was deeply embedded in an honor code even as late as the first half of the twentieth century. We thank Professor Angelo De Berardino from the Institutum Patristicum Augustinianum of Rome for oral communication about his childhood as a Catholic in southern Italy.

39. Aristotle, *Politics,* in *The Basic Works of Aristotle,* ed. Richard McKeon (New York: Random House, 1941), Book 1, chap. 12.

40. Aristotle, *Nicomachean Ethics,* Book 8, chap. 10.

41. Markus Barth, *Ephesians* (New York: Doubleday & Co., 1974), 609.

42. Ibid., 608.

43. Aristotle, *Nicomachean Ethics,* Book 8, chap. 7.

44. Ibid., chap. 11.

45. David Balch, *Let Wives Be Submissive: The Domestic Code in 1 Peter* (Atlanta: Scholars Press, 1981).

46. Ibid., 65–80.

47. Ibid., 109.

48. Frances Young, *The Theology of the Pastoral Letters* (Cambridge: Cambridge Univ. Press, 1994), 17.

49. Karl Olav Sandnes, *A New Family: Conversion and Ecclesiology in the Early Church with Cross-Cultural Comparisons* (New York: Peter Lang, 1994), 56.

50. Ibid., 62.

51. Ibid., 177–79.

52. Ibid., 179. Sandnes is following here the theory of reciprocity set forth in Marshall Sahlins, *Stone Age Economics* (London: Tavistock, 1974).

53. Ibid., 79.

54. Ibid., 71.

55. David Gilmore, *Manhood in the Making: Cultural Concepts of Masculinity* (New Haven, Conn.: Yale Univ. Press, 1990). Early work on the honor-shame framework is found in J. G. Peristiany, ed., *Honor and Shame: The Values of Mediterranean Society* (London: Routledge & Kegan Paul, 1965); Julian Pitt-Rivers, *The Fate of Shechem* (Cambridge: Cambridge Univ. Press, 1977).

56. Lawrence Stone, *Road to Divorce: England 1530–1987* (Oxford: Oxford Univ. Press, 1990), 237–39.

57. Elijah Anderson, "The Code of the Streets," *Atlantic Monthly,* May 1994:81–94.

Part 3. The Voices

Notes to Chapter 6.
Feminism, Religion, and the Family

1. Shulamith Firestone, *The Dialectic of Sex* (New York: Bantam Books, 1970).
2. Judith Stacey, "Are Feminists Afraid to Leave Home? The Challenge of Conservative Pro-Family Feminism," in *What Is Feminism? A Reexamination,* ed. Juliet Mitchell and Ann Oakley (New York: Pantheon Books, 1986), 230.
3. Jane Flax, "The Family in Contemporary Feminist Thought: A Critical Review," in *The Family in Political Thought,* ed. Jean Bethke Elshtain (Amherst: Univ. of Massachusetts Press, 1982), 253.
4. Simone de Beauvoir, *The Second Sex* (New York: Vintage Books, 1974).
5. Iris Marion Young, "Humanism, Gynocentrism and Feminist Politics," *Women's Studies International Forum* 8 (1985):173.
6. Betty Friedan, *The Feminine Mystique* (New York: Dell Publishing Co., 1974); Kate Millett, *Sexual Politics* (Garden City, N.Y.: Doubleday & Co., 1970).
7. For statistics on domestic violence, see Elisabeth Schüssler Fiorenza, "Introduction," *Concilium: Violence against Women,* ed. Schüssler Fiorenza and M. Shawn Copeland (Maryknoll, N.Y.: Orbis Books, 1994), viii–ix; see also Robert T. Ammerman and Michel Hersen, eds., *Assessment of Family Violence: A Clinical and Legal Sourcebook* (New York: John Wiley & Sons, 1992).
8. Margaret Bendroth, *Fundamentalism and Gender* (New Haven, Conn.: Yale Univ. Press, 1994), 116. See also Susan Brooks Thistlethwaite, "Every Two Minutes: Battered Women and Feminist Interpretation," in *Weaving the Vision: New Patterns in Feminist Spirituality,* ed. Judith Plaskow and Carol P. Christ (San Francisco: Harper & Row, 1989), 302–13.
9. Karen Offen, "Defining Feminism: A Comparative Historical Approach,"9 *Signs: Journal of Women in Culture and Society* 14:1 (1988): 119–57.
10. Young, "Humanism, Gynocentrism and Feminist Politics," 173.
11. Marie Ferguson Peters, "Parenting in Black Families with Young Children: A Historical Perspective," in *Black Families,* 2d ed., ed. Harriette Pipes McAdoo (Newbury Park, Calif.: Sage Publications, 1988), 236–38; see also Bonnie J. Miller-McLemore, "Family and Work: Can Anyone Have It All?" in *Religion, Feminism, and the Family,* ed. Anne Carr and Mary Stewart Van Leeuwen (Louisville, Ky.: Westminster John Knox Press, 1996), 274–292.
12. bell hooks, *Feminist Theory: From Margin to Center* (Boston: South End, 1984), see especially chaps. 2, 7, and 10; see also Patricia Morton, "Rediscovering the Black Family: New and Old Images of Motherhood," in *Disfigured Images: The Historical Assault on Afro-American Women* (New York: Praeger Publishers, 1991), 125–35; and Patricia Hill Collins, *Black Feminist Thought: Knowledge, Consciousness, and the Politics of Empowerment* (New York: Routledge & Kegan Paul, 1991).
13. Susan Moller Okin, *Justice, Gender, and the Family* (New York: Basic Books, 1989), 4, 171.

14. Ibid., 5–6.
15. Ibid., 17.
16. Iris Marion Young, *Throwing Like a Girl and Other Essays in Feminist Philosophy and Social Theory* (Bloomington: Indiana Univ. Press, 1990), 7.
17. Iris M. Young, "Pregnant Subjectivity and the Limits of Existential Phenomenology," in *Descriptions,* ed. Don Ihde and Hugh J. Silverman (Albany, N.Y.: State Univ. of New York Press, 1985), 29.
18. Iris Marion Young, "Making Single Motherhood Normal," *Dissent* (Winter 1989):91.
19. Ibid., 93.
20. Betty Friedan, *The Second Stage* (New York: Summit Books, 1981); Germaine Greer, *Sex and Destiny: The Politics of Human Fertility* (New York: Harper & Row, 1984); Jean Bethke Elshtain, *Public Man, Private Woman: Women in Social and Political Thought* (Princeton, N.J.: Princeton Univ. Press, 1981).
21. Elshtain, *Public Man, Private Woman,* xi.
22. Ibid., 333.
23. See Jean Bethke Elshtain, "Family Matters: The Plight of America's Children," *Christian Century* (July 14–21, 1993):710–12; see also *Marriage in America: A Report to the Nation.*
24. Elshtain, *Public Man, Private Woman,* 327.
25. Jean Bethke Elshtain, "The Family and Civic Life," in *Rebuilding the Nest: A New Commitment to the American Family,* ed. Elshtain, David Blankenhorn, and Steven Bayme (Milwaukee: Family Service America, 1990), 127.
26. Stacey, "Are Feminists Afraid?", 226.
27. Ibid., 230; Stacey, "New Family Values Crusaders," 112.
28. Judith Stacey, *Brave New Families* (New York: Basic Books, 1990), 260.
29. Ibid., 270, 269, 17.
30. Rosemary Ruether, "Politics and the Family: Recapturing a Lost Issue," *Christianity and Crisis* 40 (Sept. 29, 1980):264 (emphasis added).
31. Rosemary Radford Ruether, *Sexism and God-Talk: Toward a Feminist Theology* (Boston: Beacon Press, 1983), 216; see also p. 109.
32. Rosemary Radford Ruether, "Church and Family V: Feminism, Church and Family in the 1980s," *New Blackfriars* (May 1984):208.
33. Rosemary Radford Ruether, "Church and Family IV: The Family in Late Industrial Society," *New Blackfriars* (April 1984):178.
34. Ruether, *Sexism and God-Talk,* 19.
35. Ibid., 111.
36. Ibid., 177.
37. Rosemary Radford Ruether, "The Family in a Dim Light," *Christianity and Crisis* (June 27, 1983):266.
38. Ruether, *Sexism and God-Talk,* 20.
39. Rosemary Radford Ruether, "Church and Family I: Church and Family in the Scriptures and Early Christianity," *New Blackfriars* (January 1984):13; and "Church and Family V," 21; see also R. R. Ruether, "An Unrealized Revolution: Searching Scripture for a Model of the Family," *Christianity and Crisis,* Oct. 31, 1983:399–404.

40. Ruether, "Unrealized Revolution," 400.

41. Ruether, *Sexism and God-Talk,* 141–43; Ruether, "Church and Family I," 13.

42. Rosemary Radford Ruether, "Church and Family II: Church and Family in the Medieval and Reformation Periods," *New Blackfriars* (February 1984):83–84.

43. Ruether, "Church and Family V," 212; see also *Sexism and God-Talk,* 233.

44. Rosemary Radford Ruether, *New Woman/New Earth: Sexist Ideologies and Human Liberation* (New York: Seabury Press, 1975), 207–11; "Home and Work: Women's Roles and the Transformation of Values," *Theological Studies* 36:4 (1975):659; "Church and Family V," 209.

45. Christine E. Gudorf, "Parenting, Mutual Love, and Sacrifice," in *Women's Consciousness and Women's Conscience: A Reader in Feminist Ethics,* ed. Barbara Hilkert Andolsen, Christine E. Gudorf, and Mary D. Pellauer (New York: Harper & Row, 1985), 190.

46. Christine E. Gudorf, "Sacrifice and Parental Spiritualities," in *Religion, Feminism, and the Family,* ed. Anne Carr and Mary Stewart Van Leeuwen (Louisville, Ky.: Westminster John Knox Press, 1996), 299.

47. Valerie Saiving Goldstein, "The Human Situation: A Feminine View," *Journal of Religion* (April 1960):100–112.

48. Bonnie J. Miller-McLemore, *Also a Mother: Work and Family as Theological Dilemma* (Nashville: Abingdon Press, 1994), 92.

49. Christine E. Gudorf, "Dissecting Parenthood: Infertility, in Vitro, and Other Lessons in Why and How We Parent," *Conscience* 15:3 (Autumn 1994):21.

50. Christine E. Gudorf, *Body, Sex, and Pleasure: Reconstructing Christian Sexual Ethics* (Cleveland: Pilgrim Press, 1994), 66.

51. For an elaboration of this argument, see Miller-McLemore, *Also a Mother.*

52. For another example, in addition to the works already cited by Gudorf and Miller-McLemore, see Pamela Couture's *Blessed are the Poor: Women's Poverty, Family Policy, and Practical Theology* (Nashville: Abingdon Press, 1991).

53. Mary Stewart Van Leeuwen, ed., *After Eden: Facing the Challenge of Gender Reconciliation* (Grand Rapids: Wm. B. Eerdmans Publishing Co., 1993), 19–20, 578–80; see also idem, "Confessions of a Christian Feminist," *Whitworth College* (Spring 1994):22–23. Lisa Sowle Cahill, *Between the Sexes: Foundations for a Christian Ethics of Sexuality* (Philadelphia: Fortress Press, 1985), and *Women and Sexuality* (Mahwah, N.J.: Paulist Press, 1992).

54. Lisa Sowle Cahill, *Sex, Gender, and Christian Ethics* (Cambridge: Cambridge Univ. Press, 1996), 220.

55. Mary Stewart Van Leeuwen, "Opposite Sexes or Neighboring Sexes? The Importance of Gender," in *Welfare in America: Christian Perspectives on a Policy in Crisis,* ed. Stanley Carlson-Thies and James Skillen (Grand Rapids: Wm. B. Eerdmans Publishing Co., 1996), 243–76.

56. Mary Stewart Van Leeuwen, *Gender and Grace: Love, Work, and Parenting in a Changing World* (Downers Grove, Ill.: InterVarsity Press, 1990), 30, and see in general chap. 2; also Van Leeuwen, *After Eden,* 6–13. Nancy

Chodorow, *The Reproduction of Mothering: Psychoanalysis and the Sociology of Gender* (Berkeley, Calif.: Univ. of California Press, 1978).

57. Mary Stewart Van Leeuwen, "Feminism and Family at the Close of the Twentieth Century," in *Religion, Feminism, and the Family,* ed. Anne Carr and Mary Stewart Van Leeuwen (Louisville, Ky.: Westminster John Knox Press, 1996), 43–46.
58. Cahill, *Sex, Gender, and Christian Ethics,* 114–16.
59. Ibid., 206–7.
60. Ibid., 161–62.
61. Cheryl Townsend Gilkes, "The 'Loves' and 'Troubles' of African-American Women's Bodies," in *A Troubling in My Soul: Womanist Perspectives on Evil and Suffering,* ed. Emilie M. Townes (Maryknoll, N. Y.: Orbis Books 1993), 240.
62. Bonnie Thorton Dill, "Our Mother's Grief: Racial Ethnic Women and the Maintenance of Families," *Journal of Family History* 13 (1988): 415–31.
63. Cheryl Townsend Gilkes, "The Roles of Church and Community Mothers: Ambivalent American Sexism or Fragmented African Familyhood?" *Journal of Feminist Studies in Religion* 2 (Spring 1986):46.
64. Delores S. Williams, *Sisters in the Wilderness: The Challenge of Womanist God-Talk* (Maryknoll, N. Y.: Orbis Books, 1993), 2–6.
65. Gilkes, "'Loves' and 'Troubles,'" 247.
66. Jacquelyn Grant, "The Sin of Servanthood and the Deliverance of Discipleship," in *Troubling in My Soul,* 204, 213, 215–16.
67. Frances E. Wood, "'Take My Yoke Upon You': The Role of the Church in the Oppression of African-American Woman," in *Troubling in My Soul,* 240.

Notes to Chapter 7.
Families and the Therapeutic

1. Jürgen Habermas, *Communication and the Evolution of Society* (Boston: Beacon Press, 1979), 202–205.
2. Christopher Lasch, *Haven in a Heartless World: The Family Besieged* (New York: Basic Books, 1977); Robert Bellah, Richard Madsen, William Sullivan, Ann Swidler, and Steven Tipton, *Habits of the Heart: Individualism and Commitment in American Life* (Berkeley: Univ. of California Press, 1985).
3. Lasch, *Haven in a Heartless World,* xx.
4. Christopher Lasch, *The Culture of Narcissism* (New York: W. W. Norton & Co., 1978).
5. Philip Rieff, *Freud: The Mind of the Moralist* (New York: Viking Press, 1959), and idem, *The Triumph of the Therapeutic: Uses of Faith after Freud* (New York: Harper & Row, 1966).
6. Lasch, *Haven in a Heartless World,* 19.
7. Bellah et al., *Habits of the Heart,* 13–14, 76.
8. Ibid., 81.
9. Ibid., 99, 138.
10. Carl Rogers, *Client-Centered Therapy* (Boston: Houghton Mifflin Co., 1957.
11. Bellah et al., *Habits of the Heart,* 5, 16.
12. Ibid., 98, 100.

13. Alexis de Tocqueville, *Democracy in America* (Garden City, N.Y.: Anchor Books, 1969).

14. Stephanie Coontz, *The Way We Never Were: American Families and the Nostalgia Trap* (New York: Basic Books, 1992), 53; Bellah et al., *Habits of the Heart,* 40–41.

15. For ethical-egoist leanings of some of the literature of psychotherapy, see Don Browning, *Religious Thought and the Modern Psychologies* (Minneapolis: Fortress Press, 1987).

16. Professor Thomas Needham of the Graduate School of Psychology connected with Fuller Theological Seminary did the survey based on a questionnaire jointly developed by Professor Needham and Don Browning. John Wall, a graduate student of the University of Chicago, wrote the first interpretation of the data. The findings have developed into an article to be jointly published in a forthcoming professional journal under the authorship of John Wall, Thom Needham, and Don Browning.

17. The basic data on professionals' cautiousness about divorce when children are involved are as follows:

	Female Respondent	Male Respondent	Overall Mean
Psychiatrists	80 %	73.1%	74.1%
Psychologists	75 %	59 %	66.1%
Marriage-Family Therapists	69.9%	54 %	66.1%
Social Workers	57.1%	45 %	54.7%
Pastoral Counselors	43.1%	51.8%	50.0%

Data prepared by Professor Thomas Needham.

18. Bellah et al., *Habits of the Heart,* 317.

19. Carl R. Rogers, "The Implications of Client-Centered Therapy for Family Life," in *On Becoming a Person* (Boston: Houghton Mifflin Co., 1961), 328.

20. The full text of the *Ethical Principles of Psychologists* is given in Max Rosenbaum, *Ethics and Values in Psychotherapy: A Guidebook* (New York: Free Press, 1982), 439–51.

21. See, for example, the APA's 1981 *Principles of Medical Ethics,* 427–36.

22. Rogers, *Client-Centered Therapy,* 105–6, 112–13, 308–9, 351–52, 452–55.

23. Jay R. Greenberg and Stephen Mitchell, *Object Relations in Psychoanalytic Theory* (Cambridge, Mass., and London: Harvard Univ. Press, 1983), 2–3.

24. Harry Guntrip, *Psychoanalytic Theory, Therapy, and the Self* (New York: Basic Books, 1971).

25. Erik Erikson, *Childhood and Society* (New York: W. W. Norton, 1963), 72–108.

26. Erik Erikson, *Insight and Responsibility* (New York: W. W. Norton & Co., 1964), 95, 102, 117, 231. Erikson makes use of the work of René Spitz on the deprivation of physically satisfied but underattended children to posit his phylogenetic need to be recognized. He also uses the work of Robert White in *Ego and Reality in Psychoanalytic Theory* (New York: International Universities Press, 1963) to posit independent ego needs. See his *Childhood and Society,* 80.

27. Daniel N. Stern, *The Interpersonal World of the Infant* (New York: Basic Books, 1985), 10.

28. Jean Baker Miller, *Toward a New Psychology of Women* (Boston: Beacon Press, 1986), 83.

29. John Gottman, *What Predicts Divorce: The Relationship between Marital Processes and Marital Outcomes* (Hillsdale, N.J.: Lawrence Erlbaum Associates, 1994), and idem, *Why Marriages Succeed or Fail* (New York: Simon & Schuster, 1994); Howard Markman, Scott Stanley, and Susan L. Blumberg, *Fighting for Your Marriage: Positive Steps for Preventing Divorce and Preserving a Lasting Love* (San Francisco: Jossey-Bass Publishers, 1994); Harville Hendrix, *Getting the Love You Want* (New York: Henry Holt & Co., 1988).

30. Randall Mason, "Imago, Relationships, and Empathy," *Journal of Imago Relationship Therapy* 1 (1996): 1–18. We thank Randall and Margaret Mason for permitting members of our team to attend their Imago Workshop for couples.

31. Harville Hendrix, *Keeping the Love You Find* (New York: Pocket Books, 1992), 243.

32. Gottman, *Why Marriages Succeed or Fail,* 30.

33. Markman et al., *Fighting for Your Marriage,* 169.

34. Pearl Buck, quoted in Hendrix, *Getting the Love You Want,* 197.

35. Ibid., 238, 201.

36. Jessica Benjamin, *The Bonds of Love: Psychoanalysis, Feminism, and the Problem of Domination* (New York: Pantheon Books, 1989), 36, 23.

37. Ibid., 171.

38. Ibid., 177.

39. Ibid., 114.

40. Nancy Chodorow, *The Reproduction of Mothering: Psychoanalysis and the Sociology of Gender* (Berkeley, Calif.: Univ. of California, 1978), 211.

41. Carol Gilligan, *In a Different Voice: Psychological Theory and Women's Development* (Cambridge, Mass.: Harvard Univ. Press, 1982), 21, 149.

42. Salvador Minuchin and H. Charles Fishman, *Techniques of Family Therapy* (Cambridge, Mass.: Harvard Univ. Press, 1981), 193; see also Donald J. Wendorf and Robert J. Wendorf, "A Systematic View of Family Therapy Ethics," *Family Process* 24 (December 1985):447–49.

43. Evan Imber-Black, *Families and Larger Systems: A Family Therapist's Guide through the Labyrinth* (New York: Guilford, 1988), v.

44. Mary Sykes Wylie, "The Evolution of a Revolution," *The Family Therapy Networker* 16:1 (January/February 1992):20.

45. Monica McGoldrick, "Ethnicity and Family Therapy: An Overview," in *Ethnicity and Family Therapy,* ed. Monica McGoldrick, John K. Pearce, and Joseph Giordan, (New York: Guilford, 1982), 4.

46. Monica McGoldrick, Carol M. Anderson, and Froma Walsh, *Women in Families: A Framework for Family Therapy* (New York: W. W. Norton & Co., 1989).

47. Rachel Hare-Mustin, foreword to Thelma Jean Goodrich, Cheryl Rampage, Barbara Ellman, and Kris Halstead, *Feminist Family Therapy: A Casebook* (New York: W. W. Norton & Co., 1988), viii.

48. Goodrich et al., *Feminist Family Therapy,* 20–21.

49. Ivan Boszormenyi-Nagy, "The Field of Family Therapy: Review and Mandate," *AFTA Newsletter* (Winter 1995–96): 34; idem, "Commentary: Transgenerational Solidarity—Therapy's Mandate and Ethics," *Family Process* 24 (December 1985):454–60. See also Ivan Boszormenyi-Nagy and D. N. Urich, "Contextual Family Therapy," in *Handbook of Family Therapy,* ed. A. S. Gurman and D. P. Knistern (New York: Brunner/Mazel, 1981), 159–86.

50. Ivan Boszormenyi-Nagy and Barbara R. Krasner, *Between Give and Take: A Clinical Guide to Contextual Therapy* (New York: Brunner/Mazel, 1986), 17.

51. Wylie, "Evolution of a Revolution," 98.

52. See William J. Doherty, *Soul Searching: Why Psychotherapy Must Promote Moral Responsibility* (New York: Basic Books, 1995).

53. E. Brooks Holifield, *A History of Pastoral Care in America: From Salvation to Self-Realization* (Nashville: Abingdon Press, 1983).

54. Froma Walsh, "Conceptualization of Normal Family Processes," in *Normal Family Processes,* 2d ed., ed. Froma Walsh (New York: Guilford, 1993), 3–69.

55. John Patton and Brian Childs, *Christian Marriage and Family: Caring for Our Generations* (Nashville: Abingdon, 1988), 12.

56. Herbert Anderson and Susan B. W. Johnson, *Regarding Children: A New Respect for Childhood and Families* (Louisville, Ky.: Westminster/John Knox Press, 1994), 107.

57. Ibid., 70–71.

58. See Pamela D. Couture, *Blessed Are the Poor: Women's Poverty, Family Policy, and Practical Theology* (Nashville: Abingdon Press, 1991), Bonnie J. Miller-McLemore, *Also a Mother: Work and Family as Theological Dilemma* (Nashville: Abingdon Press, 1994).

Notes to Chapter 8. Christian Profamily Movements:
The Black Church, Roman Catholics, and the Christian Right

1. Timothy McNulty and Steve Daley, "Answers on Racism Appear to Lie with Individuals, not a Panel," *Chicago Tribune,* Oct. 18, 1995, sec. 1.

2. Ibid.

3. Pope John Paul II, "Homily at Aqueduct Race Track," *New York Times,* Oct. 7, 1995.

4. Ralph Reed, *Politically Incorrect: The Emerging "Faith Factor" in American Politics* (Dallas: Word Publishing, 1994).

5. Myron Magnet, *The Dream and the Nightmare: The Sixties' Legacy to the Underclass* (New York: William Morrow & Co., 1993).

6. William Bennett, *The Book of Virtues* (New York: Simon & Schuster, 1993); Gertrude Himmelfarb, *The De-Moralization of Society: From Victorian Virtues to Modern Values* (New York: Alfred A. Knopf, 1995).

7. Lee Rainwater and William L. Yancey, *The Moynihan Report and the Politics of Controversy* (Cambridge, Mass.: MIT Press, 1967), 194–215.

8. Ian Fisher, "New York Senator Stands Alone in Welfare Debate," *New York Times,* Sept. 27, 1995. sec. A.

9. Daniel Patrick Moynihan, "The Negro Family: The Case for National Action," in Rainwater and Yancey, *Moynihan Report,* 51–52.

10. Ibid., 93.

11. Ibid., 47.

12. William Julius Wilson, *The Truly Disadvantaged* (Chicago: Univ. of Chicago Press, 1987); and idem, *When Work Disappears: The World of the New Urban Poor* (New York: Alfred A. Knopf, 1996).

13. Moynihan, "Negro Family," 20.

14. Pope Leo XIII, *Rerum Novarum,* in *Proclaiming Justice and Peace: Papal Documents from Rerum Novarum through Centesimus Annus,* ed. Michael Walsh and Brian Davies (Mystic, Conn.: Twenty-Third Publications), 20, 30, 34.

15. Ibid., 54.

16. E. Franklin Frazier, *The Negro Family in the United States* (Chicago: Univ. of Chicago Press, 1939), 13, 23, 39, 107, 110, 340.

17. Kenneth Clark, *Dark Ghetto* (New York: Harper & Row, 1965).

18. Wallace Charles Smith, *The Church in the Life of the Black Family* (Valley Forge, Pa.: Judson Press, 1985).

19. Ibid., 58–59.

20. Ibid. 52.

21. Karl Barth, *Church Dogmatics* III, 4 (Edinburgh: T. & T. Clark, 1961), 164.

22. Ibid., 19–23. For a sympathetic extension of Barth's view of male-female relations yet a criticism of patriarchy, see Paul Jewett, *Man as Male and Female* (Grand Rapids: Wm. B. Eerdmans Publishing Co., 1975).

23. Smith, *Church in the Life of the Black Family,* 99.

24. Ibid., 70.

25. Ibid., 90–98.

26. Herbert Gutman, *The Black Family in Slavery and Freedom, 1750–1925* (New York: Pantheon Books, 1976), xxii, 45, 101.

27. Ibid., xviii, 450–60.

28. Andrew Billingsley, *Climbing Jacob's Ladder: The Enduring Legacy of African American Families* (New York: Simon & Schuster, 1992), 18.

29. Ibid., 23, our italics.

30. Ibid., 35, as quoted from Billingsley.

31. Ibid., 94–95.

32. See Alice and Peter Rossi, *Of Human Bonding* (Hawthorne, N.Y.: Aldine de Gruyter), 1991.

33. Melville J. Herskovitz, *The Myth of the Negro Past* (Boston: Beacon Press, 1958); Billingsley, *Climbing Jacob's Ladder,* 83, 95.

34. Billingsley, *Climbing Jacob's Ladder,* 205. After reviewing a decade of studies on African-American families, he writes, "What comes through strikingly in

a careful review of this decade of studies is that among African-American families a higher level of egalitarian relations exist than among families in the nation as a whole. For men, women, and children in these families, tasks and roles are interchangeable in ways that often vary from the traditional."

35. Donna Franklin, "Black Herstory," *New York Times,* Oct. 18, 1995, sec. A.
36. Gutman, *Black Family in Slavery and Freedom,* xxiii.
37. For a study of a black Pentecostal church with a similar pattern, see Don Browning, *A Fundamental Practical Theology* (Minneapolis: Fortress Press, 1991), 243–77.
38. Smith, *Church in the Life of the Black Family,* 67.
39. We will learn that what is Christian about these movements is actually quite diffuse. The term "pro-family," in a somewhat restricted sense of that term, gets closer to the heart of what these groups are about.
40. Margaret Bendroth, *Fundamentalism and Gender* (New Haven, Conn.: Yale Univ. Press, 1994), 46–52.
41. James Dobson, *What Wives Wish Their Husbands Knew about Women* (Wheaton, Ill.: Tyndale House Publishers, 1975), 114–17.
42. James Dobson, *Dr. Dobson Answers Your Questions about Marriage and Sexuality* (Wheaton, Ill.: Tyndale House Publishers, 1975), 75–76.
43. In Dobson's early writings, he often said the biggest problem with men and families is that men work too much, which is a way of saying that the forces of the market have overwhelmed home life. See Dobson, *Dr. Dobson Answers Your Questions about Marriage and Sexuality,* iv, 43. Promise Keepers too has accepted the analysis that industrialization has functioned to alienate males from the home. Sometimes, however, this is spoken about under the rubric of the "feminization" of the American male (a nation of "sissified" men). As fathers have become overembedded in the market, young boys have become feminized by their mothers at home. See *Seven Promises of a Promise Keeper* (Colorado Springs, Colo.: Focus on the Family Publishing, 1994), 73.
44. Tony Evans, "A Man and His Integrity," in *Seven Promises of a Promise Keeper,* 79.
45. Ibid., 80.
46. Ibid.
47. James Dobson and Gary L. Bauer, *Children at Risk: The Battle for the Hearts and Minds of Our Kids* (Dallas: Word Publishing, 1990), 33–34.
48. Ibid., 31.
49. Reed, *Politically Incorrect,* 256.
50. Ibid., 18.
51. Ibid.
52. Ralph Reed, *Active Faith: How Christians Are Changing the Soul of American Politics* (New York: Free Press, 1996), 275.
53. For an initial report of John Coleman's research, see "Under the Cross and the Flag: Reflections on Discipleship and Citizenship in America," *America* 174 (May 11, 1996):6–14. This information came from a forthcoming book on paracongregational organizations, specifically a chapter titled "Sovereign Spheres: Focus on the Family."
54. Ibid., 36–37.

55. Charles Colson and Richard John Neuhaus, *Evangelicals and Catholics Together: Toward a Common Mission* (Dallas: Word Publishing, 1989), xv–xxxiii.
56. Ibid., 13.
57. Richard Berke, "Christian Coalition Is United on Morality, but Not Politics," *New York Times,* Sept. 8, 1995, sec. A; Timothy J. McNulty, "Robertson Group Courts Catholics," *Chicago Tribune,* Sept. 10, 1995, sec. 1; Gustav Niebuhr, "The Christian Coalition Sees Recruiting Possibilities Arising from the Pope's Visit," *New York Times,* Oct. 7, 1995, sec. A.
58. Reed, *Politically Incorrect,* 12.
59. Dobson and Bauer, *Children at Risk,* 19–56.
60. Harvey Cox, "The Warring Visions of the Religious Right," *The Atlantic Monthly* (November 1995):66–69.
61. Stephen Carter, *The Culture of Disbelief* (New York: Basic Books, 1993), 49, 63–65.
62. Reed, *Politically Incorrect,* 132.
63. Ibid., 132–35.
64. Ibid., 252–53.
65. Daniel Moynihan, "Social Justice in the *Next* Century," *America* 165:6 (Sept. 14, 1991):137.
66. Karol Wojtyla (John Paul II), *Love and Responsibility* (New York: Farrar, Straus & Giroux, 1981).
67. John Paul II, "Letter to Families," *Origins: CNS Documentary Service* 23:37 (March 3, 1994):642.
68. Pope Leo XIII, *Rerum Novarum,* 19.
69. Ibid., 19.
70. Erich Fromm, *Marx's Concept of Man* (New York: Unger, 1961), 119–35.
71. Pope Leo XIII, *Rerum Novarum,* 20–21.
72. John Locke, *Two Treatises on Government* (Cambridge: Cambridge Univ. Press, 1991), II, par. 56–58.
73. Pope Leo XIII, *Rerum Novarum,* 28.
74. Ibid., 29.
75. Pope John Paul II, *Centesimus Annus,* in Walsh and Davies, ed., *Proclaiming Justice and Peace,* pars. 5–10.
76. For the roots of this thinking in Aristotle, see his *Politics,* especially Book 1, i. Aristotle taught that the family preceded the state: "Out of these two relationships between man and woman, master and slave, the first thing to arise is the family." Even before the family is the union of man and woman, which "in common with other animals and with plants" comes from the "natural desire to leave behind them an image of themselves" (Book 1, ii). Although the family precedes the state temporally and builds on natural dependencies and the desire to extend themselves through offspring, the state exceeds the family in its range of responsibilities. "But, if all communities aim at some good, the state or political community . . . embraces all the rest, aims at the good in a greater degree than any other." (Book 1, i). But the family, not the state, should have the task of raising children. "For that which is common to the greatest number has the least care bestowed upon it" (Book 2, iii). People are naturally more invested in children that

they can call "mine" (Book 2, iii). The same is true of work. In addition to having more disputes over property held in common, we exert more energy and care for what we own. "Again, how immeasurably greater is the pleasure, when a man feels a thing to be his own; for surely the love of self is a feeling implanted by nature and not given in vain, although selfishness is rightly censured" (Book 6).

77. Barth, *Church Dogmatics* III, 4, pp. 19–23.
78. Emil Brunner, *The Divine Imperative* (Philadelphia: Westminster Press, 1957), 343.
79. Ibid., 333.
80. Ibid., 335.
81. Ibid., 343.
82. John Paul II, *Familiaris Consortio* (Chicago: Archdiocese of Chicago, 1981), pars. 6, 17; see also *Gaudium et Spes, The Documents of Vatican II,* ed. Walter Abbott, S.J. (New York: Herder & Herder, 1966), par. 49.
83. John Paul II, *Familiaris Consortio,* par. 17.
84. Lisa Sowle Cahill, *Between the Sexes: Foundations for a Christian Ethics of Sexuality* (Philadelphia: Fortress Press, 1985), 121; Christine E. Gudorf, *Body, Sex, and Pleasure: Reconstructing Christian Sexual Ethics* (Cleveland: Pilgrim Press, 1994), 89–100.
85. *Gaudium et Spes,* par. 48.
86. John Paul II, "Letter to Families," 654.

Notes to Chapter 9. Economic Voices: State Family, Market Family, and Civil Society

1. Robert D. Putnam, "Bowling Alone: America's Declining Social Capital" *Journal of Democracy* 6:1 (January 1995):65–78.
2. Robert D. Putnam, "The Strange Disappearance of Civic America," *American Prospect* 24 (Winter 1996):34–49.
3. Republican spoiler Pat Buchanan is the exception to this rule; see Richard Bernstein, "Digging up the Roots of a Populist in the G.O.P.," *New York Times,* March 24, 1996.
4. Nancy Ammerman, "Bowling Together: Congregations and the American Civic Order," University Lecture in Religion: Arizona State University, 1996; Robert Wuthnow, *Christianity and Civil Society: The Contemporary Debate* (Valley Forge, Pa: Trinity Press International, 1996).
5. A. F. Robertson, *Beyond the Family: The Social Organization of Human Reproduction* (Berkeley, Calif.: Univ. of California Press, 1991), 1.
6. Ibid., 2.
7. Michel Foucault, *The History of Sexuality,* 3 vols. (New York: Random House, 1990); Thomas Laqueur, *Making Sex: Body and Gender from the Greeks to Freud* (Cambridge, Mass.: Harvard Univ. Press, 1990).
8. Ibid., 26.
9. Ibid., 27–28.
10. Alan Wolfe, *Whose Keeper? Social Science and Moral Obligation* (Berkeley, Calif.: Univ. of California Press, 1989), 5.

11. Jan Dizard and Howard Gadlin, *Minimal Family* (Amherst, Mass.: Univ. of Massachusetts Press, 1990), 187.

12. Ibid., 188.

13. Ibid., 201.

14. Ibid., 189.

15. Ibid., 191.

16. Ibid., 203.

17. Ibid., 217.

18. Shirley Zimmerman, *Family Policies and Family Well-Being* (Newbury Park, Calif.: Sage Publications, 1992), 46–53.

19. Ibid., 158.

20. Ibid., 161.

21. Mary Jo Bane and David Ellwood, *Welfare Realities: From Rhetoric to Reform* (Cambridge, Mass.: Harvard Univ. Press, 1994), 1–27.

22. David Held, *Political Theory and the Modern State* (Palo Alto, Calif.: Stanford Univ. Press, 1989), 181.

23. William Leach, *Land of Desire: Merchants, Power, and the Rise of a New American Culture* (New York: Vintage Books, 1993), 6.

24. Ibid.

25. Alan Dawley, *Struggles for Justice: Social Responsibility and the Liberal State* (Cambridge, Mass.: Belknap Press, 1991), 307.

26. Christopher Lasch, *The True and Only Heaven: Progress and Its Critics* (New York: W. W. Norton & Co., 1991).

27. Wolfe, *Whose Keeper?* 35.

28. Ibid., 32.

29. Gary Becker, *A Treatise on the Family* (Cambridge, Mass.: Harvard Univ. Press, 1991).

30. Gary Becker, *Human Capital* (New York: Columbia Univ. Press, 1975), and idem, *The Economic Approach to Human Behavior* (Chicago: Univ. of Chicago Press, 1991).

31. See Richard Posner, *The Economics of Justice* (Cambridge, Mass.: Harvard Univ. Press, 1981); idem, *Economic Analysis of the Law* (Boston: Little, Brown, & Co., 1986); idem, *The Problem of Jurisprudence* (Cambridge, Mass.: Harvard Univ. Press, 1990); idem, *Sex and Reason* (Cambridge, Mass.: Harvard Univ. Press, 1992).

32. Becker, *Economic Approach to Human Behavior,* 3–14.

33. Ibid., 5.

34. Becker, *Treatise on the Family,* 364; Posner, *Sex and Reason,* 189.

35. Becker, *Economic Approach to Human Behavior,* 169–75.

36. Becker, *Treatise on the Family,* 20–79.

37. Posner, *Problem of Jurisprudence,* 26.

38. Posner, *Sex and Reason,* 85.

39. Ibid., 88–89.

40. Ibid., 90–95.

41. Ibid., 171. Or as some African-American women say, "First you marry a man, and then you marry *the* man."

42. For a discussion of the impact of Catholic canon law on secular family law

in Western societies, see James Brundage, *Law, Sex, and Christian Society in Medieval Europe,* (Chicago: Univ. of Chicago Press, 1987) 576–94.

43. Ibid., 192.
44. James Q. Wilson, *The Moral Sense* (New York: Free Press, 1993), 175; also see David Popenoe, *Life without Father* (New York: Free Press, 1996), 215–17.
45. Linda Waite, "Does Marriage Matter?" *Demography* 32:4 (Nov. 1995): 483–507.
46. Posner, *Sex and Reason,* 151–60, 220–36.
47. Ibid., 227.
48. Don Browning, *Religious Thought and the Modern Psychologies* (Minneapolis: Fortress Press, 1987).
49. Donald McCloskey, *If You're So Smart: The Narrative of Economic Expertise* (Chicago: Univ. of Chicago Press, 1990), 1.
50. Ibid., 135–36.
51. Ibid., 140.
52. Max Weber, *The Protestant Ethic and the Spirit of Capitalism* (New York: Charles Scribner's Sons, 1958).
53. McCloskey, *If You're So Smart,* 146.
54. Amitai Etzioni, *The Moral Dimension: Toward a New Economics* (New York: Free Press, 1988).
55. Amitai Etzioni, "The Responsive Communitarian Manifesto," *The Responsive Community* 2 (Winter 1992):4–6.
56. Becker, *Economic Approach to Human Behavior,* 134.
57. Robert Putnam, "Why We're on our Worst Behavior," *Chicago Tribune,* Jan. 10, 1996, sec. 1.
58. Ammerman, "Bowling Together," 2–3.
59. Wuthnow, *Christianity and Civil Society,* 26–39.
60. James Coleman, "Social Capital in the Creation of Human Capital," *American Journal of Sociology* 94 (1988):95–120.
61. James Coleman et al., *Equality of Educational Opportunity* (Washington, D.C.: U.S. Department of Health, Education, and Welfare, Office of Education, 1966).
62. Sara McLanahan and Gary Sandefur, *Growing Up with a Single Parent* (Cambridge, Mass.: Harvard Univ. Press, 1994), 134–55.
63. See also Peter Benson and Eugene C. Roehlkepartain, "Single-Parent Families," *Source* 9:2 (June 1993):3. These authors also make the point that a wide range of community supports lower the risks to children of divided families.

Part 4. Directions

Notes to Chapter 10.
A Practical Theology of Families

1. Erik Erikson, *Young Man Luther* (New York: W. W. Norton & Co., 1958), 49–97.

2. David Rhoads and Donald Michie, *Mark as Story: An Introduction to the Narrative of a Gospel* (Minneapolis: Fortress Press, 1982), 10. The quotations of Mark are taken from the authors' translation.

3. Christine E. Gudorf, "Parenting, Mutual Love, and Sacrifice," in *Woman's Consciousness, Woman's Conscience: A Reader in Feminist Ethics*, ed. Barbara Hilkert Andolsen, Christine E. Gudorf, and Mary D. Pellauer (New York: Harper & Row, 1985) 185.

4. Barbara Andolsen, "Agape in Feminist Ethics," *Journal of Religious Ethics* 9 (Spring 1981): 69–81; Beverly Harrison, "Anger as a Work of Love: Christian Ethics for Women and Other Strangers," *Union Seminary Quarterly Review* 36 (1981):41–58; Gene Outka, *Agape: An Ethical Analysis* (New Haven, Conn.: Yale University Press), 9–13; Margaret Farley, "New Patterns of Relationship," in *Woman: New Dimensions*, ed. Walter Burkhardt (New York: Paulist Press, 1975), 51–70.

5. Victor Furnish, "Neighbor Love in the New Testament," *Journal of Religious Ethics* 10 (Fall 1982):227.

6. Gene Outka sounds like Aquinas, although he does not refer to him in the opening pages of his "Universal Love and Impartiality," in *The Love Commandments*, ed. Edmund Santurri and William Werpehowski (Washington, D.C.: Georgetown Univ. Press, 1992), 2.

7. Louis Janssens, "Norms and Priorities of a Love Ethic," *Louvain Studies* 6 (1977):219.

8. Lawrence Kohlberg, *The Philosophy of Moral Development* (San Francisco: Harper & Row, 1981), 147–68; John Rawls, *A Theory of Justice* (Cambridge, Mass.: Harvard Univ. Press, 1971).

9. Louis Janssens, "Norms and Priorities of a Love Ethic," *Louvain Studies* 6 (1977):220.

10. Ibid., 219–30.

11. Immanuel Kant, *Foundations of the Metaphysics of Morals* (New York: Bobbs-Merrill Co., 1959), 49.

12. Jürgen Habermas, *Moral Consciousness and Communicative Action* (Cambridge, Mass.: MIT Press, 1990).

13. Paul Ricoeur, "The Teleological and Deontological Structures of Action: Aristotle and/or Kant?" in *Contemporary French Philosophy*, ed. A. Phillips Griffiths (Cambridge: Cambridge Univ. Press, 1987), 106; see also Paul Ricoeur, *Oneself as Another* (Chicago: Univ. of Chicago Press, 1992), 219–27.

14. Ricoeur, "Teleological and Deontological Structures," 109.

15. William James, *The Principles of Psychology*, vol. 2 (New York: Dover Publications, 1950), 398–403; Mary Midgley, *Beast and Man* (Ithaca, NY: Cornell Univ. Press, 1978), 81–82.

16. Jürgen Habermas, *Knowledge and Human Interest* (Boston: Beacon Press, 1973).

17. Mary Beth Franklin, "Ailing System: Dramatic Rise in STDs Strains Family Clinics," *Chicago Tribune*, April 11, 1993, sec. 9.

18. Robert Shaffern, "Christianity and the Rise of the Nuclear Family," *America* (May 7, 1994):13–15.

19. Basil Mitchell, *Morality: Sacred and Secular* (Oxford: Clarendon Press,

1980). Mitchell acknowledges that there are analogies between the Christian formulation of the ground of respect, i.e., the image of God in humans, and the Kantian ground, i.e., the capacity of rationality in all persons. Mitchell believes that the Christian model, based on a sacred dimension in all humans, provides a more profound, weightier, and more motivating ground for respect or what we call equal regard.

20. For Paul Ricoeur's statement of this perspective, see his *Oneself as Another,* 140–68.

21. Alasdair MacIntyre, *After Virtue: A Theory of Morality* (Notre Dame, Ind.: Notre Dame Univ. Press, 1992), 202.

22. Ibid., 201.

23. Rosemary Radford Ruether, *Sexism and God-Talk: Toward a Feminist Theology* (Boston: Beacon Press, 1983), 137.

24. Sarah Coakley, "*Kenosis* and Subversion: On the Repression of 'Vulnerability' in Christian Feminist Writing," in *Swallowing a Fishbone? Feminist Theologians Debate Christianity,* ed. Daphne Hampson (London: SPCK, 1996).

25. Gudorf, "Parenting, Mutual Love, and Sacrifice," 182.

26. Ibid., 183; Outka, *Agape,* 278.

27. Andolsen, "Agape in Feminist Ethics," 78.

28. Harrison, "Anger as a Work of Love," 41–58.

29. For a critique of the moral horizon of rational-choice economic theory, see Don Browning, "Egos without Selves," *The Annual: Society of Christian Ethics* (Washington, D.C.: Georgetown Univ. Press, 1994), 127–46.

30. Janssens, "Norms and Priorities," 228.

31. Alfred North Whitehead, *Process and Reality* (New York: Harper Brothers, 1960); Charles Hartshorne, *Man's Vision of God and the Logic of Theism* (Chicago: Willett, Clarke & Co., 1941). Protestant theologians who extend these insights are John Cobb, *Christian Natural Theology* (Philadelphia: Westminster Press, 1965); Schubert Ogden, *The Reality of God* (New York: Harper & Row, 1966); Franklin Gamwell, *The Divine Good* (San Francisco: Harper & Row, 1990).

32. Charles Hartshorne, *The Divine Relativity* (New Haven, Conn.: Yale Univ. Press, 1964), 133.

33. Elizabeth Johnson, *She Who Is: The Mystery of God in Feminist Theological Discourse* (New York: Crossroad, 1992); Catherine LaCugna, *God for Us: The Trinity in the Christian Life* (San Francisco: HarperCollins, 1991).

34. For examples of process philosophy's understanding of the sympathetic character of all experience, feeling, and sensation and how this is unbreakable and enduring when perfectly exhibited in God, see William James, *A Pluralistic Universe* (Cambridge, Mass.: Harvard Univ. Press, 1977), 127–28; Hartshorne, *Man's Vision of God,* 7, 165–266, 273.

35. For a fuller discussion of the marriage and family life cycle, see the entire series coauthored by Herbert Anderson titled 'Family Living in Pastoral Perspective, all published by Westminster John Knox Press. The specific titles are Herbert Anderson and Kenneth Mitchell, *Leaving Home* (1993), Herbert Anderson and Robert Fite, *Becoming Married* (1993), Herbert Ander-

son and Susan B. W. Johnson, *Regarding Children* (1994), Herbert Anderson, David Hogue, Marie McCarthy, *Promising Again* (1995), and Herbert Anderson and Frieda Gardner, *Living Alone* (1996).

36. For a discussion of how Erikson demonstrated the historical and cultural content of psychological concepts such as superego, ego ideal, and ego-identity, see "Ego Development and Historical Change" and "The Problem of Ego Identity" in his *Identity and the Life Cycle* (New York: International Universities Press, 1959), 18–49, 101–64.

37. Hans-Georg Gadamer, *Truth and Method* (New York: Crossroad, 1982), 330.

38. Ibid., 273.

39. Ana Maria Rizzuto, *The Birth of the Living God* (Chicago: Univ. of Chicago Press, 1979).

40. David Gutman, *Reclaimed Powers: Toward a New Psychology of Men and Women in Later Life* (New York: Basic Books, 1987), 187.

41. Ibid., 188.

42. Ibid., 190.

43. Ibid., 194.

44. Ibid., 196.

45. Ibid., 203.

46. Bonnie J. Miller-McLemore, *Also a Mother: Work and Family as a Theological Dilemma* (Nashville: Abingdon Press, 1994), 120.

47. Ibid., 222.

48. Alice Rossi, "A Biosocial Perspective on Parenting," *Daedalus* (1977):1–25; also see idem, "Gender and Parenthood," in *Gender and the Life Course,* ed. Alice Rossi (Hawthorne, N.Y.: Aldine Publishing Co., 1985), 161–86; idem, "The Biosocial Side of Parenthood," in *Psychology of Women,* ed. Juanita Williams (New York: W. W. Norton, 1985), 381–90.

49. Rossi, "Gender and Parenthood," 183.

50. Ibid. For another summary of this research, see David Popenoe, "Modern Marriage: Revising the Cultural Script" (New York: Institute for American Values, 1992).

51. Miller-McLemore, *Also a Mother,* 144.

52. Rhona Maloney, *Kidding Ourselves: Breadwinning, Babies, and Bargaining Power* (New York: Basic Books, 1995).

53. Erik Erikson, *Childhood and Society* (New York: W.W. Norton, 1963), 267.

54. Ibid., 233.

55. Erik Erikson, *Insight and Responsibility* (New York: W. W. Norton & Co., 1964), 231.

56. Jessica Benjamin, *The Bonds of Love: Psychoanalysis, Feminism, and the Problem of Domination* (New York: Pantheon Books, 1988), 13.

57. Ibid., 14.

58. In addition to Gudorf, Benjamin's point has also been made, with special reference to the early foundations of generativity, by Miller-McLemore in *Also a Mother,* 166.

59. Erikson called this phenomenon of mutual reinforcement between parents and children a matter of cogwheeling. For an explanation of the concept,

see David Rapaport's "A Historical Survey of Psychoanalytic Ego Psychology," in Erikson's *Identity and the Life Cycle,* 15.

60. Miller-McLemore, *Also a Mother,* 167.
61. Ibid., 155.
62. In this regard, Janet Fishburn's worry about the family idolatry of the Christian right is correct. See her *Confronting the Idolatry of Family* (Nashville: Abingdon Press, 1991).
63. Aquinas, *Summa Theologica* (London: R. & T. Washbourne, 1917), 1, ii. q.26, a.7.
64. Plato, *The Republic* (New York: Basic Books, 1968), Book 5, pp. 461–65.
65. Plato, *The Laws* (London: Penguin Books, 1970), 30, 206, 249–50.
66. Aristotle, *Politics,* in *The Basic Works of Aristotle,* ed. Richard McKeon (New York: Random House, 1941), Book 1, chap. 2.
67. Aristotle, *Nicomachean Ethics,* in *The Basic Works of Aristotle, Book 3, chap. 6.*
68. Aristotle, *Politics,* Book 2: chap. 3.
69. James Q. Wilson, *The Moral Sense* (New York: The Free Press, 1993), 1–28.
70. Gordon Paul Hugenberger, *Marriage as Covenant* (Leiden: E. J. Brill, 1994), 166–67.
71. Pamela D. Couture, *Blessed are the Poor: Women's Poverty, Family Policy, and Practical Theology* (Nashville: Abingdon Press, 1991), 71.
72. For a discussion of the nature of analogical thinking in theology and practical theology, see David Tracy, *Blessed Rage for Order* (Minneapolis: Seabury Press, 1975) and Don Browning, *A Fundamental Practical Theology* (Minneapolis: Fortress Press, 1991).

Notes to Chapter 11. Critical Familism:
New Directions for Church and Society

1. Margaret Miles, "The Courage to Be Alone—In and Out of Marriage," in *The Feminist Mystic* ed. Mary E. Giles (New York: Crossroad, 1982), 84–101.
2. John Demos, *A Little Commonwealth: Family Life in Plymouth Colony* (New York: Oxford Univ. Press, 1970), 184; Michael Walzer, *The Revolution of the Saints: A Study in the Origin of Radical Politics* (Cambridge, Mass.: Harvard Univ. Press, 1965), 191–93.
3. *Follow the Way of Love: A Pastoral Message of the U.S. Catholic Bishops to Families* (National Conference of Catholic Bishops, November 1993), 4.
4. Michael McManus, *Marriage Savers: Helping Your Friends and Family Stay Married* (Grand Rapids: Zondervan Publishing House, 1993), 131.
5. Ibid., 267.
6. In an attempt to verify McManus's claims, our assistant Christie Green made approximately a dozen phone calls to different cities where the proposal has been tried. Indeed, the Modesto program is functioning, although pastors report some loss of interest. Furthermore, the mobility of pastors makes it difficult to sustain. In addition, mainline churches are seldom a part of the program. It seems that mainly evangelical and fundamentalist churches participate. One of the best programs was in Louisville,

Kentucky, with strong, knowledgeable leadership from Gary and Sherry Hendricks and Gregory Wingenbach, director of the Kentuckiana Interfaith Community, 1115 S. Fourth Street, Louisville, KY 40203-3101.

7. James Coleman, "Schools, Families, and Children," Ryerson Lecture: University of Chicago, 1985, 9–18.

8. Ibid., 18.

9. Dan Coats, "Can Congress Revive Civil Society?" *Policy Review* (January–February 1996):27.

10. Ibid., 30.

11. Norval Glenn, "The Textbook Story of American Marriages and Families," Publication No. W.P. 46: Institute for American Values, New York City, May 1996.

12. Ibid., 11; Linda Waite, "Does Marriage Matter?" *Demography* 32:4 (November 1995):483–504. She writes, after summarizing the positive consequences of marriage, "I think social scientists have an obligation to point out the benefits of marriage beyond the mostly emotional ones, which tend to push people toward marriage but may not sustain them when the honeymoon is over. We have an equally strong obligation to make policy makers aware of the stakes when they pull the policy levers that discourage marriage" (p. 500).

13. There are few careful studies of the values clarification approach to sex education that show it to be successful. This is an approach in which teachers take no stand on moral issues. Decisions are left to students about how to use information. See Barbara Dafoe Whitehead, "The Failure of Sex Education," *Atlantic Monthly* (October 1994):55–80.

14. Whitehead, "Failure of Sex Education," 55–80. A major study of sex education programs done for the Department of Health, Education, and Welfare argues that knowledge-based programs that emphasize individual decision making by students in a neutral atmosphere have little effect in decreasing disease and out-of-wedlock births. See Douglas Kirby, et al., "School-Based Programs to Reduce Sexual Risk Behaviors: A Review of Effectiveness," *Journal of the U.S. Public Health Service* 109 (May–June 1994):339–60, and Douglas Kirby, *Sex Education in Schools* (Menlo Park, Calif.: Henry Kaiser Family Foundation, 1994).

15. For information on Sex Respect, write SEX RESPECT, Respect Incorporated, P.O. Box 349 Bradley, IL 60915.

16. Marion Howard and Judith Blamey McCabe, "Helping Teenagers Postpone Sexual Involvement," *Family Planning Perspectives* 22 (January–February 1990):21–26.

17. We express appreciation to Christie Green for helping review this and the following sex education programs. For information on Teen Aid, write Teen Aid, Inc., 1330 N. Kalispel, Spokane, WA 99201.

18. For information on the American Bar Association's Partners program, write American Bar Association, Family Law Section, 750 Lake Shore Drive, Chicago, IL 60611.

19. For information on "True Love Waits," write True Love Waits, 127 9th Avenue North, Nashville, TN 37234.

20. For information on Engaged Encounter, write Dave and Millie Florijan, Engaged Encounter, 5 Tara Drive, Pittsburgh, PA 15209.

21. Paul Numrich, "A Pentecostal Megachurch on the Edge," in *Congregations and Family Ministry,* ed. Bernie Lyon and Archie Smith (Louisville, Ky.: Westminster John Knox Press, forthcoming).

22. Rosemary Barciauskas and Debra Hull, *Loving and Working: Reweaving Women's Public Lives* (Bloomington: Univ. of Indiana Press, 1989).

23. Rosalind Barnett and Caryl Rivers, *She Works/He Works: How Two-Income Families Are Happier, Healthier, and Better Off* (New York: HarperCollins, 1996).

24. Jacqueline Olds, Richard Schwartz, Susan Eisen, William Betcher, and Anthony Van Niel, "Part-Time Employment and Marital Well-Being: A Hypothesis and Pilot Study" (Belmont, Mass.: Department of Psychiatry, Harvard University, McLean Hospital, 1993).

25. Ingrid Groller, "Women and Work: Results of Our Readers' Poll," *Parents Magazine* (June 1990):107–14.

26. Helmut Thielicke, *The Ethics of Sex* (New York: Harper & Row, 1964), 163–66.

27. William J. Doherty, *Soul Searching: Why Psychotherapy Must Promote Moral Responsibility* (New York: Basic Books, 1995), 33. A more value-explicit counseling for couples has been advocated by the authors of this book; see Don Browning, *The Moral Context of Pastoral Care* (Philadelphia: Westminster Press, 1976), and Bonnie Miller-McLemore, "Will the Real Pro-Family Contestant Please Stand Up? Another Look at Families and Pastoral Care," *Journal of Pastoral Care* 49:4 (Spring 1995):61–68.

28. Michelle Weiner-Davis, *Divorce Busting* (New York: Simon & Schuster, 1995).

29. The Willow Creek Community Church, a megachurch in the northern suburbs of Chicago, is an example of a church with a strong marriage culture that promotes intact families but also has a wide range of services for the divorced, single parents, stepfamilies, and singles.

30. For an extensive discussion of this church, see Don Browning, *A Fundamental Practical Theology* (Minneapolis: Fortress Press, 1991), 243–77.

31. See Lowell Livezey's account of Carter Temple Methodist Church, titled "Family Ministries at Carter Temple CME Church," in *Congregations and Families* (Forthcoming).

32. For a discussion of the idea of dialogue as this is viewed respectively by Habermas and Ricoeur, see Ricoeur's *Hermeneutics and the Human Sciences* (Cambridge: Cambridge Univ. Press, 1981).

33. See *The Church and Human Sexuality: A Lutheran Perspective,* first draft (Chicago: Division of Church in Society, Evangelical Lutheran Church in America, 1993), 12.

34. Carl E. Schneider, "The Law and the Stability of Marriage: The Family as a Social Institution," An Institute for American Values Working Paper, New York, 1992, pp. 9–11.

35. Francis Fukuyama, *Trust: The Social Virtues and the Creation of Prosperity* (New York: Free Press, 1995); Vincent J. Schodolski, "As World Shrinks, a Chasm Develops," *Chicago Tribune,* March 31, 1996, sec. B.

36. *Free to Be Family,* (Washington, D.C.: Family Research Council, 1992), 35.

37. "Republican Contract with America," p. 17 (photocopy for public distribution).

38. *Beyond Rhetoric: A New American Agenda for Children and Families* (Washington: National Commission on Children, 1991), xxi.

39. William Mattox, "Government Tax Policy and the Family," The Family, Civil Society, and the State, a conference sponsored by The American Public Philosophy Institute, June 21–22, 1996, Washington, D.C.

40. *Free to Be Family,* 34–43; Nick Rave, "Married Couples Feel Jilted by Uncle Sam," *Chicago Tribune,* March 17, 1995, sec. C.

41. John DiIulio, "Government Welfare to Support Families—The Right Way," The Family, Civil Society, and the State, a Conference Sponsored by The American Public Philosophy Institute, June 21–22, 1996, Washington, D.C.

42. In saying this we do not mean to imply that such arrangements have not already existed. For instance, in the city of Chicago it is reported that Catholic Charities receives 60 percent of its funding from government and that nationwide, government funds make up 67 percent for Catholic welfare organizations.

43. *Free to Be Family,* 37–39.

44. Dirk Johnson, "Wisconsin Law Seeks to End Welfare," *New York Times,* April 26, 1996, sec. C; idem, "Must Work Bill OKd in Wisconsin," *New York Times* March 15, 1996.

45. Peter Kilborn and Sam Verhovek, "Clinton's Welfare Shift Ends Tortuous Journey," *New York Times,* Aug. 2, 1996.

46. David Ellwood, "Welfare Reform in Name Only," *New York Times,* July 22, 1996.

47. Barbara Vobejda, "Going Down without a Fight?" *Washington Post National Weekly Edition,* June 12–19, 1996, p. 8; R. W. Apple, "His Battle Now Lost, Moynihan Still Cries Out," *New York Times,* Aug. 2, 1996.

48. Proposals for part-time work for welfare single parents have been advanced by David Ellwood, *Poor Support: Poverty in the American Family* (New York: Basic Books, 1988), 135–37; Pamela D. Couture, *Blessed Are the Poor: Women's Poverty, Family Policy, and Political Theology* (Nashville: Abingdon Press, 1991), 178–84.

49. Benjamin Kline Hunnicutt, *Kellogg's Six-Hour Day* (Philadelphia: Temple Univ. Press, 1996).

50. Alison Mitchell, "Clinton Prods Executives to 'Do the Right Thing,'" *New York Times,* May 17, 1996, sec. C; Alison Mitchell, "Banking on Family Issues, Clinton Seeks Parents' Votes," *New York Times,* June 25, 1996, sec. C.

51. Margaret Andrews, "Developing a National Strategy of Marriage and Family Education," address given to the International Conference on the Family, University of Melbourne, July 1994; see also "Moving Counselling to Community Agencies," *Threshold: A Magazine about Marriage Education* 49 (December 1995): 3.

52. Herbert Anderson, David Hogue, and Marie McCarthy, *Promising Again* (Louisville, Ky.: Westminster John Knox, 1996), 2.

53. Brochure provided by the National Institute for Responsible Fatherhood and Family Development, p. 2. To contact, write the National Institute for Responsible Fatherhood and Family Development, 8555 Hough Ave., Cleveland, OH 44106-1545.

54. For a similar but less well known program, see the Paternal Involvement Demonstration Project, Kennedy-King College, 6800 S. Wentworth, Chicago, IL 60621; for a review of many such programs, see James A. Levine with Edward W. Pitt, *New Expectations: Community Strategies for Responsible Fatherhood* (New York: Families and Work Institute, 1995).

55. Taken from a brochure titled "Creating a Father-Friendly Neighborhood: Ten Things You Can Do," National Fatherhood Initiative, Lancaster, Penn.

56. For information, write the National Center for Fathering, P.O. Box 413888, Kansas City, MO 64141.

57. William Galston, "Beyond the Murphy Brown Debate: Ideas for Family Policy" (New York: Family Policy Symposium, Institute for American Values, 1993), 14.

58. Quoted from Richard Gill and Grandon Gill, "A Parental Bill of Rights," *Family Affairs* 6:1–2 (Winter 1994):1.

59. The Michigan Family Forum is a major mover of this legislation, which has been introduced by State Representative Jessie Dalman. See the Forum's *Breaking Up Is Easy to Do* (Lansing, Mich.: Michigan Family Forum, 1995). For information, write Michigan Family Forum, 611 South Walnut, Lansing, Michigan 48933.

60. William Galston, "The Reinstitutionalization of Marriage: Political Theory and Public Policy," An Institute for American Values Working Paper, Institute for American Values, New York, 1992); idem, "A Liberal-Democratic Case for the Two-Parent Family," *Responsive Community* (Winter 1990/91):23–25.

61. These suggestions were, to our knowledge, first put forth by Mary Ann Glendon, *Abortion and Divorce in Western Law* (Cambridge, Mass.: Harvard Univ. Press, 1987), 93–95. Later they were affirmed by Elaine Ciulla Kamarck and William Galston, "Putting Children First: A Progressive Family Policy for the 1990s," Progressive Policy Institute, Washington, D.C., 1991, p. 30.

62. Traci R. Gentilozzi, "Divorce Changes Proposed," *Michigan Lawyer's Weekly* (Feb. 19, 1996):3.

63. James Brundage, *Law, Sex, and Christian Society in Medieval Europe* (Chicago: Univ. of Chicago Press, 1987), 325–416. See also John Witte, Jr., *From Sacrament to Contract: Marriage, Religion, and Law in the Western Tradition* (Louisville, Ky.: Westminster John Knox Press, 1997).

64. Michael Medved, *Hollywood vs. America: Popular Culture and the War on Traditional Values* (New York: HarperCollins, 1992).

65. Kay S. Hymowitz, "'I Don't Know Where This is Going': What Teenagers Learn about Marriage from Television and Magazines," A Council on Families in America Working Paper, Institute of American Values, New York, 1995.

66. An excellent program sponsored by Family and Community Critical Viewing Project is unfortunately limited to violence. See *Taking Charge of Your TV:*

A Guide to Critical Viewing for Parent and Children. For information on an extensive list of resources, write Family and Community Critical Viewing Project, 1724 Massachusetts Ave., N.W., Washington, DC 20036-1969.

67. Roger Cardinal Mahony, *Film Makers, Film Viewers: Their Challenges and Opportunities* (Boston, Mass.: Daughters of St. Paul, 1992).

68. Mark Caro and Steve Johnson, "Foes of New TV Ratings Worry about 'Forbidden Fruit' Factor," *Chicago Tribune,* Dec. 23, 1996, sec. 1; Richard Morin, "Confronting Sex and Violence on TV," *Washington Post National Weekly Edition,* Dec. 23, 1996, p. 38.

Notes to the Appendix

1. Robert Bellah, Richard Madsen, William Sullivan, Ann Swidler, and Steven Tipton, *Habits of the Heart* (Berkeley, Calif.: University of California Press, 1985), 297–307; Hans-Georg Gadamer, *Truth and Method* (New York: Crossroad, 1982), 330–33.

2. Bellah et al., *Habits of the Heart,* 330.

3. Ibid., 28–31.

4. Gadamer, *Truth and Method,* 235–40.

5. Ibid., 267–74.

6. Don Browning, *A Fundamental Practical Theology* (Minneapolis: Fortress Press, 1991).

7. See ibid., 47–56, for a more expanded discussion of these four movements or steps.

8. Bonnie Miller-McLemore, *Also a Mother: Work and Family as a Theological Dilemma* (Nashville: Abingdon Press, 1994).

9. Ibid. See Pamela Couture, *Blessed Are The Poor: Women's Poverty, Family Policy, and Practical Theology* (Nashville: Abingdon Press, 1991); K. Brynolf Lyon, *Toward a Practical Theology of Aging* (Philadelphia: Fortress Press, 1985); Robert M. Franklin, *Another Day's Journey: Black Churches Confronting the American Crisis* (Minneapolis: Fortress Press, 1997).

10. Paul Ricoeur, *Hermeneutics and the Human Sciences* (Cambridge: Cambridge University Press, 1981), 61–64.

11. Kyle Pasewark and Garrett Paul, *The Emphatic Christian Center* (Nashville: Abingdon Press, 1999). We also refer the interested reader to the recent book by Robert Kinast, *What Are They Saying about Theological Reflection?* (Mahwah, N.J.: Paulist Press, 2000). In this book, Kinast provides his own guide to the methodological relation between *A Fundamental Practical Theology* and *From Culture Wars to Common Ground.*

12. For an introduction to the five dimensions, see Browning, *A Fundamental Practical Theology,* 139–70.

13. See above, pp. 107–24, for an interpretation of Aquinas where these three levels become evident.

14. See above, pp. 115–18, for Aquinas's discussion of these naturalistic conditions.

15. For this summary statement, see above, p. 2.

Index

accommodation of 164
biological 167, 175
and equality 164
gender 163–64, 166, 236
sexual 111, 164, 165, 175
see also asymmetrical reproduction
discrimination. *See* racism
divorce xi, 6, 12, 21, 29, 35–37, 40,
46, 52, 63–64, 68, 88, 98,
105, 140, 151, 159, 166, 171,
184, 198, 200, 224, 257–58
266
church response to 315, 318–20
consequences for women and children 40, 53, 54, 258, 266
of couples with children 332
culture of 45
negative effects on children 39, 45,
53–58, 319
no-fault 320
patriarchal 122, 134–35
Dizard, Jan 58, 250–53, 258, 263
Dobson, James 232–34, 236–37, 241
Doherty, William 215–16, 319
Dole, Robert 30, 41–42, 50, 265, 327
domestic violence 2, 6, 36, 45, 69, 151,
163, 315
domestic work 1, 8, 63, 85, 94, 159,
162, 165, 233
democratization of 66
division of 12, 14, 84, 169–70
need for men to participate in
233
and production of wealth 256
sharing of 11, 24, 82, 318

early Christianity 78, 129–57, 171,
181, 268, 308
alternative to honor-shame ethic
142, 176, 231
apologetic strategy minimizing gender and family change 138–39,
148–49, 175–76
criticism by surrounding communities of gender and family changes
in 138–39, 142–43, 147–149,
175–76
and "discipleship of equals" 134–41,
274

and equality between the sexes
130–32, 134–41, 146, 175
and gender ambivalence 132, 138
and gender and family change 131,
185
and the kingdom of God 132–34
Jesus movement 132–35, 137
male responsibility and servanthood
131, 176
and new model of parenthood 143
and patriarchy 129, 131, 140
and respect for children 131, 136
see also Ephesians; house churches;
Jesus Christ; Paul
Eberly, Don 35, 330
ecclesia 134, 136, 141, 148–49, 171,
175–76, 302–3, 308
and post-Pauline conservative retreat
147–49
ecology 2–3, 6, 9, 22, 29, 42, 157, 164,
167, 177, 180–81, 328
behavioral 107
of family supports 42
of fatherhood 180–81
of institutions 6, 42
moral 8, 9–18, 102
perspective on families 29, 229
view of the family 22, 174
view of parenting 248–50
see also evolutionary ecology
economics 1–5, 7, 11, 12, 16, 22, 29,
33, 38, 39, 42, 46, 49–52, 59–66,
67–71, 73, 76, 84, 91, 94, 95, 97,
130, 149, 152, 157, 172, 174,
177, 184–85, 192, 210, 223–24,
228, 245, 247–68, 277, 283, 314,
333–34
cost of family changes 32
critical voice in family debate 23,
24
family as household 46
neoclassical theories of 255, 260
overemphasized by liberals as cause
of family crisis 50
spread into families and private life
21
support of families 324–37
Economics, Chicago School of 62,
254–55, 257–58, 260–61

and mutuality 47, 210–11
see also communication; dialogue;
   equal regard
intimacy 70, 89, 107, 179, 184,
   212–13, 236, 279, 308, 317
   democratization of 50, 65, 67, 288
   see also affection; communication;
   sexuality
irony 6–7, 21, 319. *See also* ideals; realism

James, William 107, 116, 277–78, 286
Janssens, Louis 154, 256, 274–77, 279,
   283–84, 286
Jesus Christ
   critique of patriarchal family clan
   134
   harsh sayings on the family 134, 301
   on divorce 132, 134–37, 272, 318
   love command of 145, 274
   parables on household 274
   see also analogy to Christ on the
   cross
Jewett, Paul 226
John Paul II, Pope 124, 220, 238–39,
   241, 243–44, 247
Johnson, Benton 44
Johnson, Elizabeth 286
Johnson, Susan 217
Jones, Tina 195
Judaism 1, 4, 7, 15–16, 103, 106, 109,
   132, 158–59, 161, 172, 175, 213,
   229, 236, 259, 281, 290, 310,
   322, 334
justice 2, 43, 44, 74, 98, 119, 146,
   170, 212, 224, 241, 244, 268,
   279
   between families 324
   economic 30, 43–44, 67, 324
   equal regard and 2
   and the family 164–66
   and intersubjectivity 13, 276
   and love 44–45, 231, 233
   sexual 121
   within families 67, 165, 170–72,
   181, 234

Kant, Immanuel 17, 103, 238, 275–76,
   280

Kemp, Jack 41–42, 327
Kerber, Linda 81
Kierkegaard, Søren 70
kin altruism, theory of 35, 71, 80,
   108–10, 116, 117, 120, 170, 172,
   176, 178, 229–30, 238–39, 248,
   256, 262, 277, 279, 303–5, 307
kinship 46, 133, 171–72, 175, 187,
   226
   feminization of 229, 258–60
Klein, Melanie 205
Knutsen, Kate 195
Kohlberg, Lawrence 275
Kohut, Heinz 206
Kuyper, Abraham 235

La Cugna, Catherine 286
labor. *See* work
language 38, 196, 278
   of commitment 38, 193, 202, 206,
   316
   confessional and public 243
   differentiated theological 307
   moral 38, 191
   religious 38
   three levels of Christian language on
   family 322–23
Lasch, Christopher 169, 190–92, 194,
   198, 200, 210–11, 213, 251, 257,
   333
Laslett, Peter 74
law 1, 3, 44, 46, 74, 75, 79, 95, 97,
   122, 177, 228, 255, 262, 314,
   332–33
   Catholic canon law 58, 258–59, 332
   law and economics movement 255
   see also Reformation, Protestant: effect on family law
Leo XIII, Pope 88, 124, 224, 238–41,
   243, 247
Lesthaeghe, Ron 64
liberalism and liberals. *See* Christianity;
   churches; culture; politics; Protestantism; religion
life-cycle perspective 177, 180–81,
   215, 329
   on equal regard 24, 154, 271
   on mutuality 287–301
   on self-sacrifice 24, 108